CASE CLOSED

VOLUME 55

Gosho A

Case Briefing:

Subject:
Occupation:
Special Skills:
Equipment:

Jimmy Kudo, a.k.a. Conan Edogawa
High School Student/Detective
Analytical thinking and deductive reasoning, Soccer
Bow Tie Voice Transmitter, Super Sneakers,
Homing Glasses, Stretchy Suspenders

The subject is hot on the trail of a pair of suspicious men in black when he is attacked from behind and administered a strange substance which physically transforms him into a first grader. When the subject confides in the eccentric inventor Dr. Agasa, they decide to keep the subject's true identity a secret for the safety of everyone around him. Assuming the new identity of first-grader Conan Edogawa, the subject continues to assist the police force on their most baffling cases. The only problem is that most crime-solving professionals won't take a little kid's advice!

Table of Contents

CONFIDEN

CASE CLOSED

Volume 55
Shonen Sunday Edition

Story and Art by GOSHO AOYAMA

MEITANTEI CONAN Vol. 55
by Gosho AOYAMA
© 1994 Gosho AOYAMA
All rights reserved.
Original Japanese edition published by SHOGAKUKAN.
English translation rights in the United States of America, Canada,
the United Kingdom and Ireland arranged with SHOGAKUKAN.

Translation
Tetsuichiro Miyaki

Touch-up & Lettering
Freeman Wong

Cover & Graphic Design
Andrea Rice

Editor
Shaenon K. Garrity

Printed in the U.S.A.

Published by VIZ Media, LLC
P.O. Box 77010
San Francisco, CA 94107

10 9 8 7 6 5 4 3 2 1
First printing, July 2015

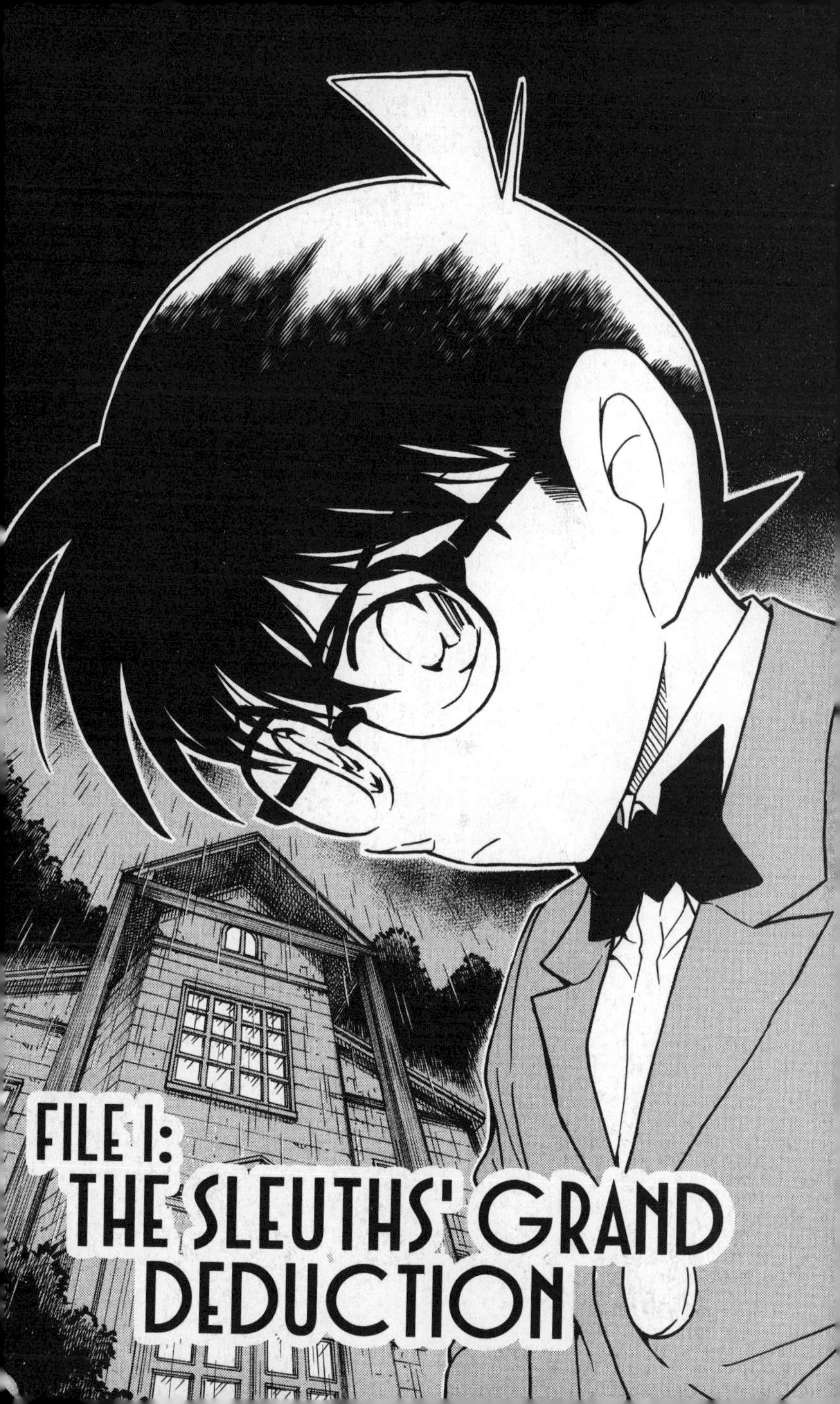
FILE 1:
THE SLEUTHS' GRAND DEDUCTION

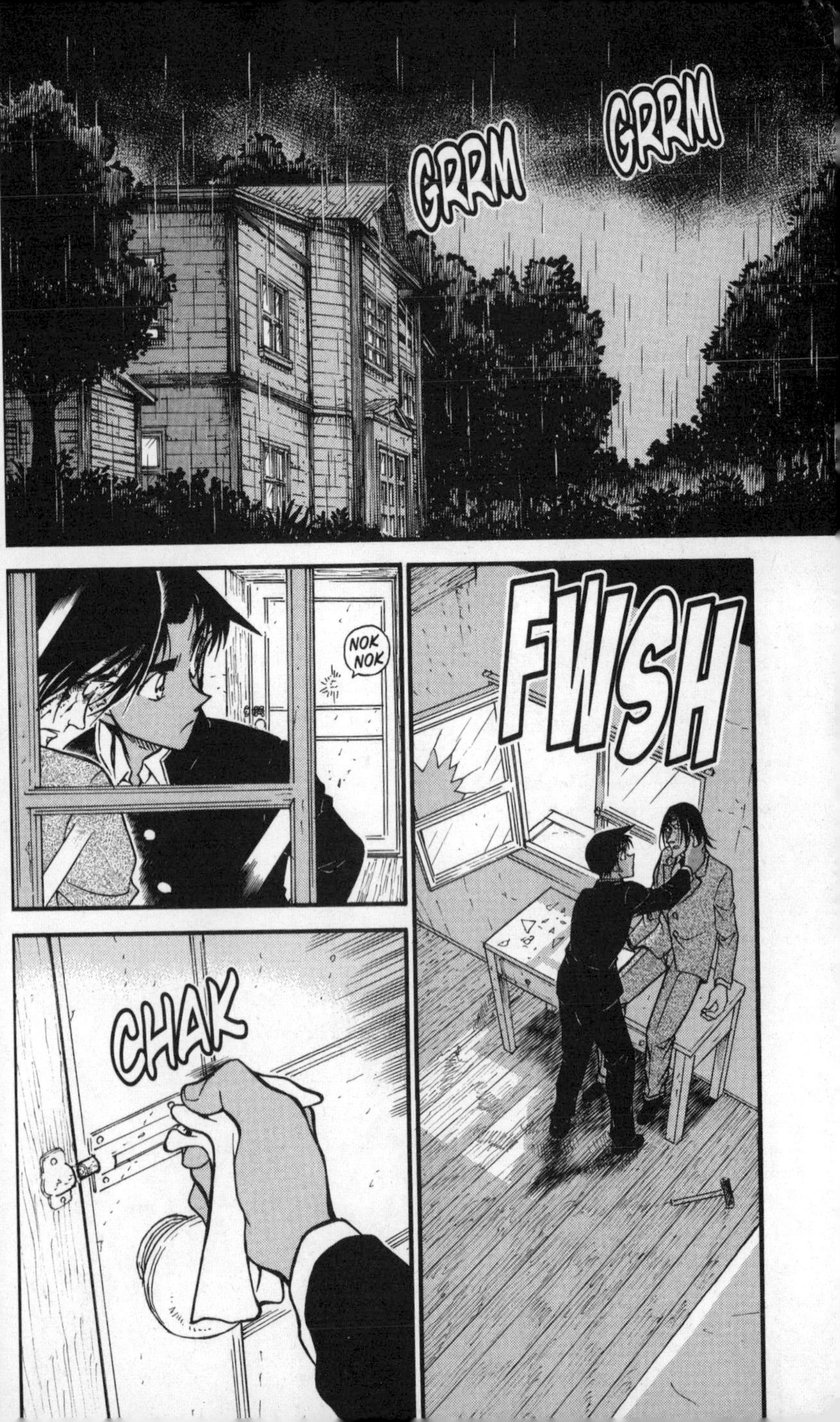
GRRM
GRRM
FWSH
NOK NOK
CHAK

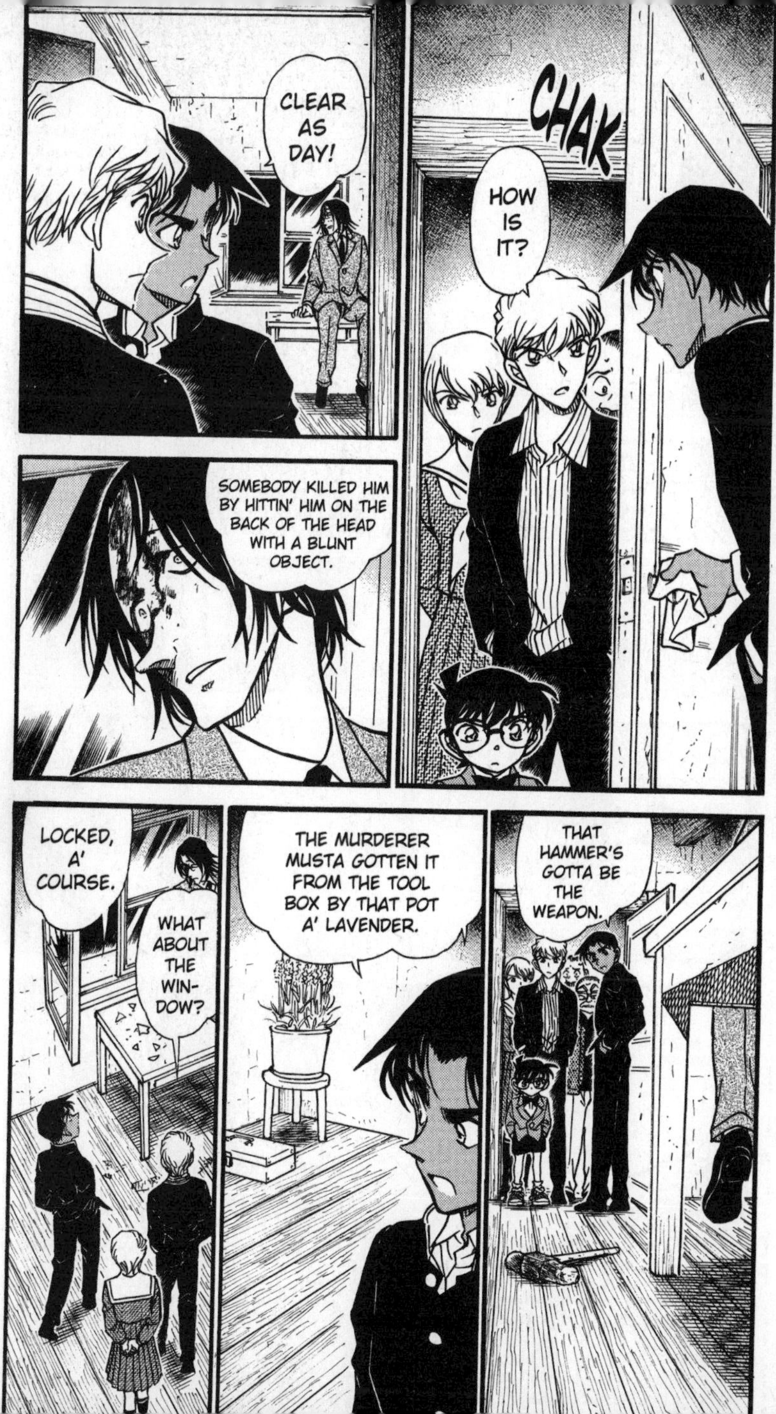
CHAK
HOW IS IT?
CLEAR AS DAY!
SOMEBODY KILLED HIM BY HITTIN' HIM ON THE BACK OF THE HEAD WITH A BLUNT OBJECT.
THAT HAMMER'S GOTTA BE THE WEAPON.
THE MURDERER MUSTA GOTTEN IT FROM THE TOOL BOX BY THAT POT A' LAVENDER.
WHAT ABOUT THE WIN-DOW?
LOCKED, A' COURSE.

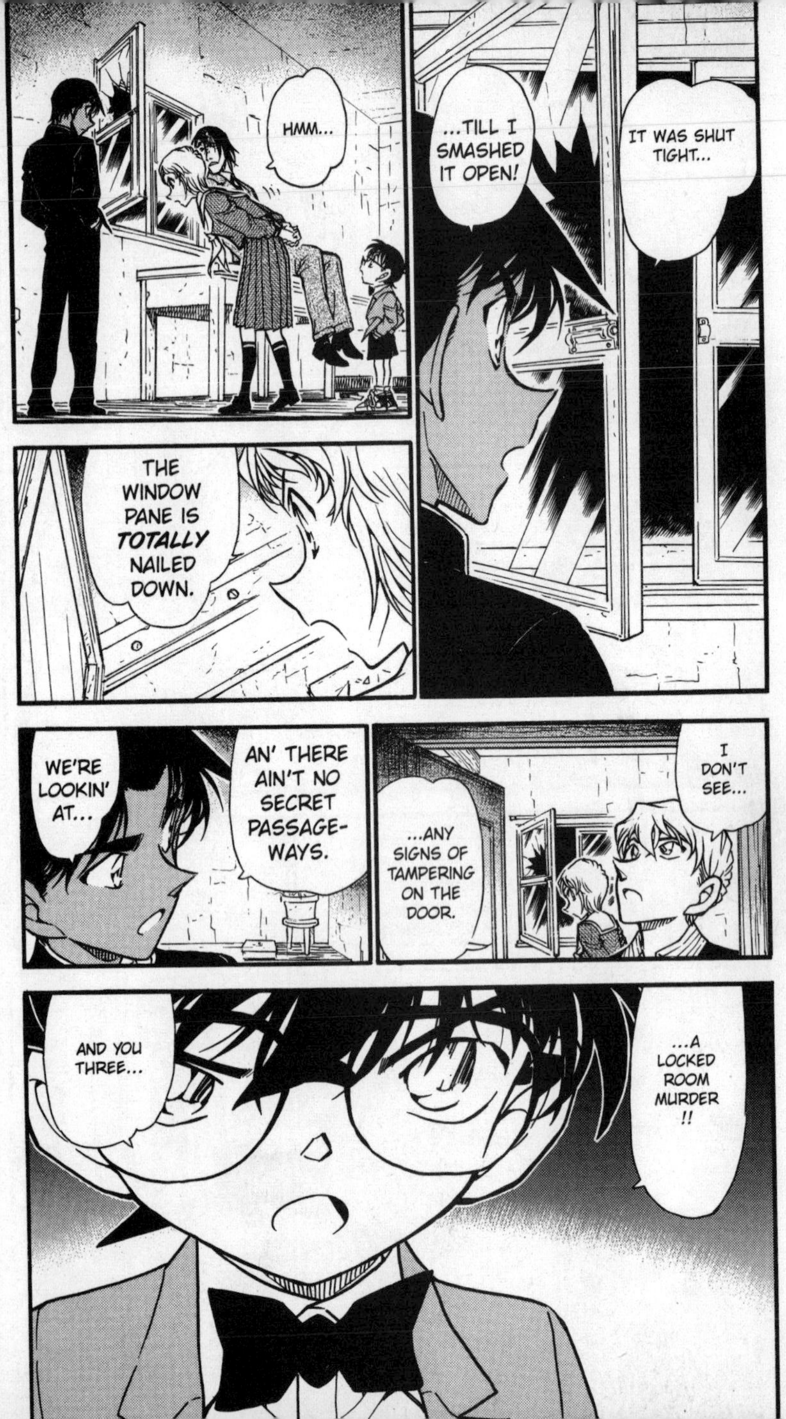

IT WAS SHUT TIGHT...
...TILL I SMASHED IT OPEN!
HMM...
THE WINDOW PANE IS TOTALLY NAILED DOWN.
I DON'T SEE...
...ANY SIGNS OF TAMPERING ON THE DOOR.
AN' THERE AIN'T NO SECRET PASSAGE-WAYS.
WE'RE LOOKIN' AT...
...A LOCKED ROOM MURDER !!
AND YOU THREE...

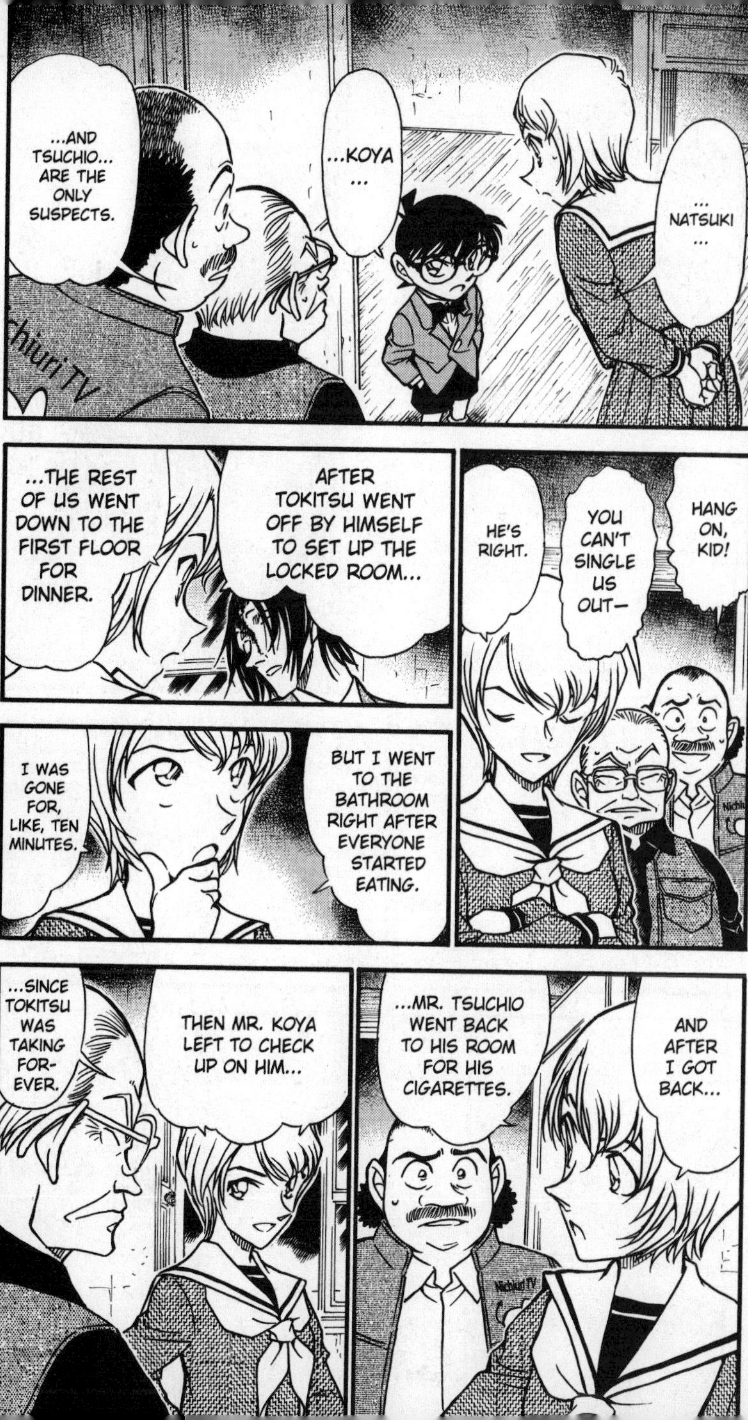
... NATSUKI ...
...KOYA ...
...AND TSUCHIO... ARE THE ONLY SUSPECTS.
HANG ON, KID!
YOU CAN'T SINGLE US OUT—
HE'S RIGHT.
AFTER TOKITSU WENT OFF BY HIMSELF TO SET UP THE LOCKED ROOM...
...THE REST OF US WENT DOWN TO THE FIRST FLOOR FOR DINNER.
BUT I WENT TO THE BATHROOM RIGHT AFTER EVERYONE STARTED EATING.
I WAS GONE FOR, LIKE, TEN MINUTES.
AND AFTER I GOT BACK...
...MR. TSUCHIO WENT BACK TO HIS ROOM FOR HIS CIGARETTES.
THEN MR. KOYA LEFT TO CHECK UP ON HIM...
...SINCE TOKITSU WAS TAKING FOR-EVER.

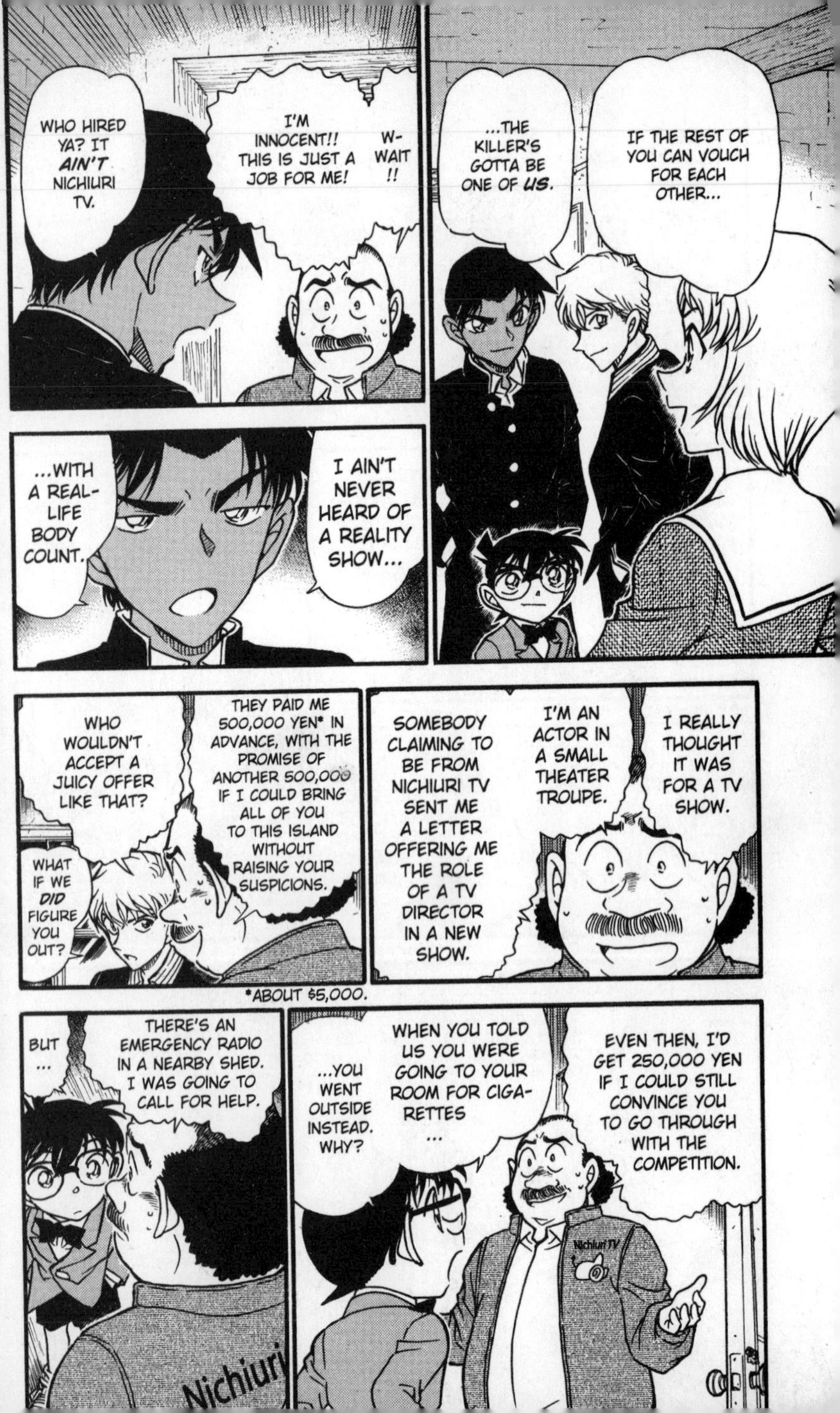
IF THE REST OF YOU CAN VOUCH FOR EACH OTHER...
...THE KILLER'S GOTTA BE ONE OF *US*.
W-WAIT !!
I'M INNOCENT!! THIS IS JUST A JOB FOR ME!
WHO HIRED YA? IT *AIN'T* NICHIURI TV.
I AIN'T NEVER HEARD OF A REALITY SHOW...
...WITH A REAL-LIFE BODY COUNT.
I REALLY THOUGHT IT WAS FOR A TV SHOW.
I'M AN ACTOR IN A SMALL THEATER TROUPE.
SOMEBODY CLAIMING TO BE FROM NICHIURI TV SENT ME A LETTER OFFERING ME THE ROLE OF A TV DIRECTOR IN A NEW SHOW.
THEY PAID ME 500,000 YEN* IN ADVANCE, WITH THE PROMISE OF ANOTHER 500,000 IF I COULD BRING ALL OF YOU TO THIS ISLAND WITHOUT RAISING YOUR SUSPICIONS.
WHO WOULDN'T ACCEPT A JUICY OFFER LIKE THAT?
WHAT IF WE *DID* FIGURE YOU OUT?
EVEN THEN, I'D GET 250,000 YEN IF I COULD STILL CONVINCE YOU TO GO THROUGH WITH THE COMPETITION.
Nichiuri TV
WHEN YOU TOLD US YOU WERE GOING TO YOUR ROOM FOR CIGA-RETTES ...
...YOU WENT OUTSIDE INSTEAD. WHY?
THERE'S AN EMERGENCY RADIO IN A NEARBY SHED. I WAS GOING TO CALL FOR HELP.
BUT ...
Nichiuri

*ABOUT $5,000.

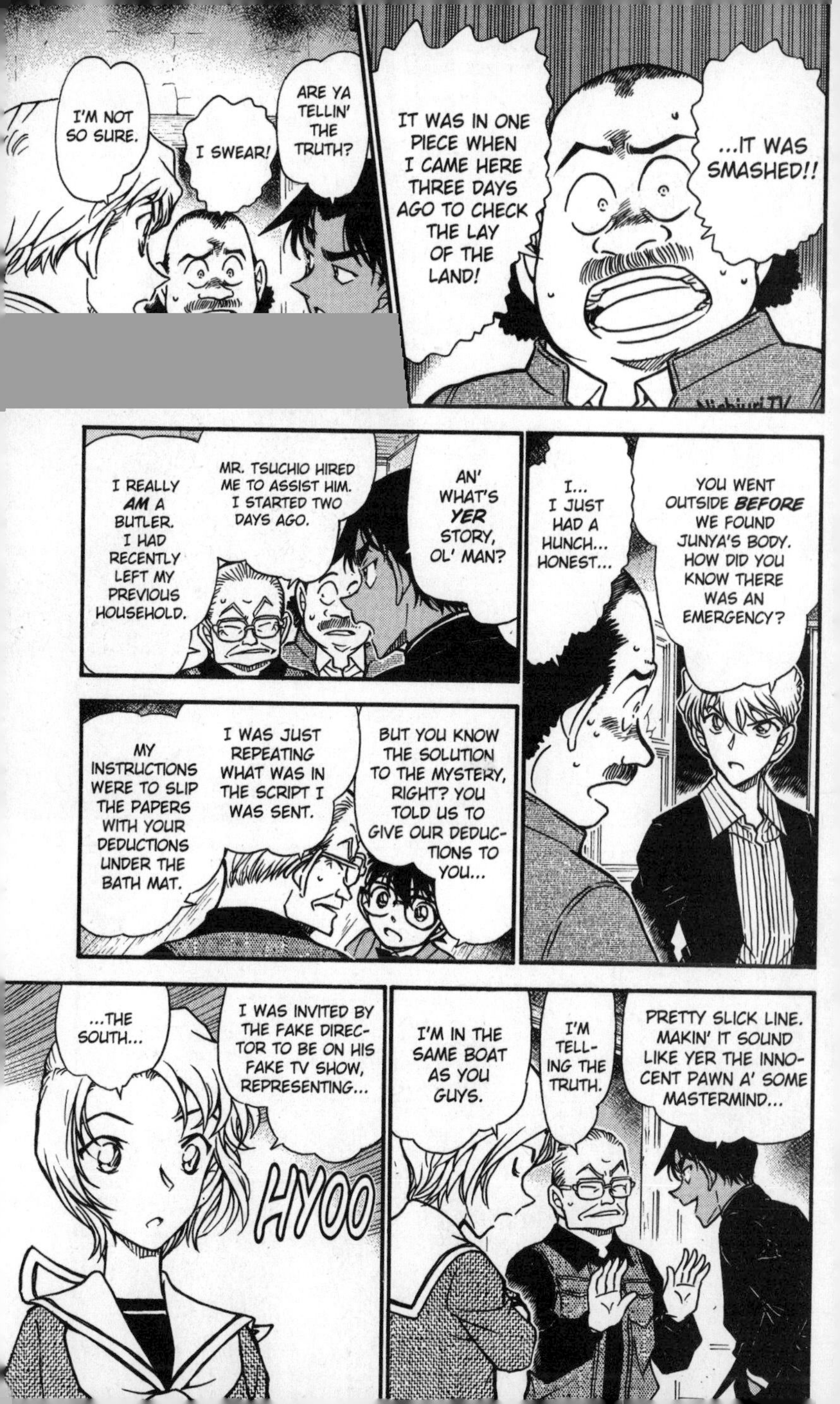
IT WAS IN ONE PIECE WHEN I CAME HERE THREE DAYS AGO TO CHECK THE LAY OF THE LAND!
...IT WAS SMASHED!!
ARE YA TELLIN' THE TRUTH?
I SWEAR!
I'M NOT SO SURE.
YOU WENT OUTSIDE **BEFORE** WE FOUND JUNYA'S BODY. HOW DID YOU KNOW THERE WAS AN EMERGENCY?
I... I JUST HAD A HUNCH... HONEST...
AN' WHAT'S **YER** STORY, OL' MAN?
MR. TSUCHIO HIRED ME TO ASSIST HIM. I STARTED TWO DAYS AGO.
I REALLY **AM** A BUTLER. I HAD RECENTLY LEFT MY PREVIOUS HOUSEHOLD.
BUT YOU KNOW THE SOLUTION TO THE MYSTERY, RIGHT? YOU TOLD US TO GIVE OUR DEDUCTIONS TO YOU...
I WAS JUST REPEATING WHAT WAS IN THE SCRIPT I WAS SENT.
MY INSTRUCTIONS WERE TO SLIP THE PAPERS WITH YOUR DEDUCTIONS UNDER THE BATH MAT.
PRETTY SLICK LINE. MAKIN' IT SOUND LIKE YER THE INNOCENT PAWN A' SOME MASTERMIND...
I'M TELLING THE TRUTH.
I'M IN THE SAME BOAT AS YOU GUYS.
I WAS INVITED BY THE FAKE DIRECTOR TO BE ON HIS FAKE TV SHOW, REPRESENTING...
...THE SOUTH...
HYOO

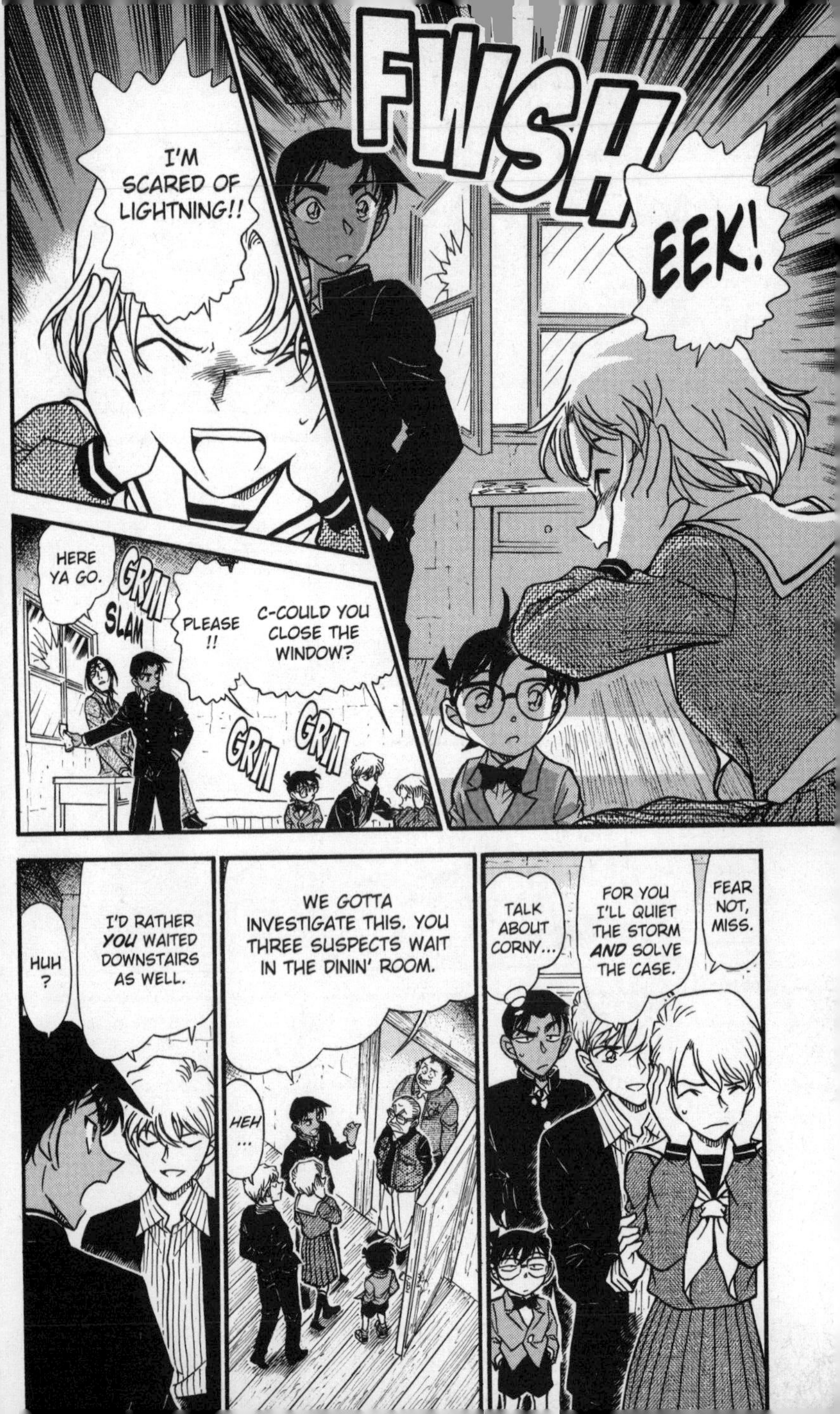
FWSH
EEK!
I'M SCARED OF LIGHTNING!!
C-COULD YOU CLOSE THE WINDOW?
PLEASE !!
GRM
SLAM
HERE YA GO.
GRM
GRM
FEAR NOT, MISS.
FOR YOU I'LL QUIET THE STORM AND SOLVE THE CASE.
TALK ABOUT CORNY...
WE GOTTA INVESTIGATE THIS. YOU THREE SUSPECTS WAIT IN THE DININ' ROOM.
HEH ...
I'D RATHER YOU WAITED DOWNSTAIRS AS WELL.
HUH ?

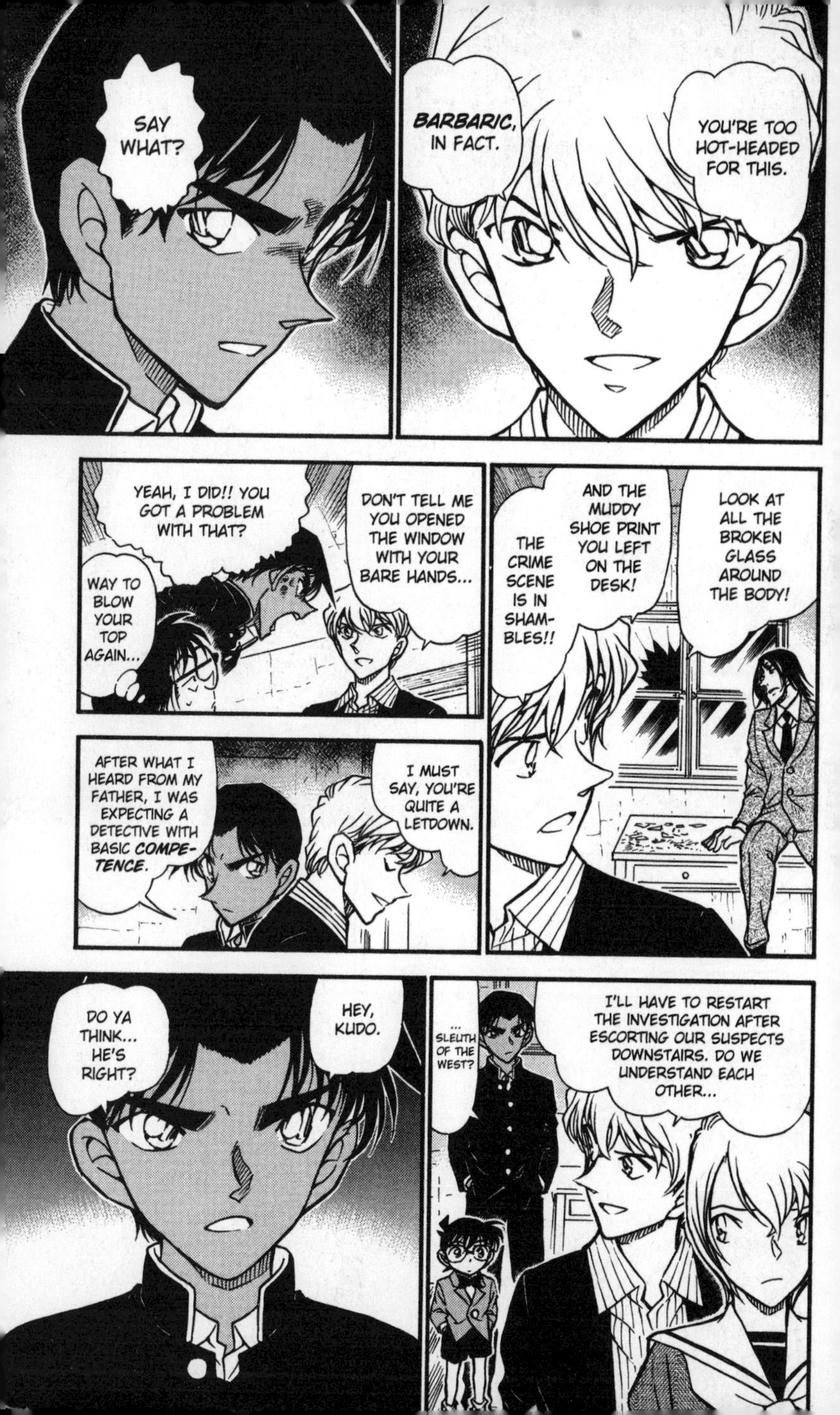
YOU'RE TOO HOT-HEADED FOR THIS.
BARBARIC, IN FACT.
SAY WHAT?
LOOK AT ALL THE BROKEN GLASS AROUND THE BODY!
AND THE MUDDY SHOE PRINT YOU LEFT ON THE DESK!
THE CRIME SCENE IS IN SHAMBLES!!
DON'T TELL ME YOU OPENED THE WINDOW WITH YOUR BARE HANDS...
YEAH, I DID!! YOU GOT A PROBLEM WITH THAT?
WAY TO BLOW YOUR TOP AGAIN...
I MUST SAY, YOU'RE QUITE A LETDOWN.
AFTER WHAT I HEARD FROM MY FATHER, I WAS EXPECTING A DETECTIVE WITH BASIC COMPETENCE.
I'LL HAVE TO RESTART THE INVESTIGATION AFTER ESCORTING OUR SUSPECTS DOWNSTAIRS. DO WE UNDERSTAND EACH OTHER...
...SLEUTH OF THE WEST?
HEY, KUDO.
DO YA THINK... HE'S RIGHT?

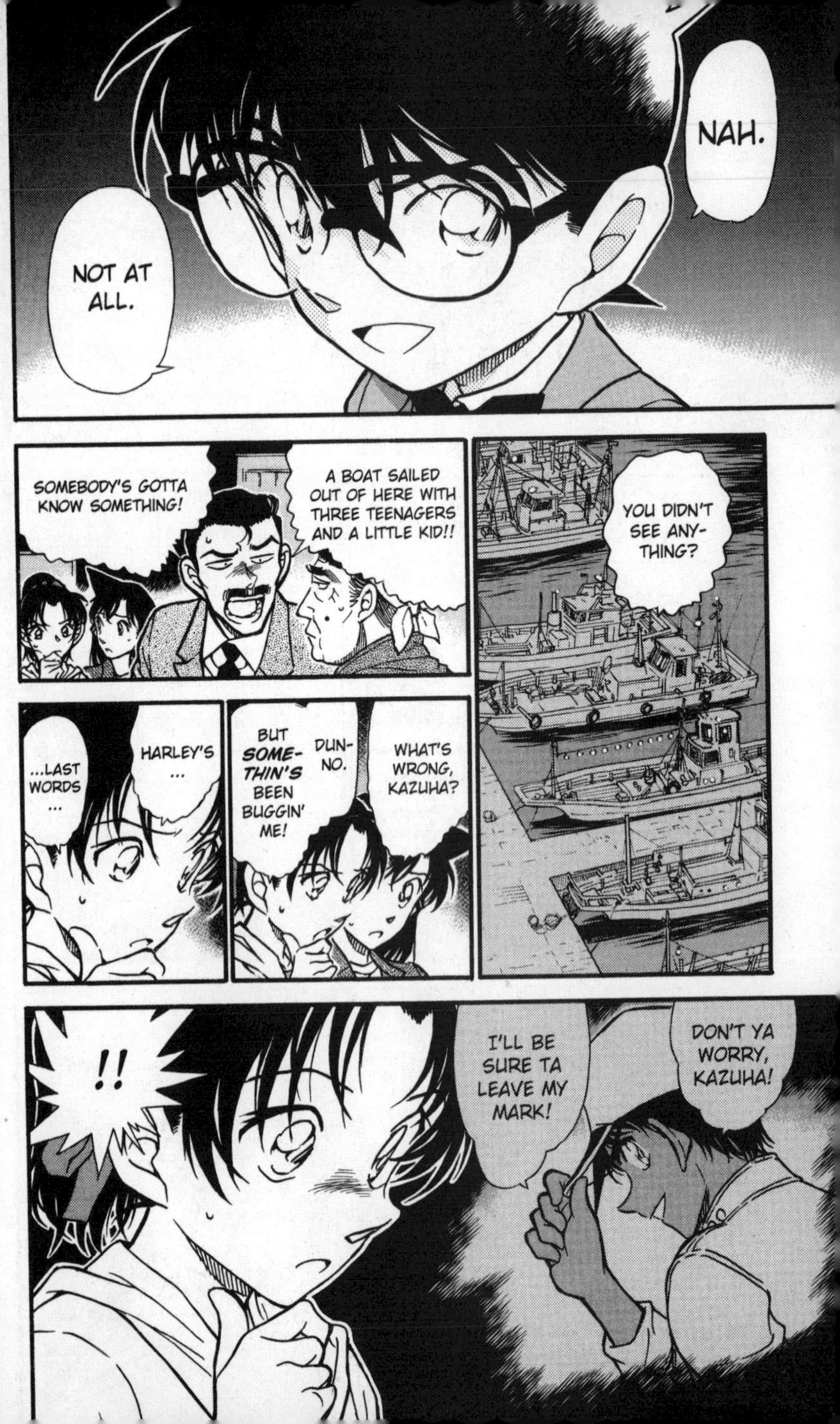
NAH.
NOT AT ALL.
YOU DIDN'T SEE ANY-THING?
A BOAT SAILED OUT OF HERE WITH THREE TEENAGERS AND A LITTLE KID!!
SOMEBODY'S GOTTA KNOW SOMETHING!
WHAT'S WRONG, KAZUHA?
DUN-NO.
BUT SOME-THIN'S BEEN BUGGIN' ME!
HARLEY'S ...
...LAST WORDS ...
DON'T YA WORRY, KAZUHA!
I'LL BE SURE TA LEAVE MY MARK!
!!

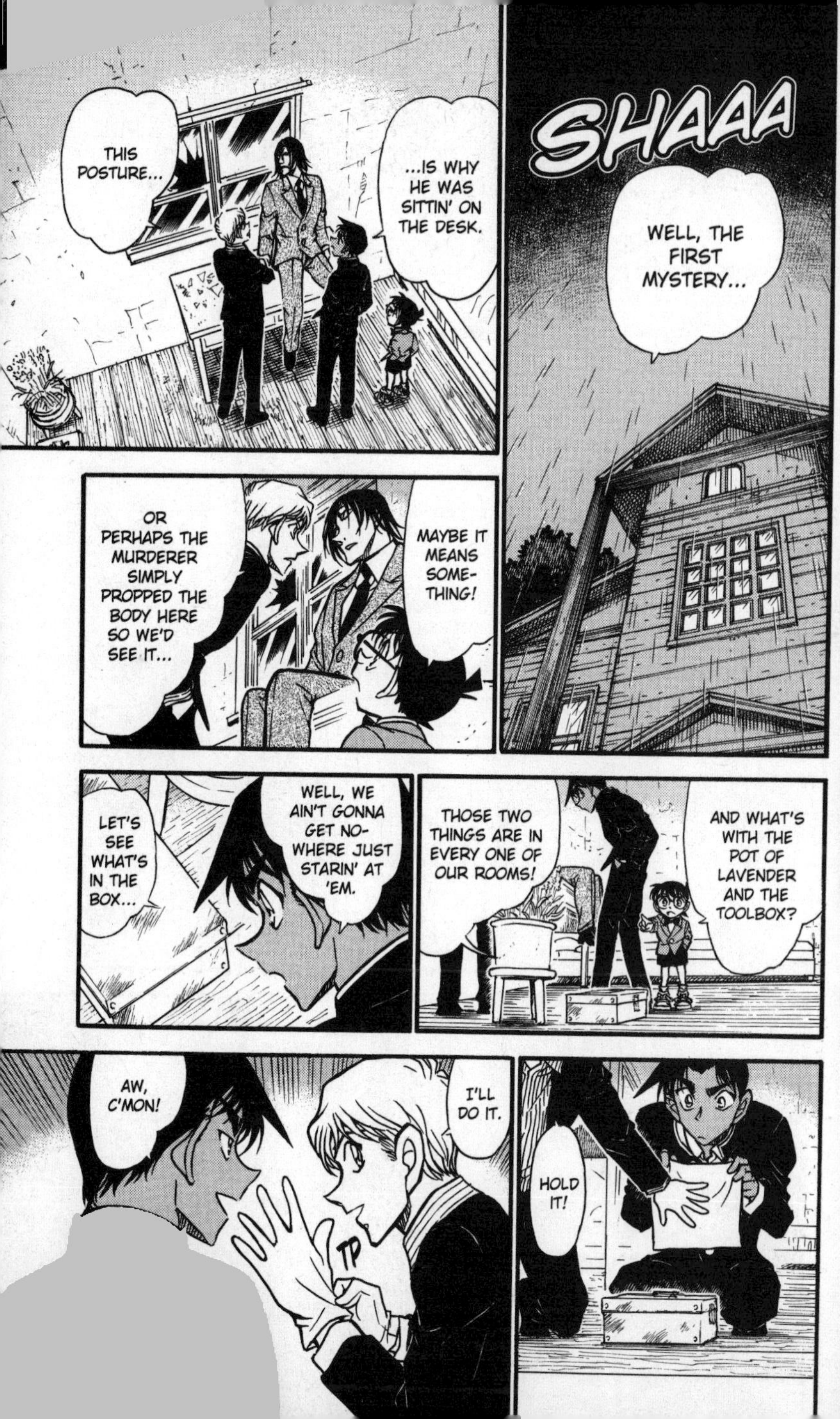
SHAAA
WELL, THE FIRST MYSTERY...
...IS WHY HE WAS SITTIN' ON THE DESK.
THIS POSTURE...
MAYBE IT MEANS SOMETHING!
OR PERHAPS THE MURDERER SIMPLY PROPPED THE BODY HERE SO WE'D SEE IT...
AND WHAT'S WITH THE POT OF LAVENDER AND THE TOOLBOX?
THOSE TWO THINGS ARE IN EVERY ONE OF OUR ROOMS!
WELL, WE AIN'T GONNA GET NOWHERE JUST STARIN' AT 'EM.
LET'S SEE WHAT'S IN THE BOX...
HOLD IT!
I'LL DO IT.
AW, C'MON!
TP

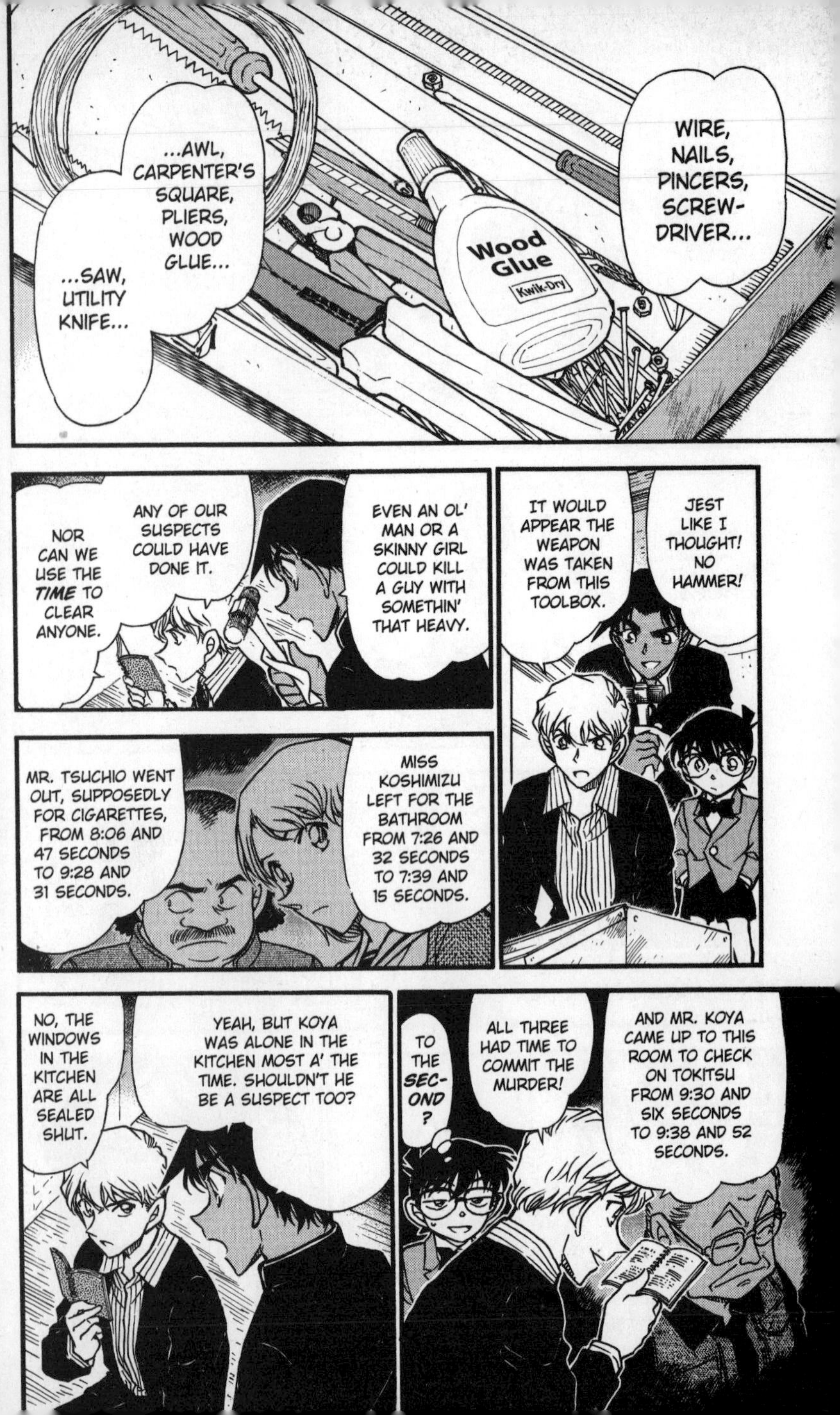
WIRE, NAILS, PINCERS, SCREW-DRIVER...
Wood Glue
Kwik-Dry
...AWL, CARPENTER'S SQUARE, PLIERS, WOOD GLUE...
...SAW, UTILITY KNIFE...
JEST LIKE I THOUGHT! NO HAMMER!
IT WOULD APPEAR THE WEAPON WAS TAKEN FROM THIS TOOLBOX.
EVEN AN OL' MAN OR A SKINNY GIRL COULD KILL A GUY WITH SOMETHIN' THAT HEAVY.
ANY OF OUR SUSPECTS COULD HAVE DONE IT.
NOR CAN WE USE THE TIME TO CLEAR ANYONE.
MISS KOSHIMIZU LEFT FOR THE BATHROOM FROM 7:26 AND 32 SECONDS TO 7:39 AND 15 SECONDS.
MR. TSUCHIO WENT OUT, SUPPOSEDLY FOR CIGARETTES, FROM 8:06 AND 47 SECONDS TO 9:28 AND 31 SECONDS.
AND MR. KOYA CAME UP TO THIS ROOM TO CHECK ON TOKITSU FROM 9:30 AND SIX SECONDS TO 9:38 AND 52 SECONDS.
ALL THREE HAD TIME TO COMMIT THE MURDER!
TO THE SEC-OND?
YEAH, BUT KOYA WAS ALONE IN THE KITCHEN MOST A' THE TIME. SHOULDN'T HE BE A SUSPECT TOO?
NO, THE WINDOWS IN THE KITCHEN ARE ALL SEALED SHUT.

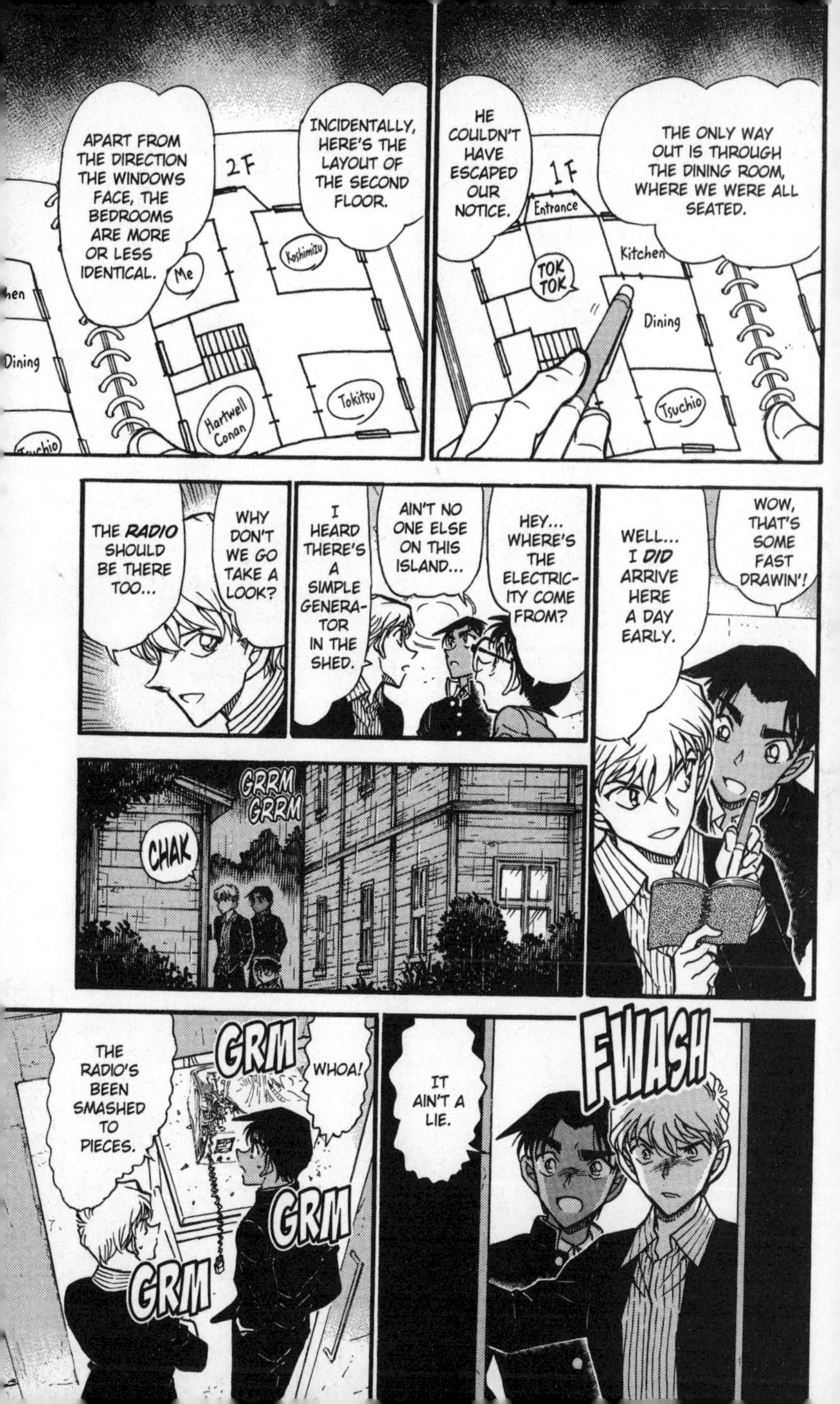
THE ONLY WAY OUT IS THROUGH THE DINING ROOM, WHERE WE WERE ALL SEATED.
HE COULDN'T HAVE ESCAPED OUR NOTICE.
1F
Entrance
Kitchen
TOK TOK
Dining
Tsuchio
INCIDENTALLY, HERE'S THE LAYOUT OF THE SECOND FLOOR.
APART FROM THE DIRECTION THE WINDOWS FACE, THE BEDROOMS ARE MORE OR LESS IDENTICAL.
2F
Koshimizu
Me
Tokitsu
Hartwell Conan
Dining
WOW, THAT'S SOME FAST DRAWIN'!
WELL... I *DID* ARRIVE HERE A DAY EARLY.
HEY... WHERE'S THE ELECTRICITY COME FROM?
AIN'T NO ONE ELSE ON THIS ISLAND...
I HEARD THERE'S A SIMPLE GENERATOR IN THE SHED.
WHY DON'T WE GO TAKE A LOOK?
THE *RADIO* SHOULD BE THERE TOO...
GRRM GRRM
CHAK
FWASH
IT AIN'T A LIE.
WHOA!
GRM
THE RADIO'S BEEN SMASHED TO PIECES.
GRM
GRM

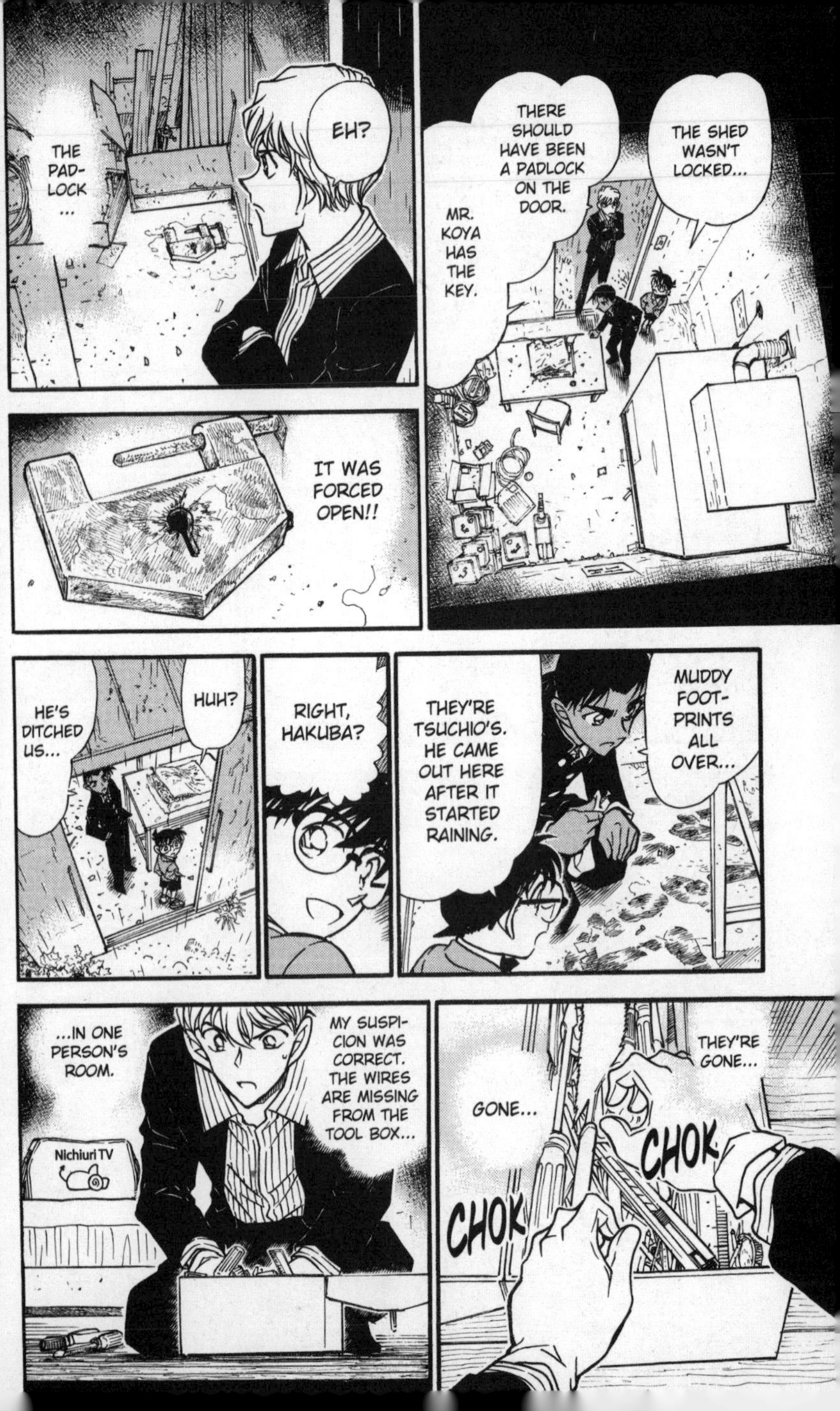
THE SHED WASN'T LOCKED...
THERE SHOULD HAVE BEEN A PADLOCK ON THE DOOR.
MR. KOYA HAS THE KEY.
EH?
THE PAD-LOCK...
IT WAS FORCED OPEN!!
MUDDY FOOT-PRINTS ALL OVER...
THEY'RE TSUCHIO'S. HE CAME OUT HERE AFTER IT STARTED RAINING.
RIGHT, HAKUBA?
HUH?
HE'S DITCHED US...
THEY'RE GONE...
GONE...
CHOK
CHOK
MY SUSPI-CION WAS CORRECT. THE WIRES ARE MISSING FROM THE TOOL BOX...
...IN ONE PERSON'S ROOM.
Nichiuri TV

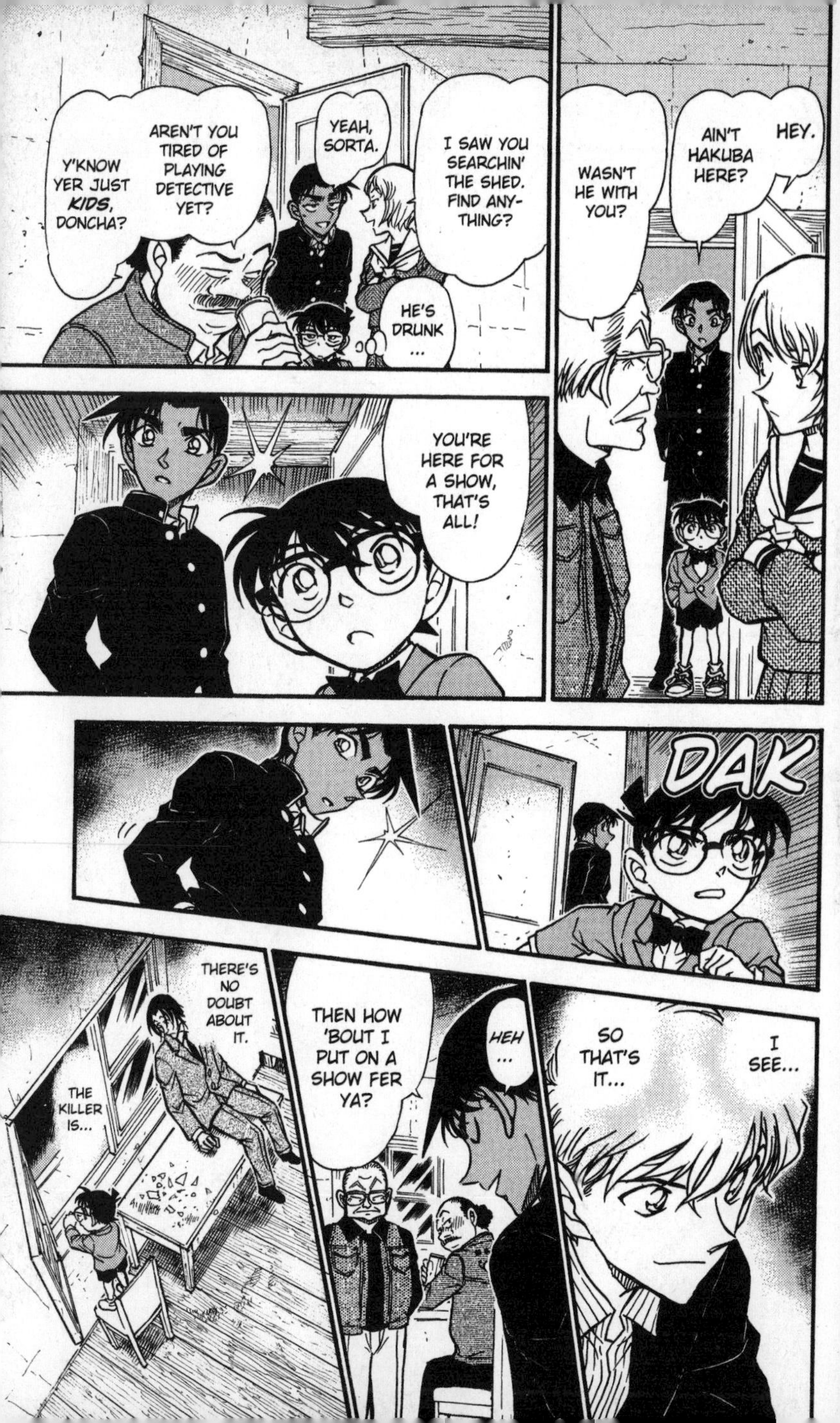
HEY.
AIN'T HAKUBA HERE?
WASN'T HE WITH YOU?
I SAW YOU SEARCHIN' THE SHED. FIND ANYTHING?
YEAH, SORTA.
AREN'T YOU TIRED OF PLAYING DETECTIVE YET?
Y'KNOW YER JUST KIDS, DONCHA?
HE'S DRUNK...
YOU'RE HERE FOR A SHOW, THAT'S ALL!
DAK
I SEE...
SO THAT'S IT...
HEH...
THEN HOW 'BOUT I PUT ON A SHOW FER YA?
THERE'S NO DOUBT ABOUT IT.
THE KILLER IS...

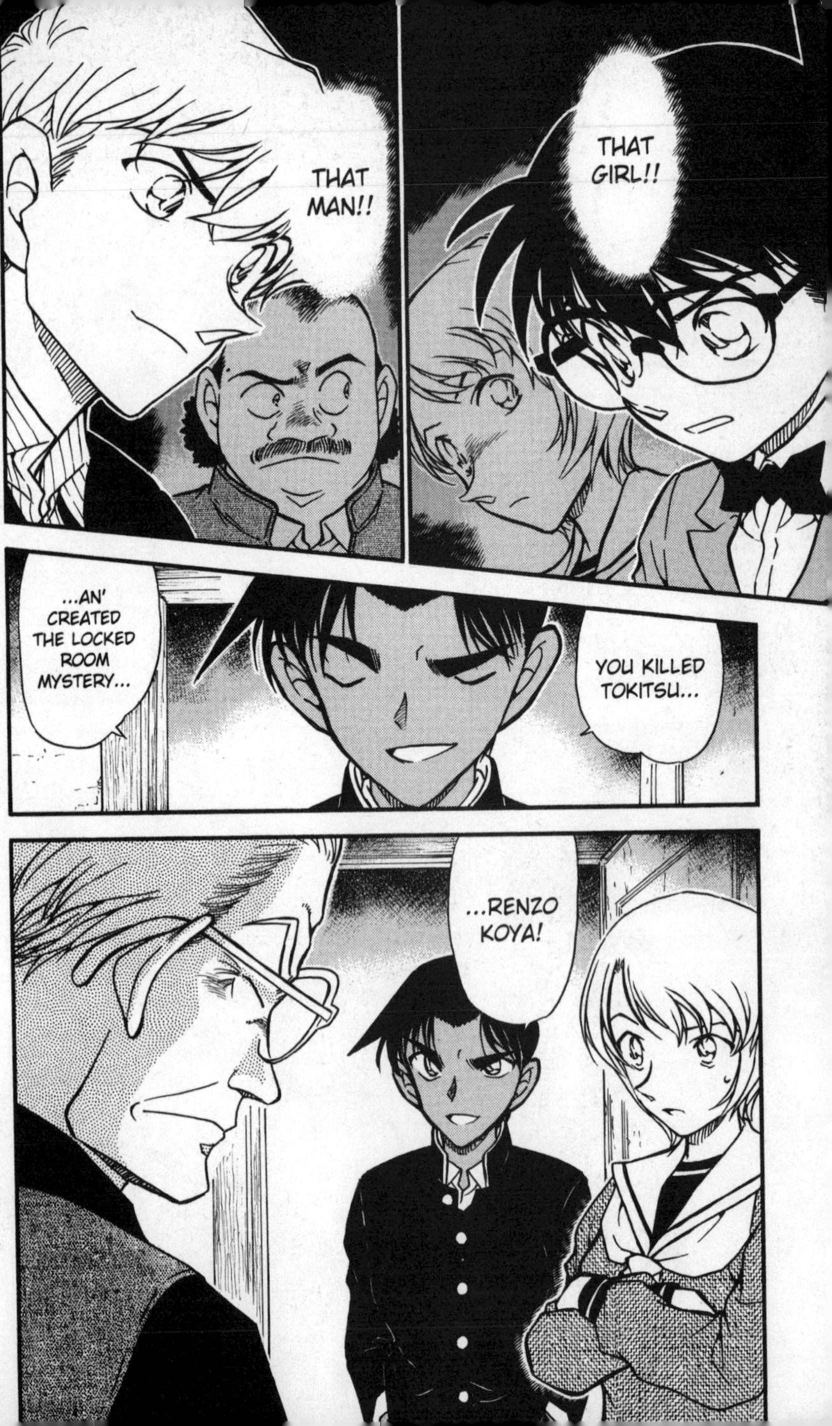
THAT GIRL!!
THAT MAN!!
YOU KILLED TOKITSU...
...AN' CREATED THE LOCKED ROOM MYSTERY...
...RENZO KOYA!

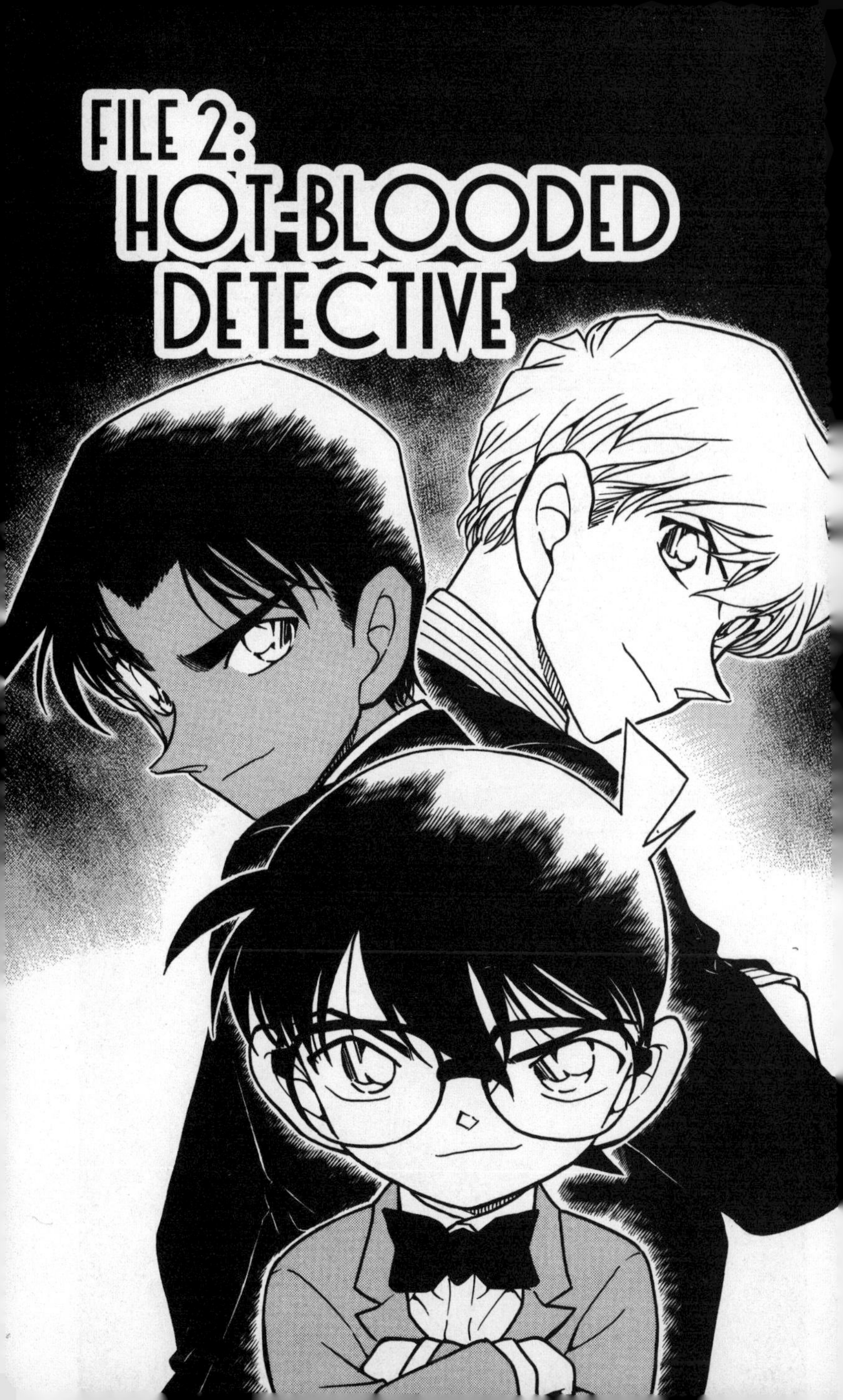
FILE 2:
HOT-BLOODED DETECTIVE

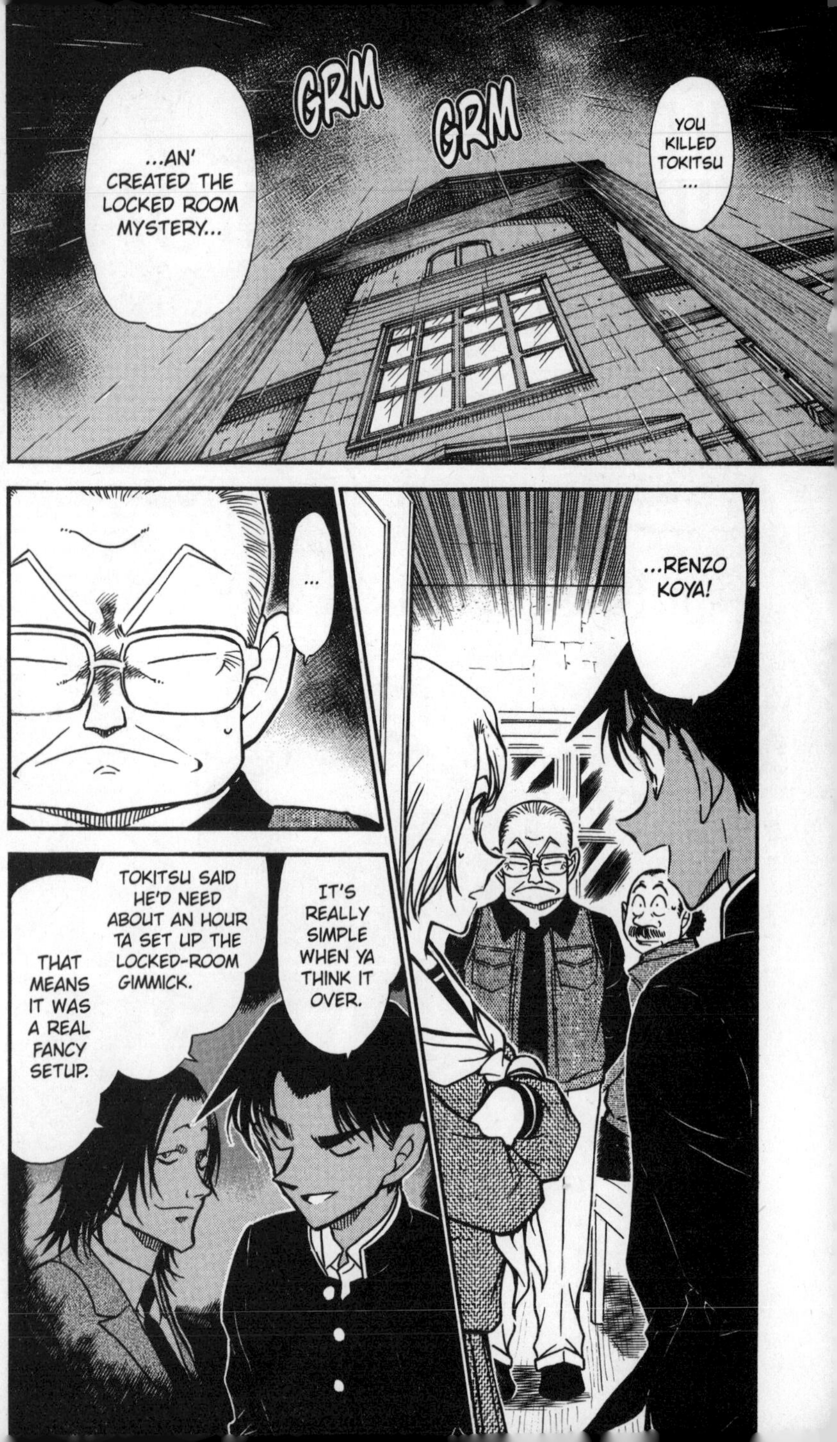
GRM GRM
YOU KILLED TOKITSU ...
...AN' CREATED THE LOCKED ROOM MYSTERY...
...RENZO KOYA!
...
IT'S REALLY SIMPLE WHEN YA THINK IT OVER.
TOKITSU SAID HE'D NEED ABOUT AN HOUR TA SET UP THE LOCKED-ROOM GIMMICK.
THAT MEANS IT WAS A REAL FANCY SETUP.

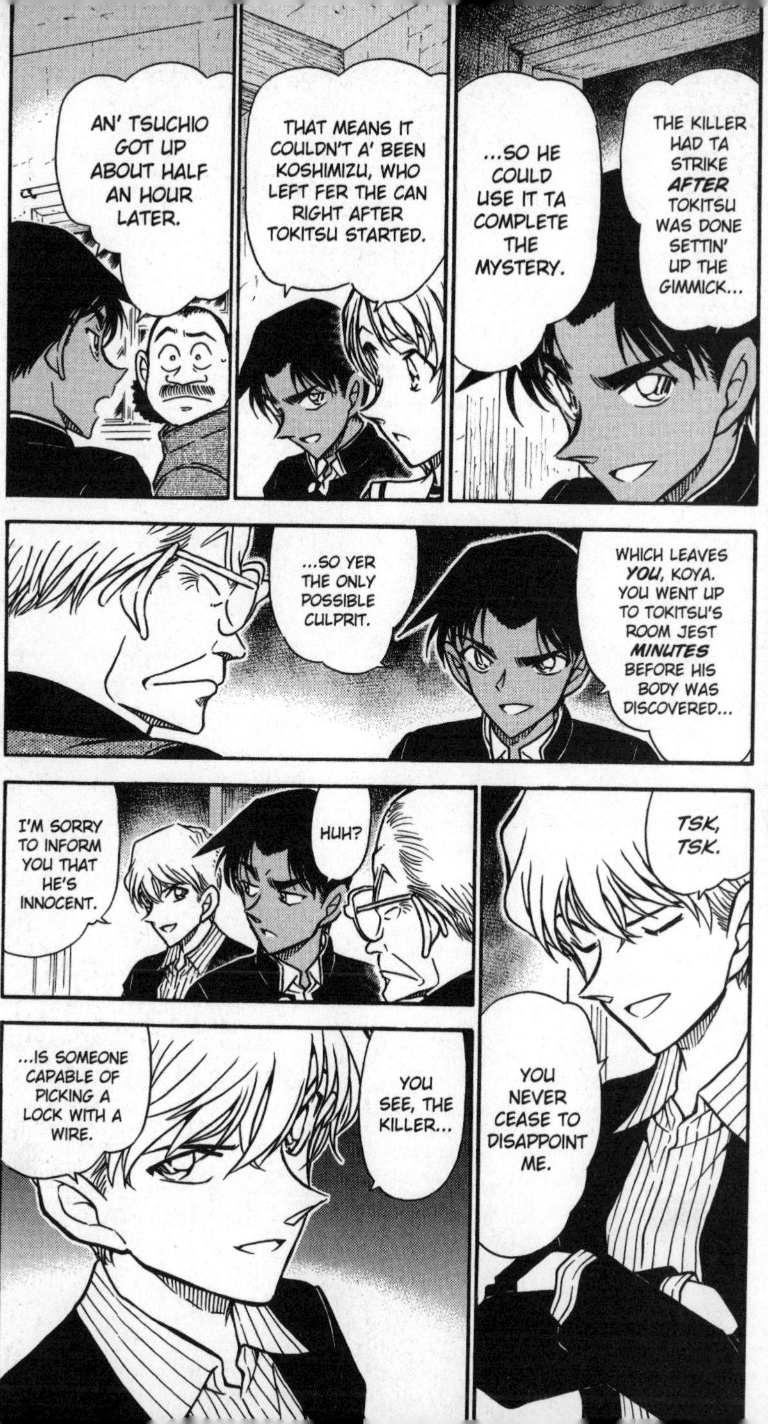
THE KILLER HAD TA STRIKE AFTER TOKITSU WAS DONE SETTIN' UP THE GIMMICK...
...SO HE COULD USE IT TA COMPLETE THE MYSTERY.
THAT MEANS IT COULDN'T A' BEEN KOSHIMIZU, WHO LEFT FER THE CAN RIGHT AFTER TOKITSU STARTED.
AN' TSUCHIO GOT UP ABOUT HALF AN HOUR LATER.
WHICH LEAVES YOU, KOYA. YOU WENT UP TO TOKITSU'S ROOM JEST MINUTES BEFORE HIS BODY WAS DISCOVERED...
...SO YER THE ONLY POSSIBLE CULPRIT.
TSK, TSK.
YOU NEVER CEASE TO DISAPPOINT ME.
HUH?
I'M SORRY TO INFORM YOU THAT HE'S INNOCENT.
YOU SEE, THE KILLER...
...IS SOMEONE CAPABLE OF PICKING A LOCK WITH A WIRE.

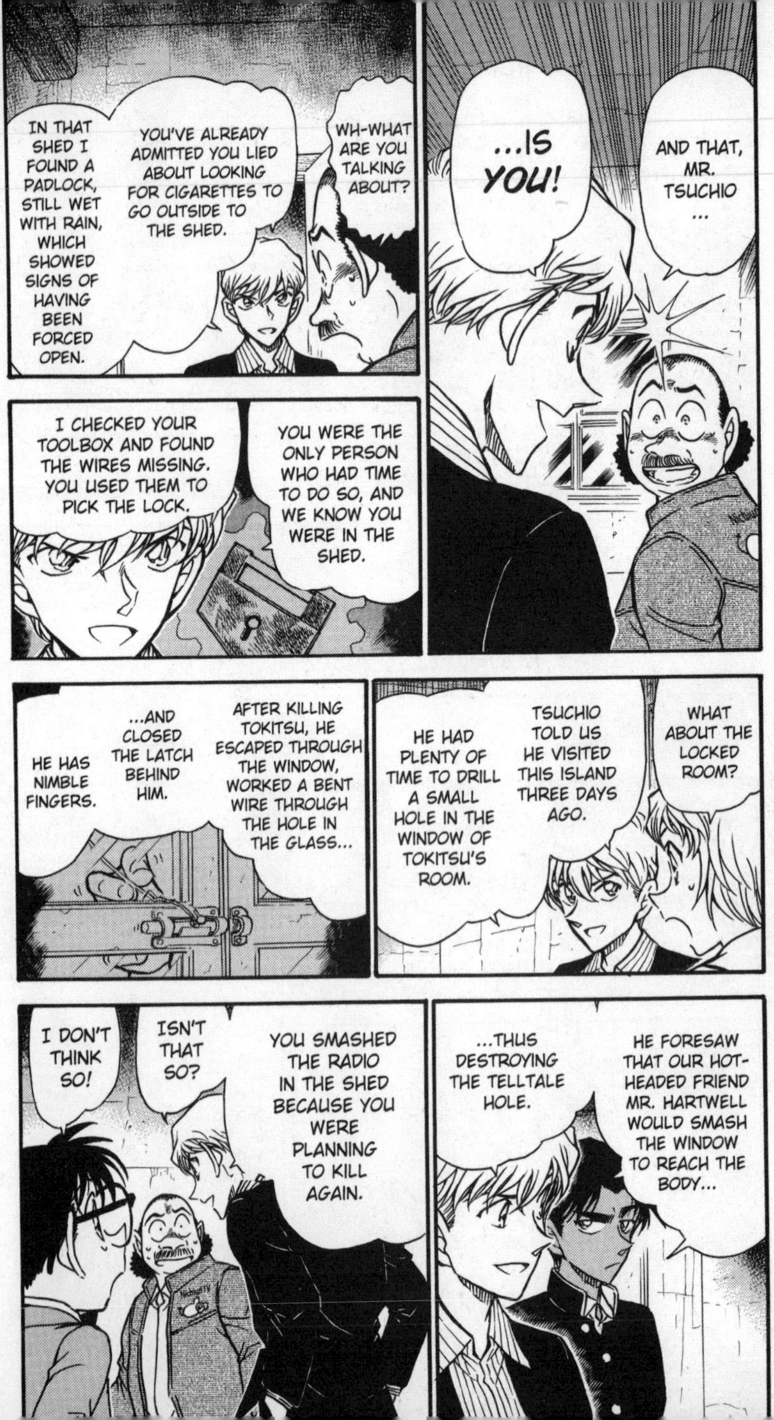
AND THAT, MR. TSUCHIO ...
...IS YOU!
WH-WHAT ARE YOU TALKING ABOUT?
YOU'VE ALREADY ADMITTED YOU LIED ABOUT LOOKING FOR CIGARETTES TO GO OUTSIDE TO THE SHED.
IN THAT SHED I FOUND A PADLOCK, STILL WET WITH RAIN, WHICH SHOWED SIGNS OF HAVING BEEN FORCED OPEN.
YOU WERE THE ONLY PERSON WHO HAD TIME TO DO SO, AND WE KNOW YOU WERE IN THE SHED.
I CHECKED YOUR TOOLBOX AND FOUND THE WIRES MISSING. YOU USED THEM TO PICK THE LOCK.
WHAT ABOUT THE LOCKED ROOM?
TSUCHIO TOLD US HE VISITED THIS ISLAND THREE DAYS AGO.
HE HAD PLENTY OF TIME TO DRILL A SMALL HOLE IN THE WINDOW OF TOKITSU'S ROOM.
AFTER KILLING TOKITSU, HE ESCAPED THROUGH THE WINDOW, WORKED A BENT WIRE THROUGH THE HOLE IN THE GLASS...
...AND CLOSED THE LATCH BEHIND HIM.
HE HAS NIMBLE FINGERS.
HE FORESAW THAT OUR HOT-HEADED FRIEND MR. HARTWELL WOULD SMASH THE WINDOW TO REACH THE BODY...
...THUS DESTROYING THE TELLTALE HOLE.
YOU SMASHED THE RADIO IN THE SHED BECAUSE YOU WERE PLANNING TO KILL AGAIN.
ISN'T THAT SO?
I DON'T THINK SO!

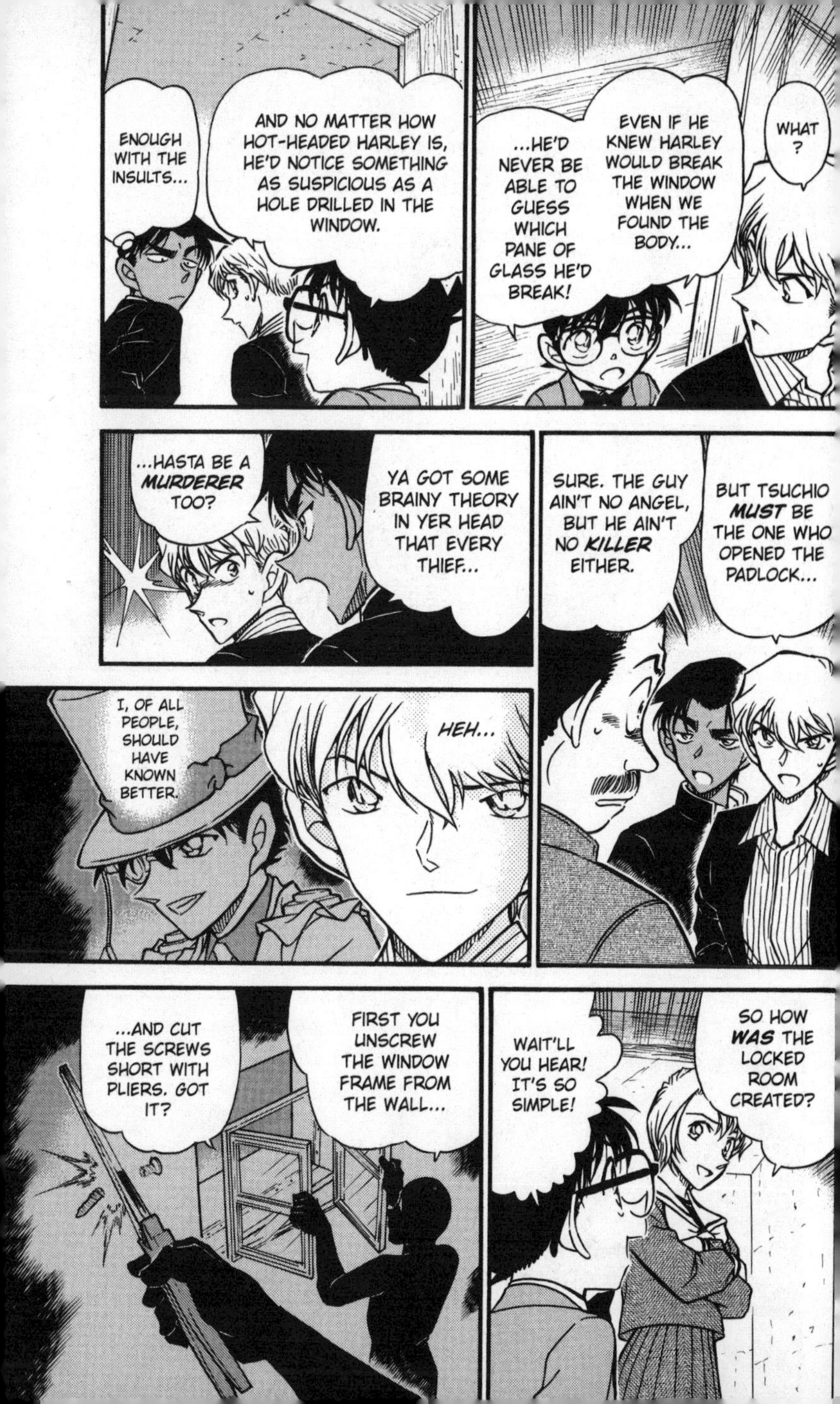
WHAT ?
EVEN IF HE KNEW HARLEY WOULD BREAK THE WINDOW WHEN WE FOUND THE BODY...
...HE'D NEVER BE ABLE TO GUESS WHICH PANE OF GLASS HE'D BREAK!
AND NO MATTER HOW HOT-HEADED HARLEY IS, HE'D NOTICE SOMETHING AS SUSPICIOUS AS A HOLE DRILLED IN THE WINDOW.
ENOUGH WITH THE INSULTS...
BUT TSUCHIO **MUST** BE THE ONE WHO OPENED THE PADLOCK...
SURE. THE GUY AIN'T NO ANGEL, BUT HE AIN'T NO ***KILLER*** EITHER.
YA GOT SOME BRAINY THEORY IN YER HEAD THAT EVERY THIEF...
...HASTA BE A ***MURDERER*** TOO?
HEH...
I, OF ALL PEOPLE, SHOULD HAVE KNOWN BETTER.
SO HOW ***WAS*** THE LOCKED ROOM CREATED?
WAIT'LL YOU HEAR! IT'S SO SIMPLE!
FIRST YOU UNSCREW THE WINDOW FRAME FROM THE WALL...
...AND CUT THE SCREWS SHORT WITH PLIERS. GOT IT?

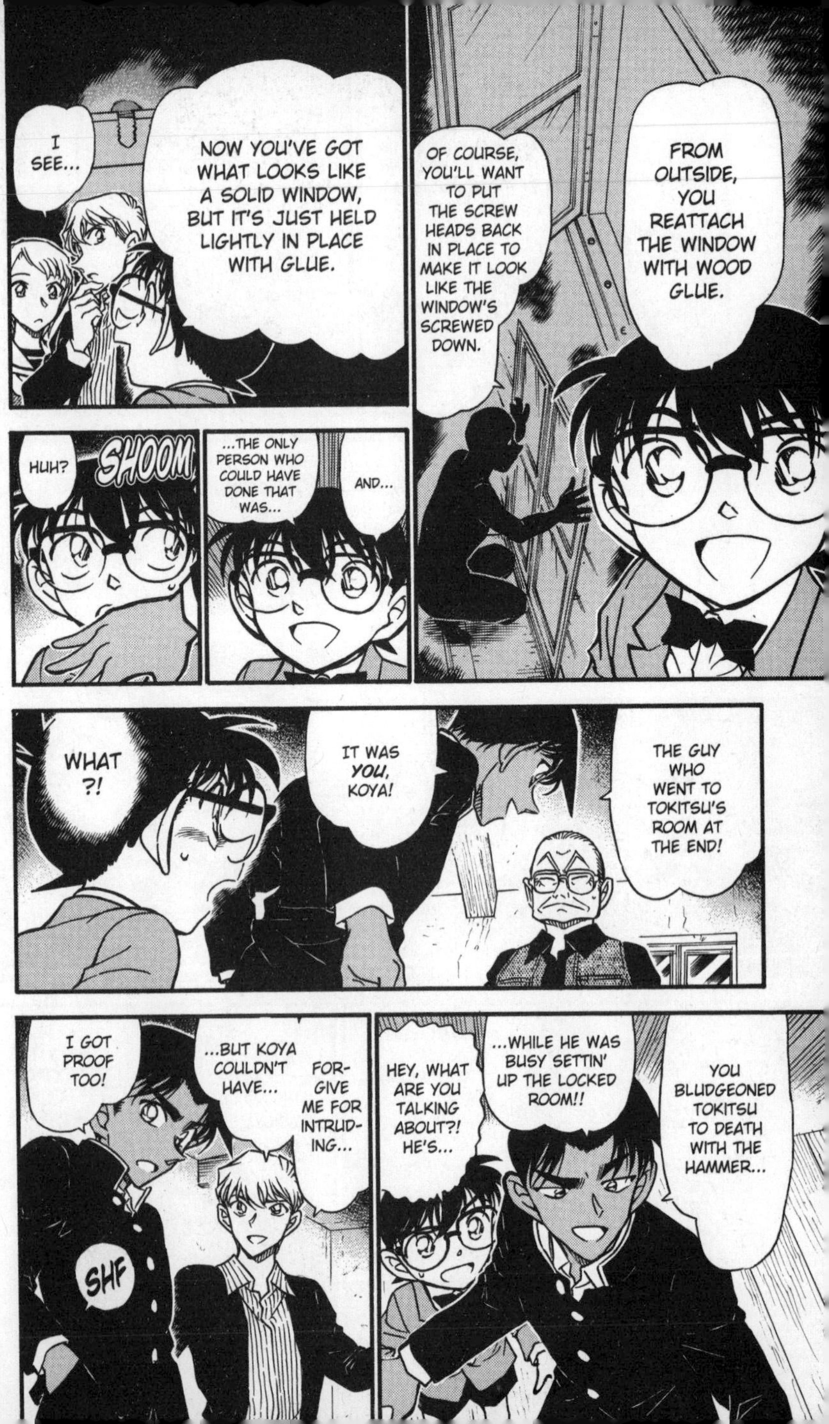

FROM OUTSIDE, YOU REATTACH THE WINDOW WITH WOOD GLUE.
OF COURSE, YOU'LL WANT TO PUT THE SCREW HEADS BACK IN PLACE TO MAKE IT LOOK LIKE THE WINDOW'S SCREWED DOWN.
NOW YOU'VE GOT WHAT LOOKS LIKE A SOLID WINDOW, BUT IT'S JUST HELD LIGHTLY IN PLACE WITH GLUE.
I SEE...
AND...
...THE ONLY PERSON WHO COULD HAVE DONE THAT WAS...
SHOOM
HUH?
THE GUY WHO WENT TO TOKITSU'S ROOM AT THE END!
IT WAS *YOU*, KOYA!
WHAT ?!
YOU BLUDGEONED TOKITSU TO DEATH WITH THE HAMMER...
...WHILE HE WAS BUSY SETTIN' UP THE LOCKED ROOM!!
HEY, WHAT ARE YOU TALKING ABOUT?! HE'S...
...BUT KOYA COULDN'T HAVE...
FOR-GIVE ME FOR INTRUD-ING...
I GOT PROOF TOO!
SHF

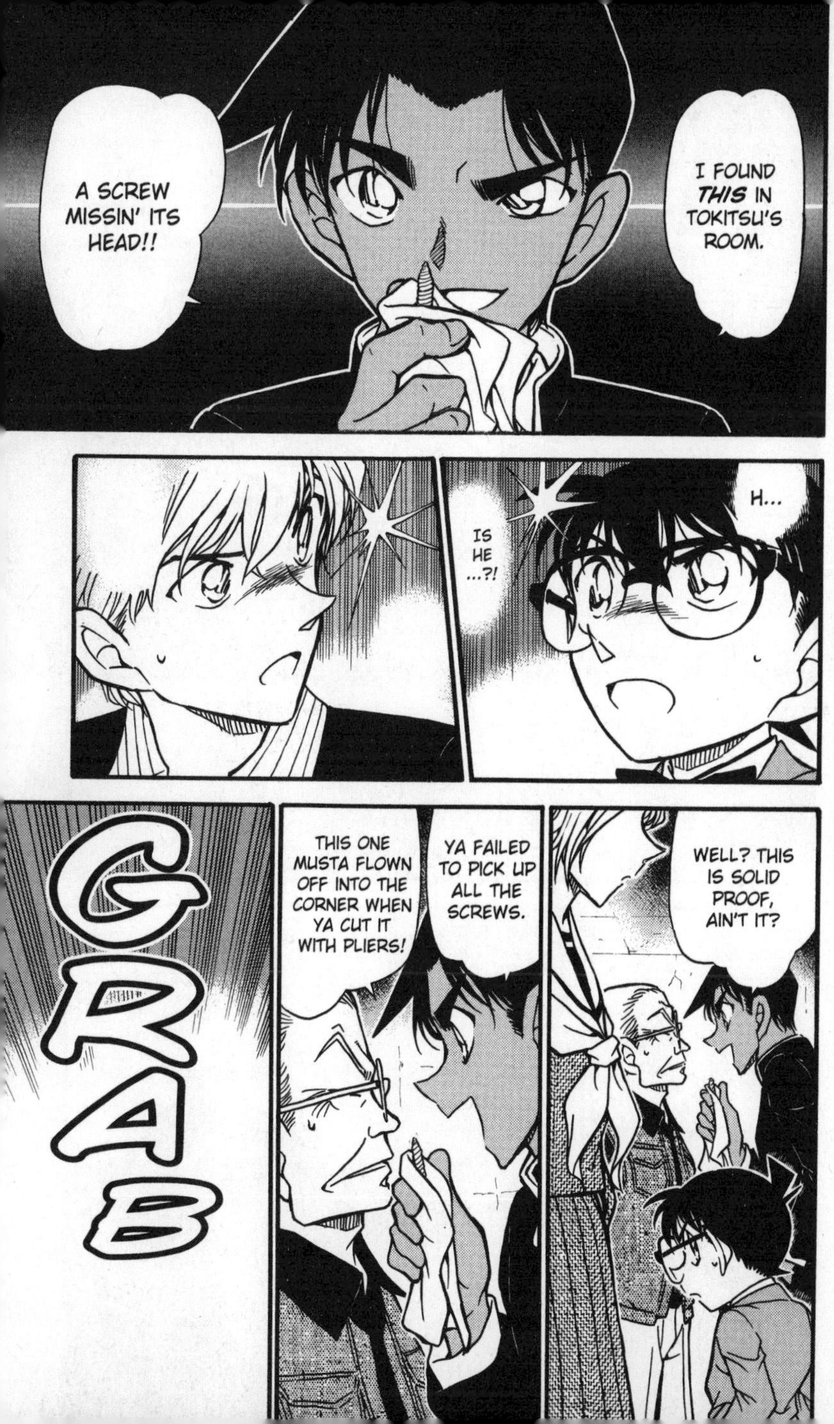
I FOUND THIS IN TOKITSU'S ROOM.
A SCREW MISSIN' ITS HEAD!!
H...
IS HE ...?!
WELL? THIS IS SOLID PROOF, AIN'T IT?
YA FAILED TO PICK UP ALL THE SCREWS.
THIS ONE MUSTA FLOWN OFF INTO THE CORNER WHEN YA CUT IT WITH PLIERS!
GRAB

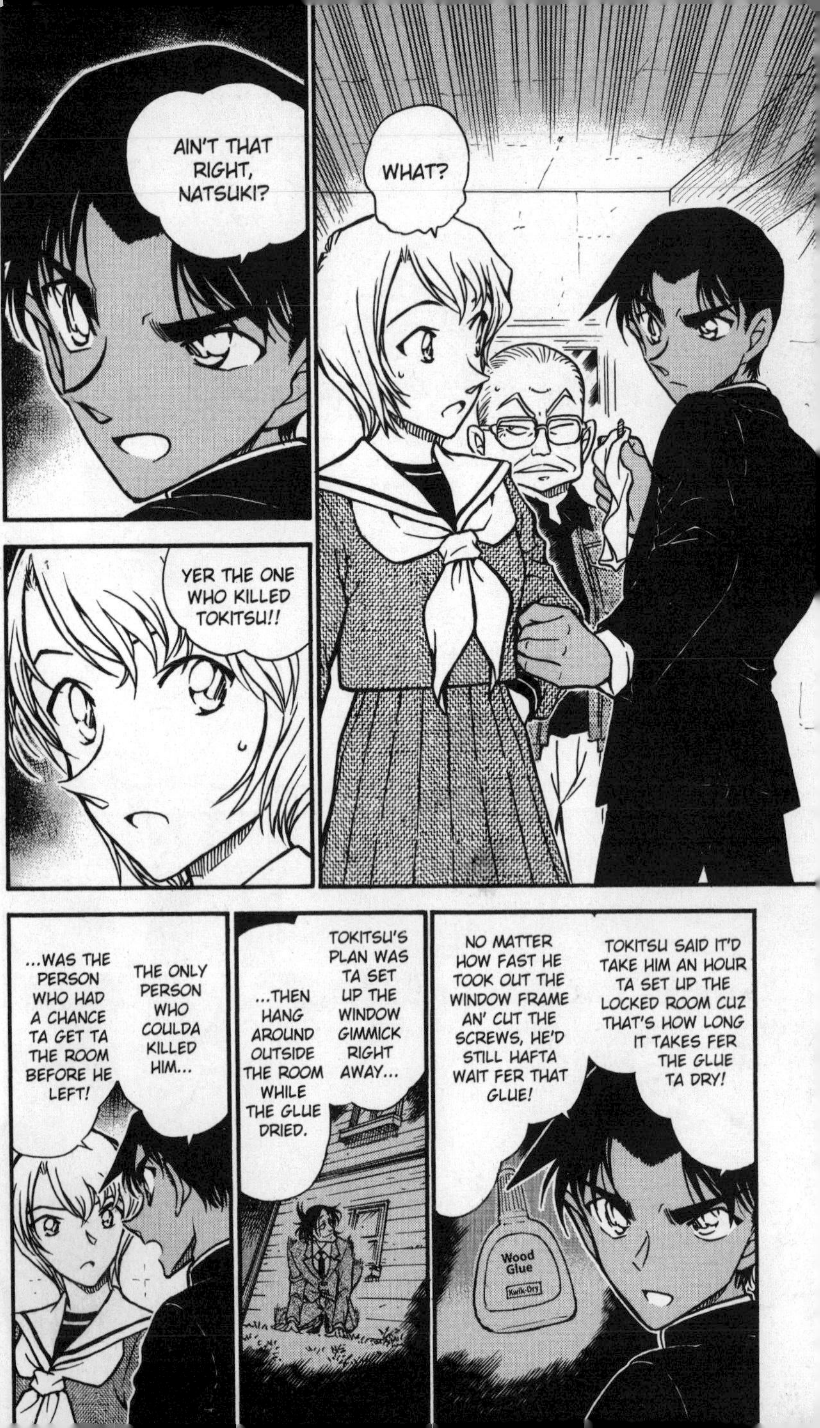
WHAT?
AIN'T THAT RIGHT, NATSUKI?
YER THE ONE WHO KILLED TOKITSU!!
TOKITSU SAID IT'D TAKE HIM AN HOUR TA SET UP THE LOCKED ROOM CUZ THAT'S HOW LONG IT TAKES FER THE GLUE TA DRY!
NO MATTER HOW FAST HE TOOK OUT THE WINDOW FRAME AN' CUT THE SCREWS, HE'D STILL HAFTA WAIT FER THAT GLUE!
Wood Glue
Kwik-Dry
TOKITSU'S PLAN WAS TA SET UP THE WINDOW GIMMICK RIGHT AWAY...
...THEN HANG AROUND OUTSIDE THE ROOM WHILE THE GLUE DRIED.
THE ONLY PERSON WHO COULDA KILLED HIM...
...WAS THE PERSON WHO HAD A CHANCE TA GET TA THE ROOM BEFORE HE LEFT!

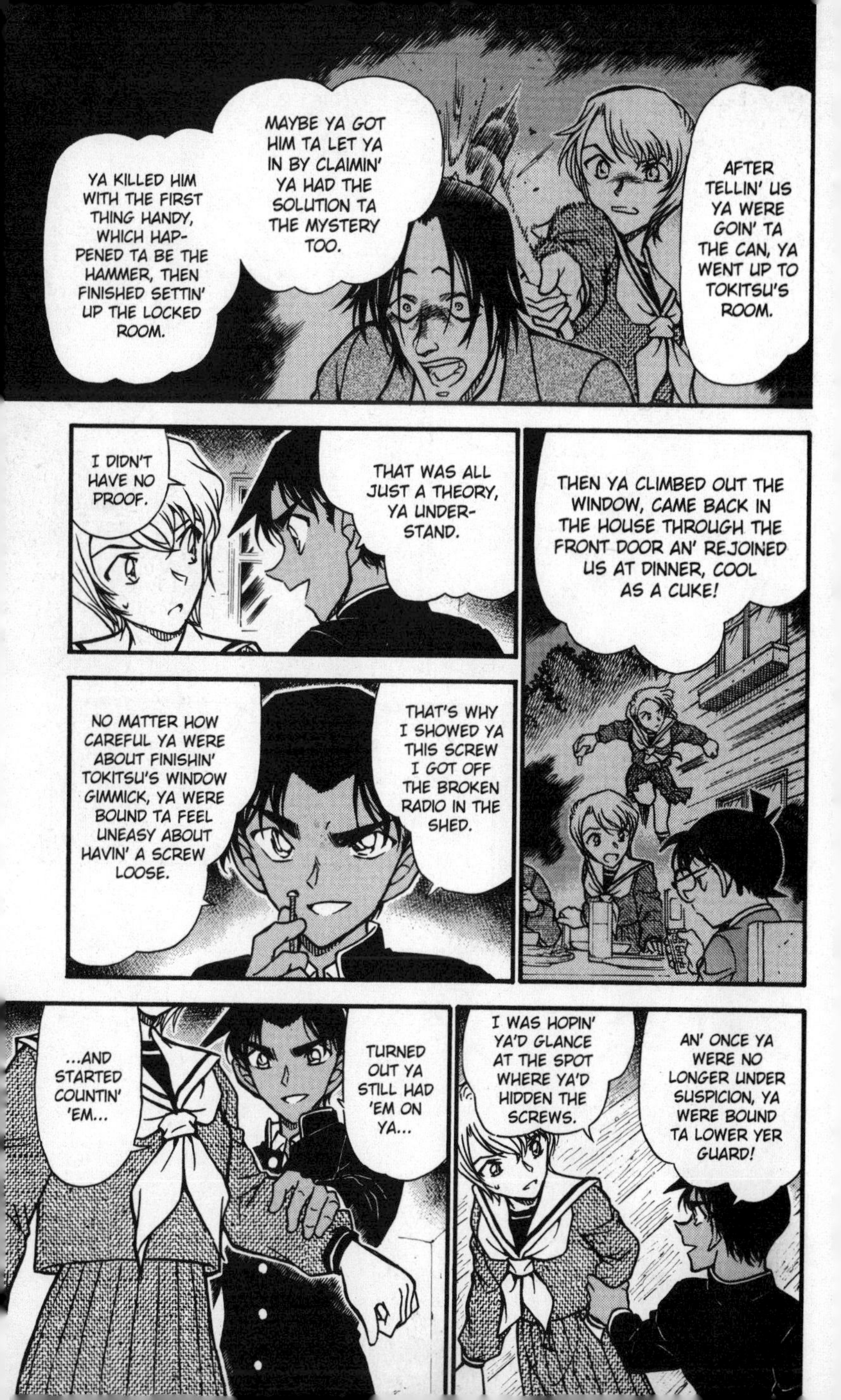
AFTER TELLIN' US YA WERE GOIN' TA THE CAN, YA WENT UP TO TOKITSU'S ROOM.
MAYBE YA GOT HIM TA LET YA IN BY CLAIMIN' YA HAD THE SOLUTION TA THE MYSTERY TOO.
YA KILLED HIM WITH THE FIRST THING HANDY, WHICH HAP-PENED TA BE THE HAMMER, THEN FINISHED SETTIN' UP THE LOCKED ROOM.
THEN YA CLIMBED OUT THE WINDOW, CAME BACK IN THE HOUSE THROUGH THE FRONT DOOR AN' REJOINED US AT DINNER, COOL AS A CUKE!
THAT WAS ALL JUST A THEORY, YA UNDER-STAND.
I DIDN'T HAVE NO PROOF.
THAT'S WHY I SHOWED YA THIS SCREW I GOT OFF THE BROKEN RADIO IN THE SHED.
NO MATTER HOW CAREFUL YA WERE ABOUT FINISHIN' TOKITSU'S WINDOW GIMMICK, YA WERE BOUND TA FEEL UNEASY ABOUT HAVIN' A SCREW LOOSE.
AN' ONCE YA WERE NO LONGER UNDER SUSPICION, YA WERE BOUND TA LOWER YER GUARD!
I WAS HOPIN' YA'D GLANCE AT THE SPOT WHERE YA'D HIDDEN THE SCREWS.
TURNED OUT YA STILL HAD 'EM ON YA...
...AND STARTED COUNTIN' 'EM...

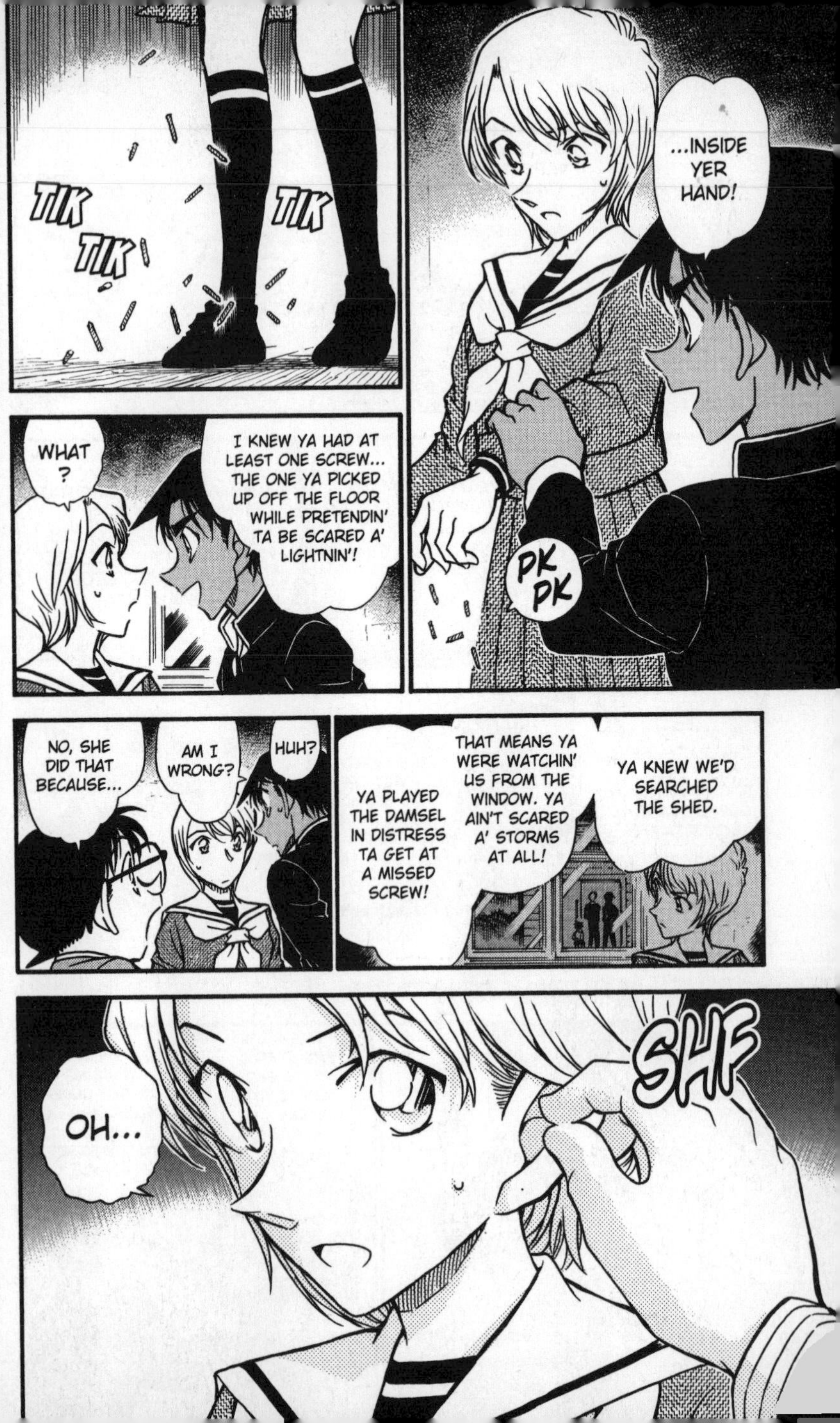
...INSIDE YER HAND!
PK PK
TIK
TIK
TIK
I KNEW YA HAD AT LEAST ONE SCREW... THE ONE YA PICKED UP OFF THE FLOOR WHILE PRETENDIN' TA BE SCARED A' LIGHTNIN'!
WHAT?
YA KNEW WE'D SEARCHED THE SHED.
THAT MEANS YA WERE WATCHIN' US FROM THE WINDOW. YA AIN'T SCARED A' STORMS AT ALL!
YA PLAYED THE DAMSEL IN DISTRESS TA GET AT A MISSED SCREW!
HUH?
AM I WRONG?
NO, SHE DID THAT BECAUSE...
SHF
OH...

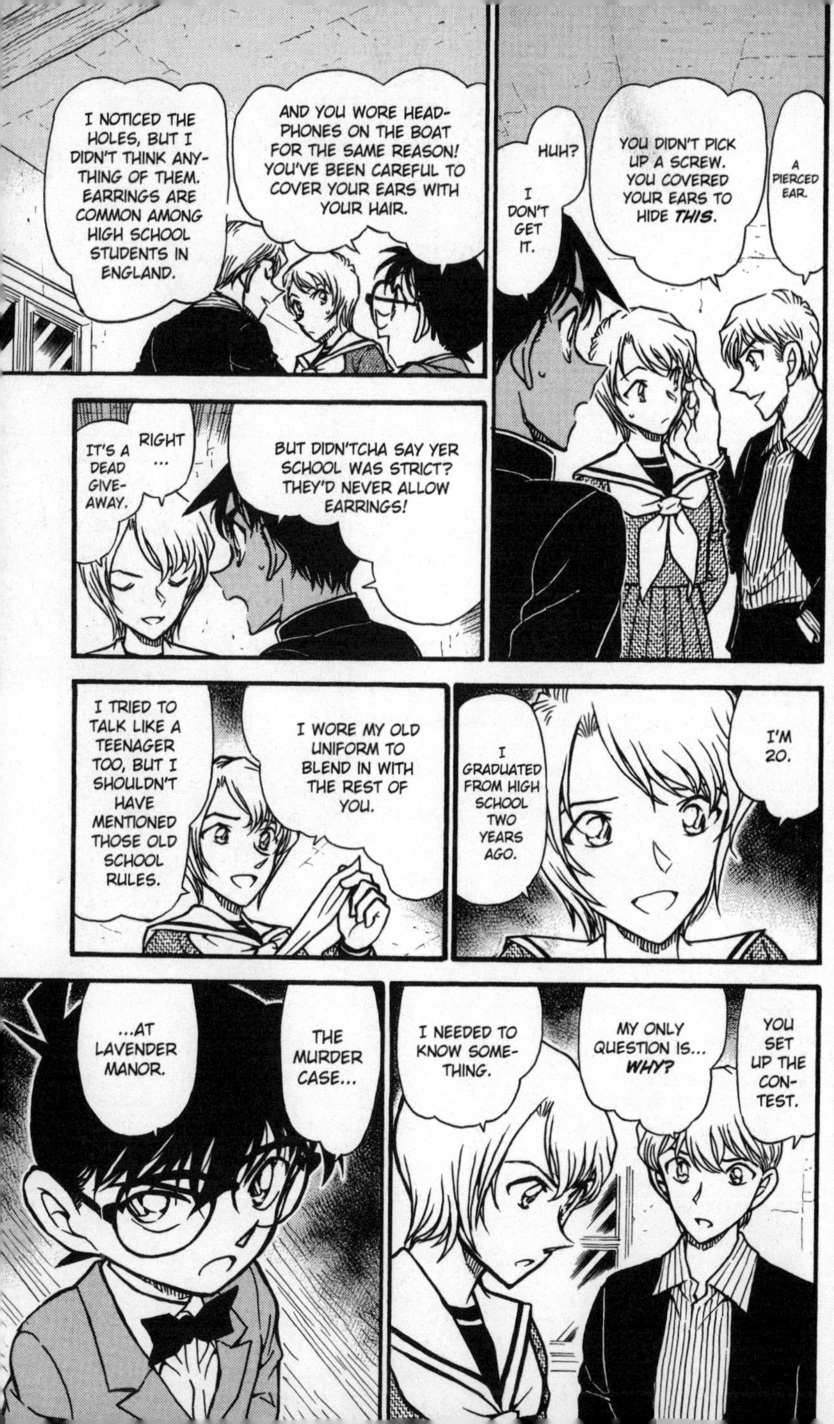
A PIERCED EAR.
YOU DIDN'T PICK UP A SCREW. YOU COVERED YOUR EARS TO HIDE ***THIS***.
HUH?
I DON'T GET IT.
AND YOU WORE HEADPHONES ON THE BOAT FOR THE SAME REASON! YOU'VE BEEN CAREFUL TO COVER YOUR EARS WITH YOUR HAIR.
I NOTICED THE HOLES, BUT I DIDN'T THINK ANYTHING OF THEM. EARRINGS ARE COMMON AMONG HIGH SCHOOL STUDENTS IN ENGLAND.
BUT DIDN'TCHA SAY YER SCHOOL WAS STRICT? THEY'D NEVER ALLOW EARRINGS!
RIGHT...
IT'S A DEAD GIVEAWAY.
I'M 20.
I GRADUATED FROM HIGH SCHOOL TWO YEARS AGO.
I WORE MY OLD UNIFORM TO BLEND IN WITH THE REST OF YOU.
I TRIED TO TALK LIKE A TEENAGER TOO, BUT I SHOULDN'T HAVE MENTIONED THOSE OLD SCHOOL RULES.
YOU SET UP THE CONTEST.
MY ONLY QUESTION IS... ***WHY?***
I NEEDED TO KNOW SOMETHING.
THE MURDER CASE...
...AT LAVENDER MANOR.

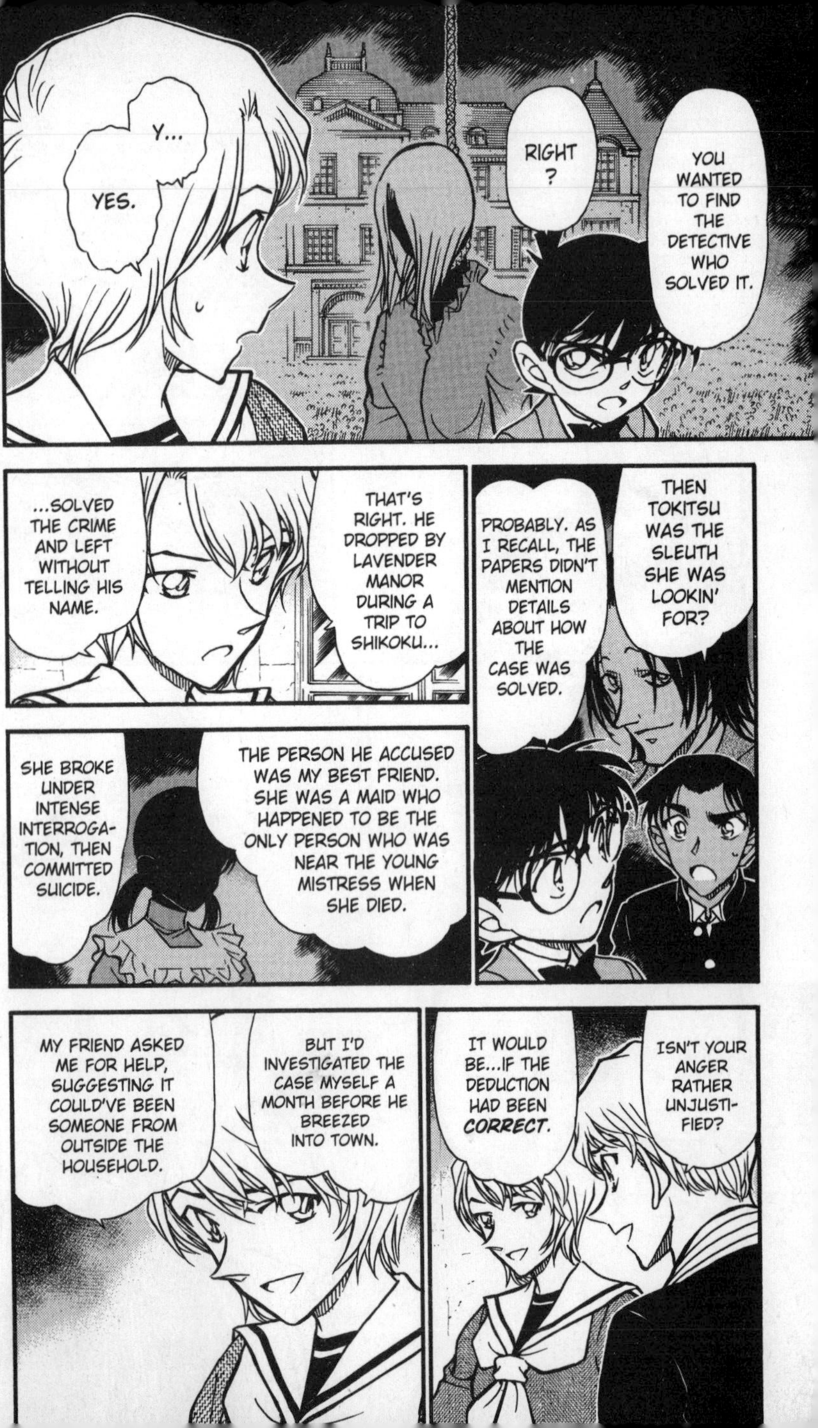
YOU WANTED TO FIND THE DETECTIVE WHO SOLVED IT.
RIGHT ?
Y... YES.
THEN TOKITSU WAS THE SLEUTH SHE WAS LOOKIN' FOR?
PROBABLY. AS I RECALL, THE PAPERS DIDN'T MENTION DETAILS ABOUT HOW THE CASE WAS SOLVED.
THAT'S RIGHT. HE DROPPED BY LAVENDER MANOR DURING A TRIP TO SHIKOKU...
...SOLVED THE CRIME AND LEFT WITHOUT TELLING HIS NAME.
THE PERSON HE ACCUSED WAS MY BEST FRIEND. SHE WAS A MAID WHO HAPPENED TO BE THE ONLY PERSON WHO WAS NEAR THE YOUNG MISTRESS WHEN SHE DIED.
SHE BROKE UNDER INTENSE INTERROGA-TION, THEN COMMITTED SUICIDE.
ISN'T YOUR ANGER RATHER UNJUSTI-FIED?
IT WOULD BE...IF THE DEDUCTION HAD BEEN ***CORRECT***.
BUT I'D INVESTIGATED THE CASE MYSELF A MONTH BEFORE HE BREEZED INTO TOWN.
MY FRIEND ASKED ME FOR HELP, SUGGESTING IT COULD'VE BEEN SOMEONE FROM OUTSIDE THE HOUSEHOLD.

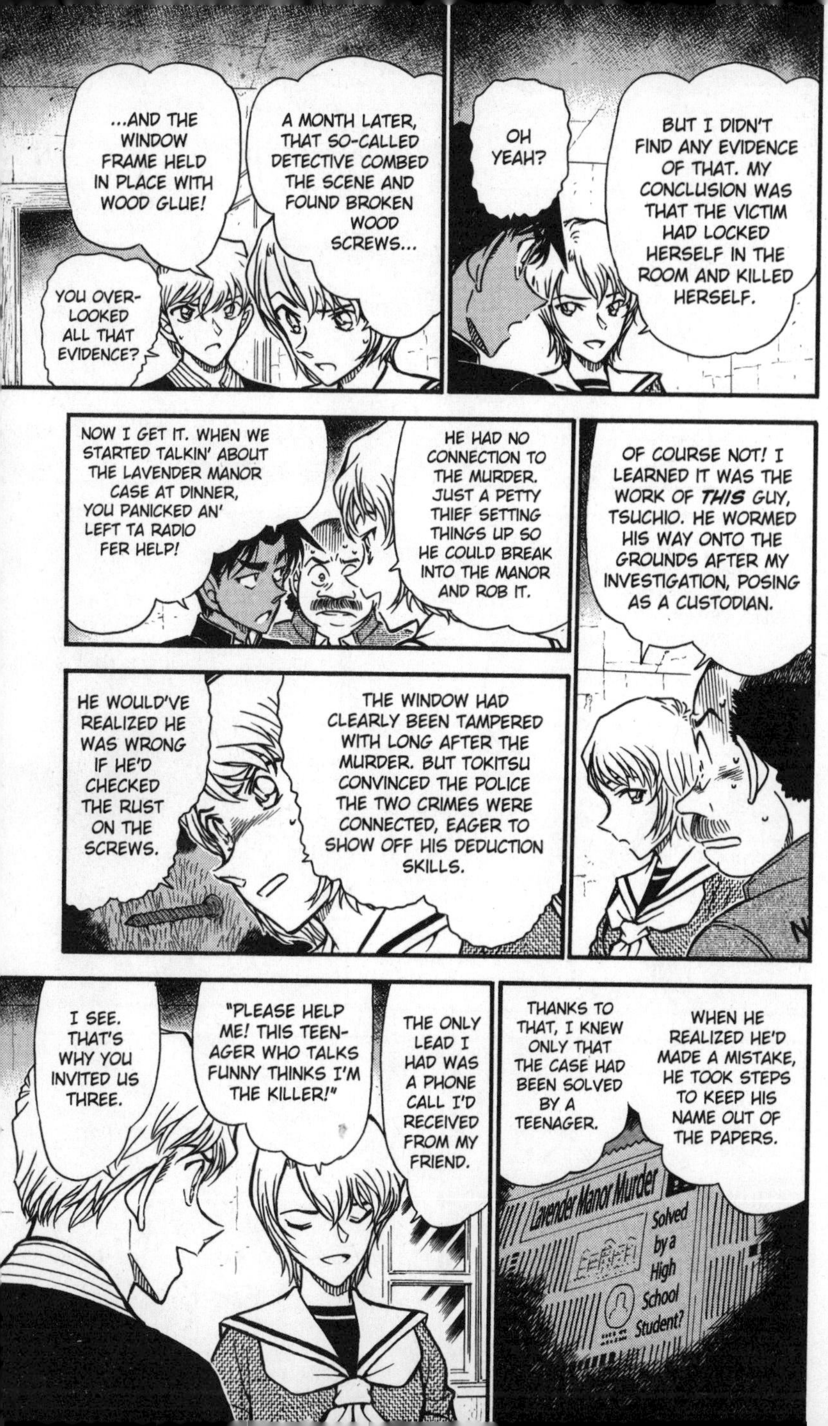
BUT I DIDN'T FIND ANY EVIDENCE OF THAT. MY CONCLUSION WAS THAT THE VICTIM HAD LOCKED HERSELF IN THE ROOM AND KILLED HERSELF.
OH YEAH?
A MONTH LATER, THAT SO-CALLED DETECTIVE COMBED THE SCENE AND FOUND BROKEN WOOD SCREWS...
...AND THE WINDOW FRAME HELD IN PLACE WITH WOOD GLUE!
YOU OVER-LOOKED ALL THAT EVIDENCE?
OF COURSE NOT! I LEARNED IT WAS THE WORK OF *THIS* GUY, TSUCHIO. HE WORMED HIS WAY ONTO THE GROUNDS AFTER MY INVESTIGATION, POSING AS A CUSTODIAN.
HE HAD NO CONNECTION TO THE MURDER. JUST A PETTY THIEF SETTING THINGS UP SO HE COULD BREAK INTO THE MANOR AND ROB IT.
NOW I GET IT. WHEN WE STARTED TALKIN' ABOUT THE LAVENDER MANOR CASE AT DINNER, YOU PANICKED AN' LEFT TA RADIO FER HELP!
THE WINDOW HAD CLEARLY BEEN TAMPERED WITH LONG AFTER THE MURDER. BUT TOKITSU CONVINCED THE POLICE THE TWO CRIMES WERE CONNECTED, EAGER TO SHOW OFF HIS DEDUCTION SKILLS.
HE WOULD'VE REALIZED HE WAS WRONG IF HE'D CHECKED THE RUST ON THE SCREWS.
WHEN HE REALIZED HE'D MADE A MISTAKE, HE TOOK STEPS TO KEEP HIS NAME OUT OF THE PAPERS.
THANKS TO THAT, I KNEW ONLY THAT THE CASE HAD BEEN SOLVED BY A TEENAGER.
Lavender Manor Murder
Solved by a High School Student?
THE ONLY LEAD I HAD WAS A PHONE CALL I'D RECEIVED FROM MY FRIEND.
"PLEASE HELP ME! THIS TEEN-AGER WHO TALKS FUNNY THINKS I'M THE KILLER!"
I SEE. THAT'S WHY YOU INVITED US THREE.

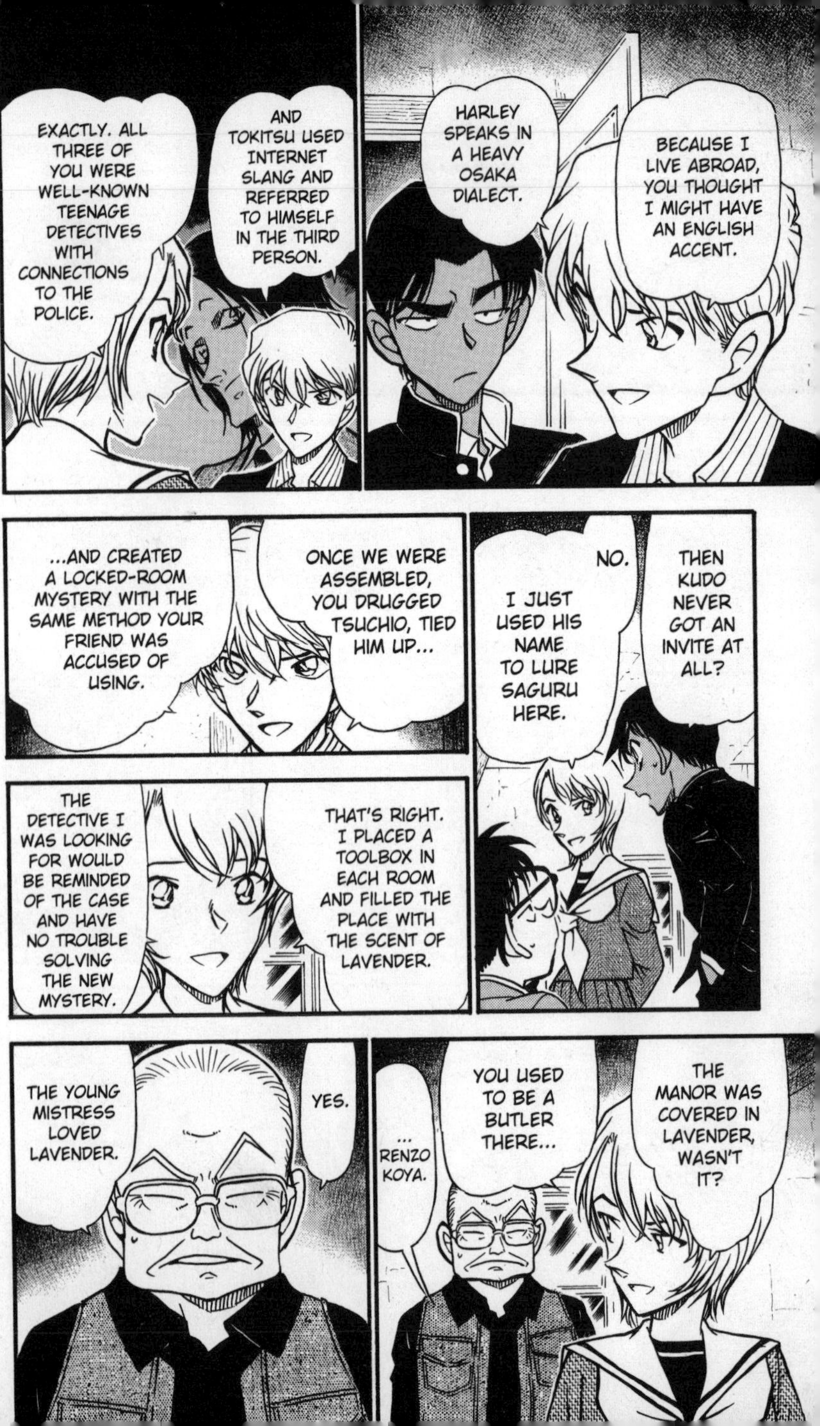
BECAUSE I LIVE ABROAD, YOU THOUGHT I MIGHT HAVE AN ENGLISH ACCENT.
HARLEY SPEAKS IN A HEAVY OSAKA DIALECT.
AND TOKITSU USED INTERNET SLANG AND REFERRED TO HIMSELF IN THE THIRD PERSON.
EXACTLY. ALL THREE OF YOU WERE WELL-KNOWN TEENAGE DETECTIVES WITH CONNECTIONS TO THE POLICE.
THEN KUDO NEVER GOT AN INVITE AT ALL?
NO.
I JUST USED HIS NAME TO LURE SAGURU HERE.
ONCE WE WERE ASSEMBLED, YOU DRUGGED TSUCHIO, TIED HIM UP...
...AND CREATED A LOCKED-ROOM MYSTERY WITH THE SAME METHOD YOUR FRIEND WAS ACCUSED OF USING.
THAT'S RIGHT. I PLACED A TOOLBOX IN EACH ROOM AND FILLED THE PLACE WITH THE SCENT OF LAVENDER.
THE DETECTIVE I WAS LOOKING FOR WOULD BE REMINDED OF THE CASE AND HAVE NO TROUBLE SOLVING THE NEW MYSTERY.
THE MANOR WAS COVERED IN LAVENDER, WASN'T IT?
YOU USED TO BE A BUTLER THERE...
...RENZO KOYA.
YES.
THE YOUNG MISTRESS LOVED LAVENDER.

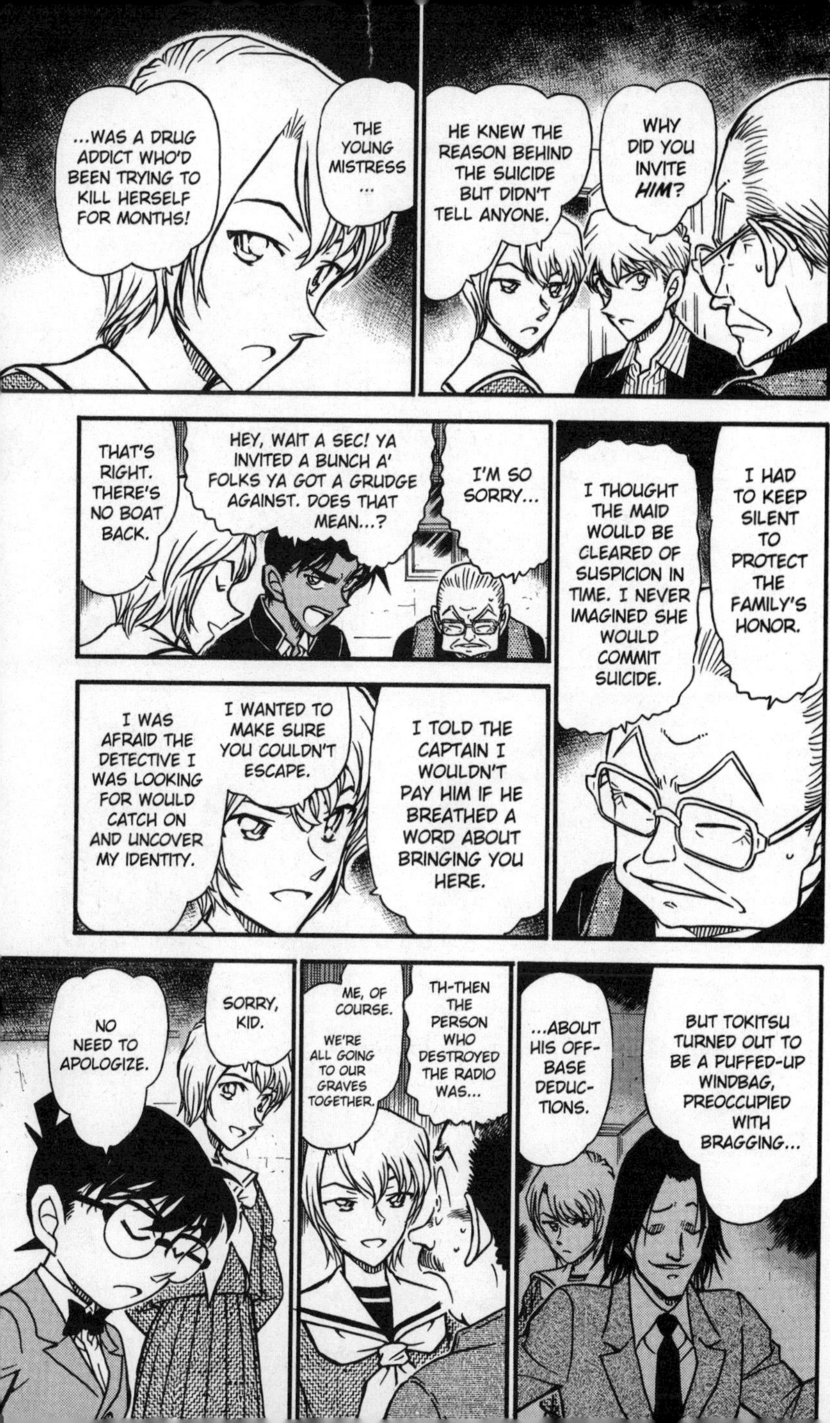
WHY DID YOU INVITE *HIM*?
HE KNEW THE REASON BEHIND THE SUICIDE BUT DIDN'T TELL ANYONE.
THE YOUNG MISTRESS...
...WAS A DRUG ADDICT WHO'D BEEN TRYING TO KILL HERSELF FOR MONTHS!
I HAD TO KEEP SILENT TO PROTECT THE FAMILY'S HONOR.
I THOUGHT THE MAID WOULD BE CLEARED OF SUSPICION IN TIME. I NEVER IMAGINED SHE WOULD COMMIT SUICIDE.
I'M SO SORRY...
HEY, WAIT A SEC! YA INVITED A BUNCH A' FOLKS YA GOT A GRUDGE AGAINST. DOES THAT MEAN...?
THAT'S RIGHT. THERE'S NO BOAT BACK.
I TOLD THE CAPTAIN I WOULDN'T PAY HIM IF HE BREATHED A WORD ABOUT BRINGING YOU HERE.
I WANTED TO MAKE SURE YOU COULDN'T ESCAPE.
I WAS AFRAID THE DETECTIVE I WAS LOOKING FOR WOULD CATCH ON AND UNCOVER MY IDENTITY.
BUT TOKITSU TURNED OUT TO BE A PUFFED-UP WINDBAG, PREOCCUPIED WITH BRAGGING...
...ABOUT HIS OFF-BASE DEDUCTIONS.
TH-THEN THE PERSON WHO DESTROYED THE RADIO WAS...
ME, OF COURSE.
WE'RE ALL GOING TO OUR GRAVES TOGETHER.
SORRY, KID.
NO NEED TO APOLOGIZE.

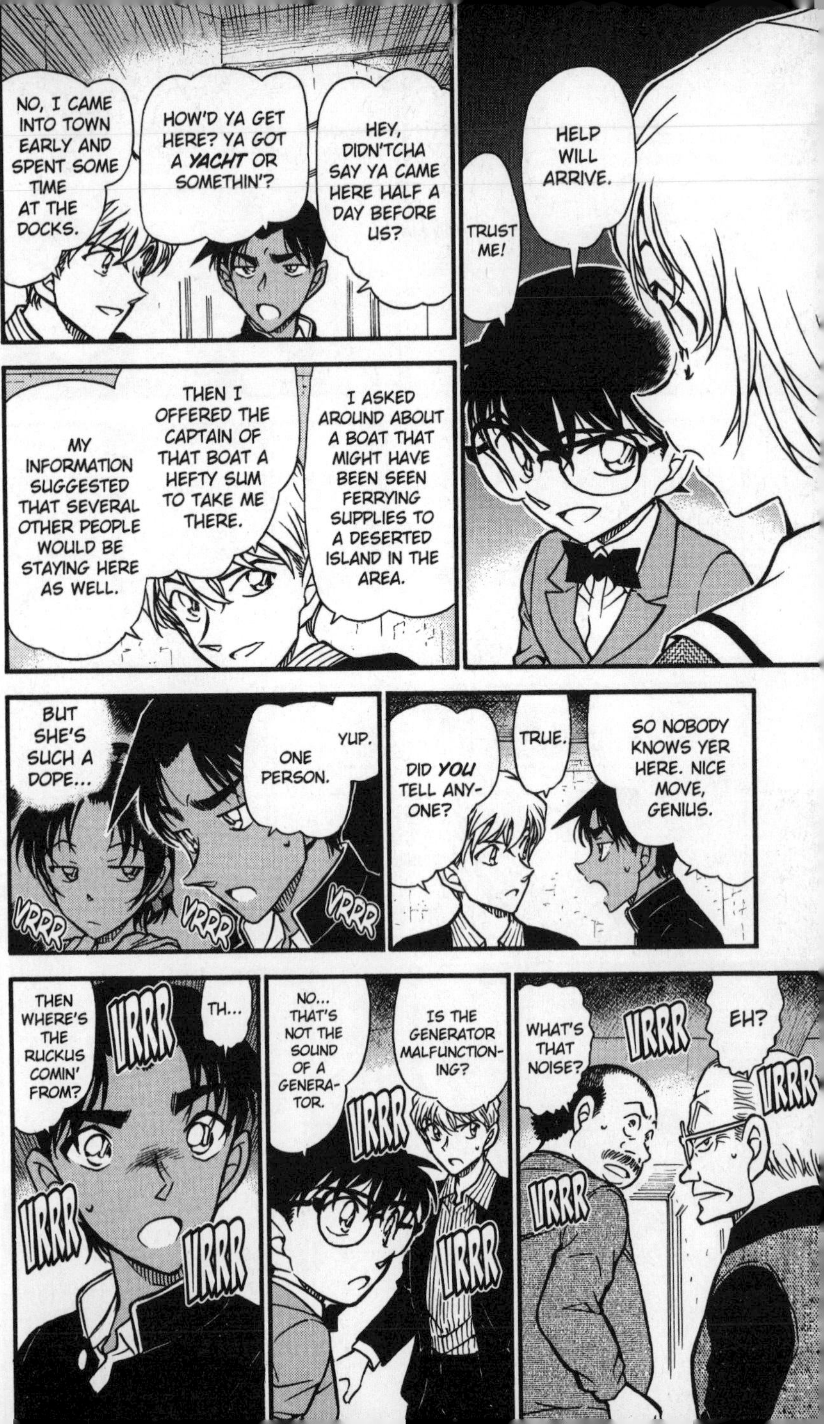
HELP WILL ARRIVE.
TRUST ME!
HEY, DIDN'TCHA SAY YA CAME HERE HALF A DAY BEFORE US?
HOW'D YA GET HERE? YA GOT A *YACHT* OR SOMETHIN'?
NO, I CAME INTO TOWN EARLY AND SPENT SOME TIME AT THE DOCKS.
I ASKED AROUND ABOUT A BOAT THAT MIGHT HAVE BEEN SEEN FERRYING SUPPLIES TO A DESERTED ISLAND IN THE AREA.
THEN I OFFERED THE CAPTAIN OF THAT BOAT A HEFTY SUM TO TAKE ME THERE.
MY INFORMATION SUGGESTED THAT SEVERAL OTHER PEOPLE WOULD BE STAYING HERE AS WELL.
SO NOBODY KNOWS YER HERE. NICE MOVE, GENIUS.
TRUE.
DID *YOU* TELL ANYONE?
YUP.
ONE PERSON.
BUT SHE'S SUCH A DOPE...
VRRR
VRRR
VRRR
EH?
VRRR
WHAT'S THAT NOISE?
VRRR
VRRR
IS THE GENERATOR MALFUNCTIONING?
NO... THAT'S NOT THE SOUND OF A GENERATOR.
VRRR
VRRR
TH...
VRRR
THEN WHERE'S THE RUCKUS COMIN' FROM?
VRRR
VRRR

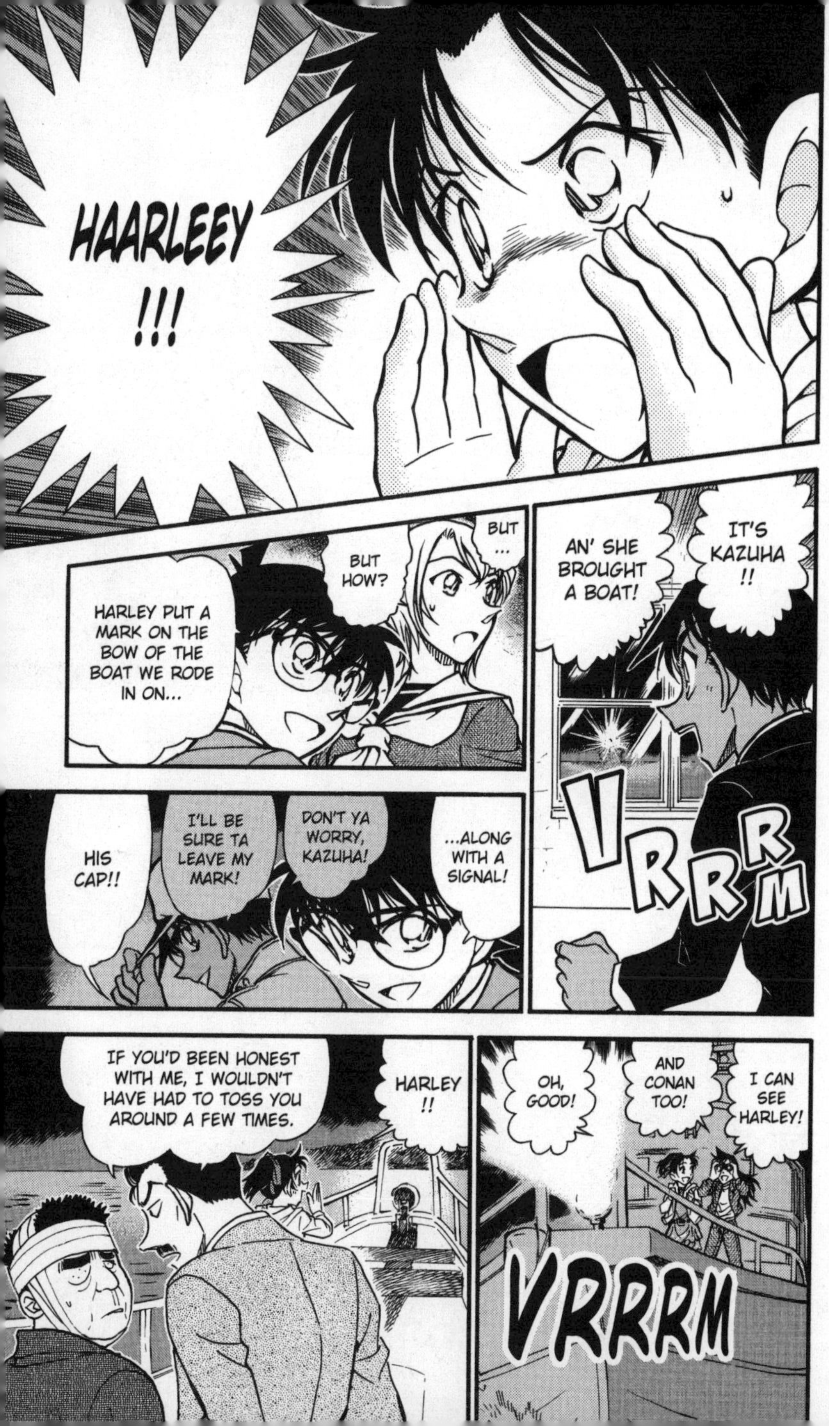
HAARLEEY !!!
IT'S KAZUHA !!
AN' SHE BROUGHT A BOAT!
VRRRM
BUT ...
BUT HOW?
HARLEY PUT A MARK ON THE BOW OF THE BOAT WE RODE IN ON...
...ALONG WITH A SIGNAL!
DON'T YA WORRY, KAZUHA!
I'LL BE SURE TA LEAVE MY MARK!
HIS CAP!!
I CAN SEE HARLEY!
AND CONAN TOO!
OH, GOOD!
VRRRM
HARLEY !!
IF YOU'D BEEN HONEST WITH ME, I WOULDN'T HAVE HAD TO TOSS YOU AROUND A FEW TIMES.

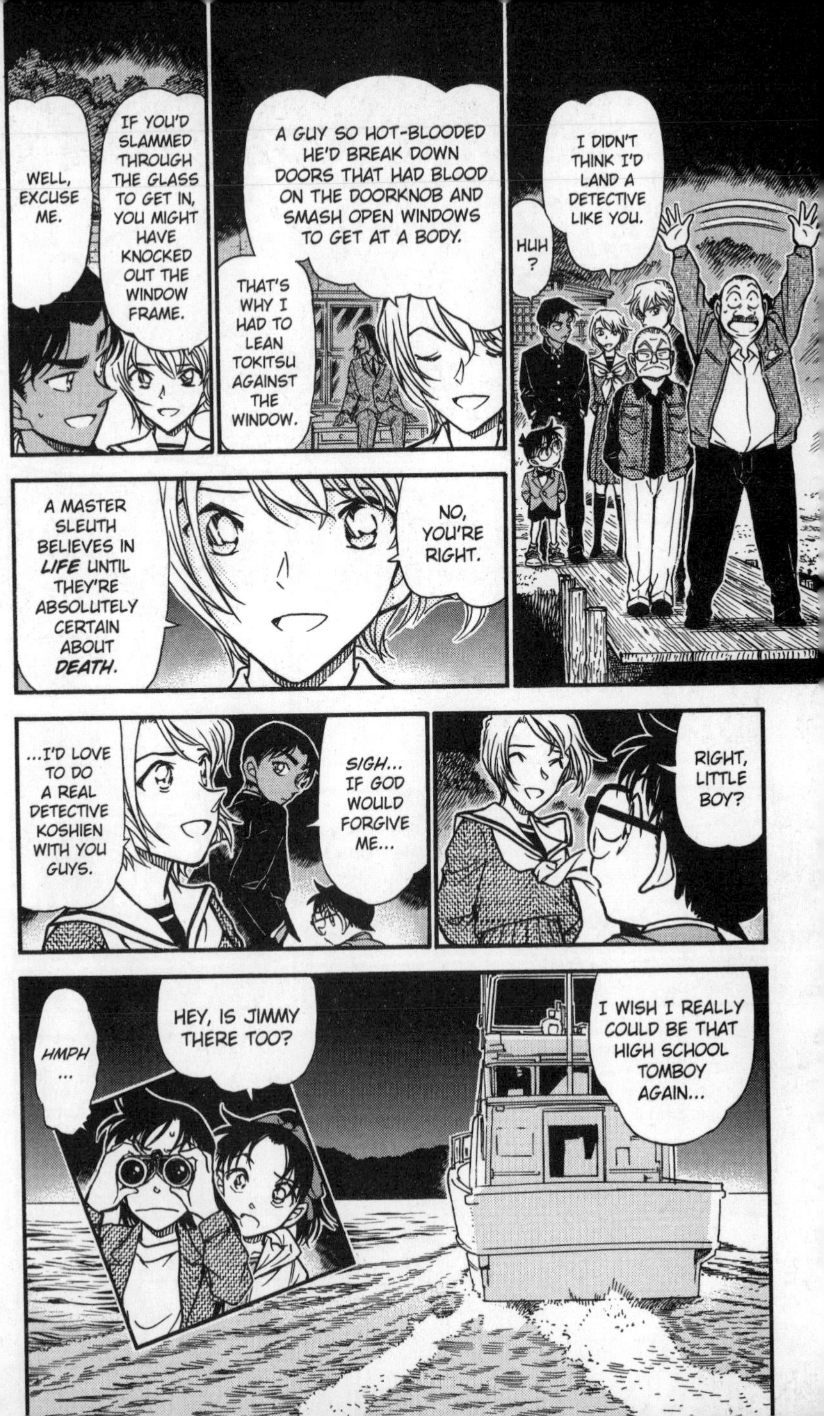
I DIDN'T THINK I'D LAND A DETECTIVE LIKE YOU.
HUH?
A GUY SO HOT-BLOODED HE'D BREAK DOWN DOORS THAT HAD BLOOD ON THE DOORKNOB AND SMASH OPEN WINDOWS TO GET AT A BODY.
THAT'S WHY I HAD TO LEAN TOKITSU AGAINST THE WINDOW.
IF YOU'D SLAMMED THROUGH THE GLASS TO GET IN, YOU MIGHT HAVE KNOCKED OUT THE WINDOW FRAME.
WELL, EXCUSE ME.
NO, YOU'RE RIGHT.
A MASTER SLEUTH BELIEVES IN ***LIFE*** UNTIL THEY'RE ABSOLUTELY CERTAIN ABOUT ***DEATH***.
RIGHT, LITTLE BOY?
SIGH... IF GOD WOULD FORGIVE ME...
...I'D LOVE TO DO A REAL DETECTIVE KOSHIEN WITH YOU GUYS.
I WISH I REALLY COULD BE THAT HIGH SCHOOL TOMBOY AGAIN...
HEY, IS JIMMY THERE TOO?
HMPH...

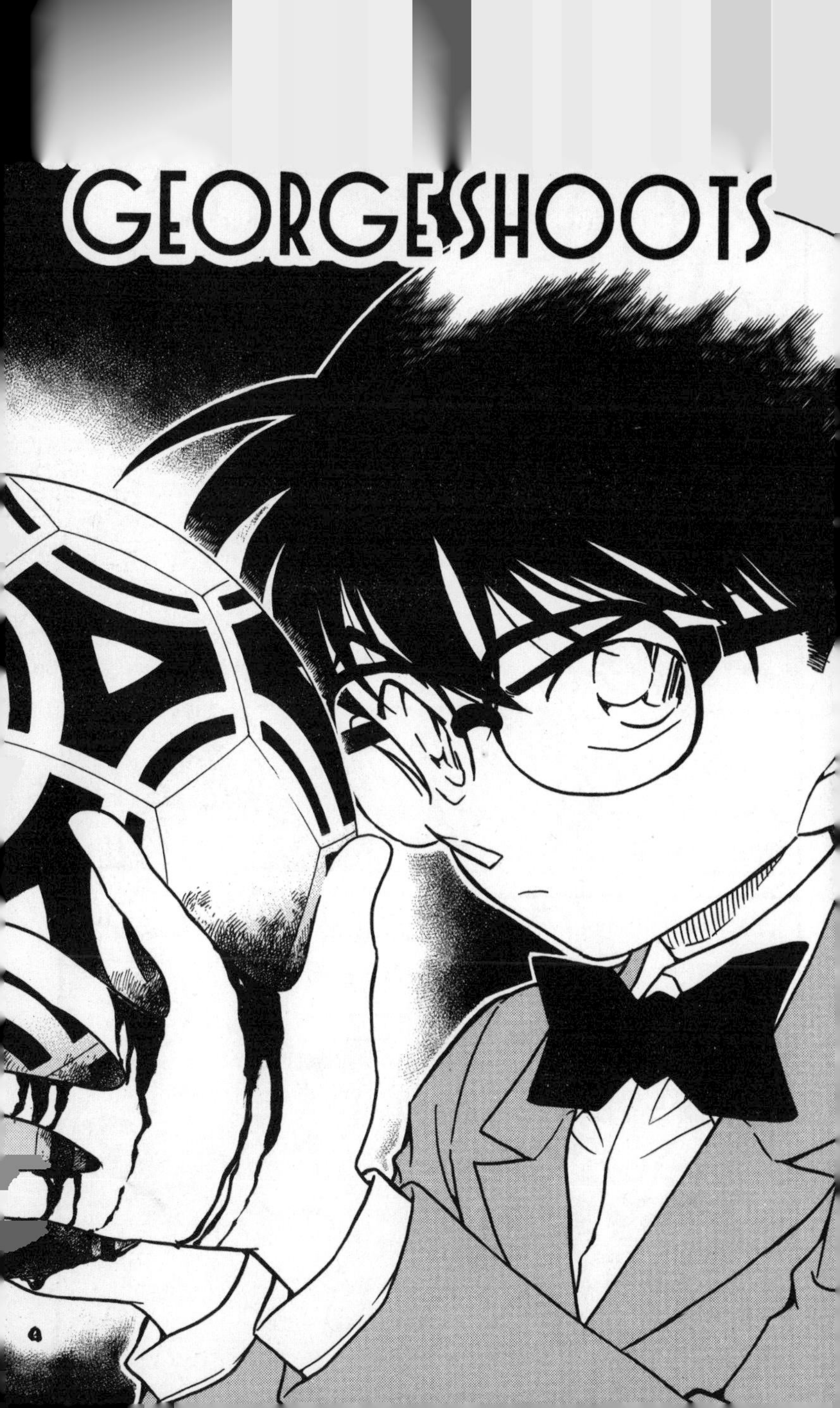
GEORGE SHOOTS

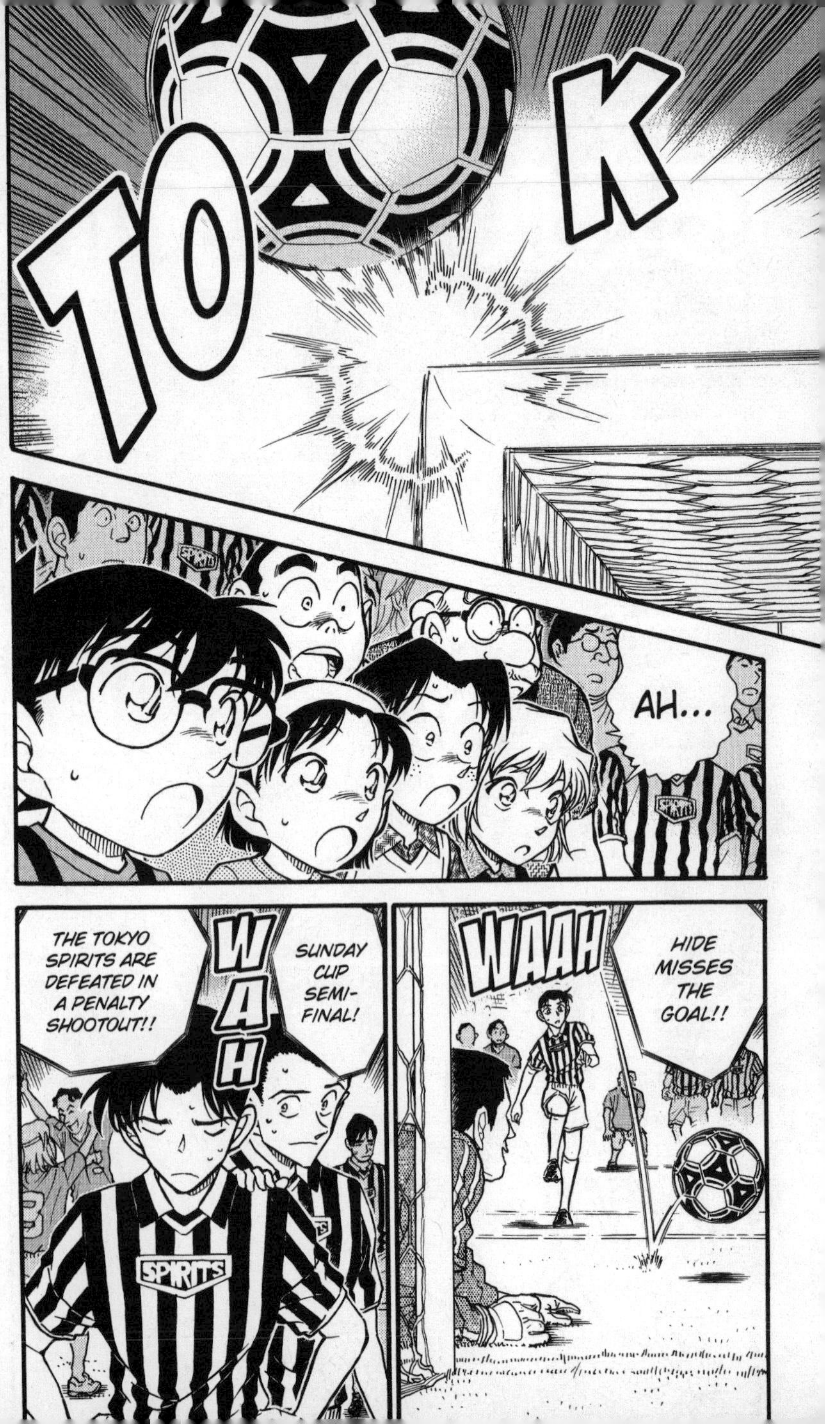
TO K
AH...
WAAH
HIDE MISSES THE GOAL!!
SUNDAY CUP SEMI-FINAL!
WAH
THE TOKYO SPIRITS ARE DEFEATED IN A PENALTY SHOOTOUT!!

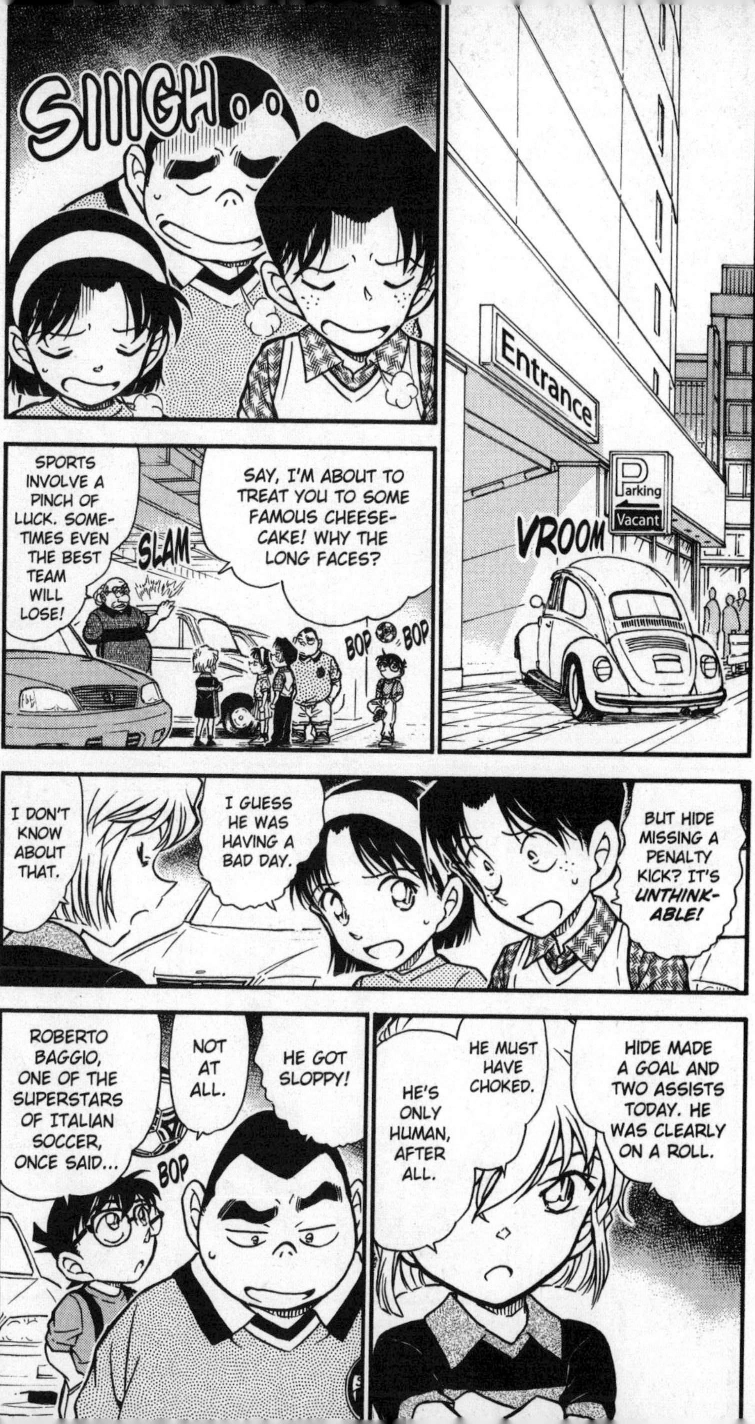
Entrance
Parking
Vacant
VROOM
SIIIGH...
SAY, I'M ABOUT TO TREAT YOU TO SOME FAMOUS CHEESE-CAKE! WHY THE LONG FACES?
SPORTS INVOLVE A PINCH OF LUCK. SOME-TIMES EVEN THE BEST TEAM WILL LOSE!
SLAM
BOP BOP
BUT HIDE MISSING A PENALTY KICK? IT'S *UNTHINK-ABLE!*
I GUESS HE WAS HAVING A BAD DAY.
I DON'T KNOW ABOUT THAT.
HIDE MADE A GOAL AND TWO ASSISTS TODAY. HE WAS CLEARLY ON A ROLL.
HE MUST HAVE CHOKED.
HE'S ONLY HUMAN, AFTER ALL.
HE GOT SLOPPY!
NOT AT ALL.
ROBERTO BAGGIO, ONE OF THE SUPERSTARS OF ITALIAN SOCCER, ONCE SAID...
BOP

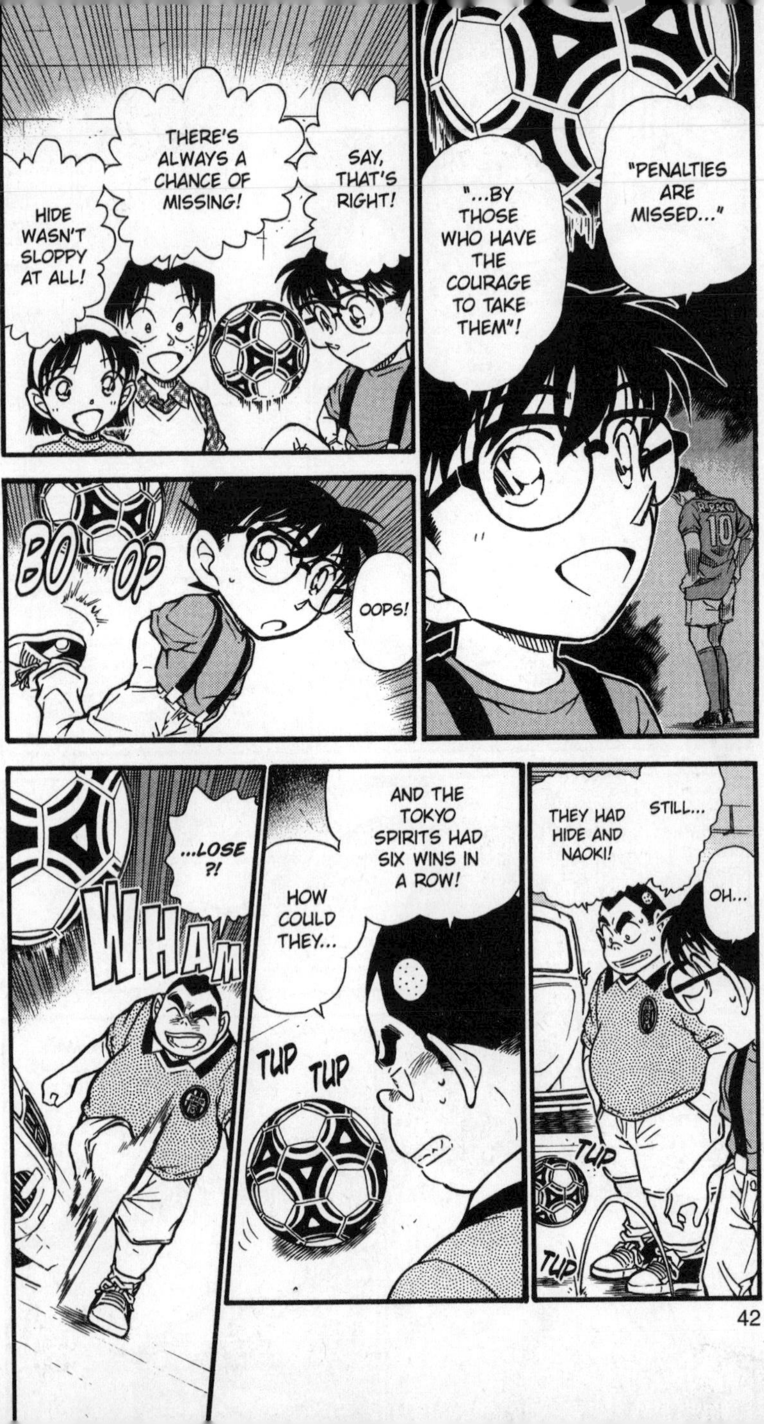
"PENALTIES ARE MISSED..."
"...BY THOSE WHO HAVE THE COURAGE TO TAKE THEM"!
SAY, THAT'S RIGHT!
THERE'S ALWAYS A CHANCE OF MISSING!
HIDE WASN'T SLOPPY AT ALL!
OOPS!
BOOP
STILL...
OH...
THEY HAD HIDE AND NAOKI!
TUP
TUP
AND THE TOKYO SPIRITS HAD SIX WINS IN A ROW!
HOW COULD THEY...
TUP
TUP
...LOSE?!
WHAM

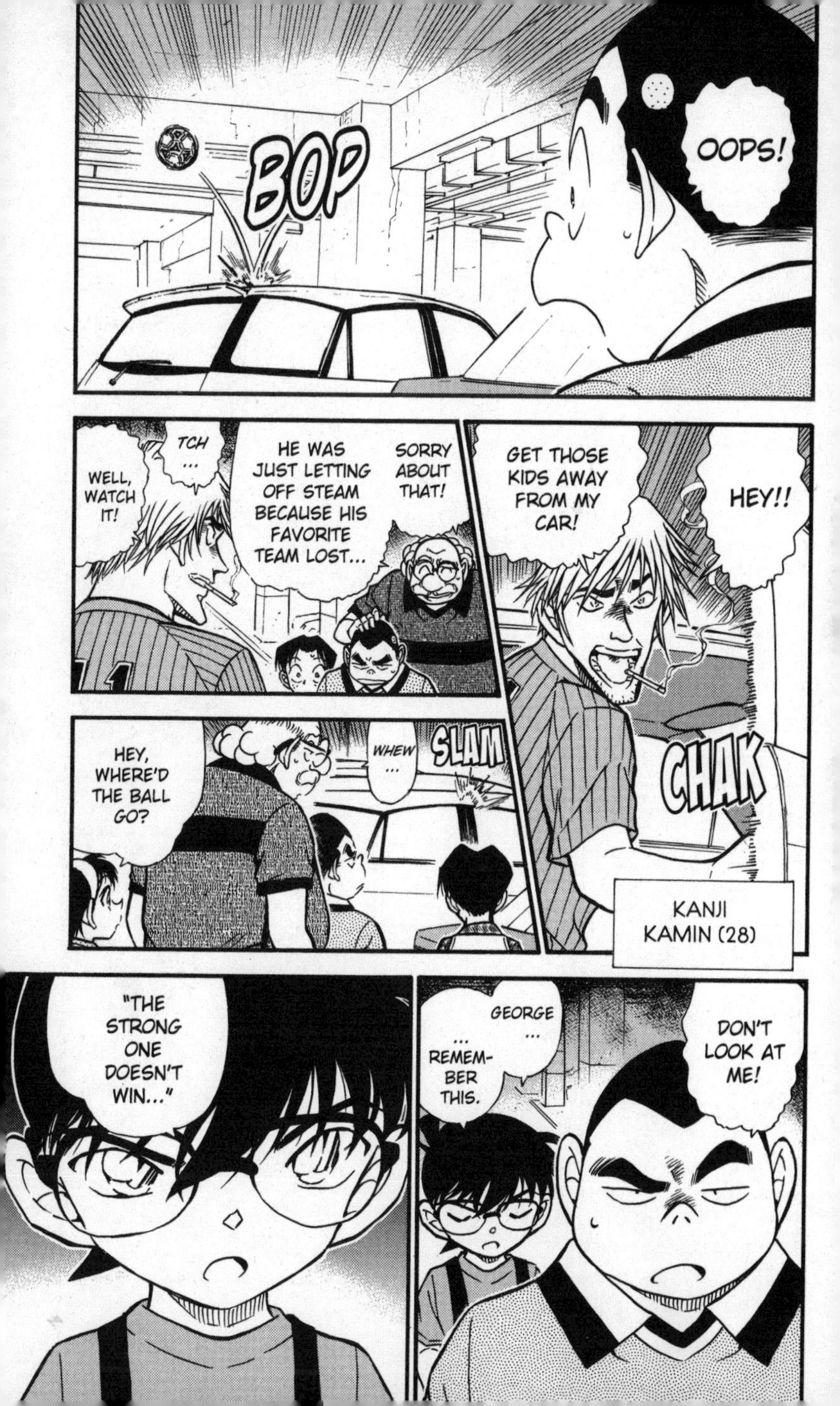
OOPS!
BOP
HEY!!
GET THOSE KIDS AWAY FROM MY CAR!
CHAK
KANJI KAMIN (28)
SORRY ABOUT THAT!
HE WAS JUST LETTING OFF STEAM BECAUSE HIS FAVORITE TEAM LOST...
TCH...
WELL, WATCH IT!
SLAM
WHEW...
HEY, WHERE'D THE BALL GO?
DON'T LOOK AT ME!
GEORGE...
...REMEMBER THIS.
"THE STRONG ONE DOESN'T WIN..."

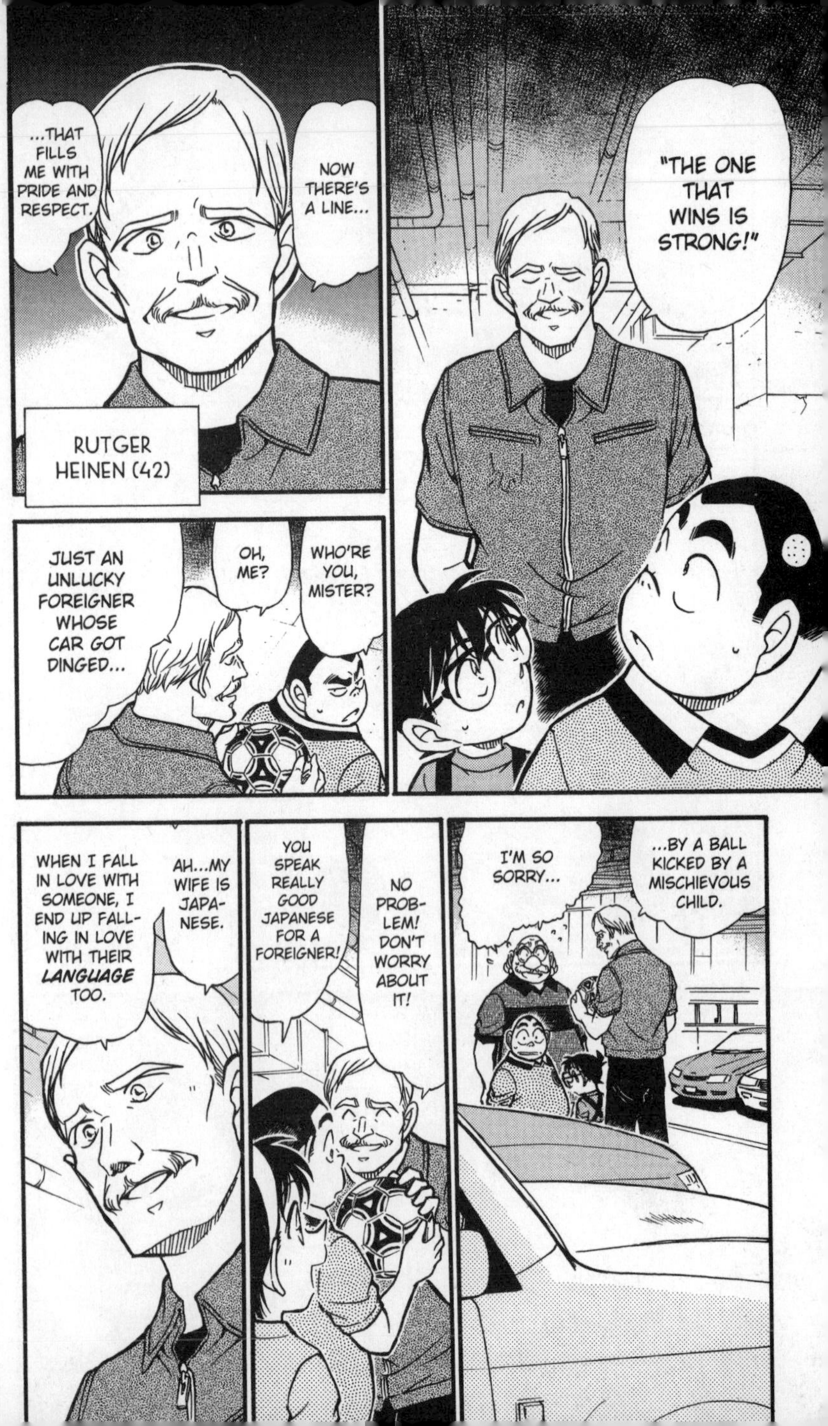
"THE ONE THAT WINS IS STRONG!"
NOW THERE'S A LINE...
...THAT FILLS ME WITH PRIDE AND RESPECT.
RUTGER HEINEN (42)
WHO'RE YOU, MISTER?
OH, ME?
JUST AN UNLUCKY FOREIGNER WHOSE CAR GOT DINGED...
...BY A BALL KICKED BY A MISCHIEVOUS CHILD.
I'M SO SORRY...
NO PROBLEM! DON'T WORRY ABOUT IT!
YOU SPEAK REALLY GOOD JAPANESE FOR A FOREIGNER!
AH...MY WIFE IS JAPANESE.
WHEN I FALL IN LOVE WITH SOMEONE, I END UP FALLING IN LOVE WITH THEIR **LANGUAGE** TOO.

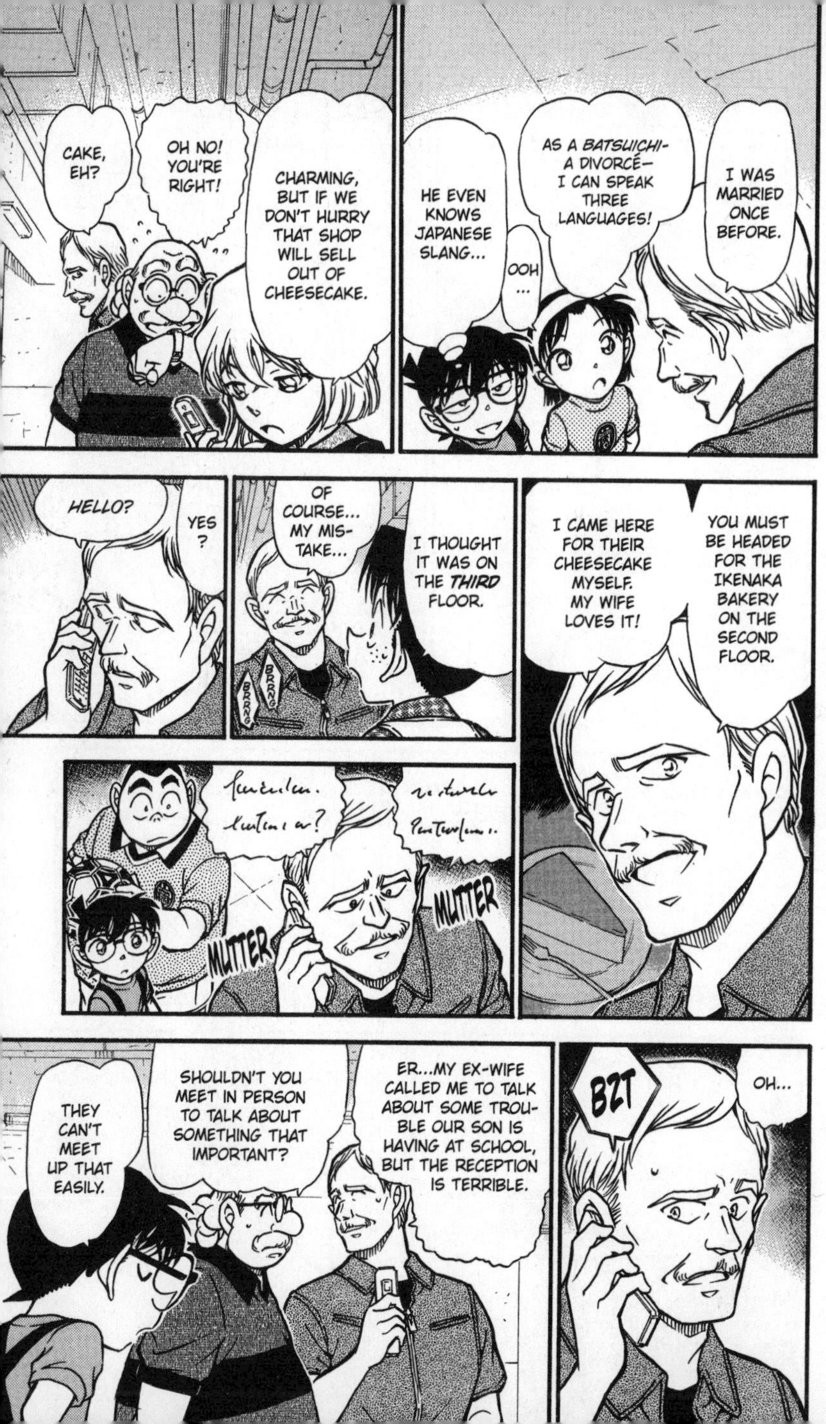
I WAS MARRIED ONCE BEFORE.
AS A *BATSUICHI*–A DIVORCÉ–I CAN SPEAK THREE LANGUAGES!
OOH...
HE EVEN KNOWS JAPANESE SLANG...
CHARMING, BUT IF WE DON'T HURRY THAT SHOP WILL SELL OUT OF CHEESECAKE.
OH NO! YOU'RE RIGHT!
CAKE, EH?
YOU MUST BE HEADED FOR THE IKENAKA BAKERY ON THE SECOND FLOOR.
I CAME HERE FOR THEIR CHEESECAKE MYSELF. MY WIFE LOVES IT!
I THOUGHT IT WAS ON THE *THIRD* FLOOR.
OF COURSE... MY MIS-TAKE...
BRRNG
BRRNG
YES?
HELLO?
MUTTER
MUTTER
OH...
BZT
ER...MY EX-WIFE CALLED ME TO TALK ABOUT SOME TROU-BLE OUR SON IS HAVING AT SCHOOL, BUT THE RECEPTION IS TERRIBLE.
SHOULDN'T YOU MEET IN PERSON TO TALK ABOUT SOMETHING THAT IMPORTANT?
THEY CAN'T MEET UP THAT EASILY.

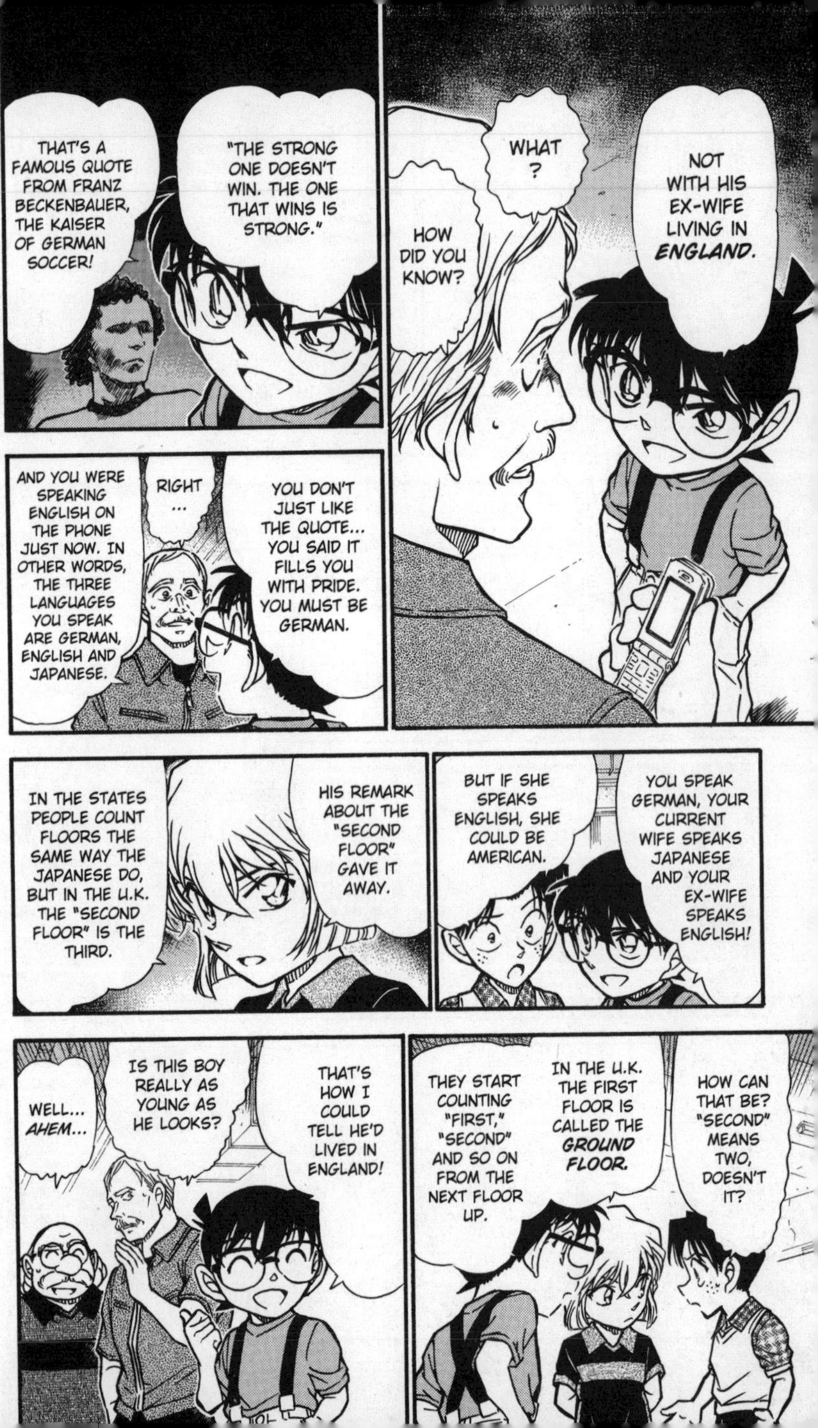
NOT WITH HIS EX-WIFE LIVING IN **ENGLAND.**
WHAT?
HOW DID YOU KNOW?
"THE STRONG ONE DOESN'T WIN. THE ONE THAT WINS IS STRONG."
THAT'S A FAMOUS QUOTE FROM FRANZ BECKENBAUER, THE KAISER OF GERMAN SOCCER!
YOU DON'T JUST LIKE THE QUOTE... YOU SAID IT FILLS YOU WITH PRIDE. YOU MUST BE GERMAN.
RIGHT...
AND YOU WERE SPEAKING ENGLISH ON THE PHONE JUST NOW. IN OTHER WORDS, THE THREE LANGUAGES YOU SPEAK ARE GERMAN, ENGLISH AND JAPANESE.
YOU SPEAK GERMAN, YOUR CURRENT WIFE SPEAKS JAPANESE AND YOUR EX-WIFE SPEAKS ENGLISH!
BUT IF SHE SPEAKS ENGLISH, SHE COULD BE AMERICAN.
HIS REMARK ABOUT THE "SECOND FLOOR" GAVE IT AWAY.
IN THE STATES PEOPLE COUNT FLOORS THE SAME WAY THE JAPANESE DO, BUT IN THE U.K. THE "SECOND FLOOR" IS THE THIRD.
HOW CAN THAT BE? "SECOND" MEANS TWO, DOESN'T IT?
IN THE U.K. THE FIRST FLOOR IS CALLED THE ***GROUND FLOOR.***
THEY START COUNTING "FIRST," "SECOND" AND SO ON FROM THE NEXT FLOOR UP.
THAT'S HOW I COULD TELL HE'D LIVED IN ENGLAND!
IS THIS BOY REALLY AS YOUNG AS HE LOOKS?
WELL... *AHEM...*

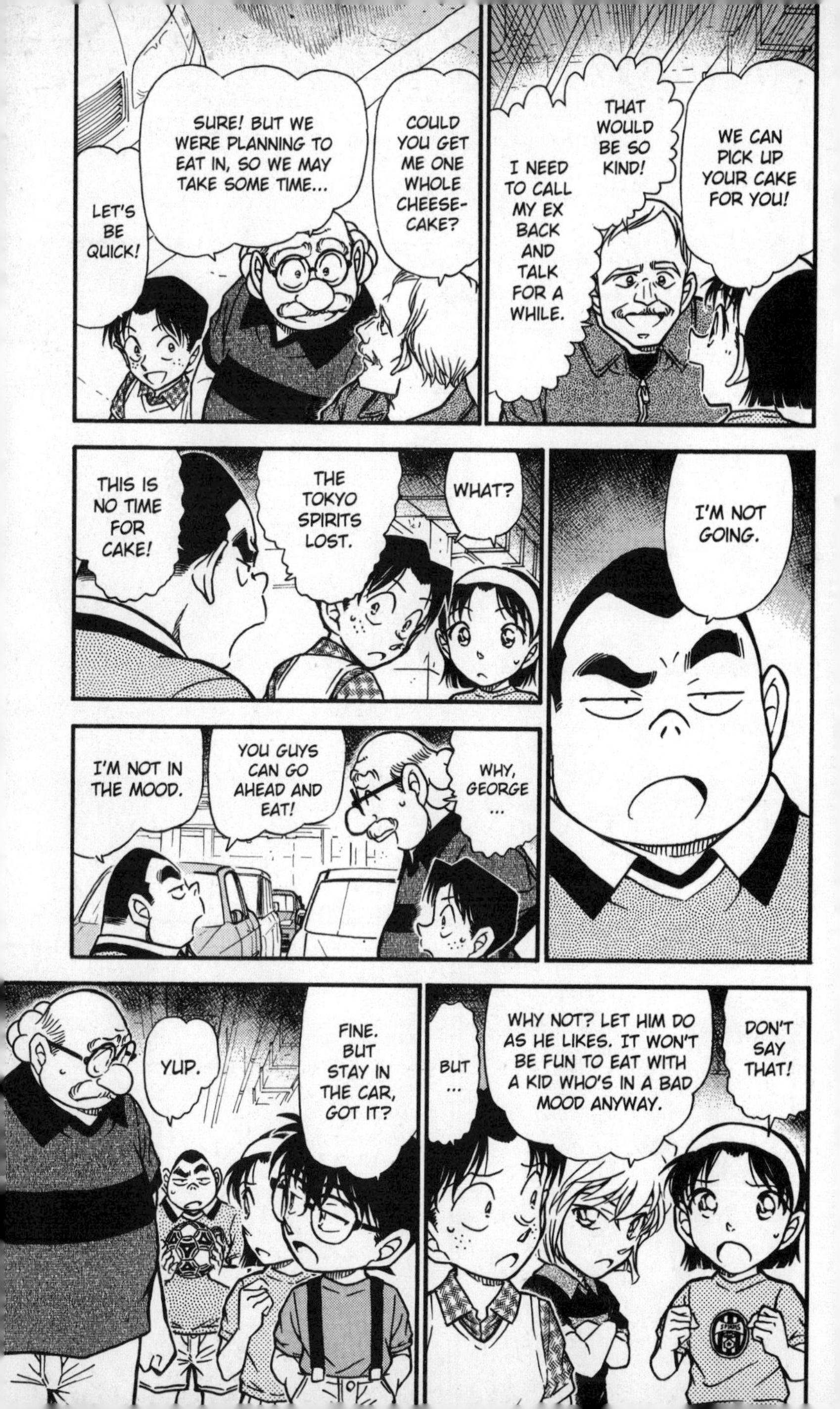
WE CAN PICK UP YOUR CAKE FOR YOU!
THAT WOULD BE SO KIND!
I NEED TO CALL MY EX BACK AND TALK FOR A WHILE.
COULD YOU GET ME ONE WHOLE CHEESE-CAKE?
SURE! BUT WE WERE PLANNING TO EAT IN, SO WE MAY TAKE SOME TIME...
LET'S BE QUICK!
I'M NOT GOING.
WHAT?
THE TOKYO SPIRITS LOST.
THIS IS NO TIME FOR CAKE!
WHY, GEORGE ...
YOU GUYS CAN GO AHEAD AND EAT!
I'M NOT IN THE MOOD.
DON'T SAY THAT!
WHY NOT? LET HIM DO AS HE LIKES. IT WON'T BE FUN TO EAT WITH A KID WHO'S IN A BAD MOOD ANYWAY.
BUT ...
FINE. BUT STAY IN THE CAR, GOT IT?
YUP.

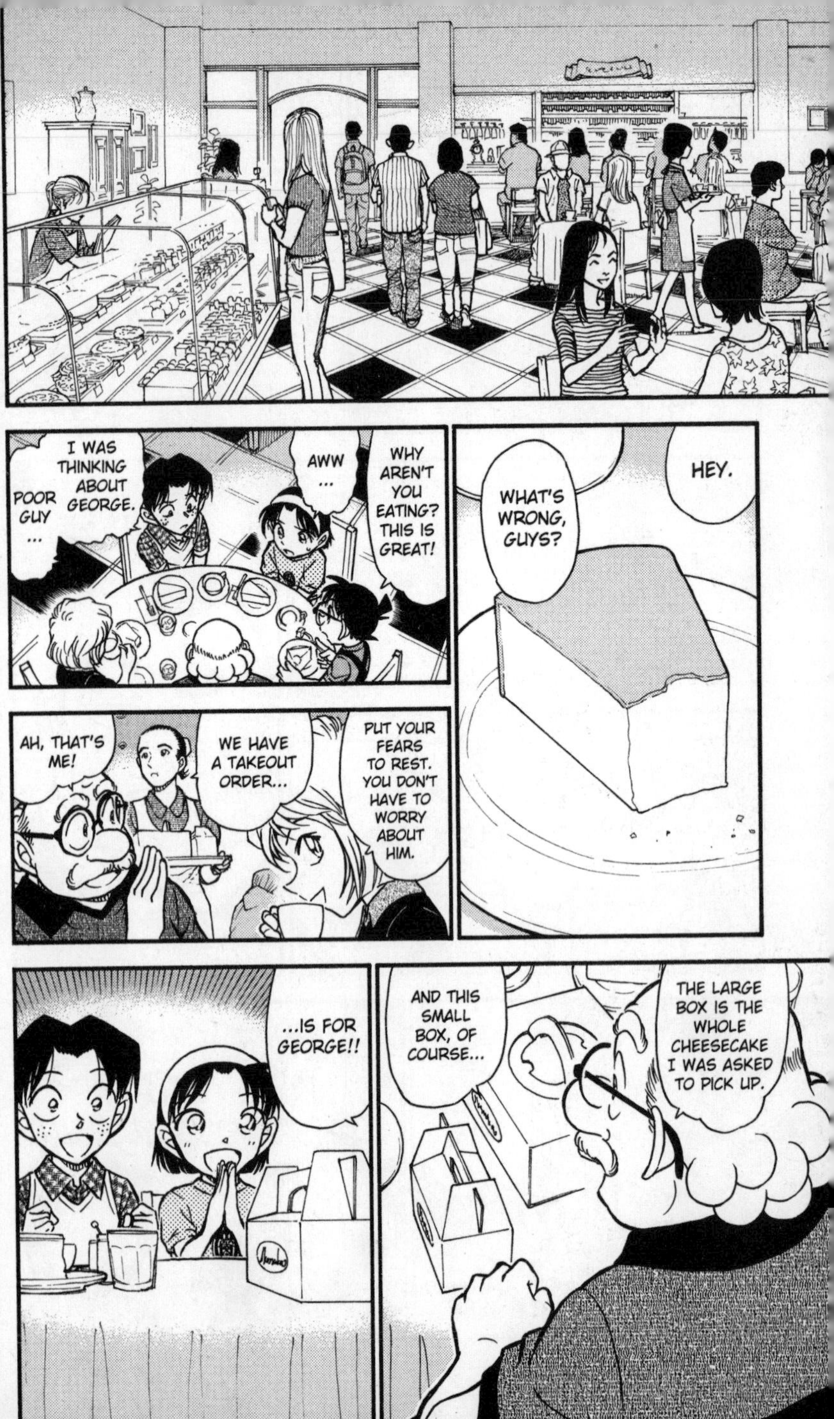
HEY.
WHAT'S WRONG, GUYS?
WHY AREN'T YOU EATING? THIS IS GREAT!
AWW...
I WAS THINKING ABOUT GEORGE.
POOR GUY...
PUT YOUR FEARS TO REST. YOU DON'T HAVE TO WORRY ABOUT HIM.
WE HAVE A TAKEOUT ORDER...
AH, THAT'S ME!
THE LARGE BOX IS THE WHOLE CHEESECAKE I WAS ASKED TO PICK UP.
AND THIS SMALL BOX, OF COURSE...
...IS FOR GEORGE!!

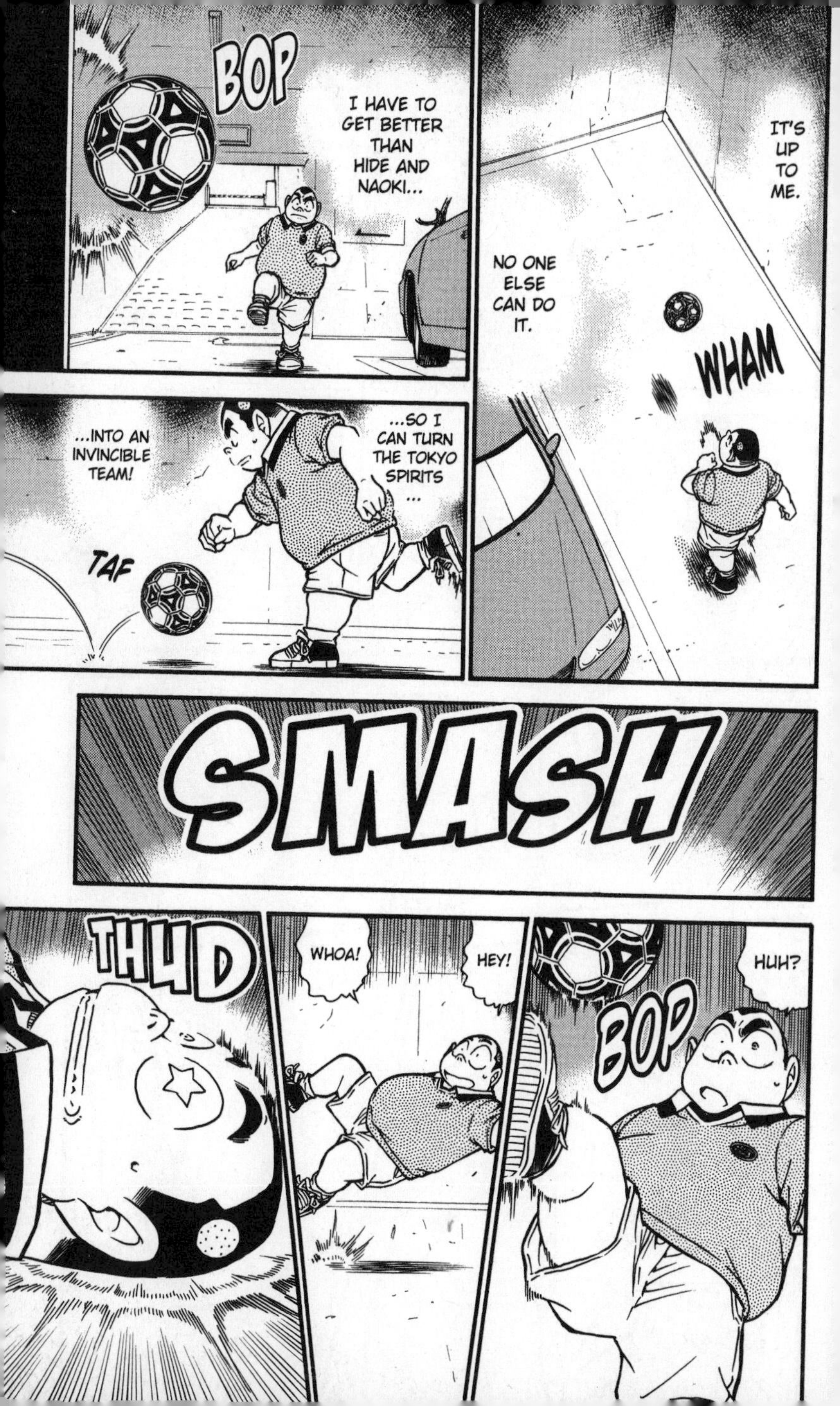
IT'S UP TO ME.
NO ONE ELSE CAN DO IT.
WHAM
I HAVE TO GET BETTER THAN HIDE AND NAOKI...
BOP
...SO I CAN TURN THE TOKYO SPIRITS ...
...INTO AN INVINCIBLE TEAM!
TAF
SMASH
HUH?
BOP
HEY!
WHOA!
THUD

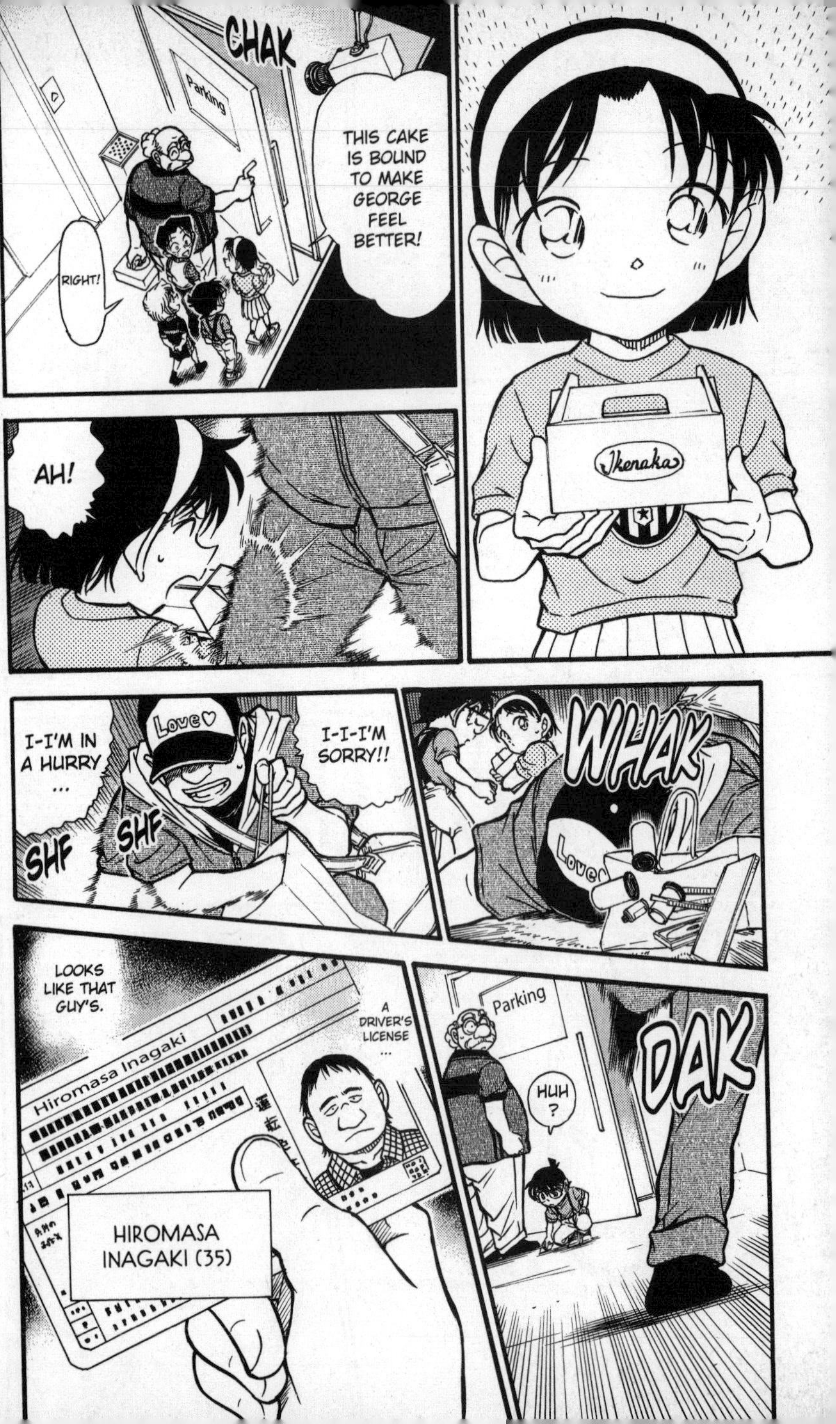

Ikenaka
CHAK
Parking
THIS CAKE IS BOUND TO MAKE GEORGE FEEL BETTER!
RIGHT!
AH!
WHAK
Love
I-I-I'M SORRY!!
Love♡
I-I'M IN A HURRY ...
SHF
SHF
Parking
DAK
HUH?
A DRIVER'S LICENSE ...
LOOKS LIKE THAT GUY'S.
Hiromasa Inagaki
HIROMASA INAGAKI (35)

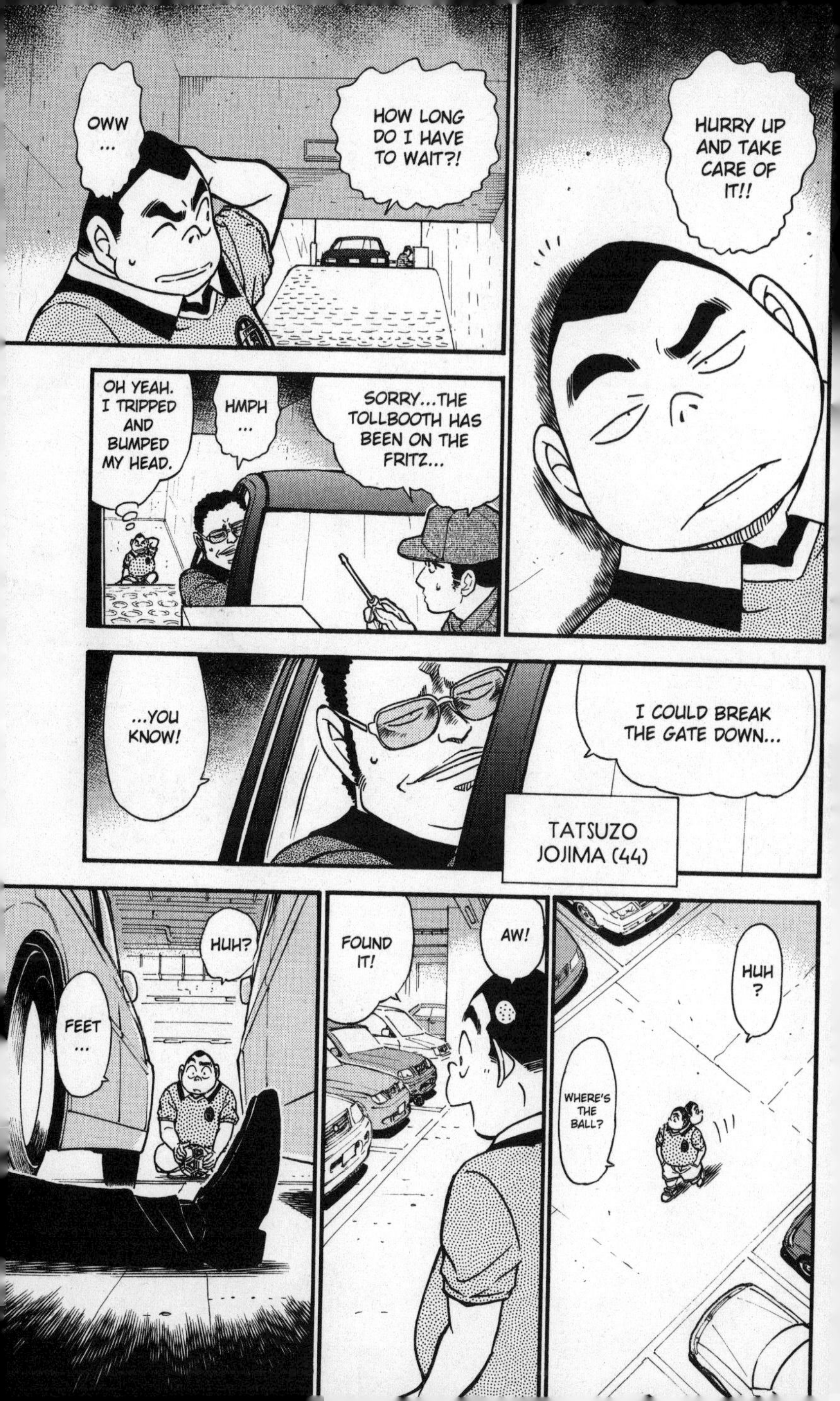
HURRY UP AND TAKE CARE OF IT!!
HOW LONG DO I HAVE TO WAIT?!
OWW ...
SORRY...THE TOLLBOOTH HAS BEEN ON THE FRITZ...
HMPH ...
OH YEAH. I TRIPPED AND BUMPED MY HEAD.
I COULD BREAK THE GATE DOWN...
TATSUZO JOJIMA (44)
...YOU KNOW!
HUH ?
WHERE'S THE BALL?
AW!
FOUND IT!
HUH?
FEET ...

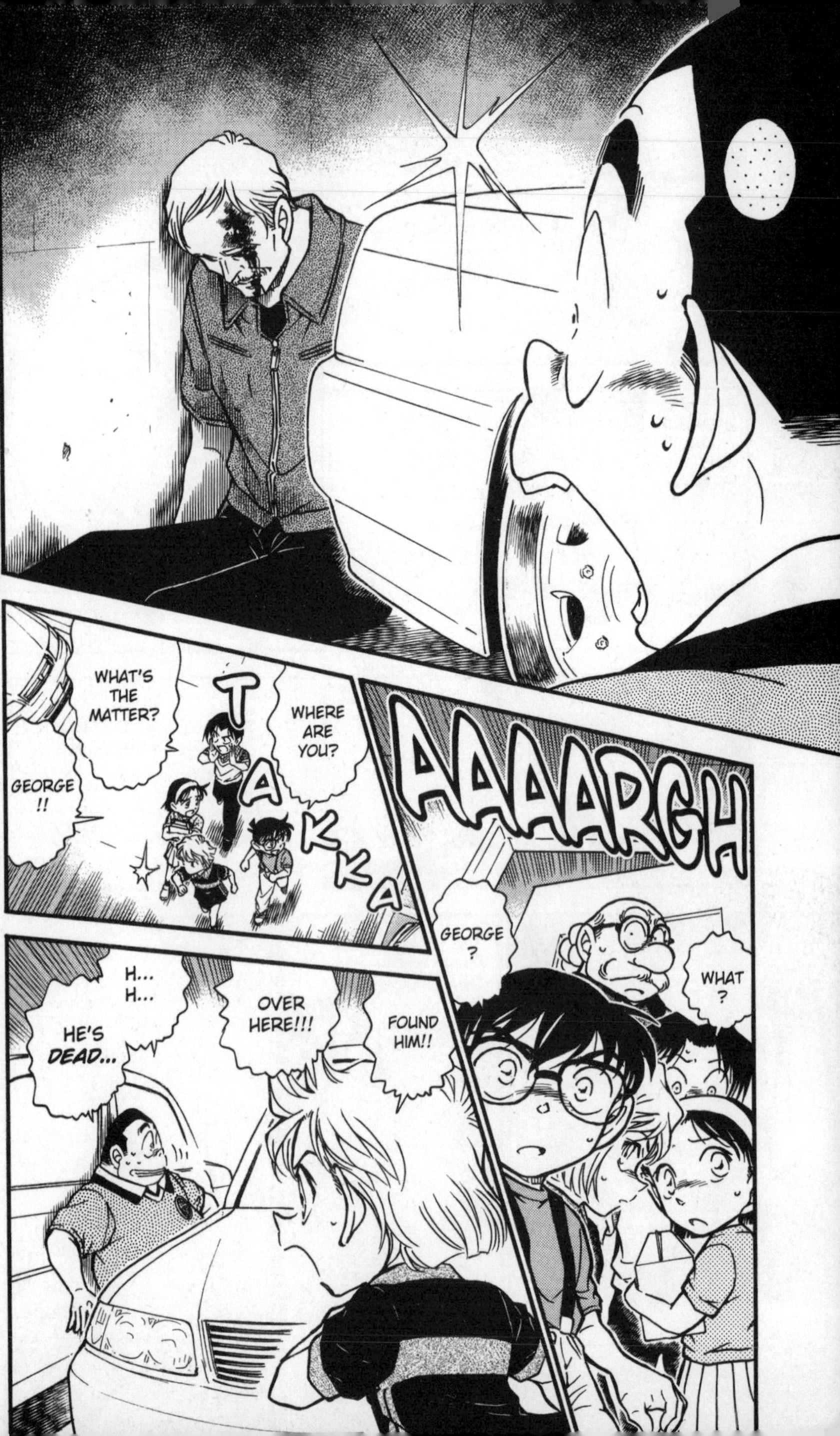
AAAARGH
WHAT?
GEORGE?
WHERE ARE YOU?
TAKKA
WHAT'S THE MATTER?
GEORGE!!
FOUND HIM!!
OVER HERE!!!
H... H...
HE'S *DEAD...*

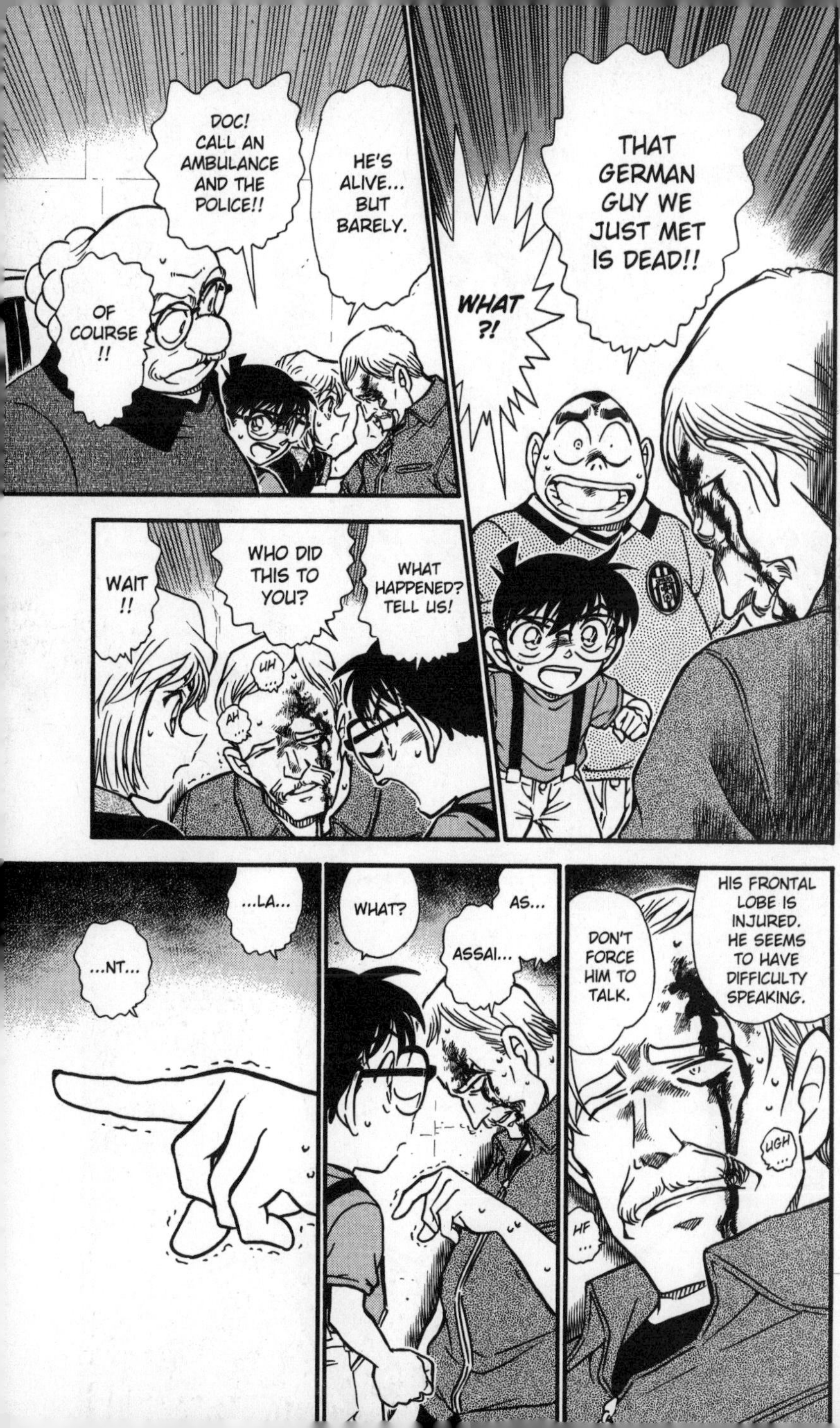
THAT GERMAN GUY WE JUST MET IS DEAD!!
WHAT?!
HE'S ALIVE... BUT BARELY.
DOC! CALL AN AMBULANCE AND THE POLICE!!
OF COURSE!!
WHAT HAPPENED? TELL US!
WHO DID THIS TO YOU?
WAIT!!
UH
AH...
HIS FRONTAL LOBE IS INJURED. HE SEEMS TO HAVE DIFFICULTY SPEAKING.
DON'T FORCE HIM TO TALK.
UGH...
HF...
AS...
ASSAI...
WHAT?
...LA...
...NT...

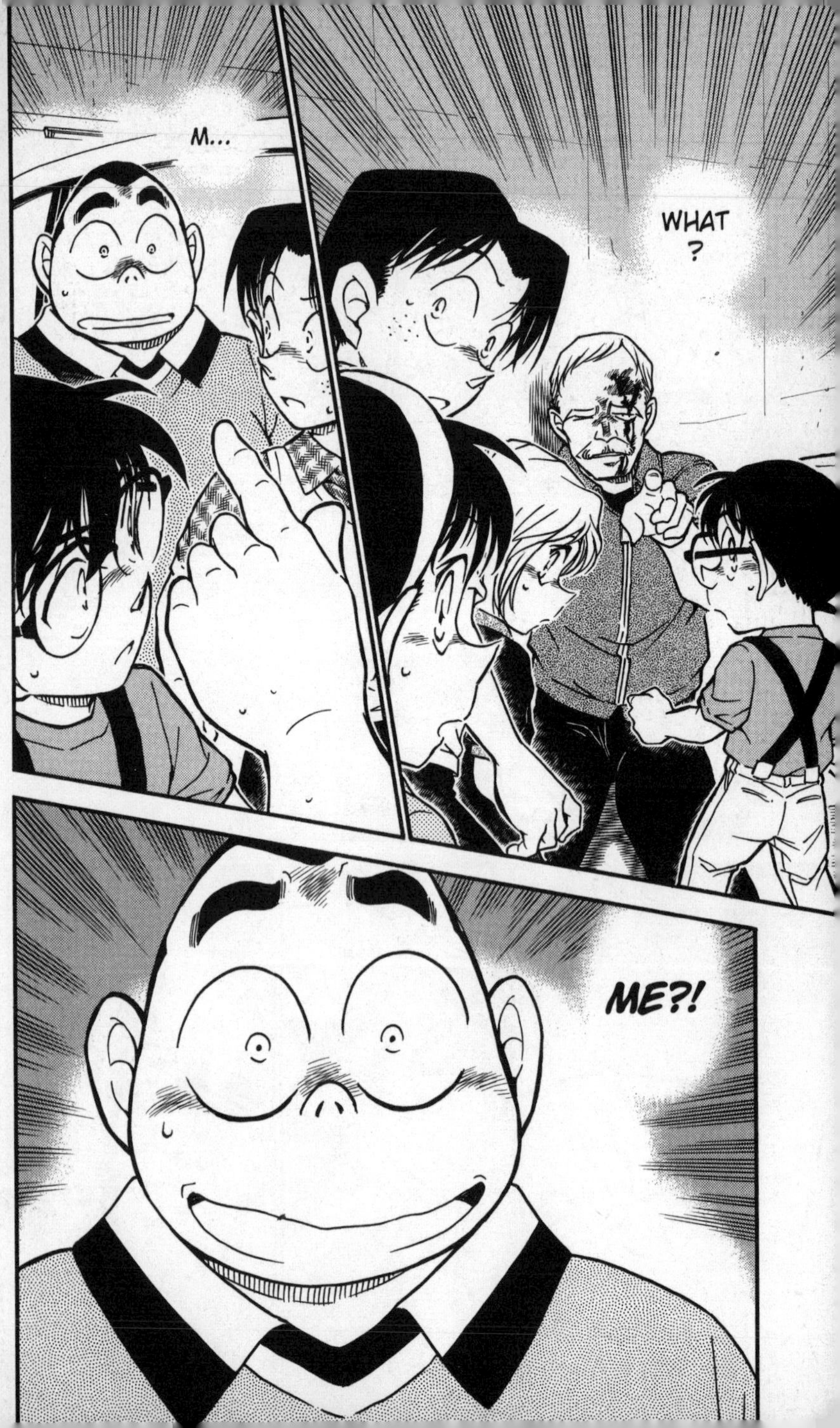
WHAT?
M...
ME?!

FILE 4: GEORGE AND EL

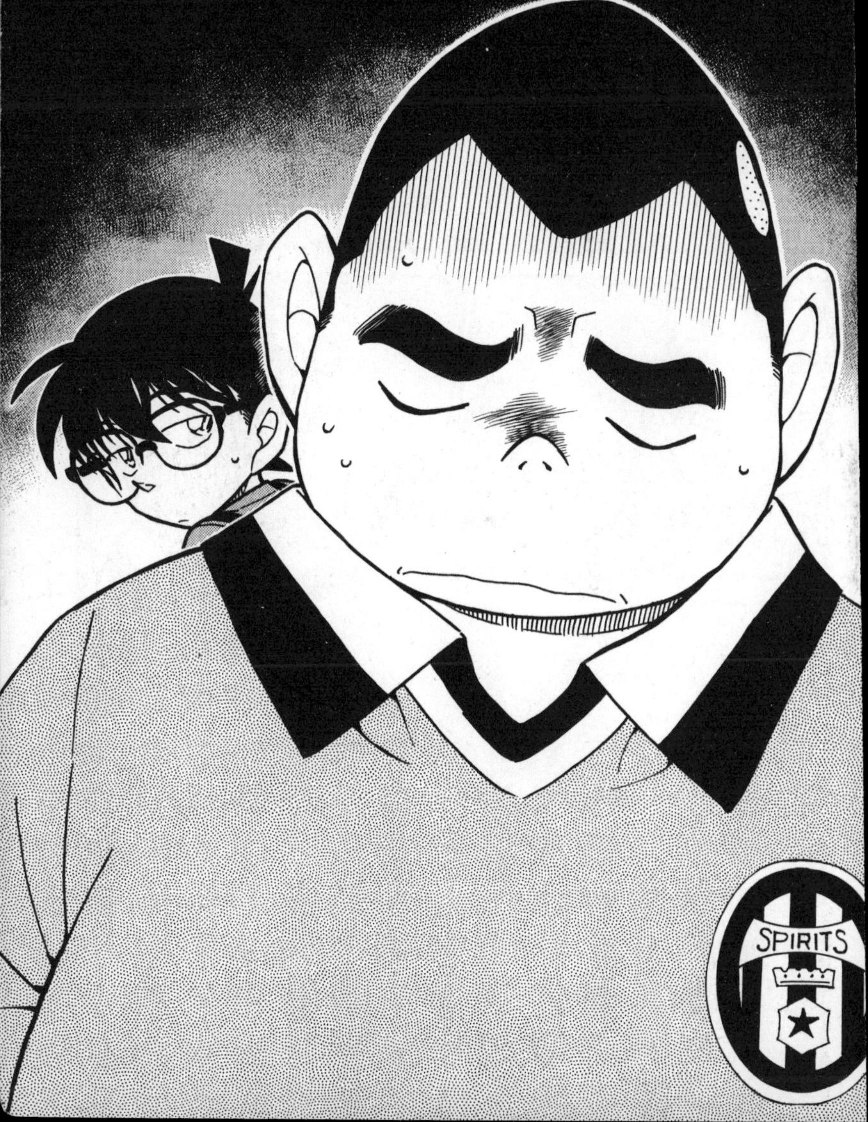
SPIRITS

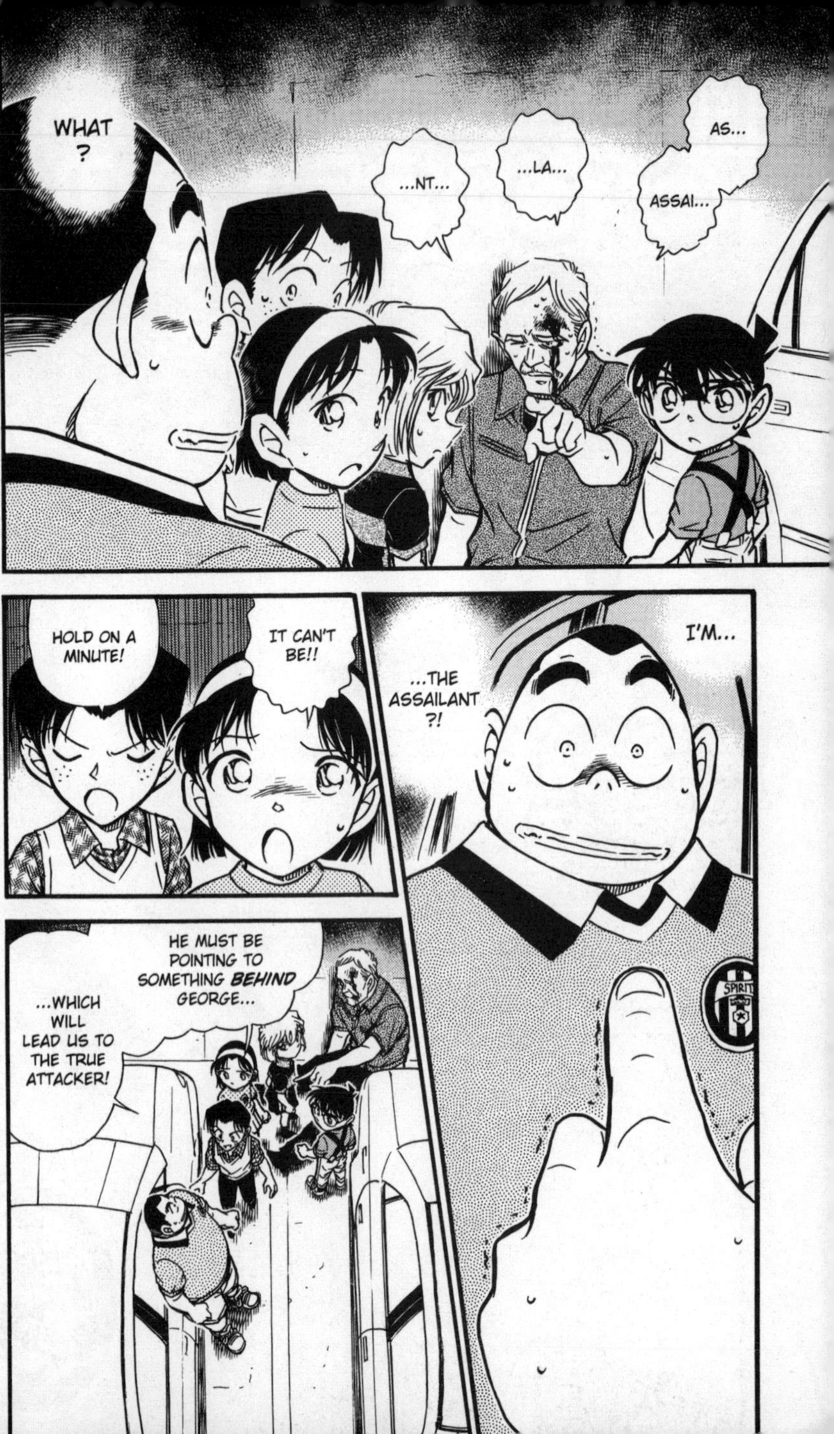
AS...
ASSAI...
...LA...
...NT...
WHAT ?
I'M...
...THE ASSAILANT ?!
SPIRIT
IT CAN'T BE!!
HOLD ON A MINUTE!
HE MUST BE POINTING TO SOMETHING *BEHIND* GEORGE...
...WHICH WILL LEAD US TO THE TRUE ATTACKER!

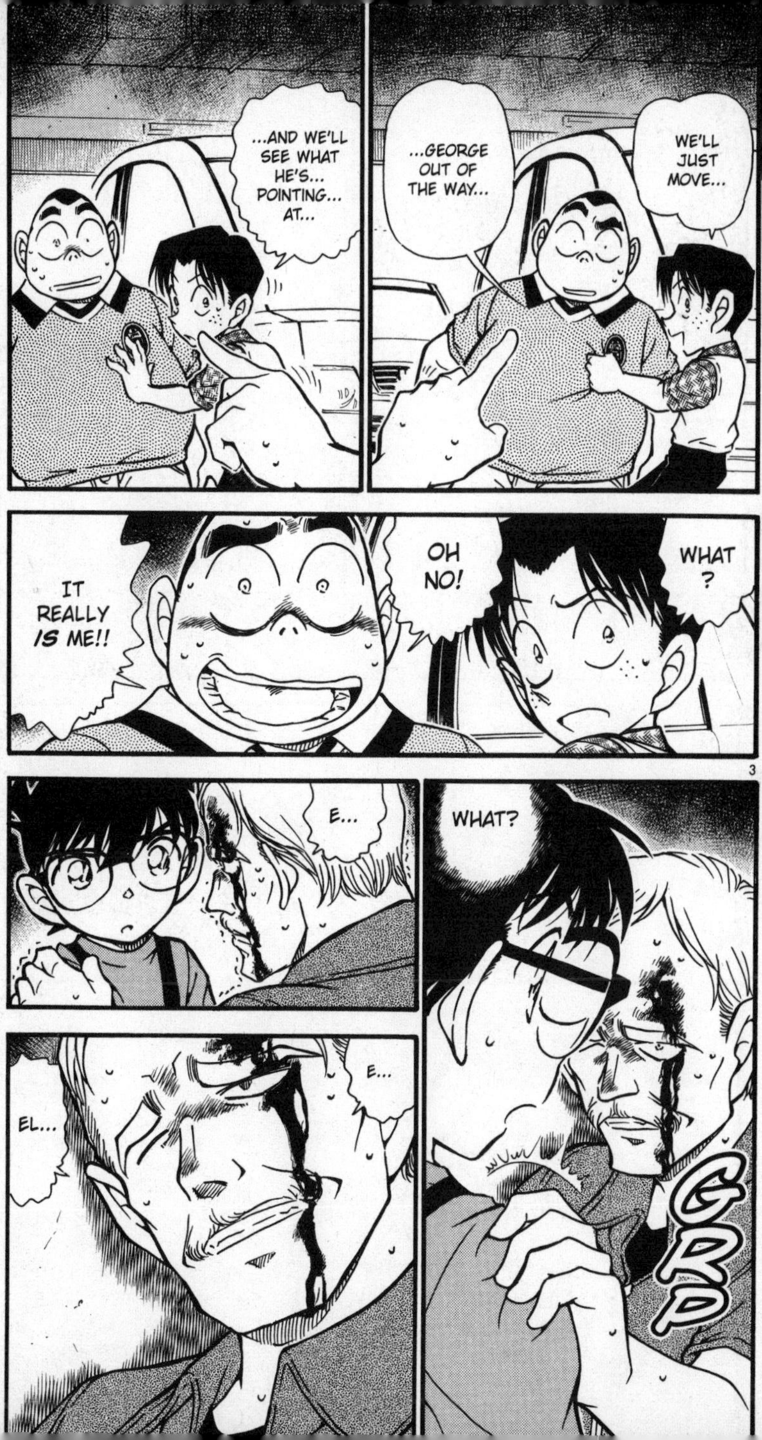
WE'LL JUST MOVE...
...GEORGE OUT OF THE WAY...
...AND WE'LL SEE WHAT HE'S... POINTING... AT...
WHAT ?
OH NO!
IT REALLY *IS* ME!!
WHAT?
GRP
E...
E...
EL...

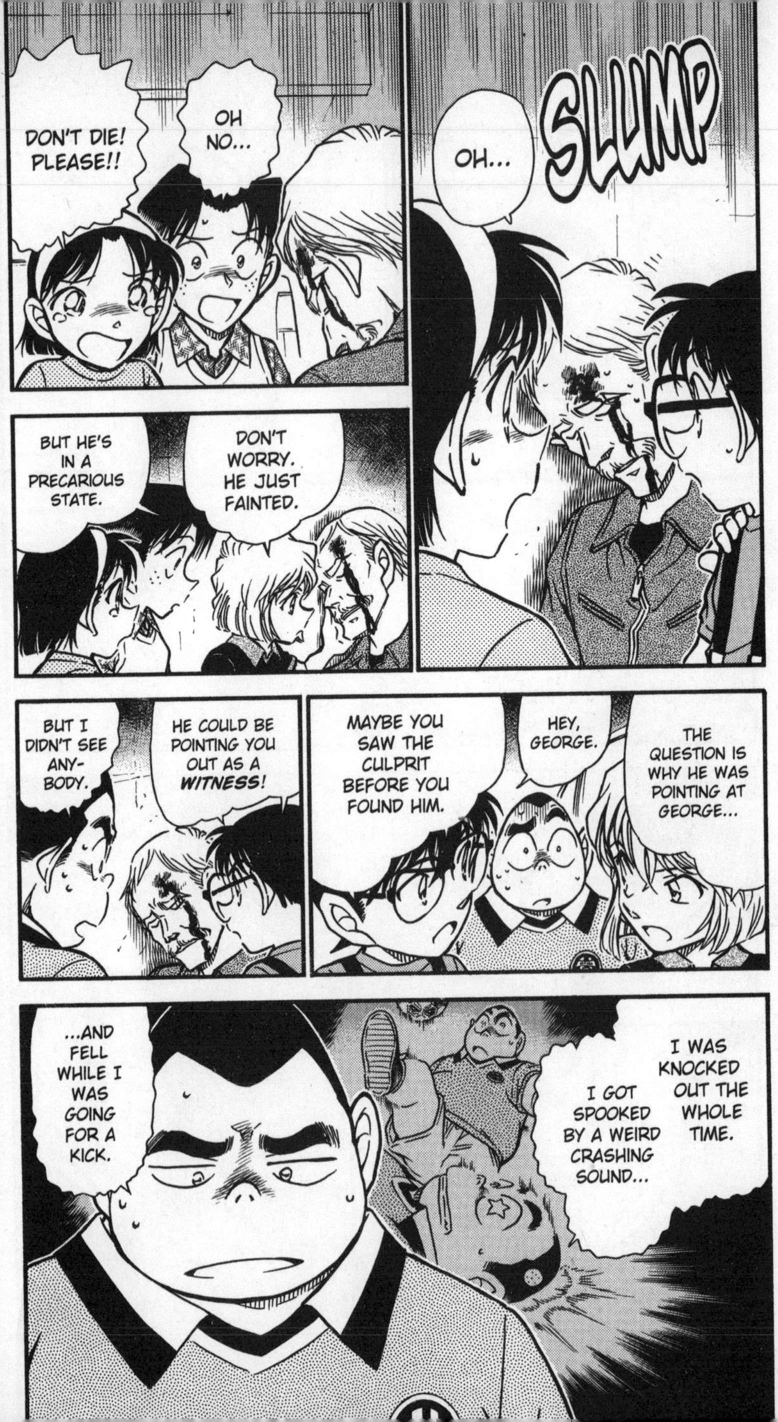
SLUMP
OH...
OH NO...
DON'T DIE! PLEASE!!
DON'T WORRY. HE JUST FAINTED.
BUT HE'S IN A PRECARIOUS STATE.
THE QUESTION IS WHY HE WAS POINTING AT GEORGE...
HEY, GEORGE.
MAYBE YOU SAW THE CULPRIT BEFORE YOU FOUND HIM.
HE COULD BE POINTING YOU OUT AS A *WITNESS*!
BUT I DIDN'T SEE ANY-BODY.
I WAS KNOCKED OUT THE WHOLE TIME.
I GOT SPOOKED BY A WEIRD CRASHING SOUND...
...AND FELL WHILE I WAS GOING FOR A KICK.

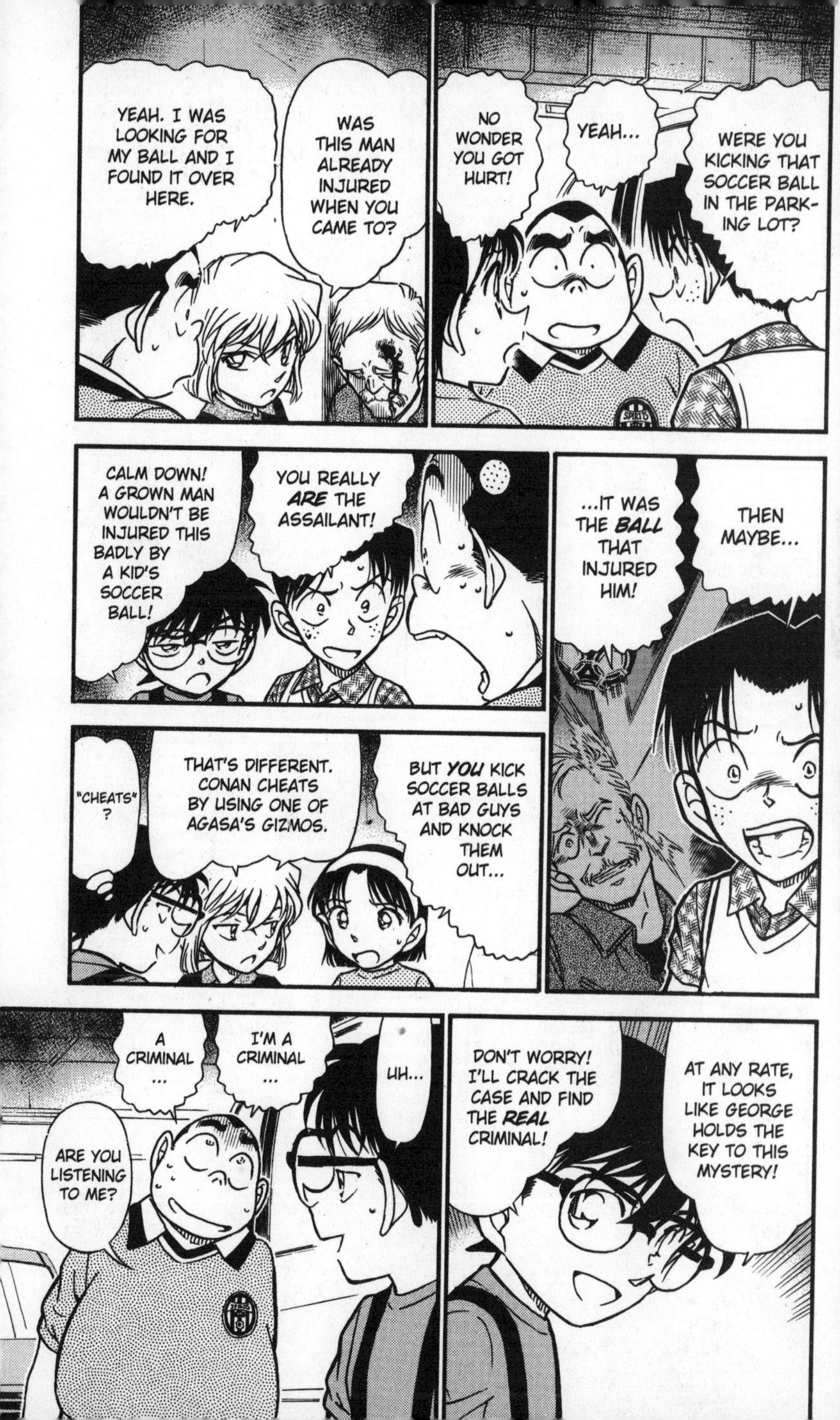
WERE YOU KICKING THAT SOCCER BALL IN THE PARK-ING LOT?
YEAH...
NO WONDER YOU GOT HURT!
WAS THIS MAN ALREADY INJURED WHEN YOU CAME TO?
YEAH. I WAS LOOKING FOR MY BALL AND I FOUND IT OVER HERE.
THEN MAYBE...
...IT WAS THE BALL THAT INJURED HIM!
YOU REALLY ARE THE ASSAILANT!
CALM DOWN! A GROWN MAN WOULDN'T BE INJURED THIS BADLY BY A KID'S SOCCER BALL!
BUT YOU KICK SOCCER BALLS AT BAD GUYS AND KNOCK THEM OUT...
THAT'S DIFFERENT. CONAN CHEATS BY USING ONE OF AGASA'S GIZMOS.
"CHEATS"?
AT ANY RATE, IT LOOKS LIKE GEORGE HOLDS THE KEY TO THIS MYSTERY!
DON'T WORRY! I'LL CRACK THE CASE AND FIND THE REAL CRIMINAL!
UH...
I'M A CRIMINAL...
A CRIMINAL...
ARE YOU LISTENING TO ME?

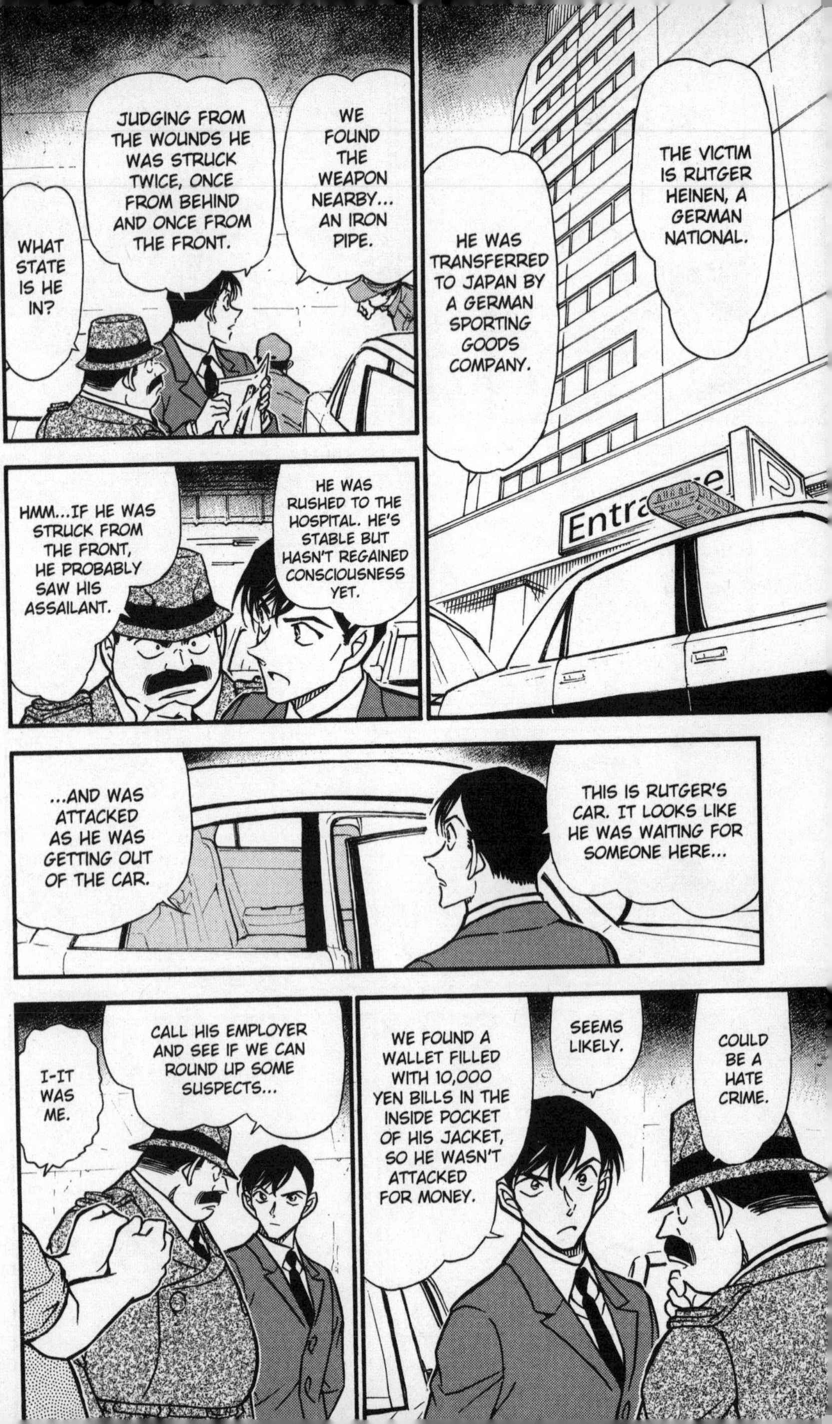
THE VICTIM IS RUTGER HEINEN, A GERMAN NATIONAL.
HE WAS TRANSFERRED TO JAPAN BY A GERMAN SPORTING GOODS COMPANY.
WE FOUND THE WEAPON NEARBY... AN IRON PIPE.
JUDGING FROM THE WOUNDS HE WAS STRUCK TWICE, ONCE FROM BEHIND AND ONCE FROM THE FRONT.
WHAT STATE IS HE IN?
HE WAS RUSHED TO THE HOSPITAL. HE'S STABLE BUT HASN'T REGAINED CONSCIOUSNESS YET.
HMM...IF HE WAS STRUCK FROM THE FRONT, HE PROBABLY SAW HIS ASSAILANT.
THIS IS RUTGER'S CAR. IT LOOKS LIKE HE WAS WAITING FOR SOMEONE HERE...
...AND WAS ATTACKED AS HE WAS GETTING OUT OF THE CAR.
COULD BE A HATE CRIME.
SEEMS LIKELY.
WE FOUND A WALLET FILLED WITH 10,000 YEN BILLS IN THE INSIDE POCKET OF HIS JACKET, SO HE WASN'T ATTACKED FOR MONEY.
CALL HIS EMPLOYER AND SEE IF WE CAN ROUND UP SOME SUSPECTS...
I-IT WAS ME.

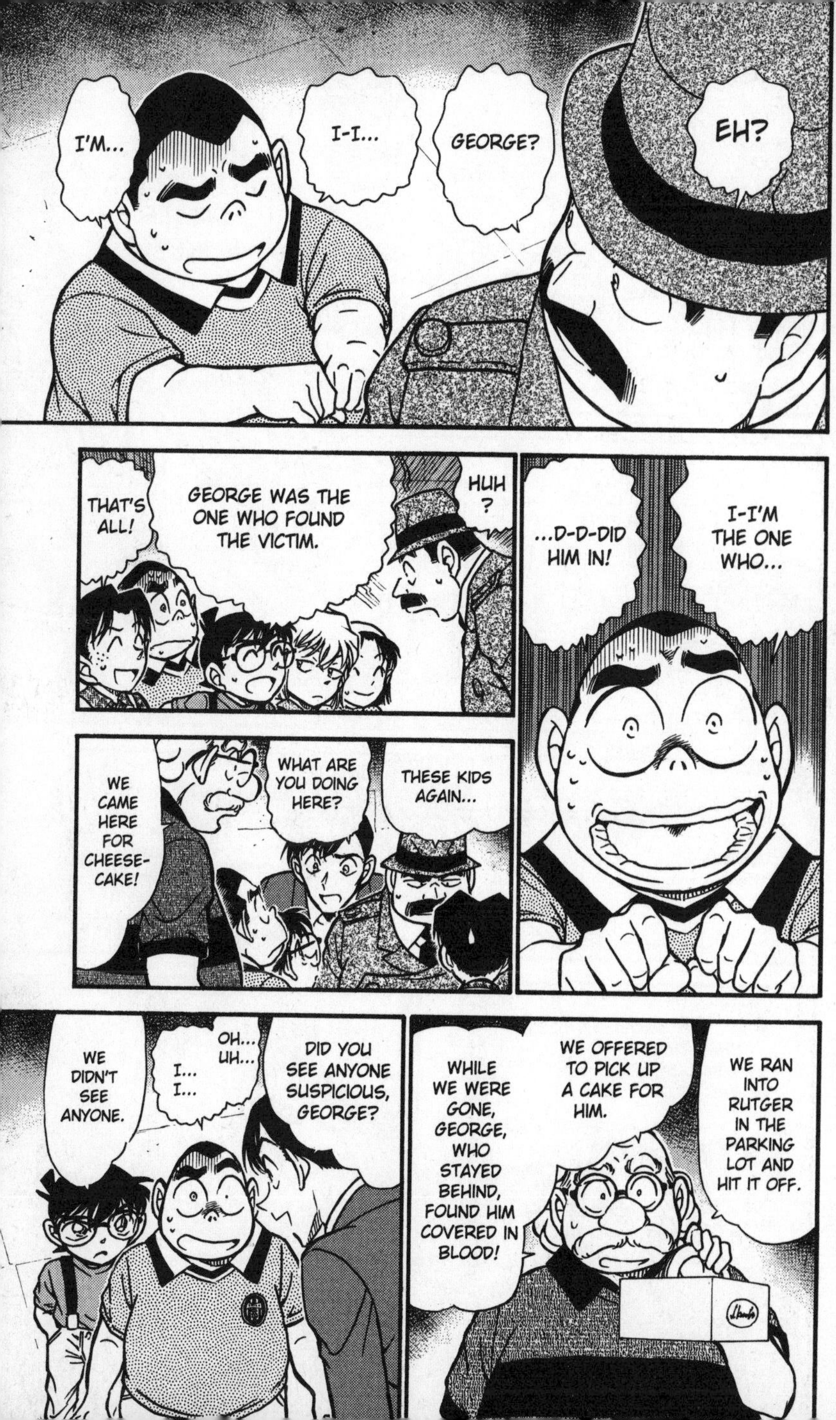
EH?
GEORGE?
I-I...
I'M...
I-I'M THE ONE WHO...
...D-D-DID HIM IN!
HUH ?
GEORGE WAS THE ONE WHO FOUND THE VICTIM.
THAT'S ALL!
THESE KIDS AGAIN...
WHAT ARE YOU DOING HERE?
WE CAME HERE FOR CHEESE-CAKE!
WE RAN INTO RUTGER IN THE PARKING LOT AND HIT IT OFF.
WE OFFERED TO PICK UP A CAKE FOR HIM.
WHILE WE WERE GONE, GEORGE, WHO STAYED BEHIND, FOUND HIM COVERED IN BLOOD!
DID YOU SEE ANYONE SUSPICIOUS, GEORGE?
OH... UH...
I... I...
WE DIDN'T SEE ANYONE.

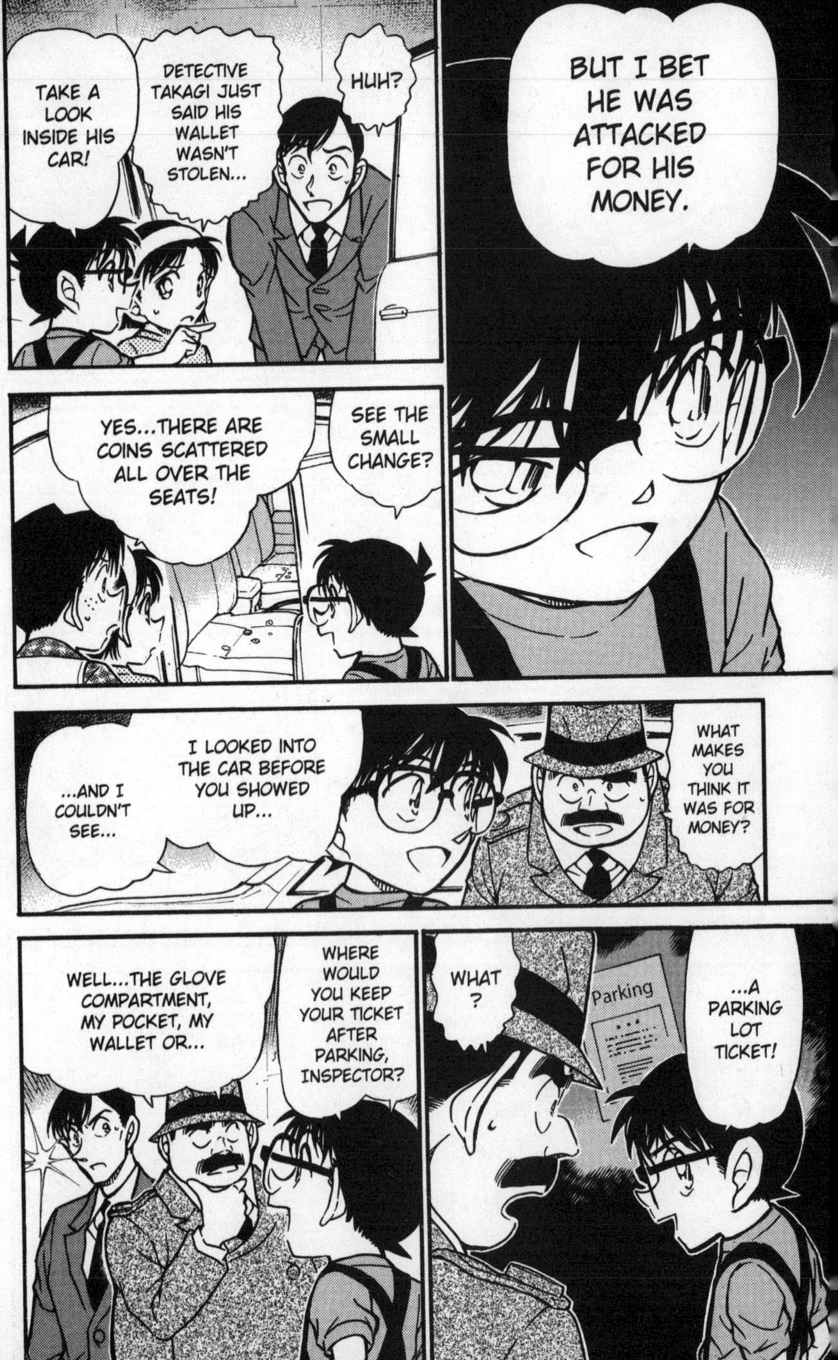
BUT I BET HE WAS ATTACKED FOR HIS MONEY.
HUH?
DETECTIVE TAKAGI JUST SAID HIS WALLET WASN'T STOLEN...
TAKE A LOOK INSIDE HIS CAR!
SEE THE SMALL CHANGE?
YES...THERE ARE COINS SCATTERED ALL OVER THE SEATS!
WHAT MAKES YOU THINK IT WAS FOR MONEY?
I LOOKED INTO THE CAR BEFORE YOU SHOWED UP...
...AND I COULDN'T SEE...
...A PARKING LOT TICKET!
Parking
WHAT?
WHERE WOULD YOU KEEP YOUR TICKET AFTER PARKING, INSPECTOR?
WELL...THE GLOVE COMPARTMENT, MY POCKET, MY WALLET OR...

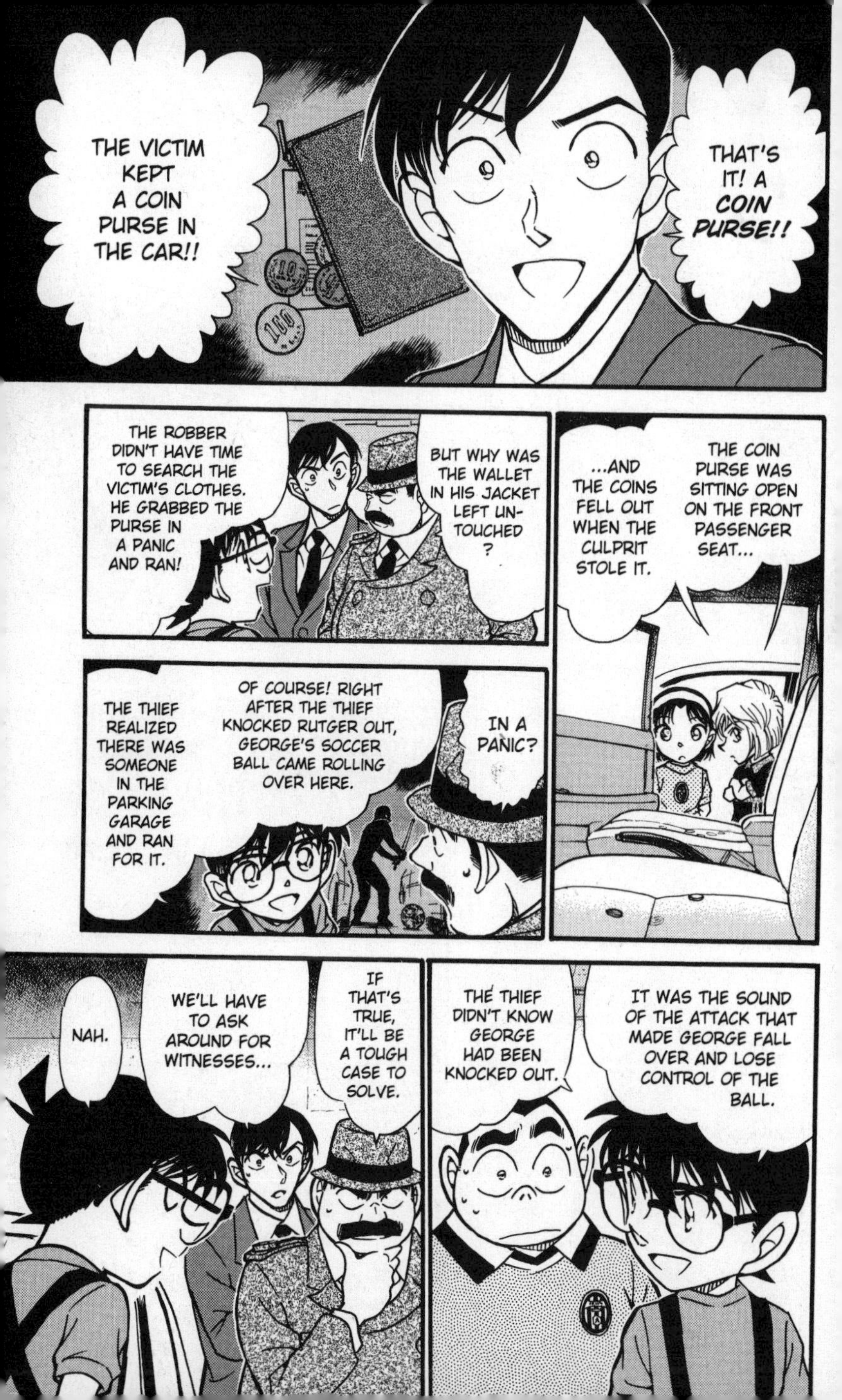

THAT'S IT! A COIN PURSE!!
THE VICTIM KEPT A COIN PURSE IN THE CAR!!
THE COIN PURSE WAS SITTING OPEN ON THE FRONT PASSENGER SEAT...
...AND THE COINS FELL OUT WHEN THE CULPRIT STOLE IT.
BUT WHY WAS THE WALLET IN HIS JACKET LEFT UN-TOUCHED?
THE ROBBER DIDN'T HAVE TIME TO SEARCH THE VICTIM'S CLOTHES. HE GRABBED THE PURSE IN A PANIC AND RAN!
IN A PANIC?
OF COURSE! RIGHT AFTER THE THIEF KNOCKED RUTGER OUT, GEORGE'S SOCCER BALL CAME ROLLING OVER HERE.
THE THIEF REALIZED THERE WAS SOMEONE IN THE PARKING GARAGE AND RAN FOR IT.
IT WAS THE SOUND OF THE ATTACK THAT MADE GEORGE FALL OVER AND LOSE CONTROL OF THE BALL.
THE THIEF DIDN'T KNOW GEORGE HAD BEEN KNOCKED OUT.
IF THAT'S TRUE, IT'LL BE A TOUGH CASE TO SOLVE.
WE'LL HAVE TO ASK AROUND FOR WITNESSES...
NAH.

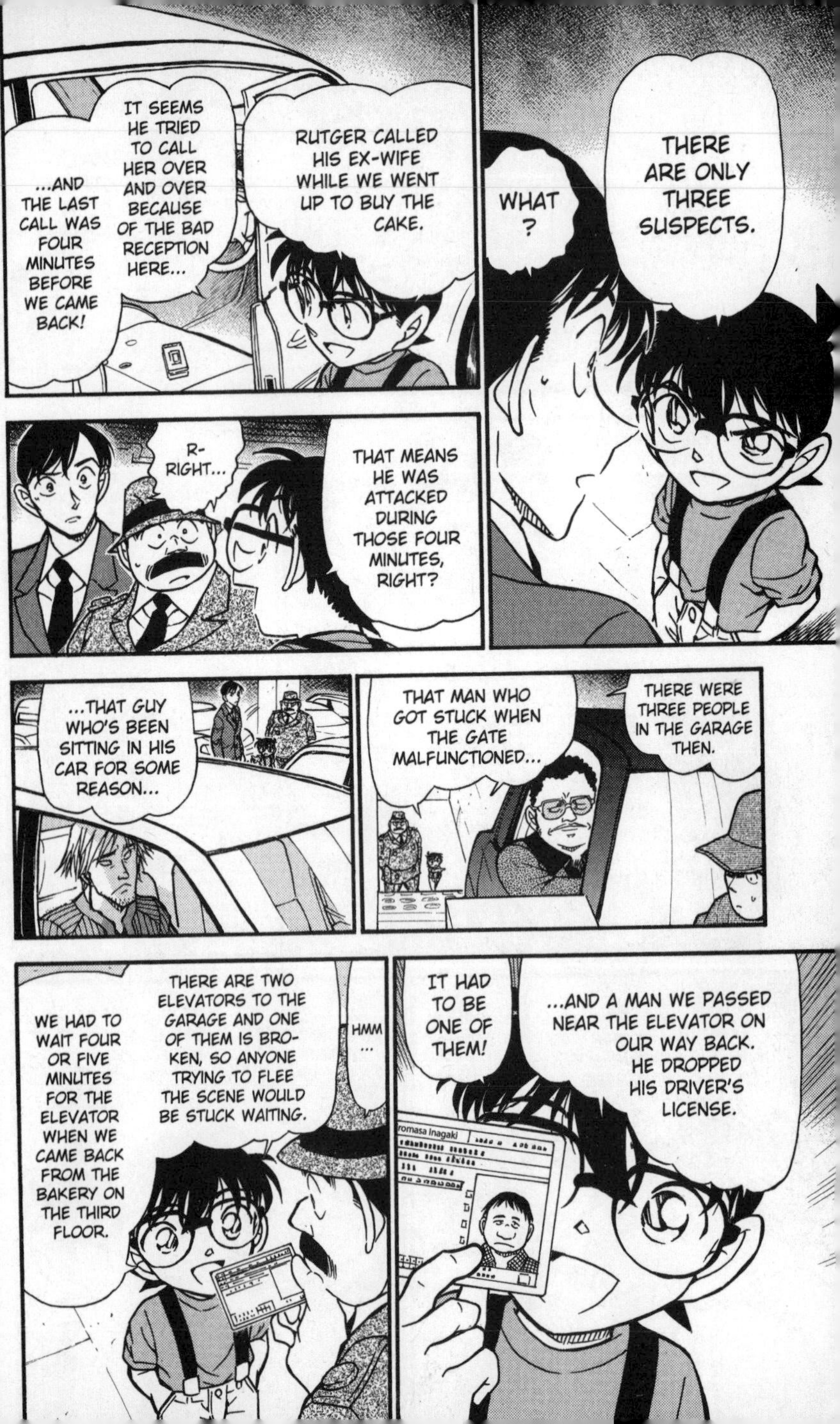
THERE ARE ONLY THREE SUSPECTS.
WHAT?
RUTGER CALLED HIS EX-WIFE WHILE WE WENT UP TO BUY THE CAKE.
IT SEEMS HE TRIED TO CALL HER OVER AND OVER BECAUSE OF THE BAD RECEPTION HERE...
...AND THE LAST CALL WAS FOUR MINUTES BEFORE WE CAME BACK!
THAT MEANS HE WAS ATTACKED DURING THOSE FOUR MINUTES, RIGHT?
R-RIGHT...
THERE WERE THREE PEOPLE IN THE GARAGE THEN.
THAT MAN WHO GOT STUCK WHEN THE GATE MALFUNCTIONED...
...THAT GUY WHO'S BEEN SITTING IN HIS CAR FOR SOME REASON...
...AND A MAN WE PASSED NEAR THE ELEVATOR ON OUR WAY BACK. HE DROPPED HIS DRIVER'S LICENSE.
IT HAD TO BE ONE OF THEM!
HMM...
THERE ARE TWO ELEVATORS TO THE GARAGE AND ONE OF THEM IS BRO-KEN, SO ANYONE TRYING TO FLEE THE SCENE WOULD BE STUCK WAITING.
WE HAD TO WAIT FOUR OR FIVE MINUTES FOR THE ELEVATOR WHEN WE CAME BACK FROM THE BAKERY ON THE THIRD FLOOR.

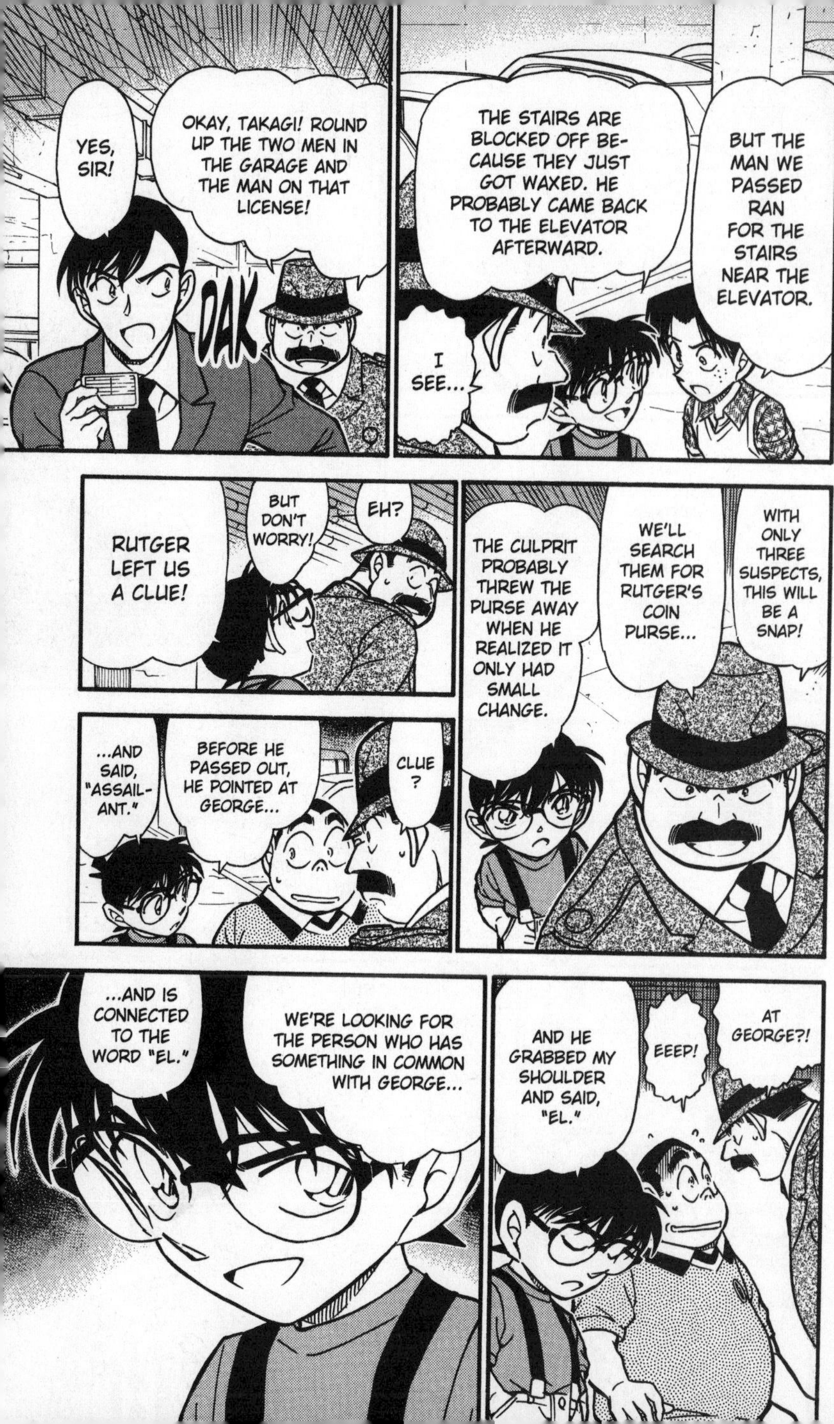
BUT THE MAN WE PASSED RAN FOR THE STAIRS NEAR THE ELEVATOR.
THE STAIRS ARE BLOCKED OFF BE-CAUSE THEY JUST GOT WAXED. HE PROBABLY CAME BACK TO THE ELEVATOR AFTERWARD.
I SEE...
OKAY, TAKAGI! ROUND UP THE TWO MEN IN THE GARAGE AND THE MAN ON THAT LICENSE!
YES, SIR!
DAK
WITH ONLY THREE SUSPECTS, THIS WILL BE A SNAP!
WE'LL SEARCH THEM FOR RUTGER'S COIN PURSE...
THE CULPRIT PROBABLY THREW THE PURSE AWAY WHEN HE REALIZED IT ONLY HAD SMALL CHANGE.
EH?
BUT DON'T WORRY!
RUTGER LEFT US A CLUE!
CLUE?
BEFORE HE PASSED OUT, HE POINTED AT GEORGE...
...AND SAID, "ASSAIL-ANT."
AT GEORGE?!
EEEP!
AND HE GRABBED MY SHOULDER AND SAID, "EL."
WE'RE LOOKING FOR THE PERSON WHO HAS SOMETHING IN COMMON WITH GEORGE...
...AND IS CONNECTED TO THE WORD "EL."

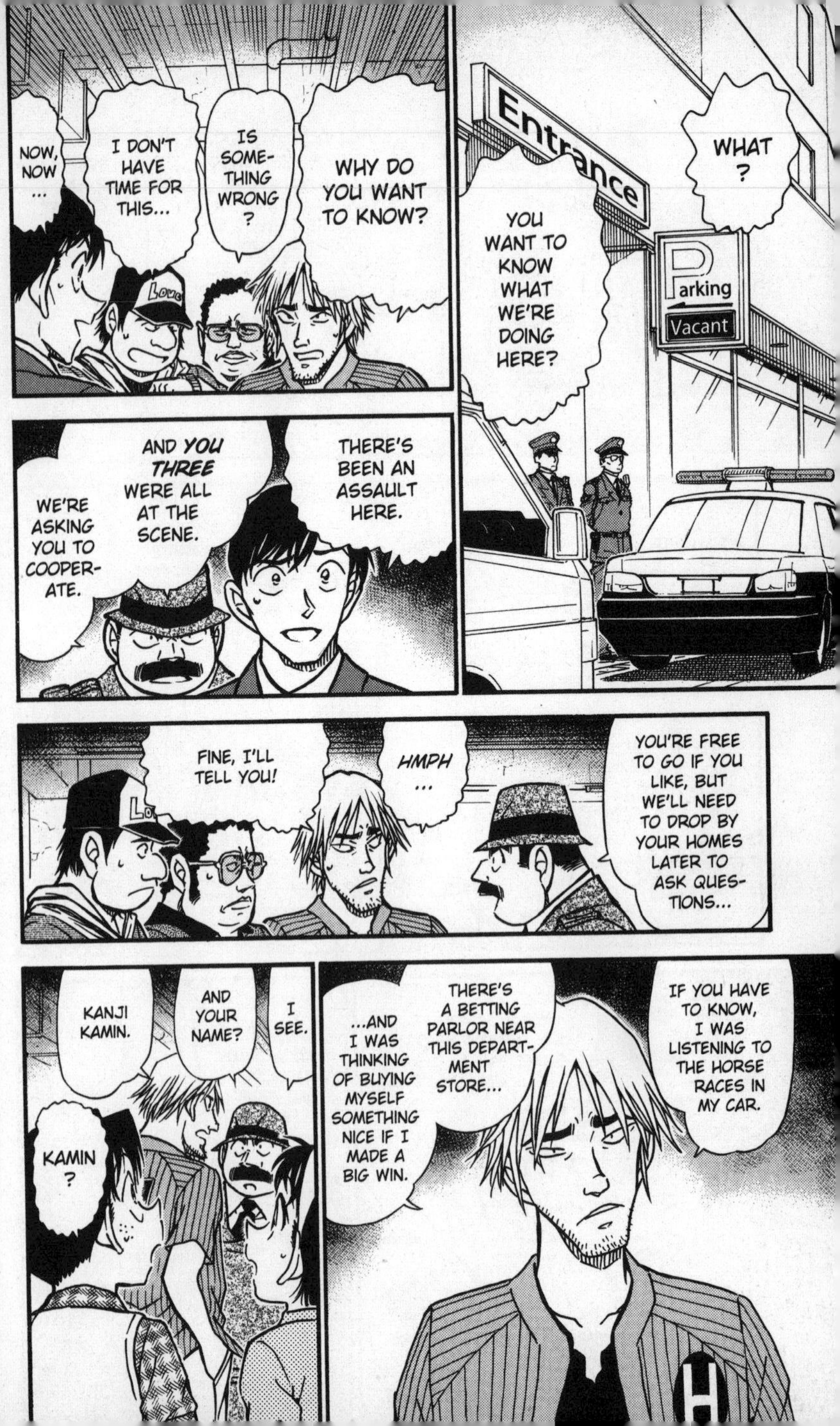
WHAT?
Entrance
YOU WANT TO KNOW WHAT WE'RE DOING HERE?
Parking
Vacant
WHY DO YOU WANT TO KNOW?
IS SOMETHING WRONG?
I DON'T HAVE TIME FOR THIS...
NOW, NOW...
THERE'S BEEN AN ASSAULT HERE.
AND *YOU THREE* WERE ALL AT THE SCENE.
WE'RE ASKING YOU TO COOPERATE.
YOU'RE FREE TO GO IF YOU LIKE, BUT WE'LL NEED TO DROP BY YOUR HOMES LATER TO ASK QUESTIONS...
HMPH...
FINE, I'LL TELL YOU!
IF YOU HAVE TO KNOW, I WAS LISTENING TO THE HORSE RACES IN MY CAR.
THERE'S A BETTING PARLOR NEAR THIS DEPARTMENT STORE...
...AND I WAS THINKING OF BUYING MYSELF SOMETHING NICE IF I MADE A BIG WIN.
I SEE.
AND YOUR NAME?
KANJI KAMIN.
KAMIN?

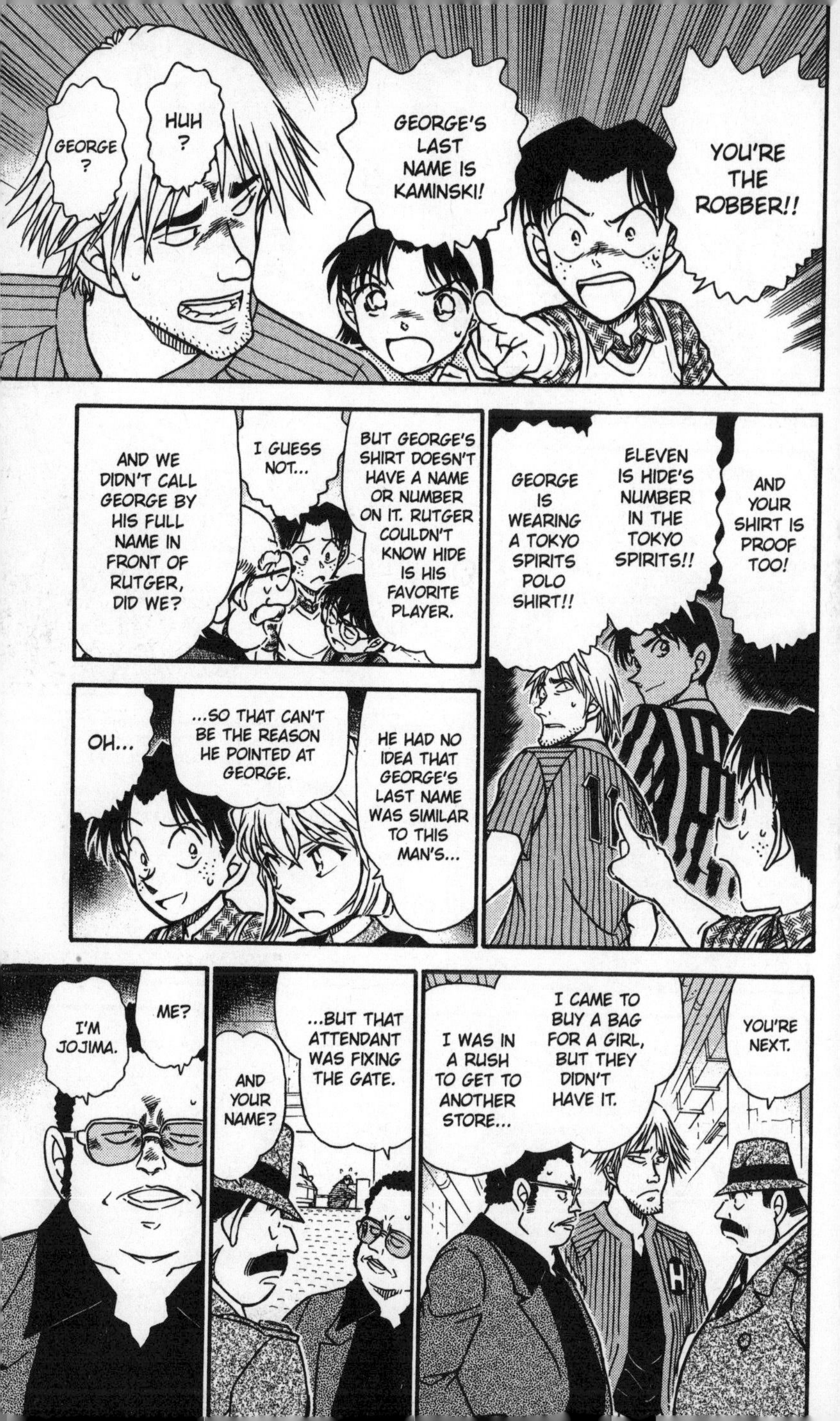
YOU'RE THE ROBBER!!
GEORGE'S LAST NAME IS KAMINSKI!
HUH?
GEORGE?
AND YOUR SHIRT IS PROOF TOO!
ELEVEN IS HIDE'S NUMBER IN THE TOKYO SPIRITS!!
GEORGE IS WEARING A TOKYO SPIRITS POLO SHIRT!!
BUT GEORGE'S SHIRT DOESN'T HAVE A NAME OR NUMBER ON IT. RUTGER COULDN'T KNOW HIDE IS HIS FAVORITE PLAYER.
I GUESS NOT...
AND WE DIDN'T CALL GEORGE BY HIS FULL NAME IN FRONT OF RUTGER, DID WE?
HE HAD NO IDEA THAT GEORGE'S LAST NAME WAS SIMILAR TO THIS MAN'S...
...SO THAT CAN'T BE THE REASON HE POINTED AT GEORGE.
OH...
YOU'RE NEXT.
I CAME TO BUY A BAG FOR A GIRL, BUT THEY DIDN'T HAVE IT.
I WAS IN A RUSH TO GET TO ANOTHER STORE...
...BUT THAT ATTENDANT WAS FIXING THE GATE.
AND YOUR NAME?
ME?
I'M JOJIMA.

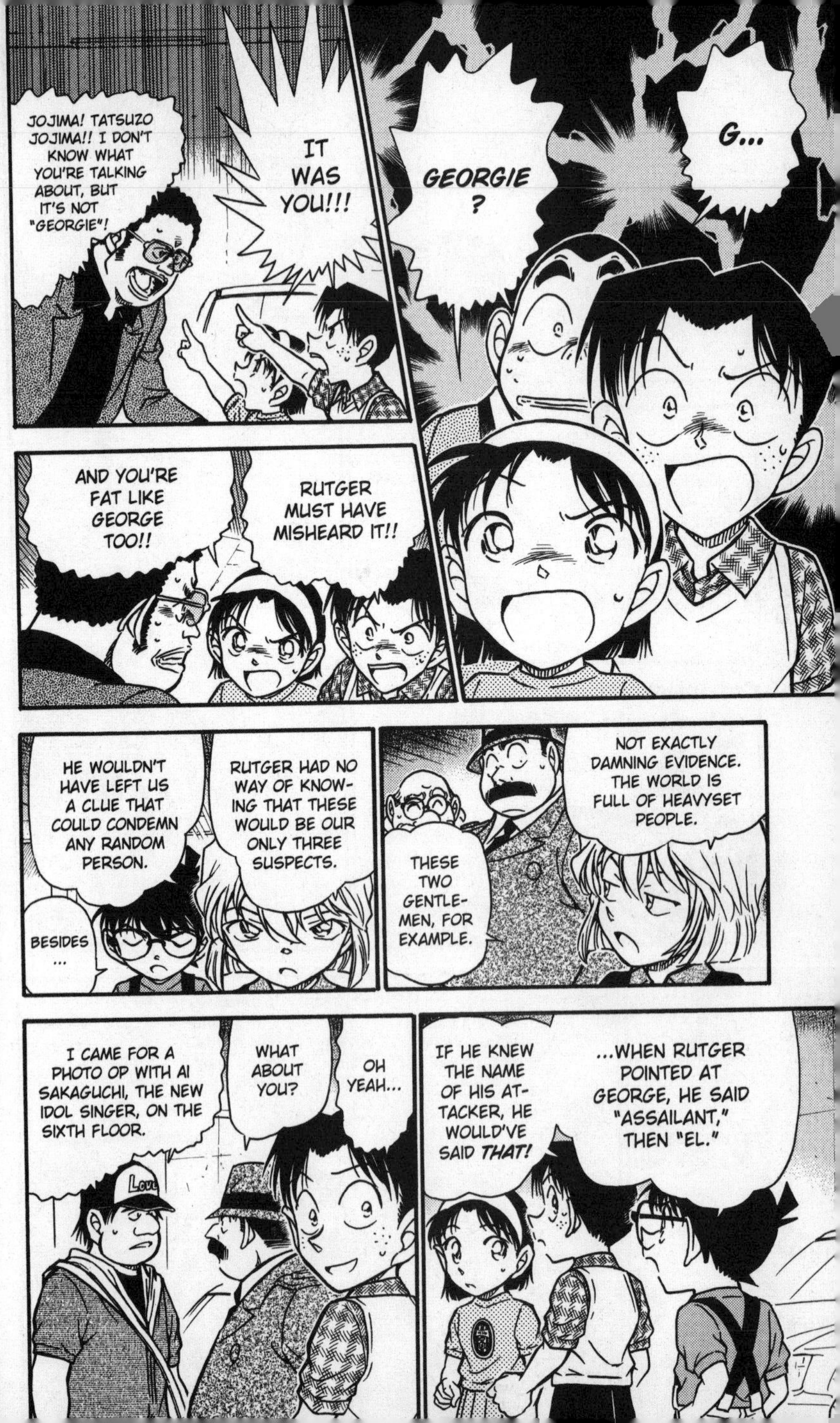
G...
GEORGIE ?
IT WAS YOU!!!
JOJIMA! TATSUZO JOJIMA!! I DON'T KNOW WHAT YOU'RE TALKING ABOUT, BUT IT'S NOT "GEORGIE"!
RUTGER MUST HAVE MISHEARD IT!!
AND YOU'RE FAT LIKE GEORGE TOO!!
NOT EXACTLY DAMNING EVIDENCE. THE WORLD IS FULL OF HEAVYSET PEOPLE.
THESE TWO GENTLE-MEN, FOR EXAMPLE.
RUTGER HAD NO WAY OF KNOW-ING THAT THESE WOULD BE OUR ONLY THREE SUSPECTS.
HE WOULDN'T HAVE LEFT US A CLUE THAT COULD CONDEMN ANY RANDOM PERSON.
BESIDES ...
...WHEN RUTGER POINTED AT GEORGE, HE SAID "ASSAILANT," THEN "EL."
IF HE KNEW THE NAME OF HIS AT-TACKER, HE WOULD'VE SAID THAT!
OH YEAH...
WHAT ABOUT YOU?
I CAME FOR A PHOTO OP WITH AI SAKAGUCHI, THE NEW IDOL SINGER, ON THE SIXTH FLOOR.

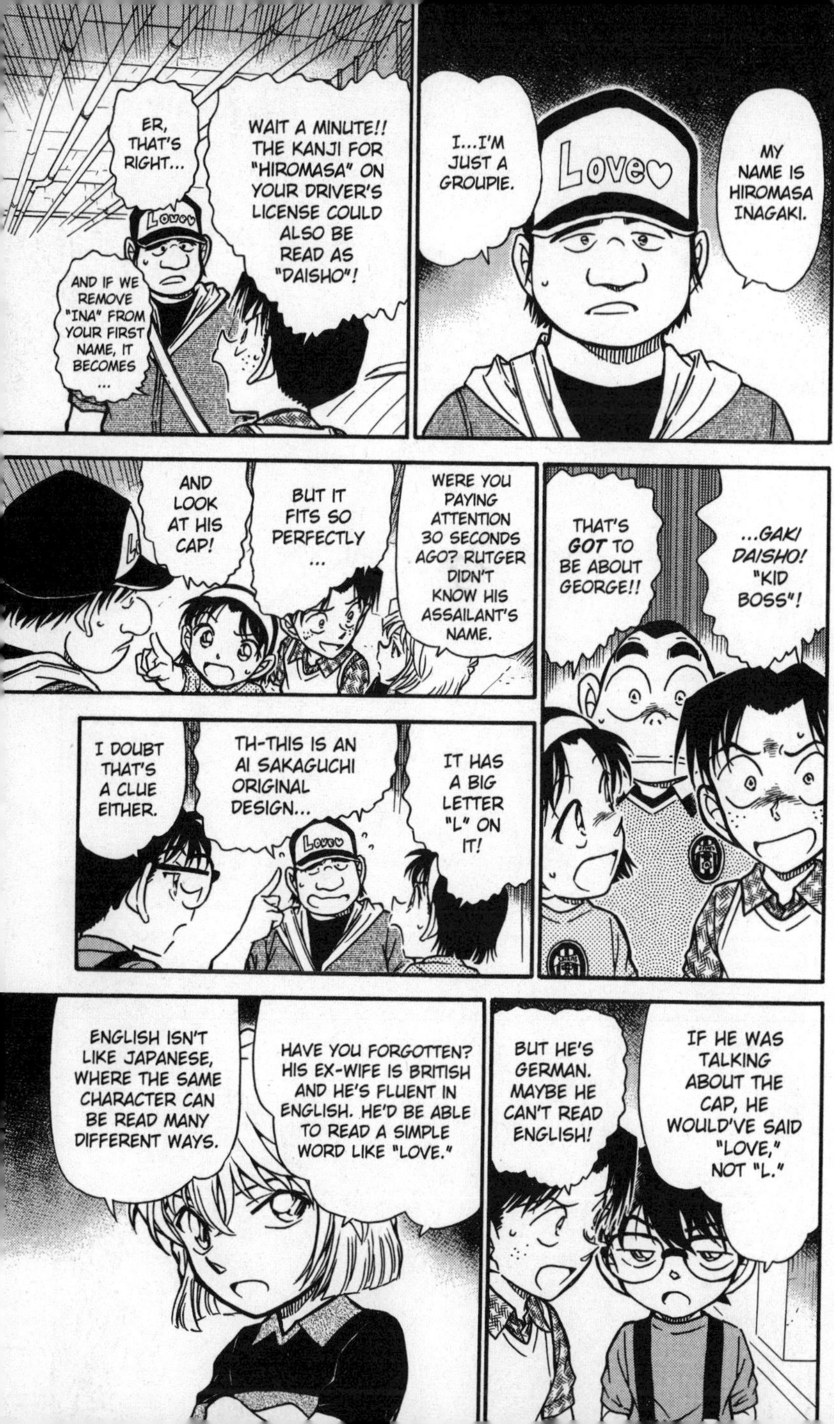
MY NAME IS HIROMASA INAGAKI.
I...I'M JUST A GROUPIE.
WAIT A MINUTE!! THE KANJI FOR "HIROMASA" ON YOUR DRIVER'S LICENSE COULD ALSO BE READ AS "DAISHO"!
ER, THAT'S RIGHT...
AND IF WE REMOVE "INA" FROM YOUR FIRST NAME, IT BECOMES ...
...GAKI DAISHO! "KID BOSS"!
THAT'S **GOT** TO BE ABOUT GEORGE!!
WERE YOU PAYING ATTENTION 30 SECONDS AGO? RUTGER DIDN'T KNOW HIS ASSAILANT'S NAME.
BUT IT FITS SO PERFECTLY ...
AND LOOK AT HIS CAP!
IT HAS A BIG LETTER "L" ON IT!
TH-THIS IS AN AI SAKAGUCHI ORIGINAL DESIGN...
I DOUBT THAT'S A CLUE EITHER.
IF HE WAS TALKING ABOUT THE CAP, HE WOULD'VE SAID "LOVE," NOT "L."
BUT HE'S GERMAN. MAYBE HE CAN'T READ ENGLISH!
HAVE YOU FORGOTTEN? HIS EX-WIFE IS BRITISH AND HE'S FLUENT IN ENGLISH. HE'D BE ABLE TO READ A SIMPLE WORD LIKE "LOVE."
ENGLISH ISN'T LIKE JAPANESE, WHERE THE SAME CHARACTER CAN BE READ MANY DIFFERENT WAYS.

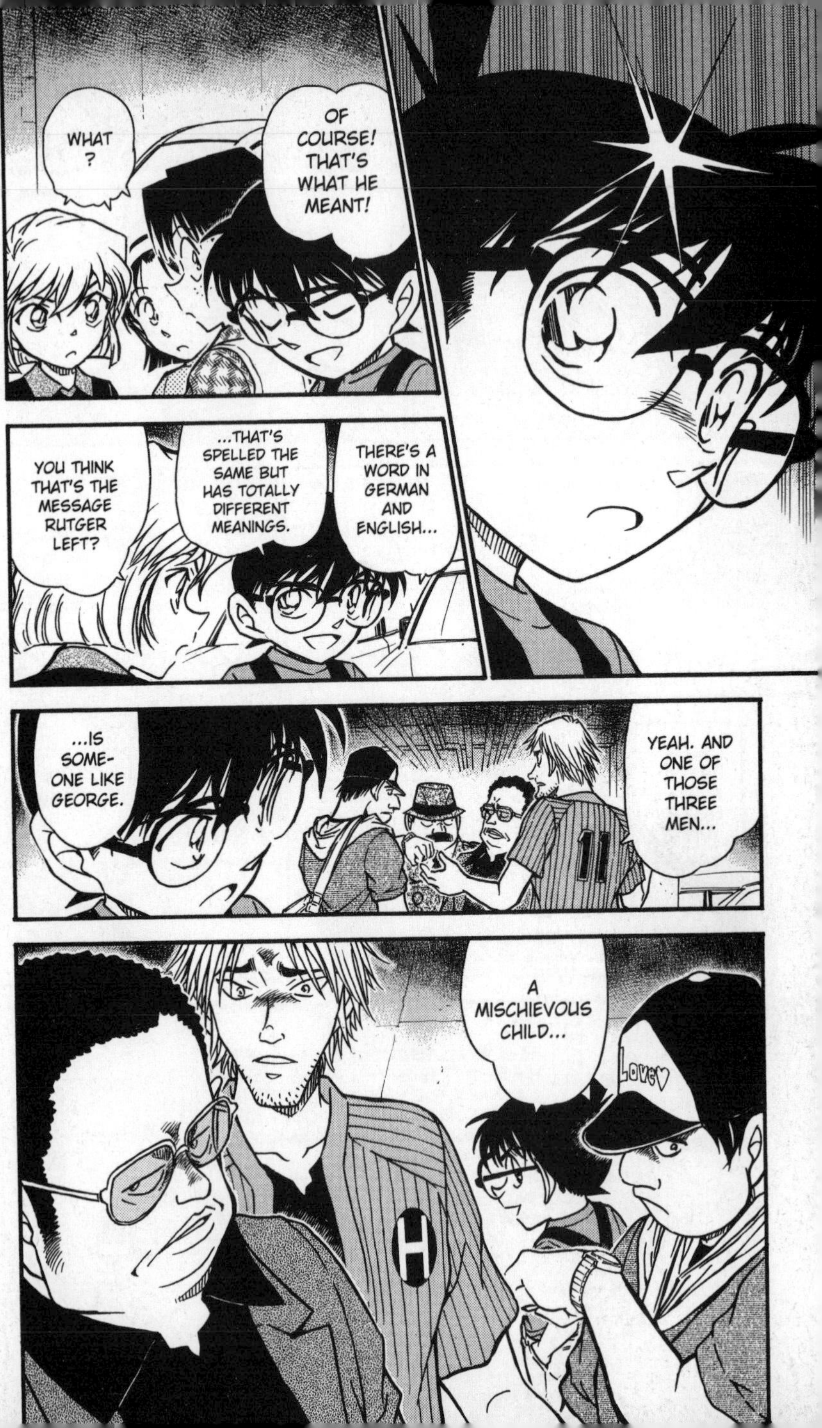
OF COURSE! THAT'S WHAT HE MEANT!
WHAT?
THERE'S A WORD IN GERMAN AND ENGLISH...
...THAT'S SPELLED THE SAME BUT HAS TOTALLY DIFFERENT MEANINGS.
YOU THINK THAT'S THE MESSAGE RUTGER LEFT?
YEAH. AND ONE OF THOSE THREE MEN...
...IS SOME-ONE LIKE GEORGE.
A MISCHIEVOUS CHILD...
Love♡

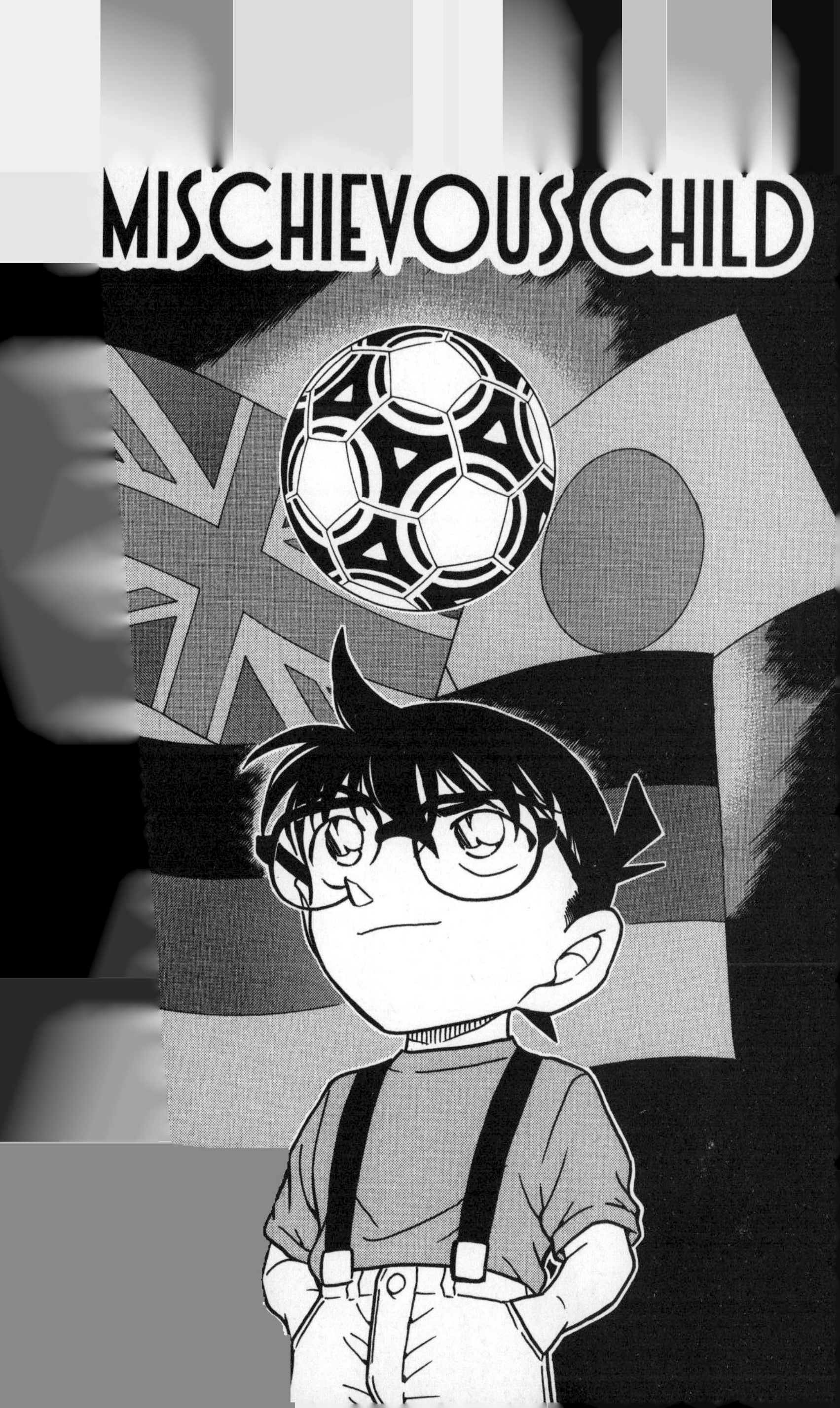
MISCHIEVOUS CHILD

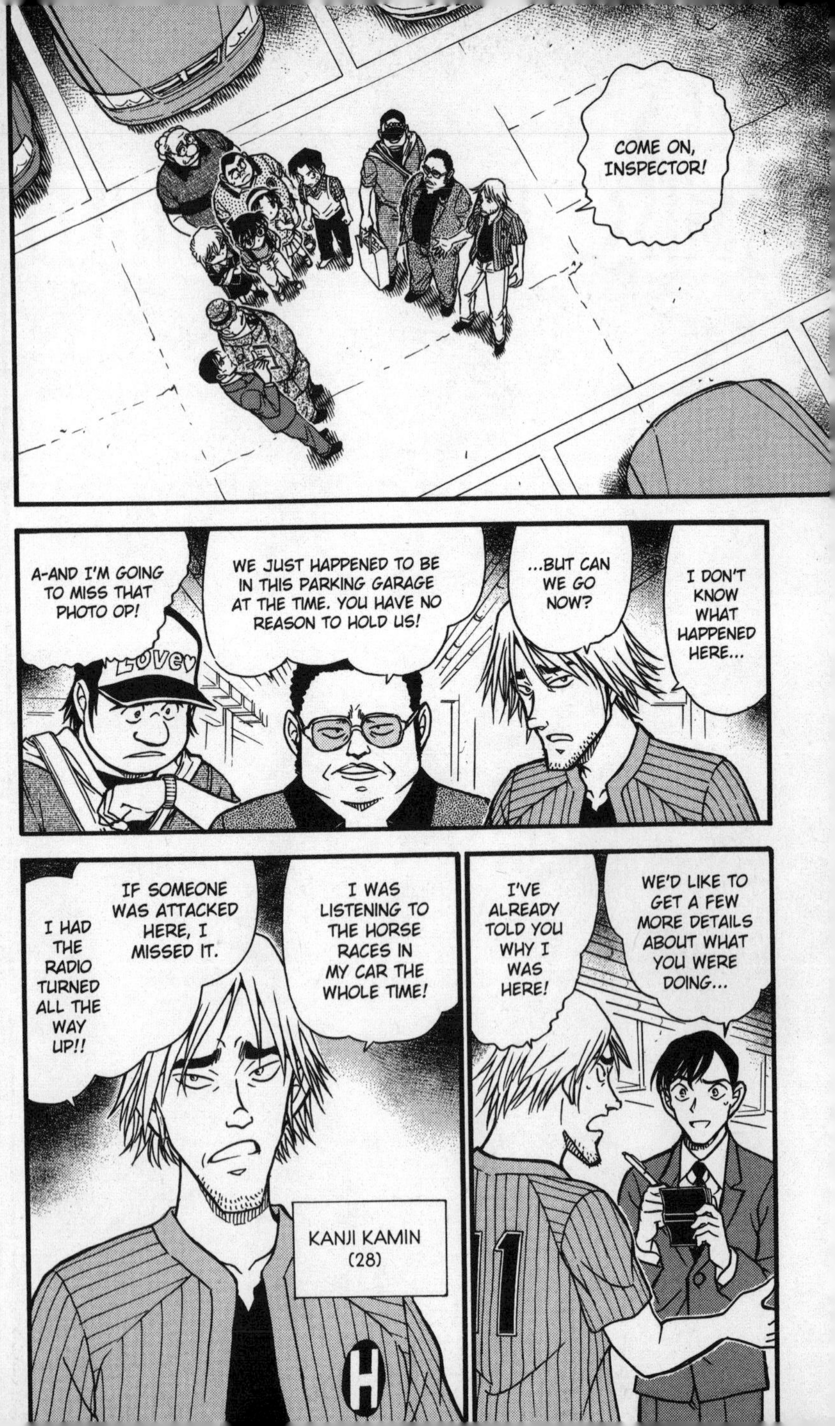
COME ON, INSPECTOR!
I DON'T KNOW WHAT HAPPENED HERE...
...BUT CAN WE GO NOW?
WE JUST HAPPENED TO BE IN THIS PARKING GARAGE AT THE TIME. YOU HAVE NO REASON TO HOLD US!
A-AND I'M GOING TO MISS THAT PHOTO OP!
WE'D LIKE TO GET A FEW MORE DETAILS ABOUT WHAT YOU WERE DOING...
I'VE ALREADY TOLD YOU WHY I WAS HERE!
I WAS LISTENING TO THE HORSE RACES IN MY CAR THE WHOLE TIME!
IF SOMEONE WAS ATTACKED HERE, I MISSED IT.
I HAD THE RADIO TURNED ALL THE WAY UP!!
KANJI KAMIN (28)

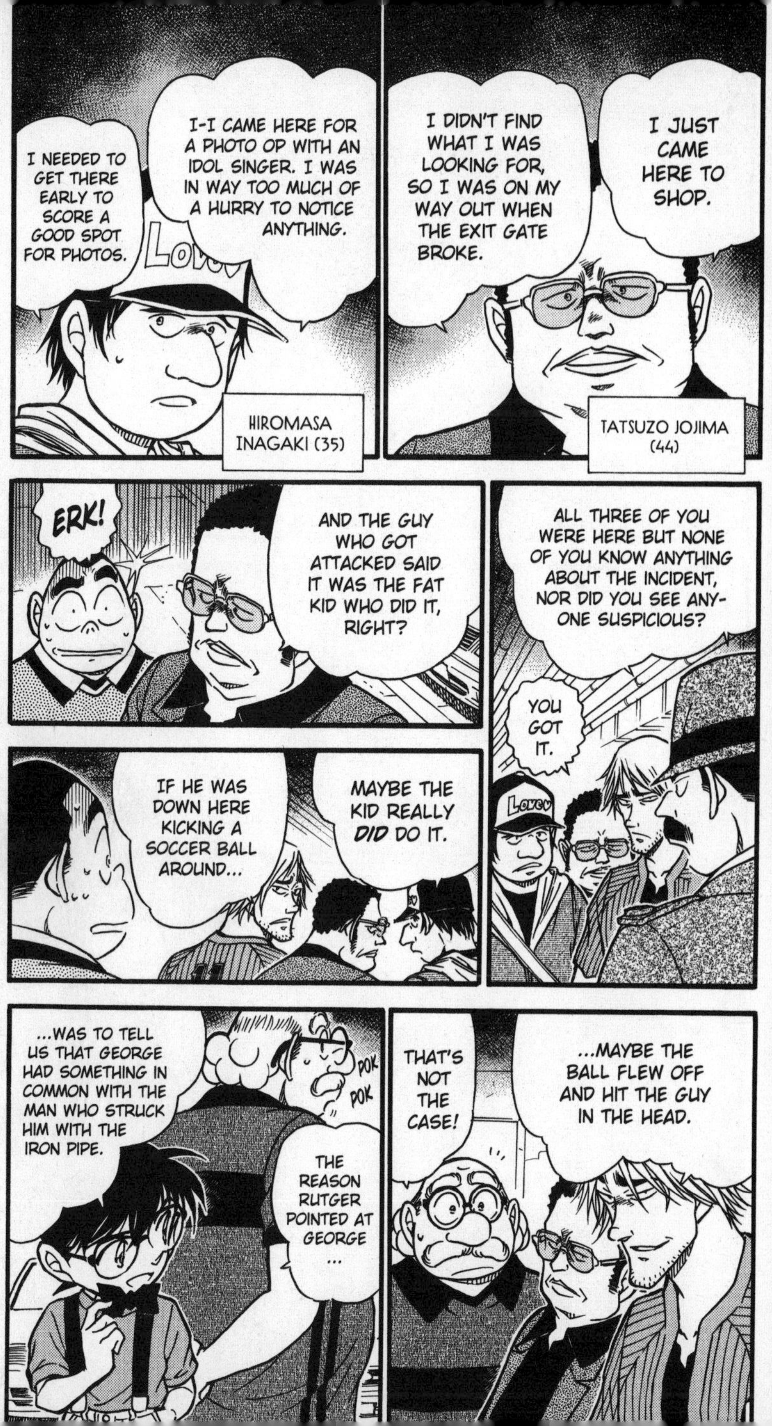
I JUST CAME HERE TO SHOP.
I DIDN'T FIND WHAT I WAS LOOKING FOR, SO I WAS ON MY WAY OUT WHEN THE EXIT GATE BROKE.
TATSUZO JOJIMA (44)
I-I CAME HERE FOR A PHOTO OP WITH AN IDOL SINGER. I WAS IN WAY TOO MUCH OF A HURRY TO NOTICE ANYTHING.
I NEEDED TO GET THERE EARLY TO SCORE A GOOD SPOT FOR PHOTOS.
HIROMASA INAGAKI (35)
ALL THREE OF YOU WERE HERE BUT NONE OF YOU KNOW ANYTHING ABOUT THE INCIDENT, NOR DID YOU SEE ANY-ONE SUSPICIOUS?
YOU GOT IT.
AND THE GUY WHO GOT ATTACKED SAID IT WAS THE FAT KID WHO DID IT, RIGHT?
ERK!
MAYBE THE KID REALLY *DID* DO IT.
IF HE WAS DOWN HERE KICKING A SOCCER BALL AROUND...
...MAYBE THE BALL FLEW OFF AND HIT THE GUY IN THE HEAD.
THAT'S NOT THE CASE!
POK POK
THE REASON RUTGER POINTED AT GEORGE...
...WAS TO TELL US THAT GEORGE HAD SOMETHING IN COMMON WITH THE MAN WHO STRUCK HIM WITH THE IRON PIPE.

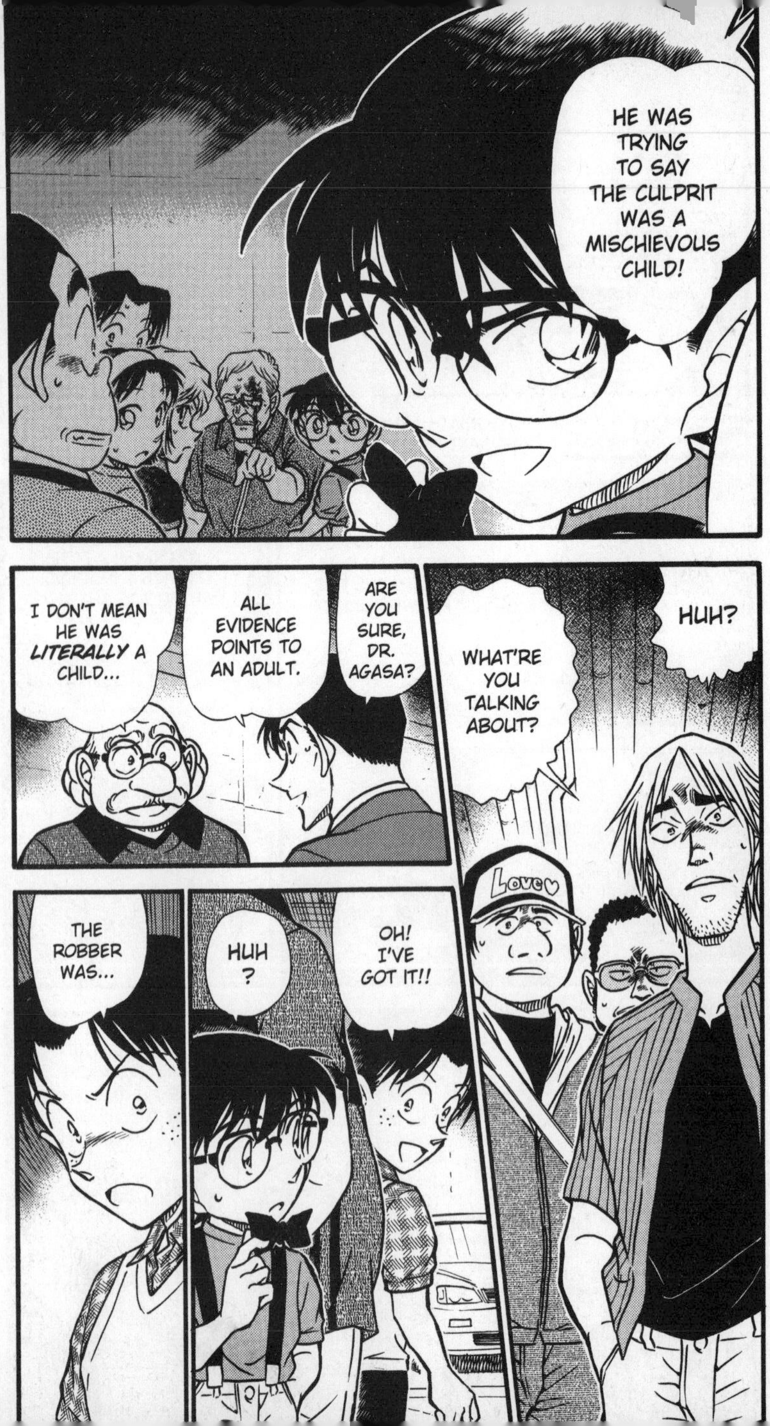
HE WAS TRYING TO SAY THE CULPRIT WAS A MISCHIEVOUS CHILD!
HUH?
WHAT'RE YOU TALKING ABOUT?
ARE YOU SURE, DR. AGASA?
ALL EVIDENCE POINTS TO AN ADULT.
I DON'T MEAN HE WAS *LITERALLY* A CHILD...
OH! I'VE GOT IT!!
HUH ?
THE ROBBER WAS...

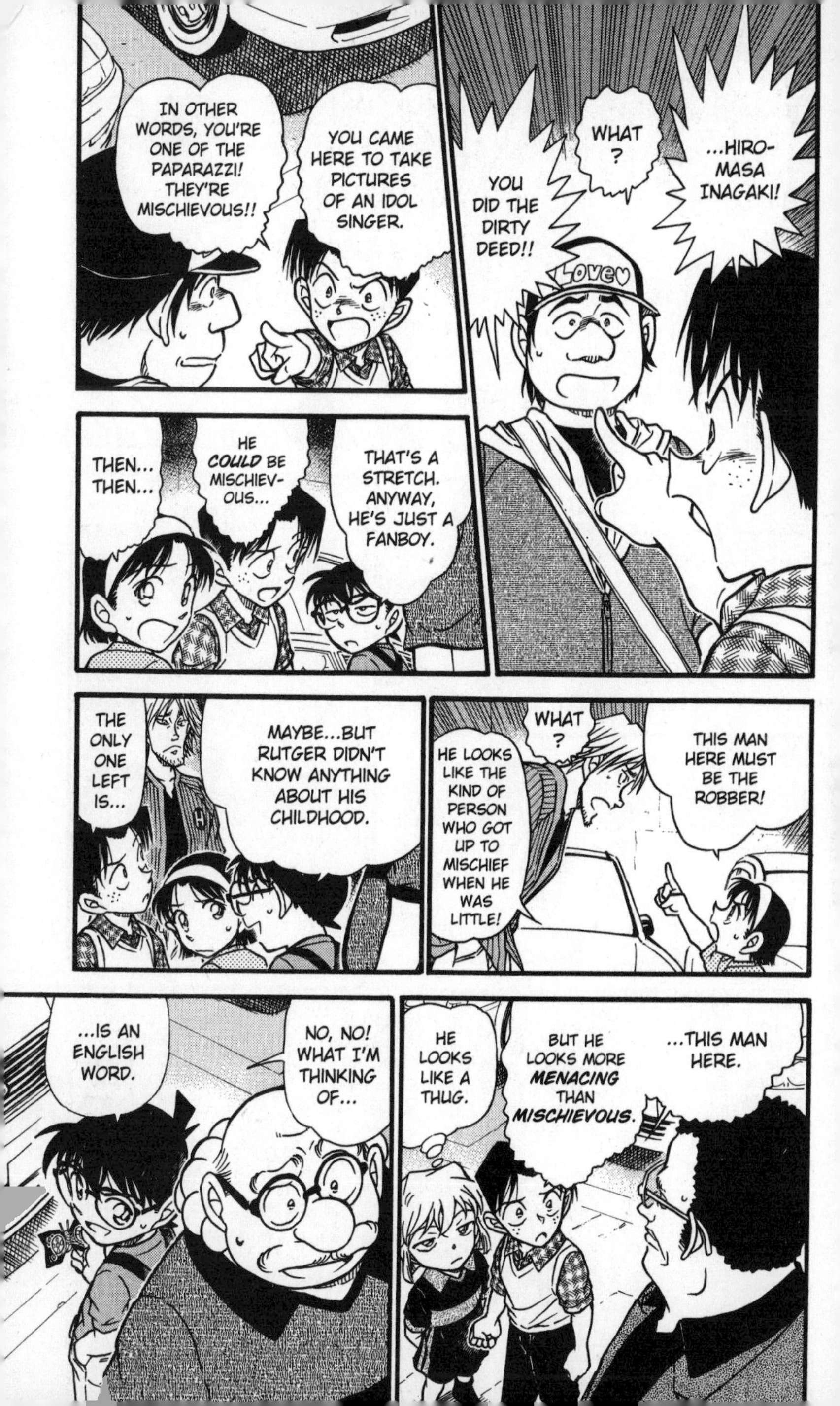
...HIRO-MASA INAGAKI!
YOU DID THE DIRTY DEED!!
WHAT ?
YOU CAME HERE TO TAKE PICTURES OF AN IDOL SINGER.
IN OTHER WORDS, YOU'RE ONE OF THE PAPARAZZI! THEY'RE MISCHIEVOUS!!
THAT'S A STRETCH. ANYWAY, HE'S JUST A FANBOY.
HE *COULD* BE MISCHIEV-OUS...
THEN... THEN...
THIS MAN HERE MUST BE THE ROBBER!
WHAT ?
HE LOOKS LIKE THE KIND OF PERSON WHO GOT UP TO MISCHIEF WHEN HE WAS LITTLE!
MAYBE...BUT RUTGER DIDN'T KNOW ANYTHING ABOUT HIS CHILDHOOD.
THE ONLY ONE LEFT IS...
...THIS MAN HERE.
BUT HE LOOKS MORE ***MENACING*** THAN ***MISCHIEVOUS***.
HE LOOKS LIKE A THUG.
NO, NO! WHAT I'M THINKING OF...
...IS AN ENGLISH WORD.

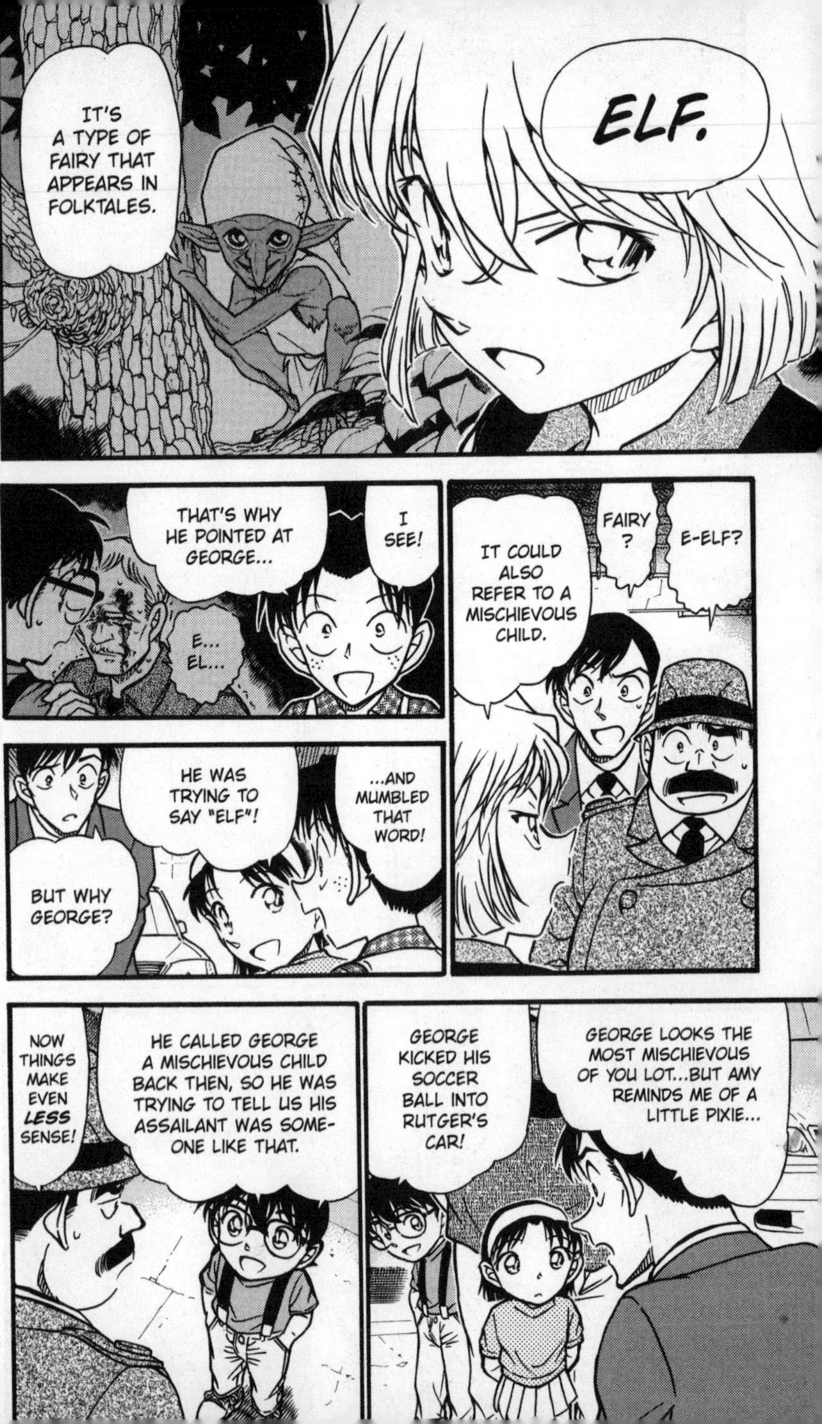
ELF.
IT'S A TYPE OF FAIRY THAT APPEARS IN FOLKTALES.
E-ELF?
FAIRY?
IT COULD ALSO REFER TO A MISCHIEVOUS CHILD.
I SEE!
THAT'S WHY HE POINTED AT GEORGE...
E... EL...
...AND MUMBLED THAT WORD!
HE WAS TRYING TO SAY "ELF"!
BUT WHY GEORGE?
GEORGE LOOKS THE MOST MISCHIEVOUS OF YOU LOT...BUT AMY REMINDS ME OF A LITTLE PIXIE...
GEORGE KICKED HIS SOCCER BALL INTO RUTGER'S CAR!
HE CALLED GEORGE A MISCHIEVOUS CHILD BACK THEN, SO HE WAS TRYING TO TELL US HIS ASSAILANT WAS SOME-ONE LIKE THAT.
NOW THINGS MAKE EVEN LESS SENSE!

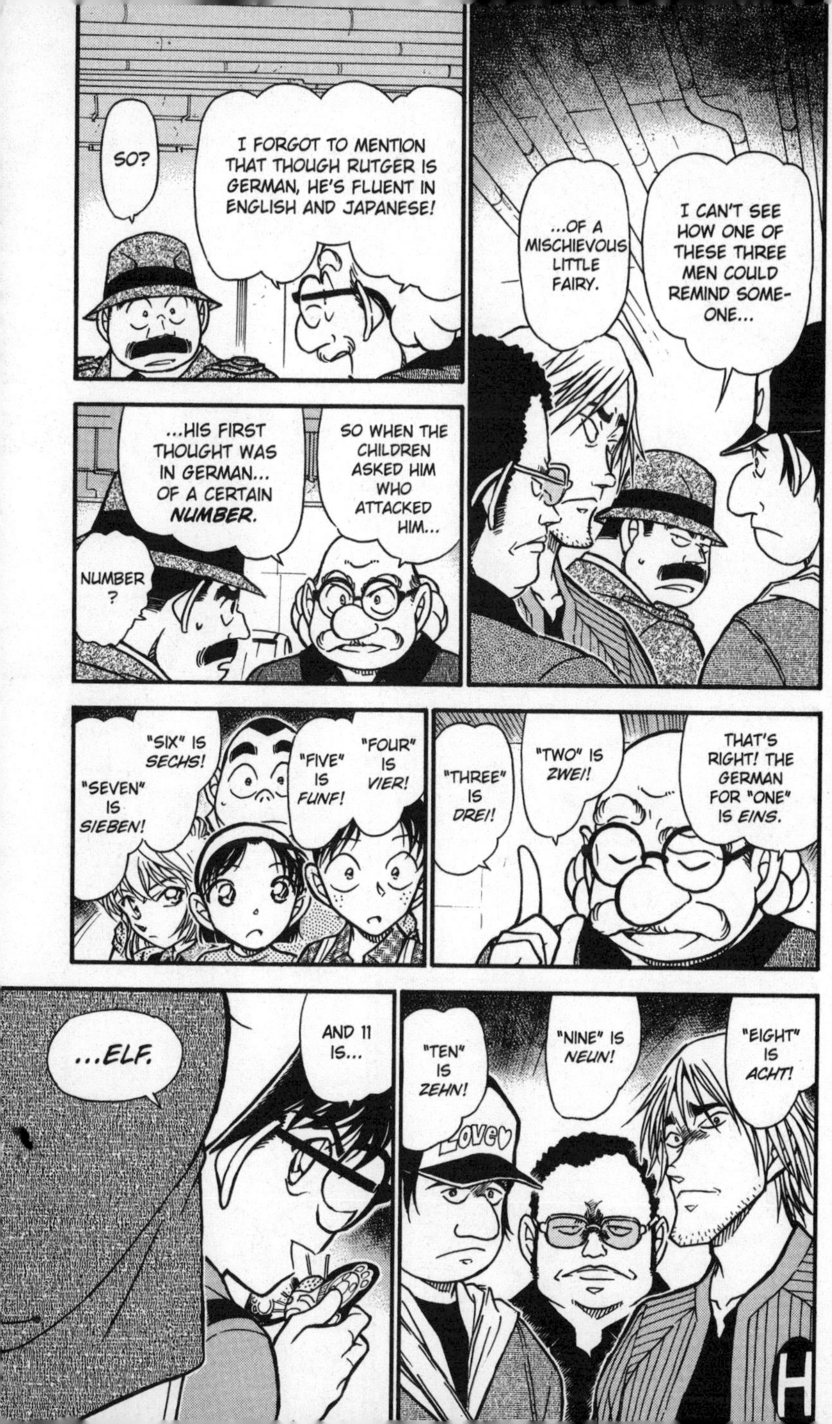
I CAN'T SEE HOW ONE OF THESE THREE MEN COULD REMIND SOME-ONE...
...OF A MISCHIEVOUS LITTLE FAIRY.
I FORGOT TO MENTION THAT THOUGH RUTGER IS GERMAN, HE'S FLUENT IN ENGLISH AND JAPANESE!
SO?
SO WHEN THE CHILDREN ASKED HIM WHO ATTACKED HIM...
...HIS FIRST THOUGHT WAS IN GERMAN... OF A CERTAIN **NUMBER.**
NUMBER?
THAT'S RIGHT! THE GERMAN FOR "ONE" IS *EINS.*
"TWO" IS *ZWEI!*
"THREE" IS *DREI!*
"FOUR" IS *VIER!*
"FIVE" IS *FUNF!*
"SIX" IS *SECHS!*
"SEVEN" IS *SIEBEN!*
"EIGHT" IS *ACHT!*
"NINE" IS *NEUN!*
"TEN" IS *ZEHN!*
LOVE
AND 11 IS...
...ELF.

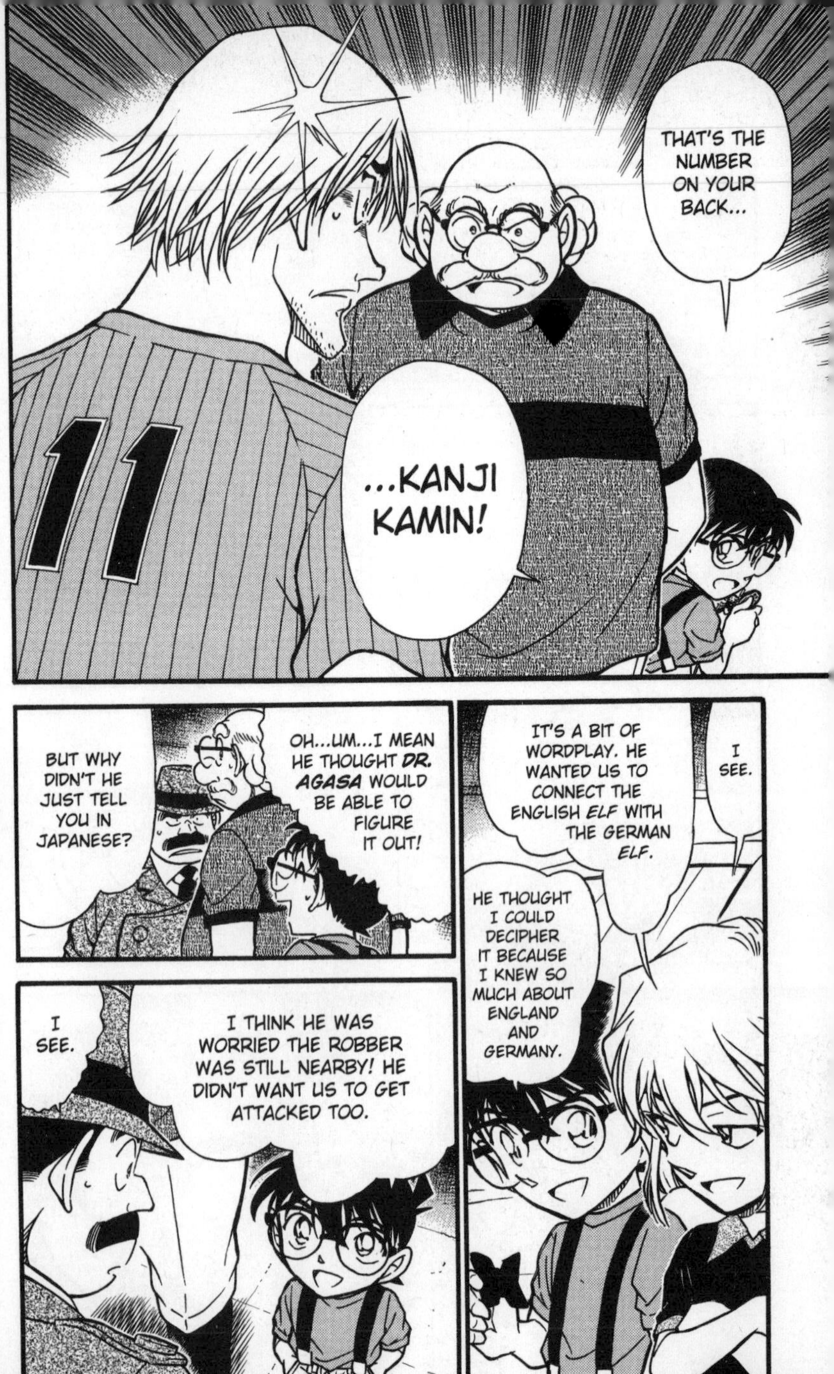
THAT'S THE NUMBER ON YOUR BACK...
...KANJI KAMIN!
I SEE.
IT'S A BIT OF WORDPLAY. HE WANTED US TO CONNECT THE ENGLISH *ELF* WITH THE GERMAN *ELF*.
HE THOUGHT I COULD DECIPHER IT BECAUSE I KNEW SO MUCH ABOUT ENGLAND AND GERMANY.
OH...UM...I MEAN HE THOUGHT ***DR. AGASA*** WOULD BE ABLE TO FIGURE IT OUT!
BUT WHY DIDN'T HE JUST TELL YOU IN JAPANESE?
I THINK HE WAS WORRIED THE ROBBER WAS STILL NEARBY! HE DIDN'T WANT US TO GET ATTACKED TOO.
I SEE.

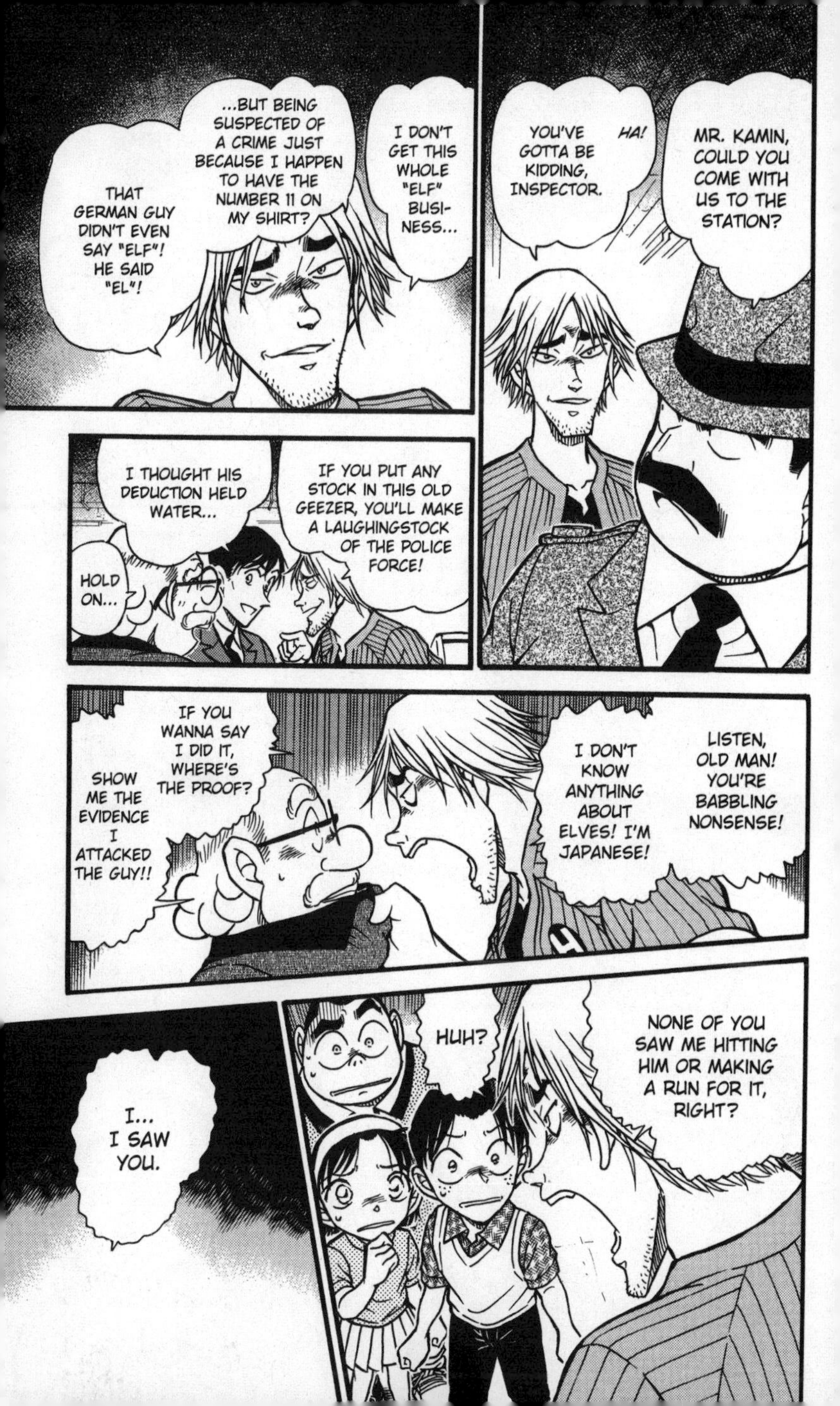
MR. KAMIN, COULD YOU COME WITH US TO THE STATION?
HA!
YOU'VE GOTTA BE KIDDING, INSPECTOR.
I DON'T GET THIS WHOLE "ELF" BUSINESS...
...BUT BEING SUSPECTED OF A CRIME JUST BECAUSE I HAPPEN TO HAVE THE NUMBER 11 ON MY SHIRT?
THAT GERMAN GUY DIDN'T EVEN SAY "ELF"! HE SAID "EL"!
IF YOU PUT ANY STOCK IN THIS OLD GEEZER, YOU'LL MAKE A LAUGHINGSTOCK OF THE POLICE FORCE!
I THOUGHT HIS DEDUCTION HELD WATER...
HOLD ON...
LISTEN, OLD MAN! YOU'RE BABBLING NONSENSE!
I DON'T KNOW ANYTHING ABOUT ELVES! I'M JAPANESE!
IF YOU WANNA SAY I DID IT, WHERE'S THE PROOF?
SHOW ME THE EVIDENCE I ATTACKED THE GUY!!
NONE OF YOU SAW ME HITTING HIM OR MAKING A RUN FOR IT, RIGHT?
HUH?
I... I SAW YOU.

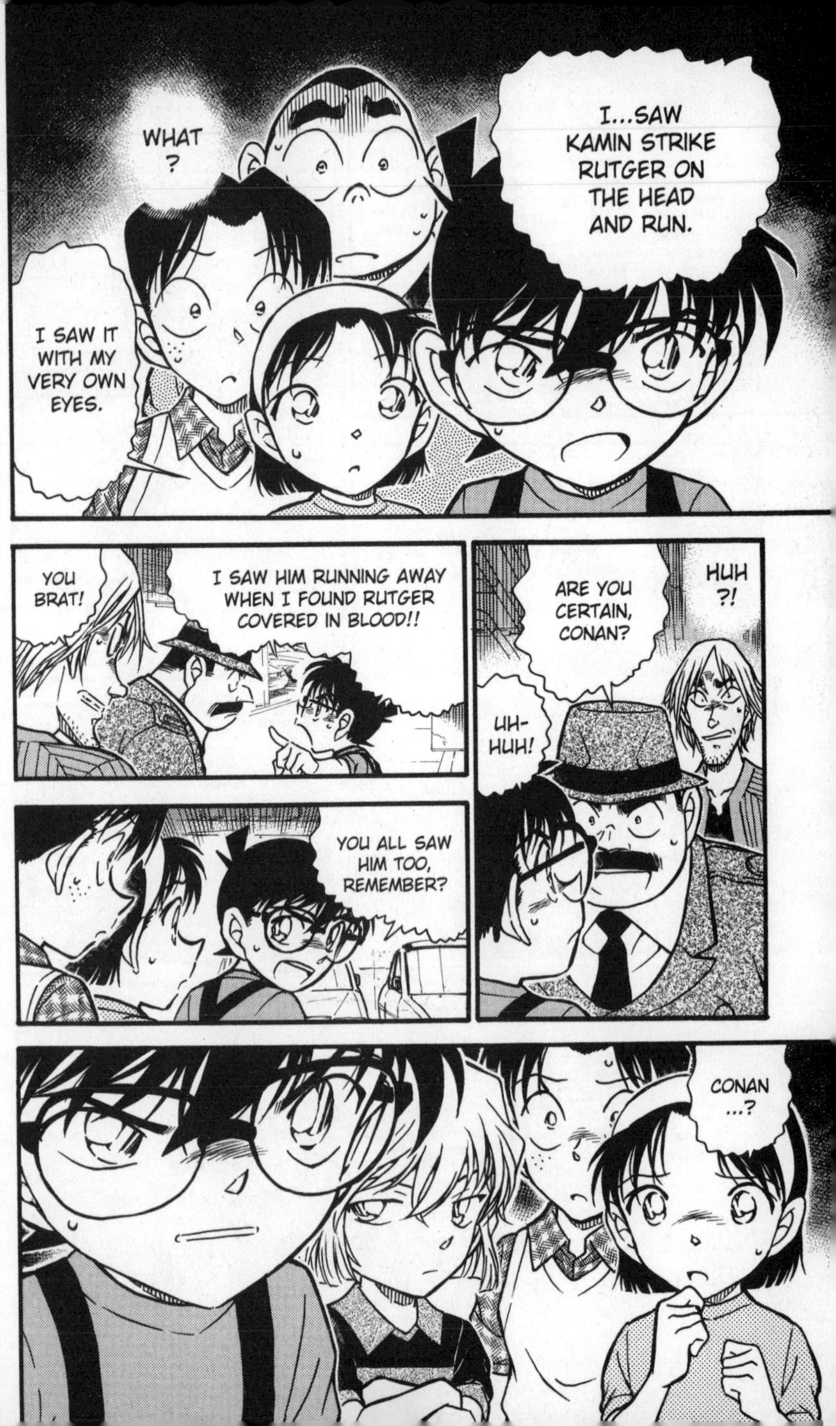
I...SAW KAMIN STRIKE RUTGER ON THE HEAD AND RUN.
WHAT?
I SAW IT WITH MY VERY OWN EYES.
HUH?!
ARE YOU CERTAIN, CONAN?
UH-HUH!
I SAW HIM RUNNING AWAY WHEN I FOUND RUTGER COVERED IN BLOOD!!
YOU BRAT!
YOU ALL SAW HIM TOO, REMEMBER?
CONAN...?

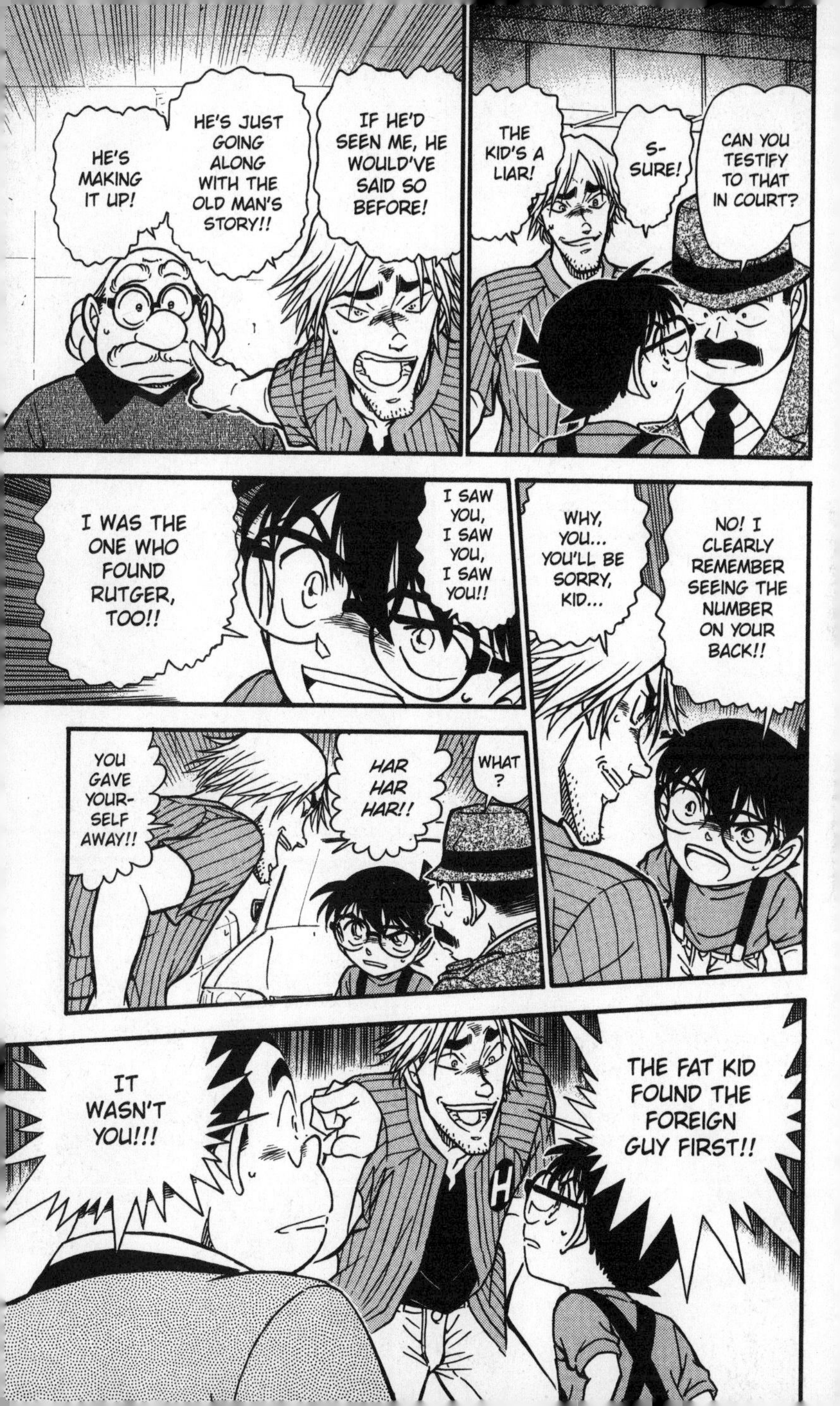
CAN YOU TESTIFY TO THAT IN COURT?
S-SURE!
THE KID'S A LIAR!
IF HE'D SEEN ME, HE WOULD'VE SAID SO BEFORE!
HE'S JUST GOING ALONG WITH THE OLD MAN'S STORY!!
HE'S MAKING IT UP!
NO! I CLEARLY REMEMBER SEEING THE NUMBER ON YOUR BACK!!
WHY, YOU... YOU'LL BE SORRY, KID...
I SAW YOU, I SAW YOU, I SAW YOU!!
I WAS THE ONE WHO FOUND RUTGER, TOO!!
WHAT?
HAR HAR HAR!!
YOU GAVE YOURSELF AWAY!!
THE FAT KID FOUND THE FOREIGN GUY FIRST!!
IT WASN'T YOU!!!

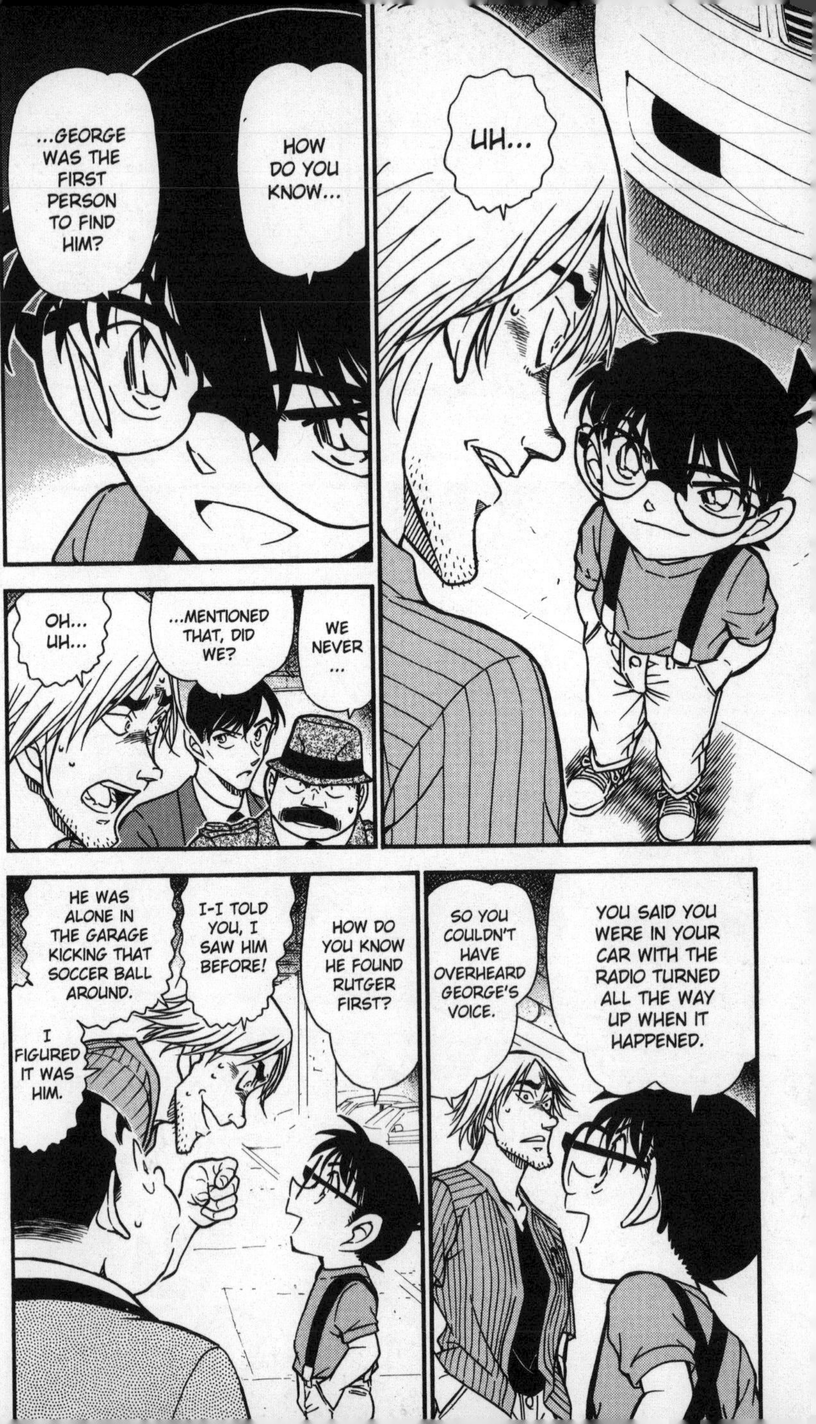
UH...
HOW DO YOU KNOW...
...GEORGE WAS THE FIRST PERSON TO FIND HIM?
WE NEVER ...
...MENTIONED THAT, DID WE?
OH... UH...
YOU SAID YOU WERE IN YOUR CAR WITH THE RADIO TURNED ALL THE WAY UP WHEN IT HAPPENED.
SO YOU COULDN'T HAVE OVERHEARD GEORGE'S VOICE.
HOW DO YOU KNOW HE FOUND RUTGER FIRST?
I-I TOLD YOU, I SAW HIM BEFORE!
HE WAS ALONE IN THE GARAGE KICKING THAT SOCCER BALL AROUND.
I FIGURED IT WAS HIM.

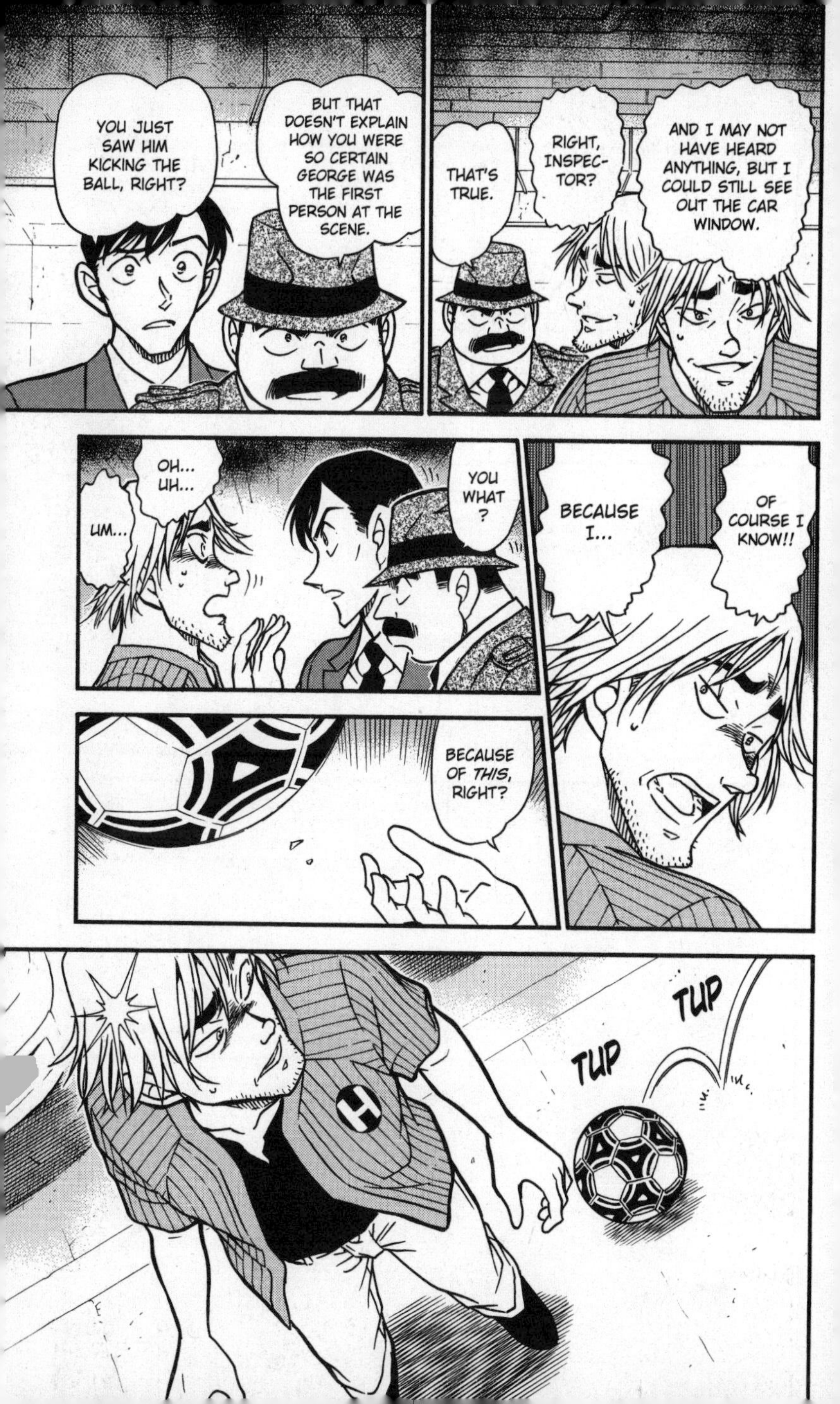
AND I MAY NOT HAVE HEARD ANYTHING, BUT I COULD STILL SEE OUT THE CAR WINDOW.
RIGHT, INSPECTOR?
THAT'S TRUE.
BUT THAT DOESN'T EXPLAIN HOW YOU WERE SO CERTAIN GEORGE WAS THE FIRST PERSON AT THE SCENE.
YOU JUST SAW HIM KICKING THE BALL, RIGHT?
OF COURSE I KNOW!!
BECAUSE I...
YOU WHAT?
OH... UH...
UM...
BECAUSE OF *THIS*, RIGHT?
TUP
TUP

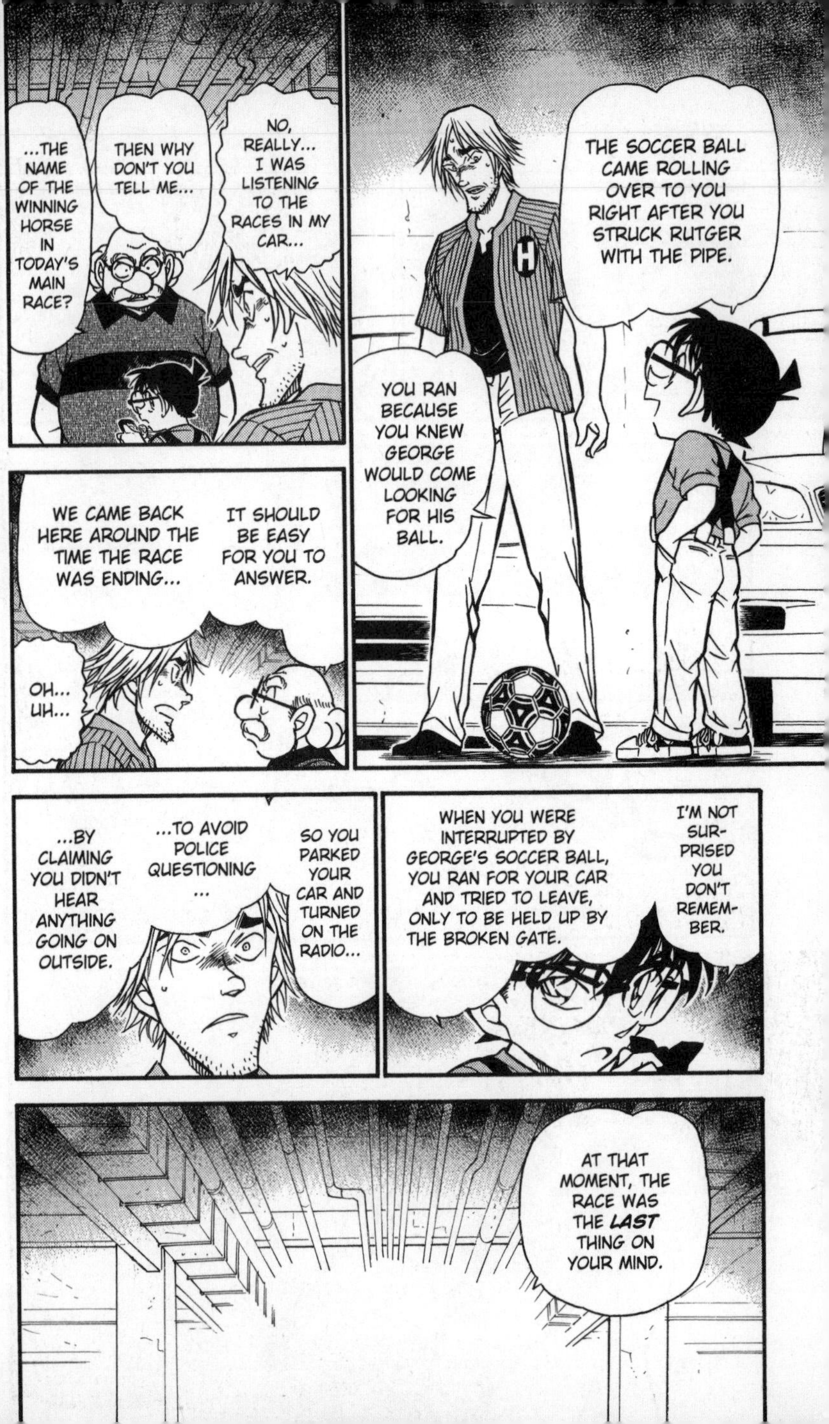
THE SOCCER BALL CAME ROLLING OVER TO YOU RIGHT AFTER YOU STRUCK RUTGER WITH THE PIPE.
YOU RAN BECAUSE YOU KNEW GEORGE WOULD COME LOOKING FOR HIS BALL.
NO, REALLY... I WAS LISTENING TO THE RACES IN MY CAR...
THEN WHY DON'T YOU TELL ME...
...THE NAME OF THE WINNING HORSE IN TODAY'S MAIN RACE?
WE CAME BACK HERE AROUND THE TIME THE RACE WAS ENDING...
IT SHOULD BE EASY FOR YOU TO ANSWER.
OH... UH...
I'M NOT SURPRISED YOU DON'T REMEMBER.
WHEN YOU WERE INTERRUPTED BY GEORGE'S SOCCER BALL, YOU RAN FOR YOUR CAR AND TRIED TO LEAVE, ONLY TO BE HELD UP BY THE BROKEN GATE.
SO YOU PARKED YOUR CAR AND TURNED ON THE RADIO...
...TO AVOID POLICE QUESTIONING...
...BY CLAIMING YOU DIDN'T HEAR ANYTHING GOING ON OUTSIDE.
AT THAT MOMENT, THE RACE WAS THE LAST THING ON YOUR MIND.

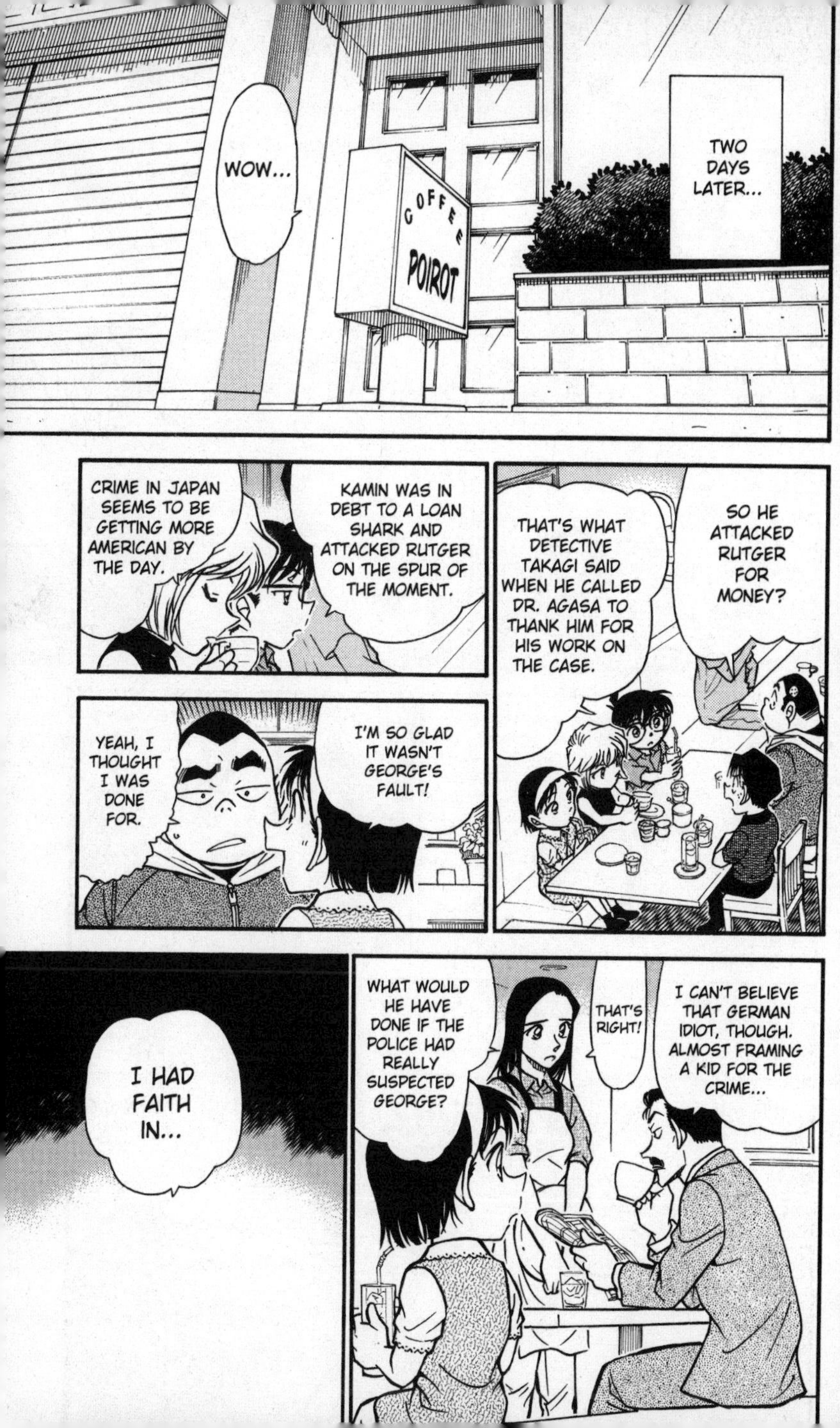
TWO DAYS LATER...
WOW...
COFFEE POIROT
SO HE ATTACKED RUTGER FOR MONEY?
THAT'S WHAT DETECTIVE TAKAGI SAID WHEN HE CALLED DR. AGASA TO THANK HIM FOR HIS WORK ON THE CASE.
KAMIN WAS IN DEBT TO A LOAN SHARK AND ATTACKED RUTGER ON THE SPUR OF THE MOMENT.
CRIME IN JAPAN SEEMS TO BE GETTING MORE AMERICAN BY THE DAY.
I'M SO GLAD IT WASN'T GEORGE'S FAULT!
YEAH, I THOUGHT I WAS DONE FOR.
I CAN'T BELIEVE THAT GERMAN IDIOT, THOUGH. ALMOST FRAMING A KID FOR THE CRIME...
THAT'S RIGHT!
WHAT WOULD HE HAVE DONE IF THE POLICE HAD REALLY SUSPECTED GEORGE?
I HAD FAITH IN...

THAT'S GREAT!!

YES, I'M FINE.

IS YOUR HEAD ALL RIGHT?

IT'S YOU!

...THESE LITTLE DETECTIVES!

N-NO PROB...

I'M SORRY, YOUNG MAN!

LOOKS LIKE IT...

THIS IS THE GUY?

...THE STRONG ONE DOESN'T WIN...

MR. MOORE...

OH, C'MON! HOW'D A BROKEN-DOWN NAG LIKE *THAT* WIN? THIS RACE SHOULD'VE BEEN EASY MONEY FOR ME!!

WAAH

EH?

THE CHEESE-CAKE FROM THAT SHOP!

I BROUGHT YOU A THANK-YOU GIFT.

?

THE ONE THAT WINS IS STRONG!!!

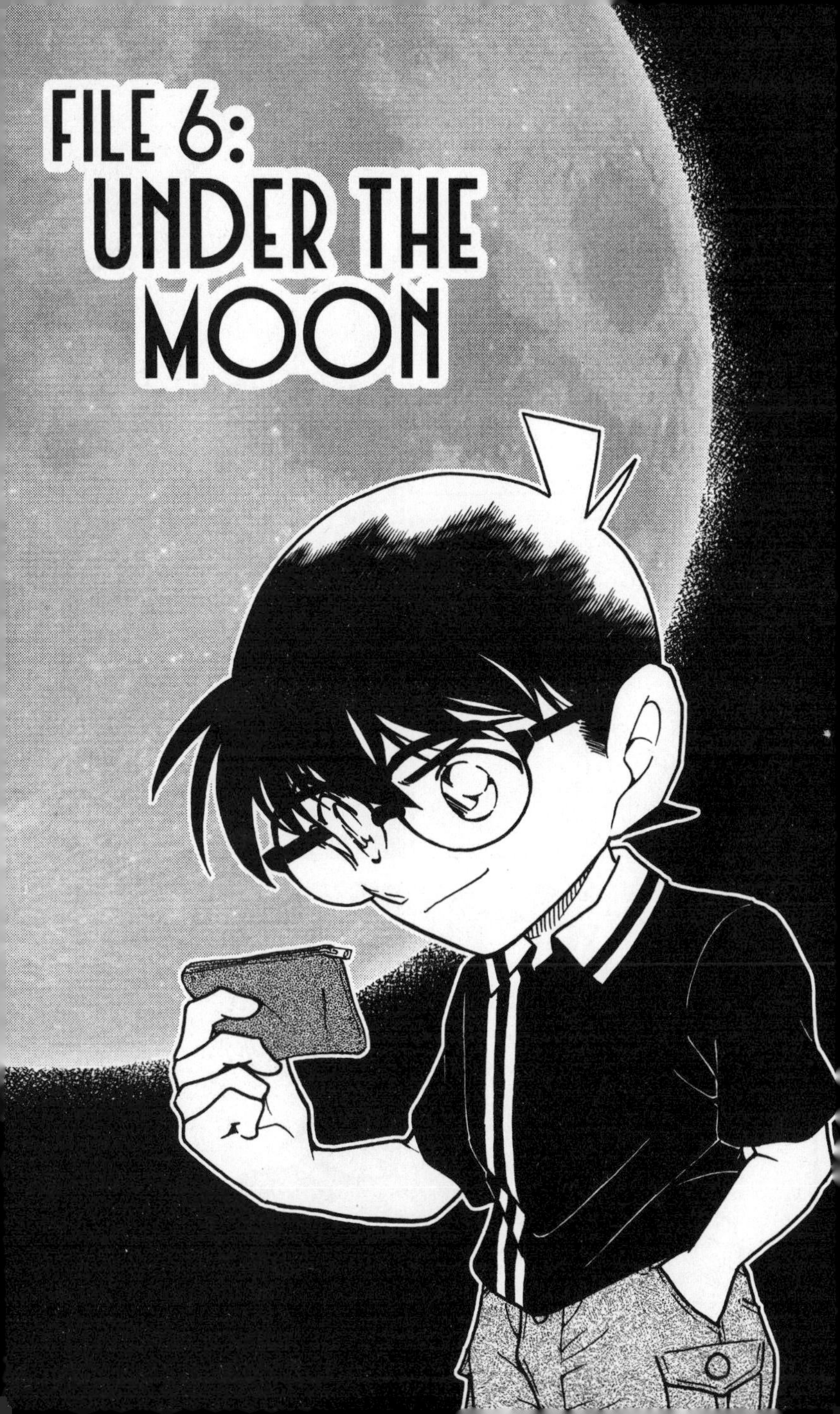
FILE 6:
UNDER THE
MOON

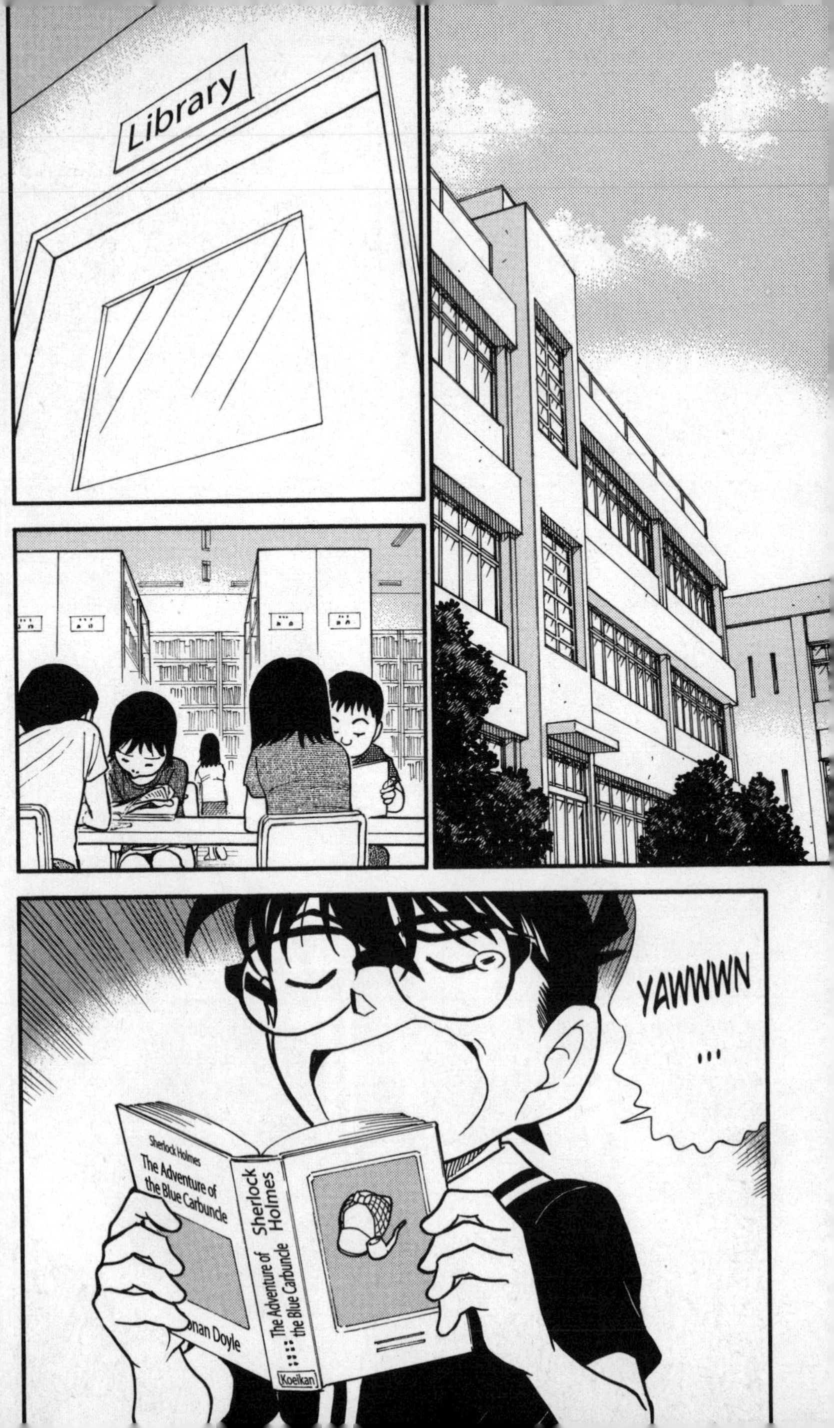
Library
YAWWWN
...
Sherlock Holmes
The Adventure of the Blue Carbuncle
onan Doyle
Sherlock Holmes
The Adventure of the Blue Carbuncle
Koeikan

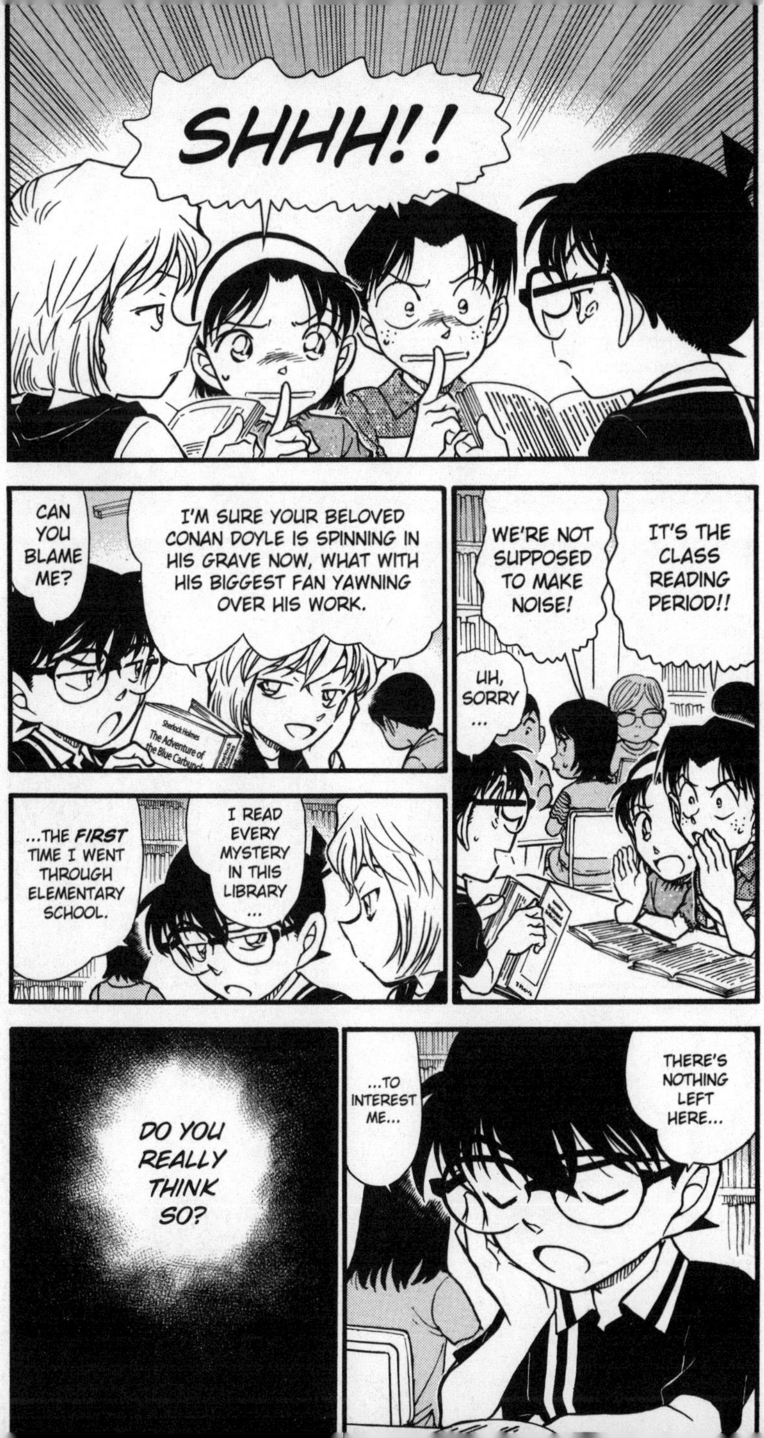
SHHH!!
IT'S THE CLASS READING PERIOD!!
WE'RE NOT SUPPOSED TO MAKE NOISE!
UH, SORRY...
I'M SURE YOUR BELOVED CONAN DOYLE IS SPINNING IN HIS GRAVE NOW, WHAT WITH HIS BIGGEST FAN YAWNING OVER HIS WORK.
CAN YOU BLAME ME?
Sherlock Holmes The Adventure of the Blue Carbuncle
I READ EVERY MYSTERY IN THIS LIBRARY...
...THE *FIRST* TIME I WENT THROUGH ELEMENTARY SCHOOL.
THERE'S NOTHING LEFT HERE...
...TO INTEREST ME...
DO YOU REALLY THINK SO?

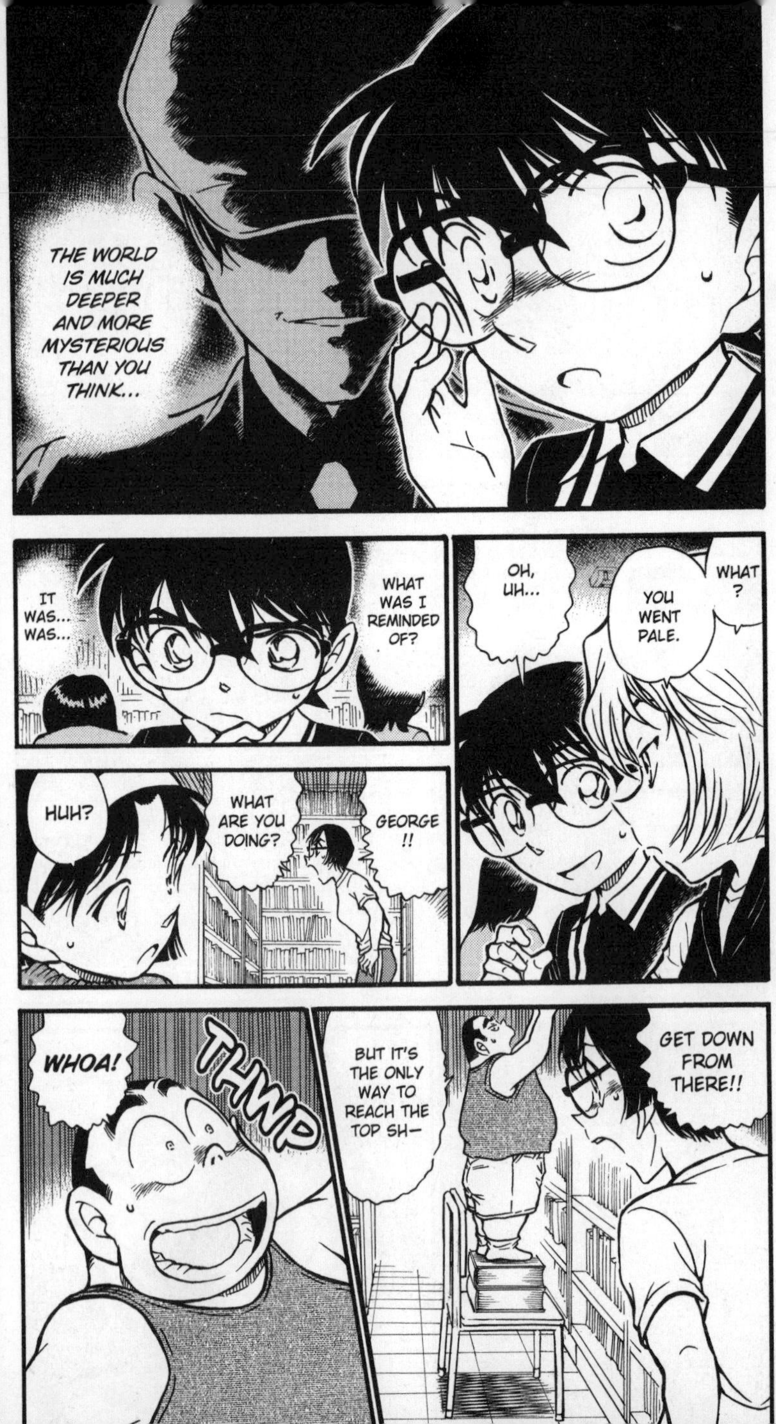
THE WORLD IS MUCH DEEPER AND MORE MYSTERIOUS THAN YOU THINK...
WHAT?
YOU WENT PALE.
OH, UH...
WHAT WAS I REMINDED OF?
IT WAS... WAS...
GEORGE!!
WHAT ARE YOU DOING?
HUH?
GET DOWN FROM THERE!!
BUT IT'S THE ONLY WAY TO REACH THE TOP SH—
THWP
WHOA!

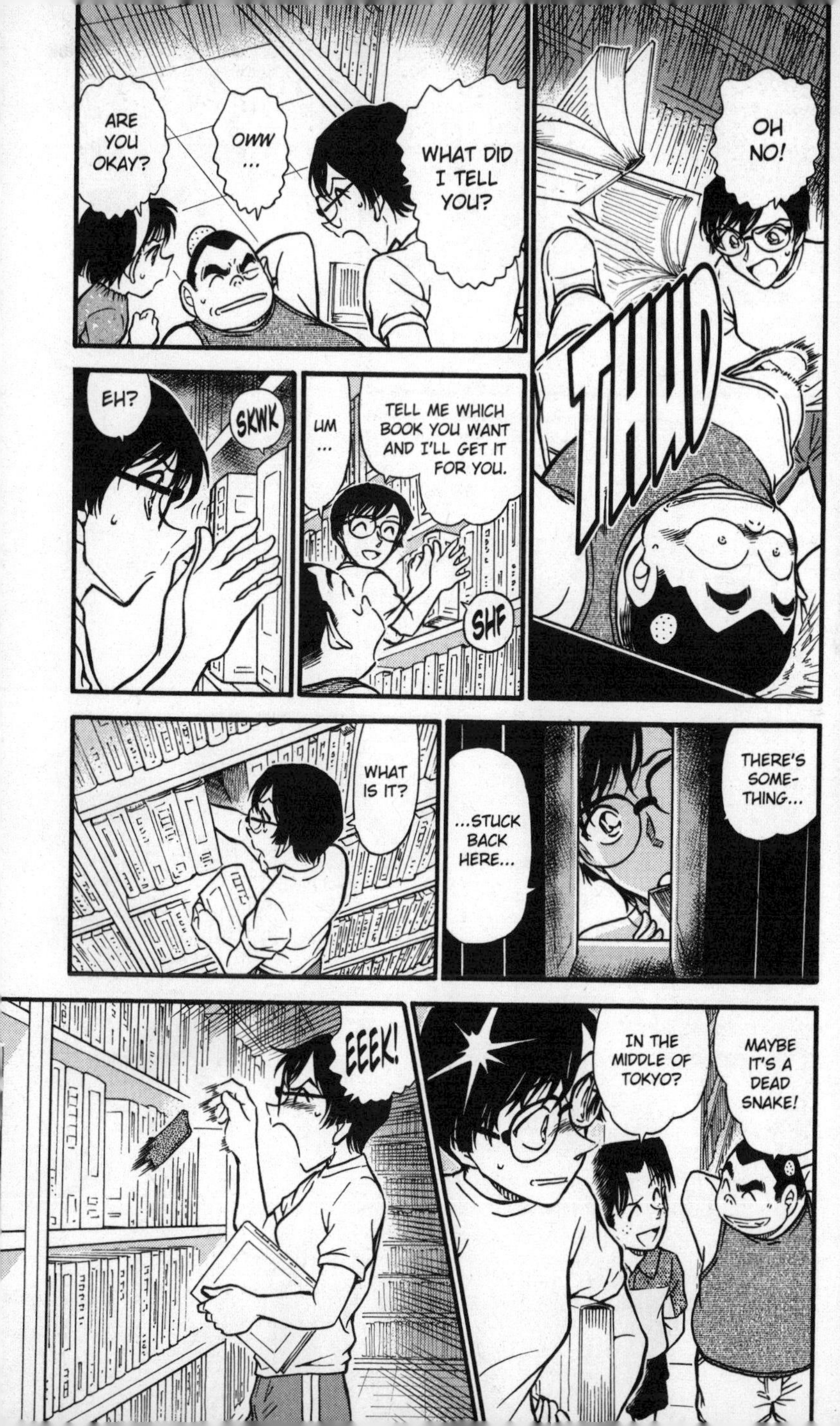
OH NO!
THUD
WHAT DID I TELL YOU?
OWW ...
ARE YOU OKAY?
TELL ME WHICH BOOK YOU WANT AND I'LL GET IT FOR YOU.
UM ...
SHF
SKWK
EH?
THERE'S SOME-THING...
...STUCK BACK HERE...
WHAT IS IT?
MAYBE IT'S A DEAD SNAKE!
IN THE MIDDLE OF TOKYO?
EEEK!

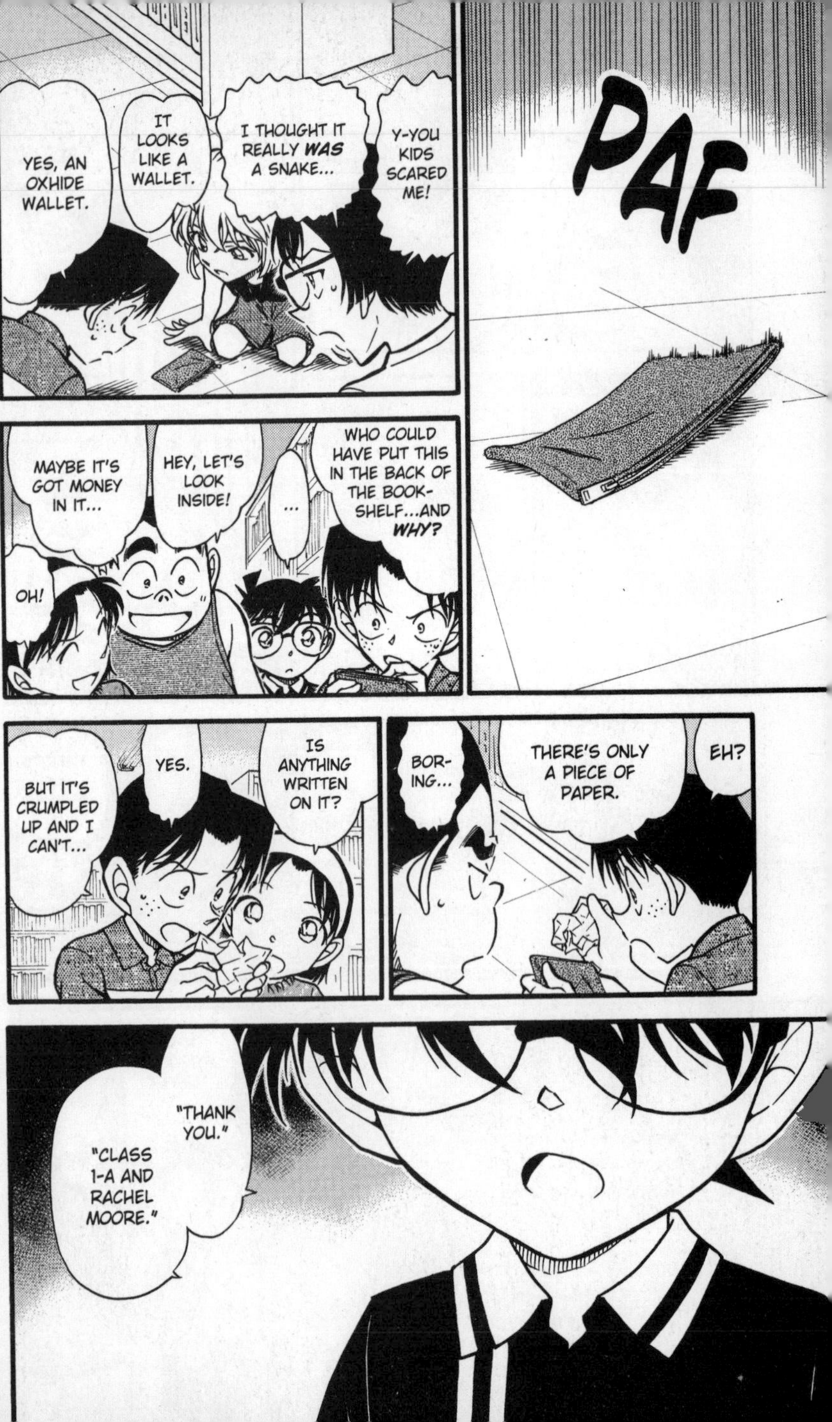
PAF
Y-YOU KIDS SCARED ME!
I THOUGHT IT REALLY WAS A SNAKE...
IT LOOKS LIKE A WALLET.
YES, AN OXHIDE WALLET.
WHO COULD HAVE PUT THIS IN THE BACK OF THE BOOK-SHELF...AND WHY?
...
HEY, LET'S LOOK INSIDE!
MAYBE IT'S GOT MONEY IN IT...
OH!
EH?
THERE'S ONLY A PIECE OF PAPER.
BOR-ING...
IS ANYTHING WRITTEN ON IT?
YES.
BUT IT'S CRUMPLED UP AND I CAN'T...
"THANK YOU."
"CLASS 1-A AND RACHEL MOORE."

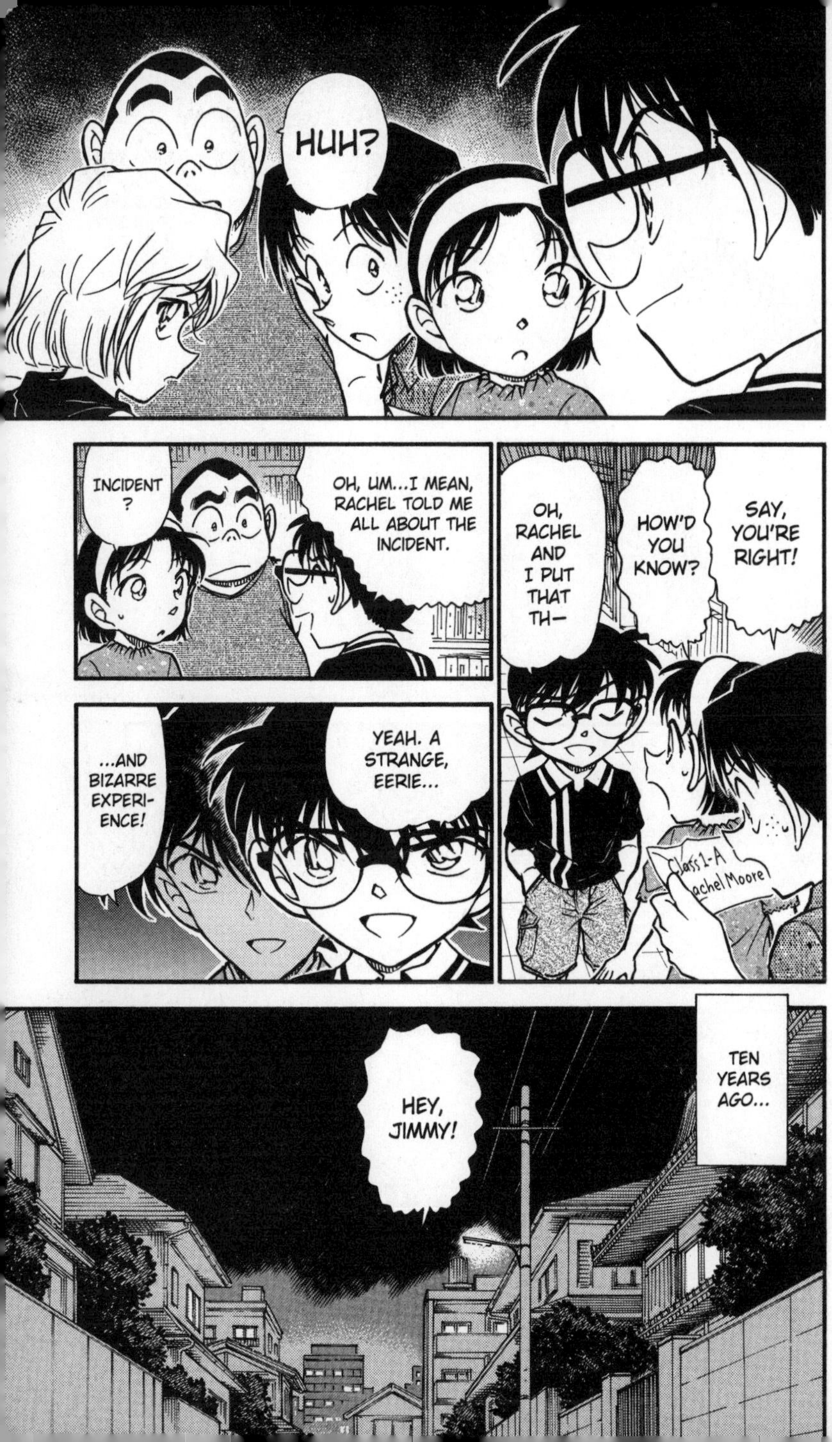
HUH?
SAY, YOU'RE RIGHT!
HOW'D YOU KNOW?
OH, RACHEL AND I PUT THAT TH—
Class 1-A
achel Moore
OH, UM...I MEAN, RACHEL TOLD ME ALL ABOUT THE INCIDENT.
INCIDENT ?
YEAH. A STRANGE, EERIE...
...AND BIZARRE EXPERIENCE!
TEN YEARS AGO...
HEY, JIMMY!

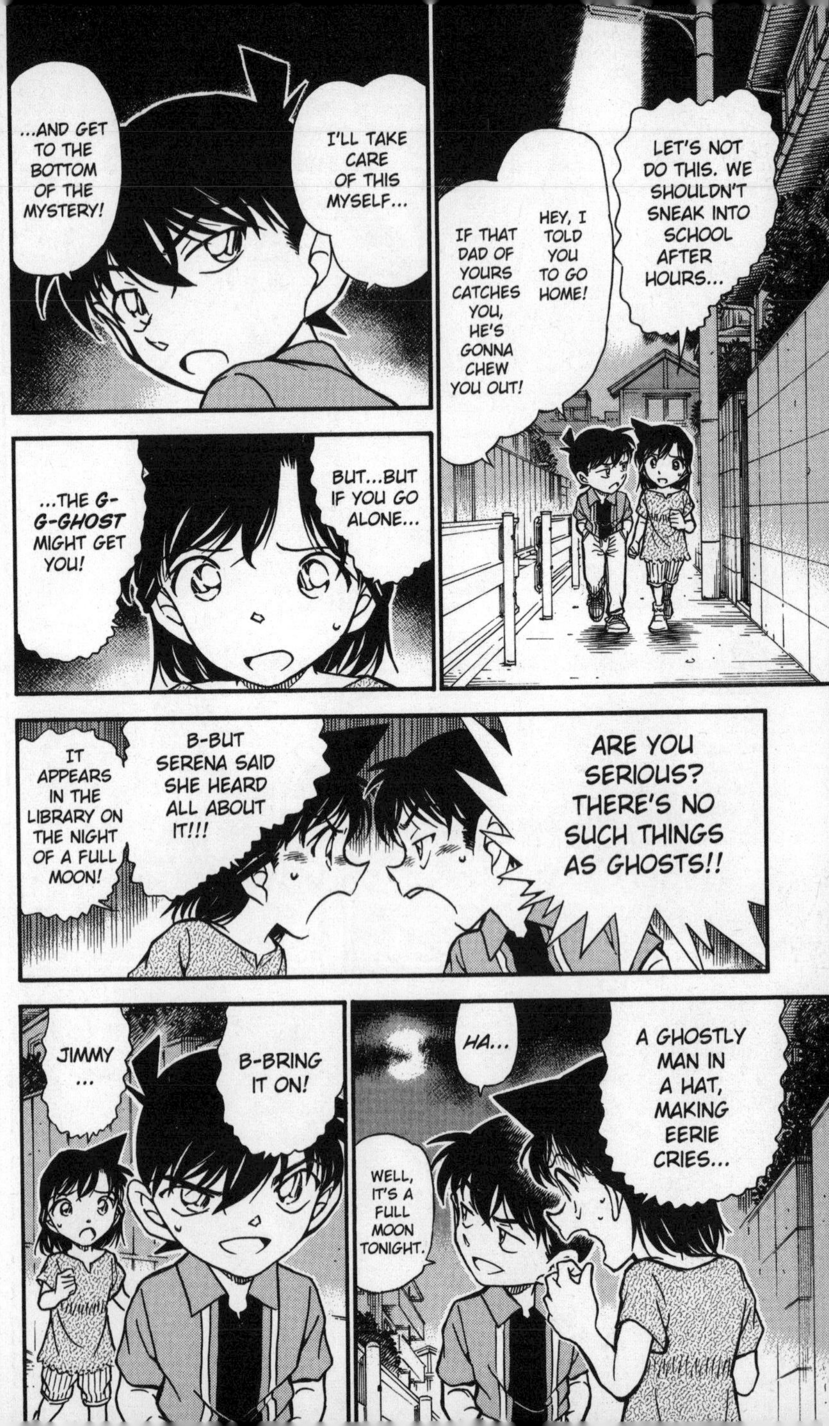
LET'S NOT DO THIS. WE SHOULDN'T SNEAK INTO SCHOOL AFTER HOURS...
HEY, I TOLD YOU TO GO HOME!
IF THAT DAD OF YOURS CATCHES YOU, HE'S GONNA CHEW YOU OUT!
I'LL TAKE CARE OF THIS MYSELF...
...AND GET TO THE BOTTOM OF THE MYSTERY!
BUT...BUT IF YOU GO ALONE...
...THE G-G-GHOST MIGHT GET YOU!
ARE YOU SERIOUS? THERE'S NO SUCH THINGS AS GHOSTS!!
B-BUT SERENA SAID SHE HEARD ALL ABOUT IT!!!
IT APPEARS IN THE LIBRARY ON THE NIGHT OF A FULL MOON!
A GHOSTLY MAN IN A HAT, MAKING EERIE CRIES...
HA...
WELL, IT'S A FULL MOON TONIGHT.
B-BRING IT ON!
JIMMY ...

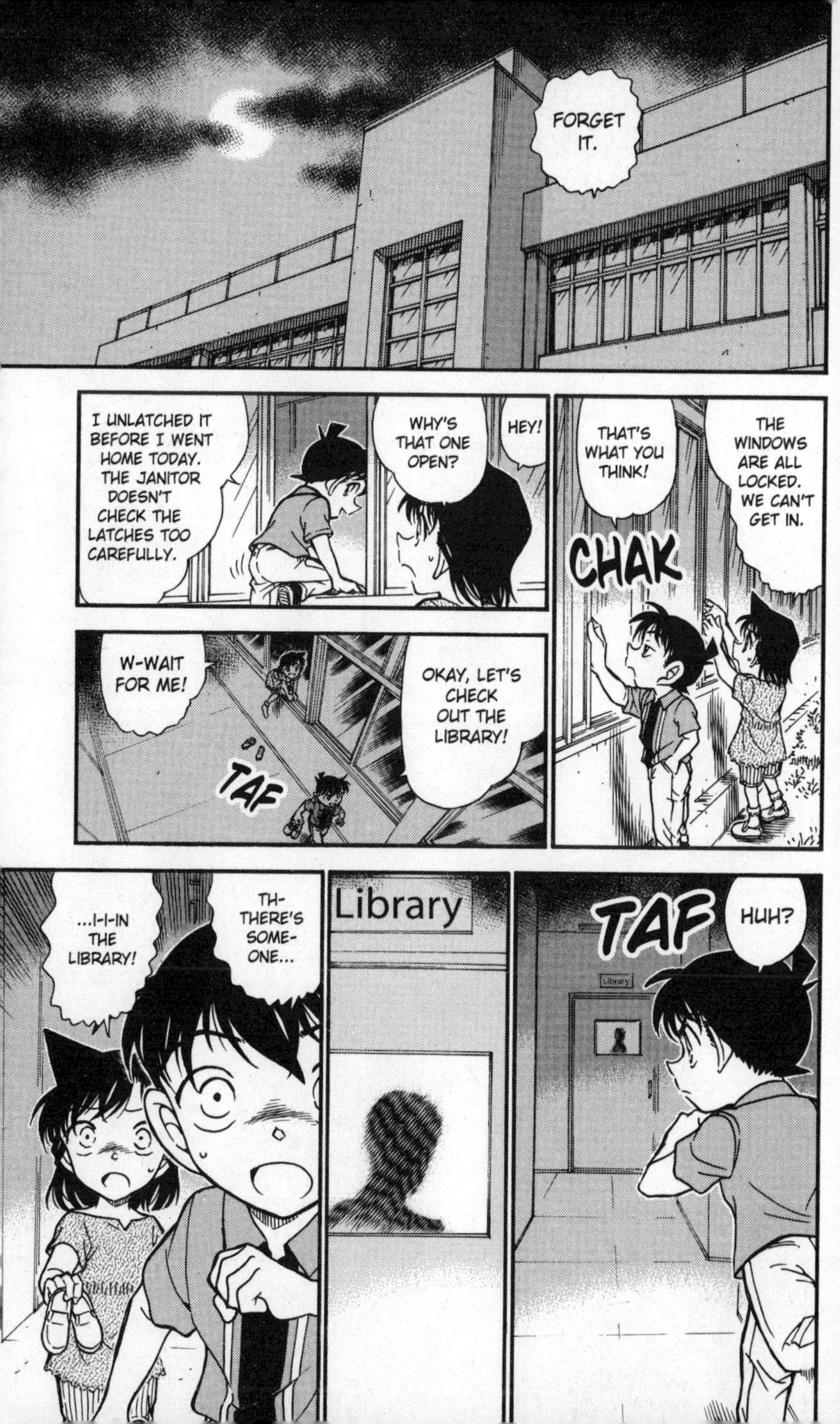
FORGET IT.
THE WINDOWS ARE ALL LOCKED. WE CAN'T GET IN.
THAT'S WHAT YOU THINK!
CHAK
HEY!
WHY'S THAT ONE OPEN?
I UNLATCHED IT BEFORE I WENT HOME TODAY. THE JANITOR DOESN'T CHECK THE LATCHES TOO CAREFULLY.
OKAY, LET'S CHECK OUT THE LIBRARY!
W-WAIT FOR ME!
TAF
HUH?
TAF
Library
Library
TH- THERE'S SOME-ONE...
...I-I-IN THE LIBRARY!

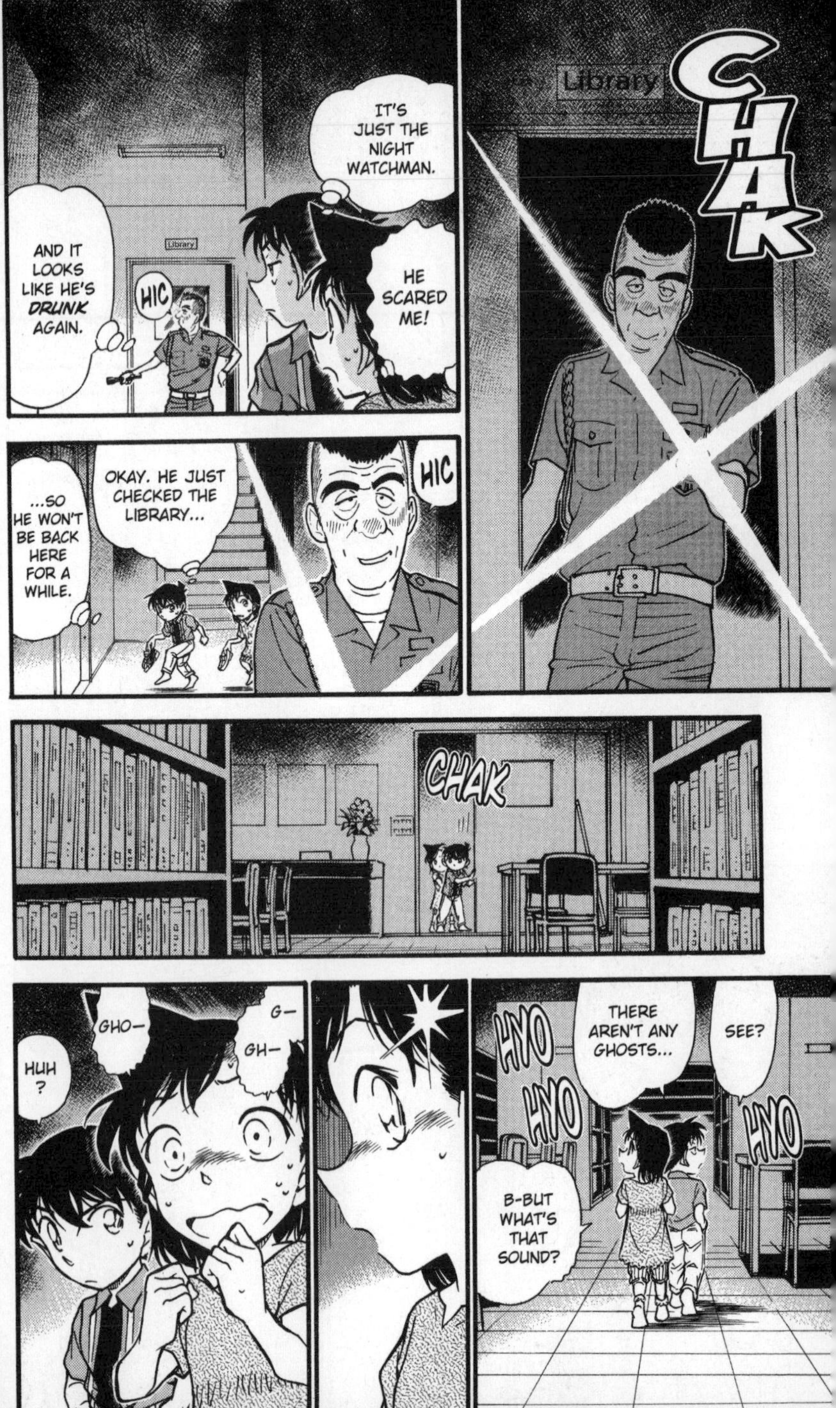

Library
CHAK
IT'S JUST THE NIGHT WATCHMAN.
HE SCARED ME!
HIC
AND IT LOOKS LIKE HE'S *DRUNK* AGAIN.
HIC
OKAY. HE JUST CHECKED THE LIBRARY...
...SO HE WON'T BE BACK HERE FOR A WHILE.
CHAK
SEE?
HYO
THERE AREN'T ANY GHOSTS...
HYO
HYO
B-BUT WHAT'S THAT SOUND?
G— GH—
GHO—
HUH?

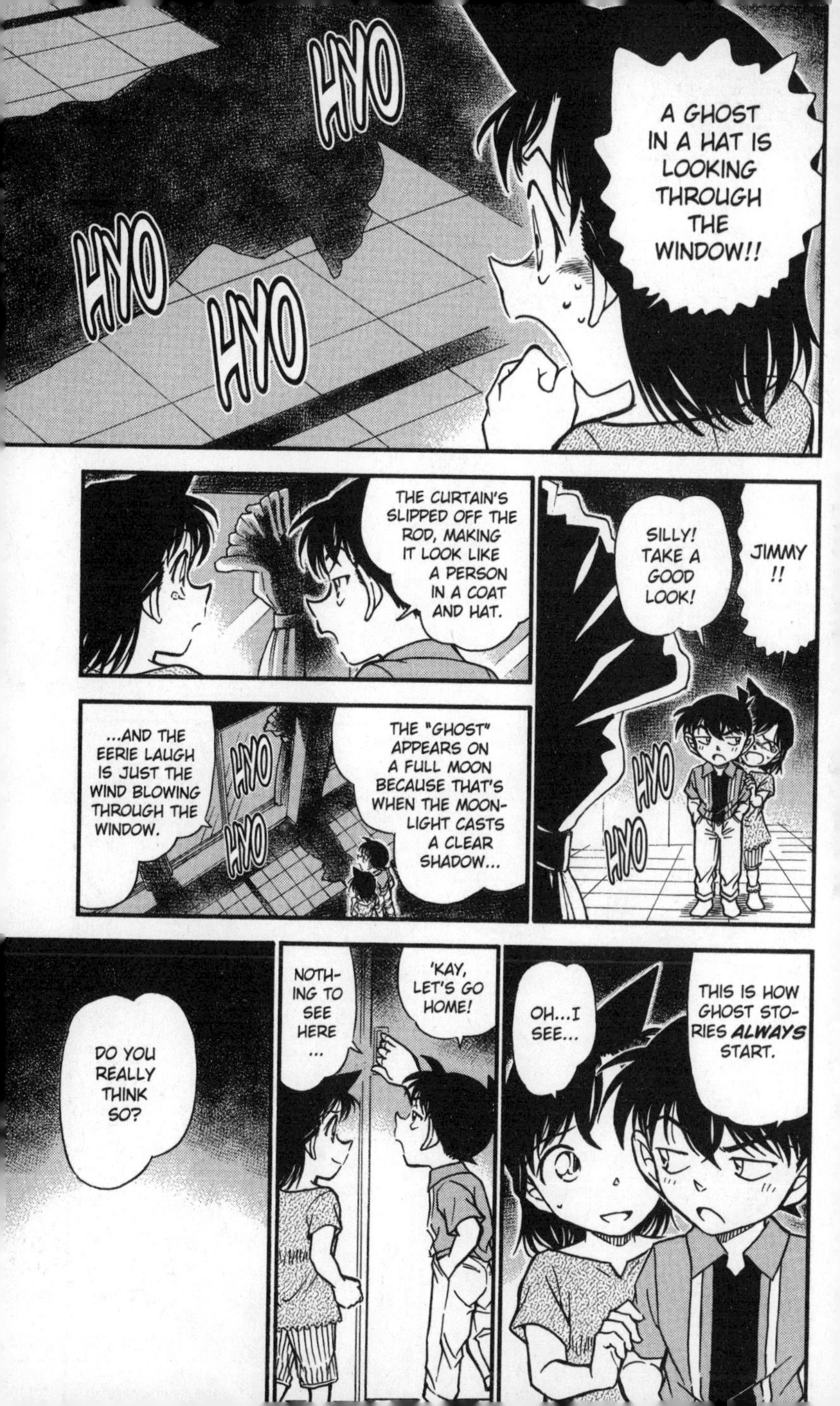
A GHOST IN A HAT IS LOOKING THROUGH THE WINDOW!!
HYO
HYO
HYO
JIMMY!!
SILLY! TAKE A GOOD LOOK!
HYO
HYO
THE CURTAIN'S SLIPPED OFF THE ROD, MAKING IT LOOK LIKE A PERSON IN A COAT AND HAT.
THE "GHOST" APPEARS ON A FULL MOON BECAUSE THAT'S WHEN THE MOON-LIGHT CASTS A CLEAR SHADOW...
HYO
HYO
...AND THE EERIE LAUGH IS JUST THE WIND BLOWING THROUGH THE WINDOW.
THIS IS HOW GHOST STO-RIES ***ALWAYS*** START.
OH...I SEE...
'KAY, LET'S GO HOME!
NOTH-ING TO SEE HERE ...
DO YOU REALLY THINK SO?

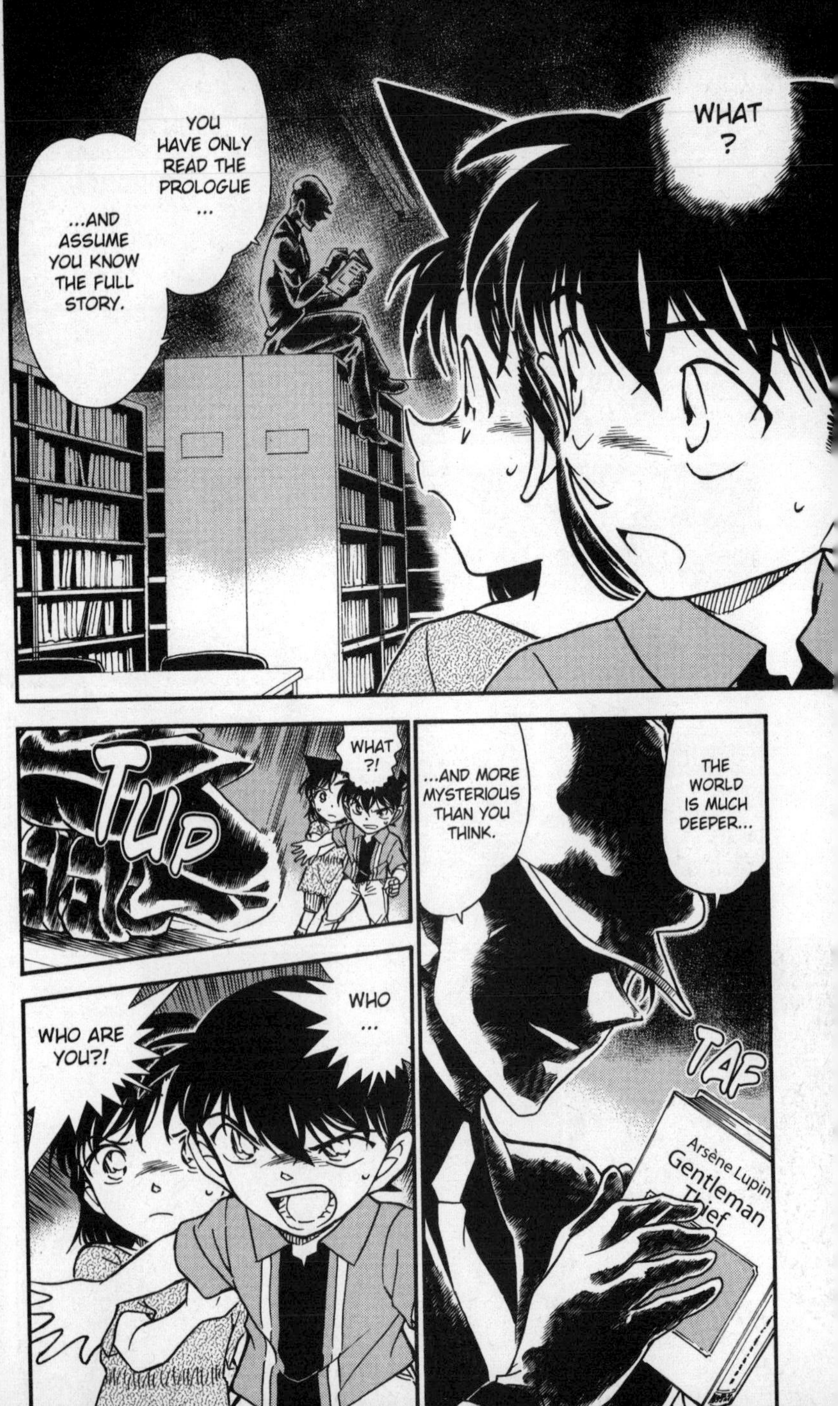
WHAT ?
YOU HAVE ONLY READ THE PROLOGUE ...
...AND ASSUME YOU KNOW THE FULL STORY.
THE WORLD IS MUCH DEEPER...
...AND MORE MYSTERIOUS THAN YOU THINK.
TAF
Arsène Lupin
Gentleman Thief
WHAT ?!
TUP
WHO ...
WHO ARE YOU?!

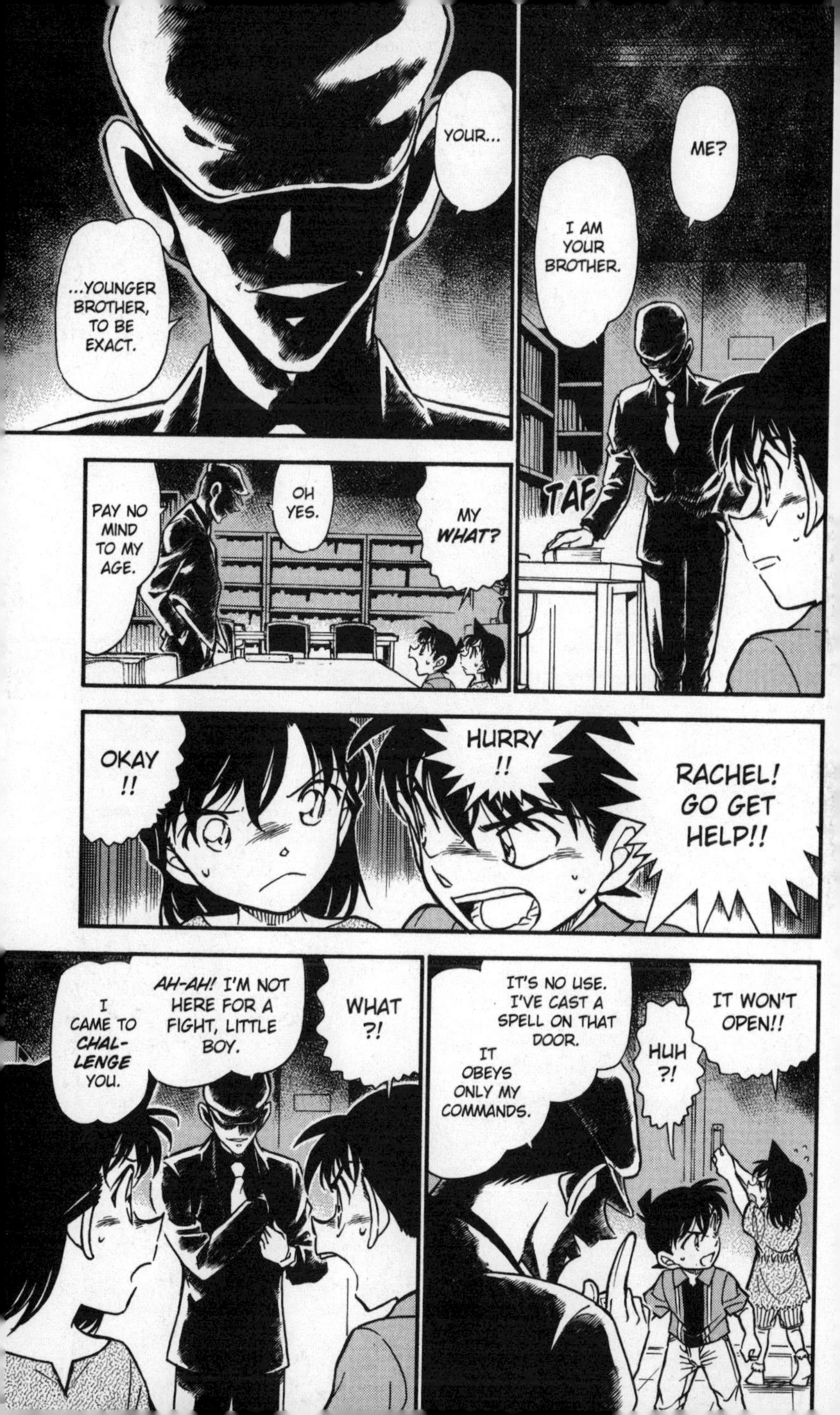
ME?
I AM YOUR BROTHER.
TAF
YOUR...
...YOUNGER BROTHER, TO BE EXACT.
MY *WHAT?*
OH YES.
PAY NO MIND TO MY AGE.
RACHEL! GO GET HELP!!
HURRY!!
OKAY!!
IT WON'T OPEN!!
HUH?!
IT'S NO USE. I'VE CAST A SPELL ON THAT DOOR.
IT OBEYS ONLY MY COMMANDS.
WHAT?!
AH-AH! I'M NOT HERE FOR A FIGHT, LITTLE BOY.
I CAME TO *CHALLENGE* YOU.

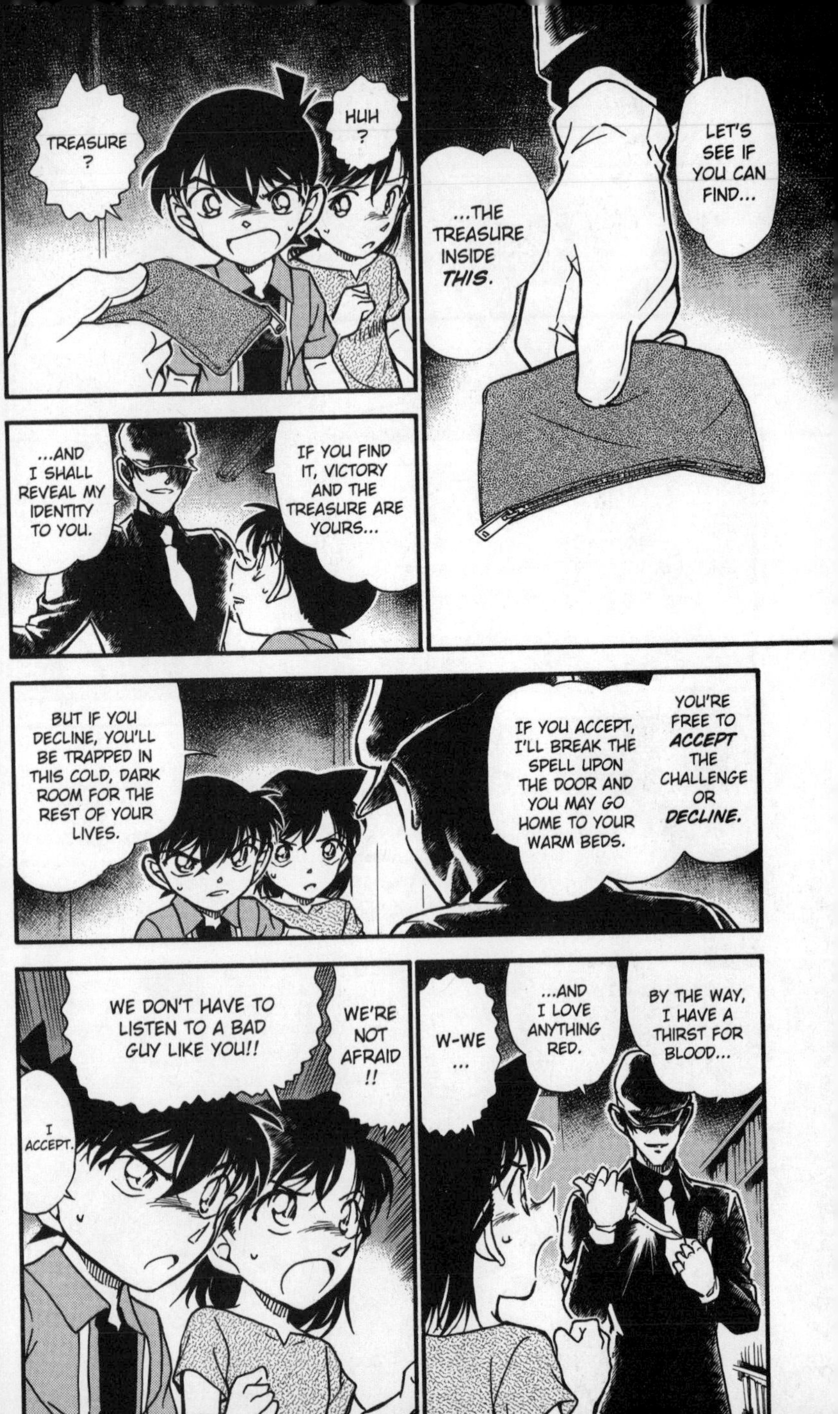
LET'S SEE IF YOU CAN FIND...
...THE TREASURE INSIDE THIS.
HUH ?
TREASURE ?
IF YOU FIND IT, VICTORY AND THE TREASURE ARE YOURS...
...AND I SHALL REVEAL MY IDENTITY TO YOU.
YOU'RE FREE TO ACCEPT THE CHALLENGE OR DECLINE.
IF YOU ACCEPT, I'LL BREAK THE SPELL UPON THE DOOR AND YOU MAY GO HOME TO YOUR WARM BEDS.
BUT IF YOU DECLINE, YOU'LL BE TRAPPED IN THIS COLD, DARK ROOM FOR THE REST OF YOUR LIVES.
BY THE WAY, I HAVE A THIRST FOR BLOOD...
...AND I LOVE ANYTHING RED.
W-WE ...
WE'RE NOT AFRAID !!
WE DON'T HAVE TO LISTEN TO A BAD GUY LIKE YOU!!
I ACCEPT.

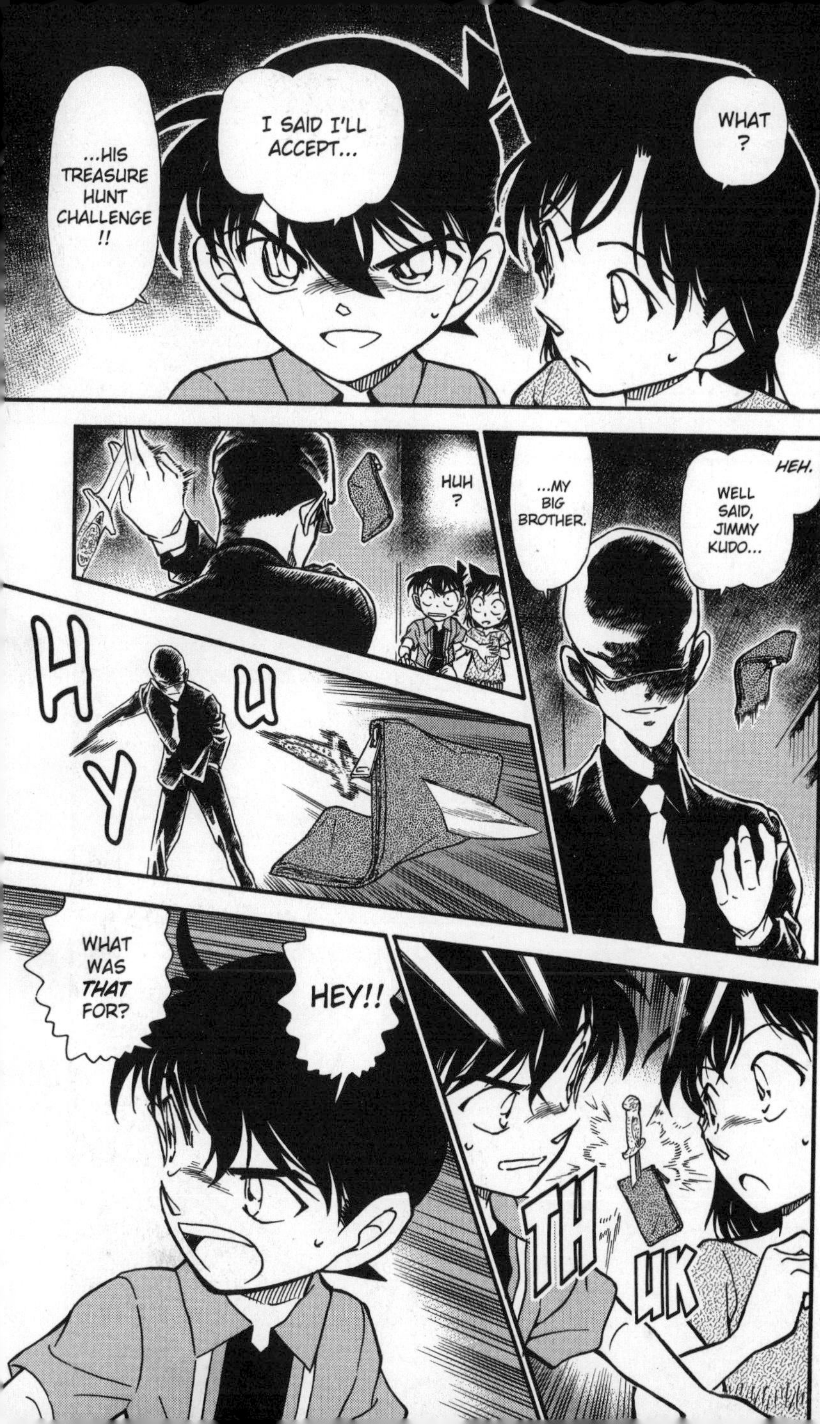
WHAT ?
I SAID I'LL ACCEPT...
...HIS TREASURE HUNT CHALLENGE !!
HEH.
WELL SAID, JIMMY KUDO...
...MY BIG BROTHER.
HUH ?
HYU
TH UK
HEY!!
WHAT WAS *THAT* FOR?

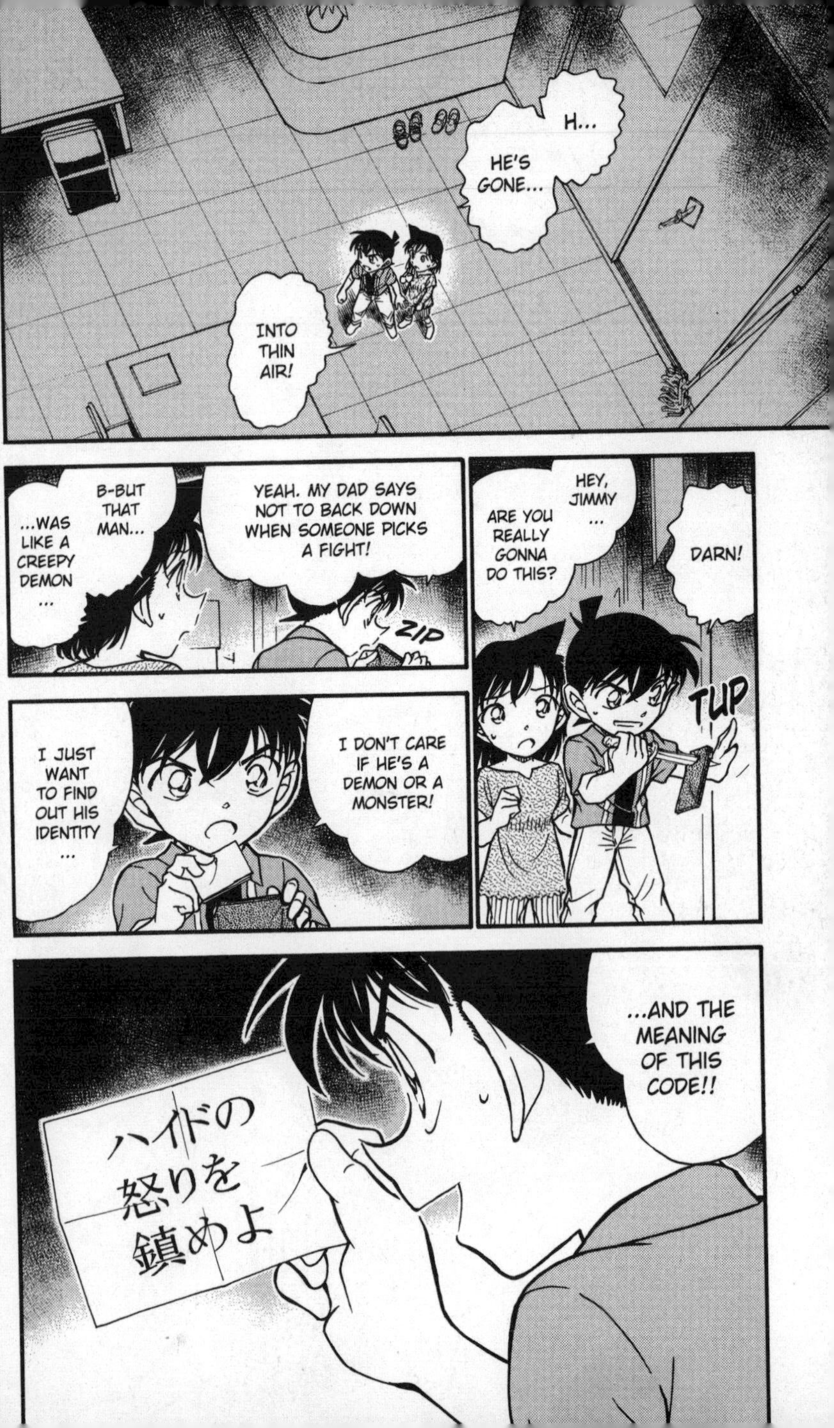
H...
HE'S GONE...
INTO THIN AIR!
DARN!
HEY, JIMMY ...
ARE YOU REALLY GONNA DO THIS?
TUP
YEAH. MY DAD SAYS NOT TO BACK DOWN WHEN SOMEONE PICKS A FIGHT!
ZIP
B-BUT THAT MAN...
...WAS LIKE A CREEPY DEMON ...
I DON'T CARE IF HE'S A DEMON OR A MONSTER!
I JUST WANT TO FIND OUT HIS IDENTITY ...
...AND THE MEANING OF THIS CODE!!
ハイドの怒りを鎮めよ

FILE 7: DAWN

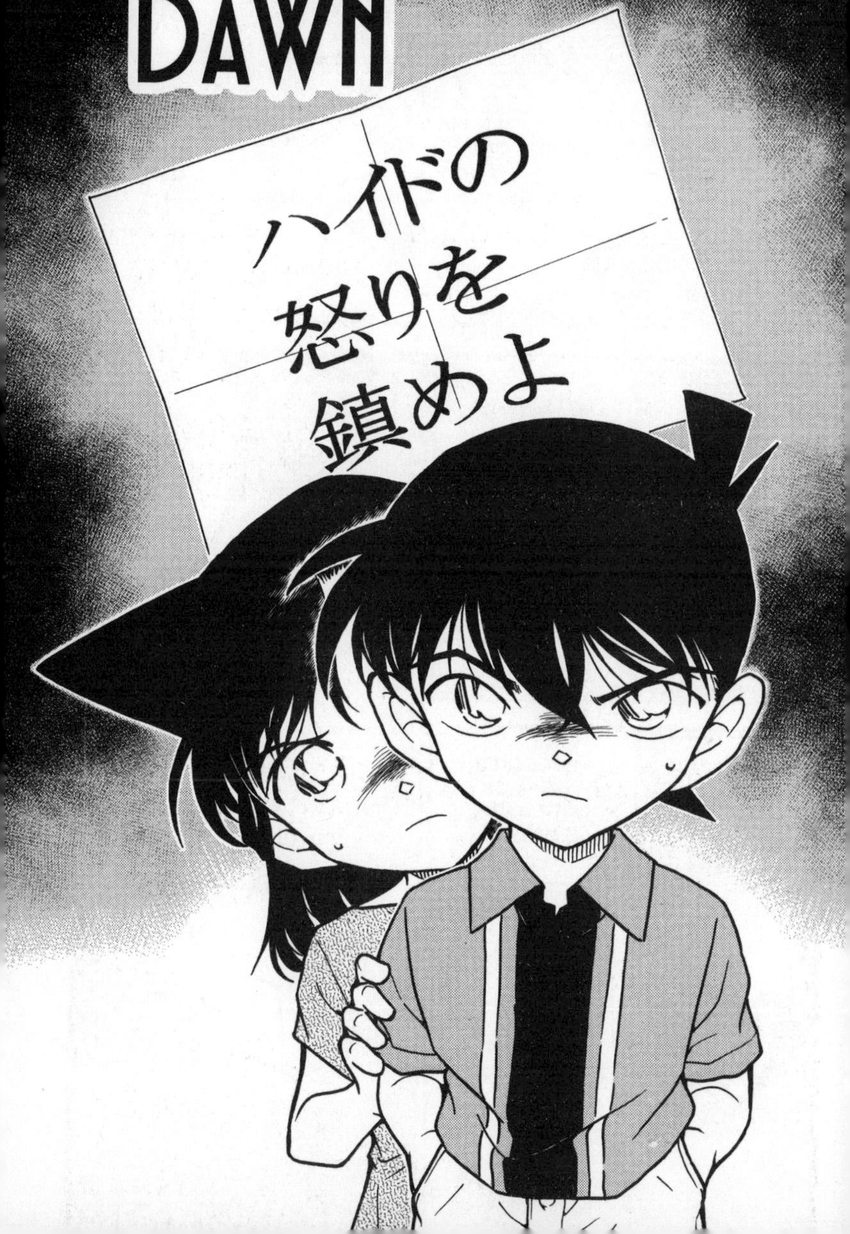

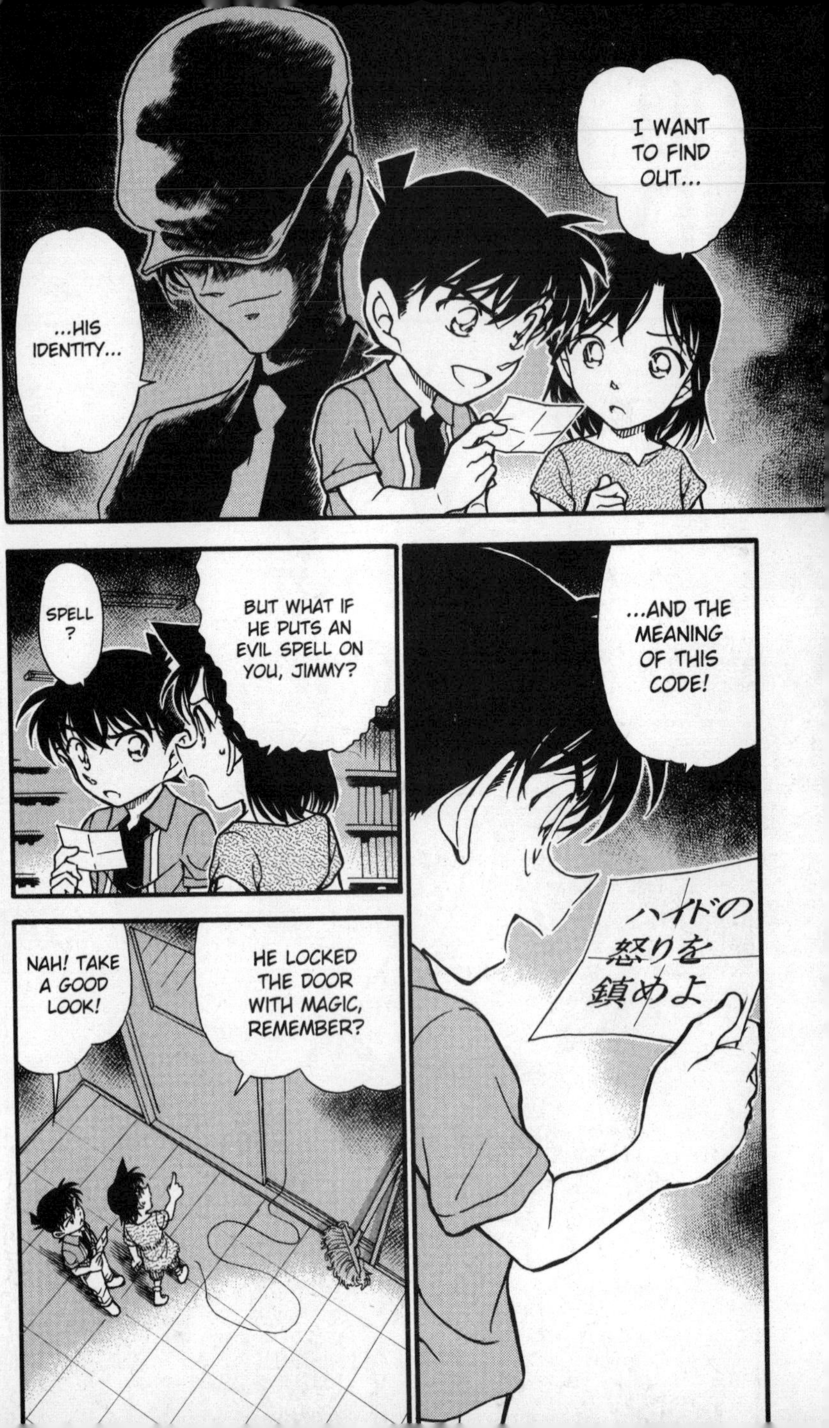
I WANT TO FIND OUT...
...HIS IDENTITY...
...AND THE MEANING OF THIS CODE!
ハイドの怒りを鎮めよ
BUT WHAT IF HE PUTS AN EVIL SPELL ON YOU, JIMMY?
SPELL ?
HE LOCKED THE DOOR WITH MAGIC, REMEMBER?
NAH! TAKE A GOOD LOOK!

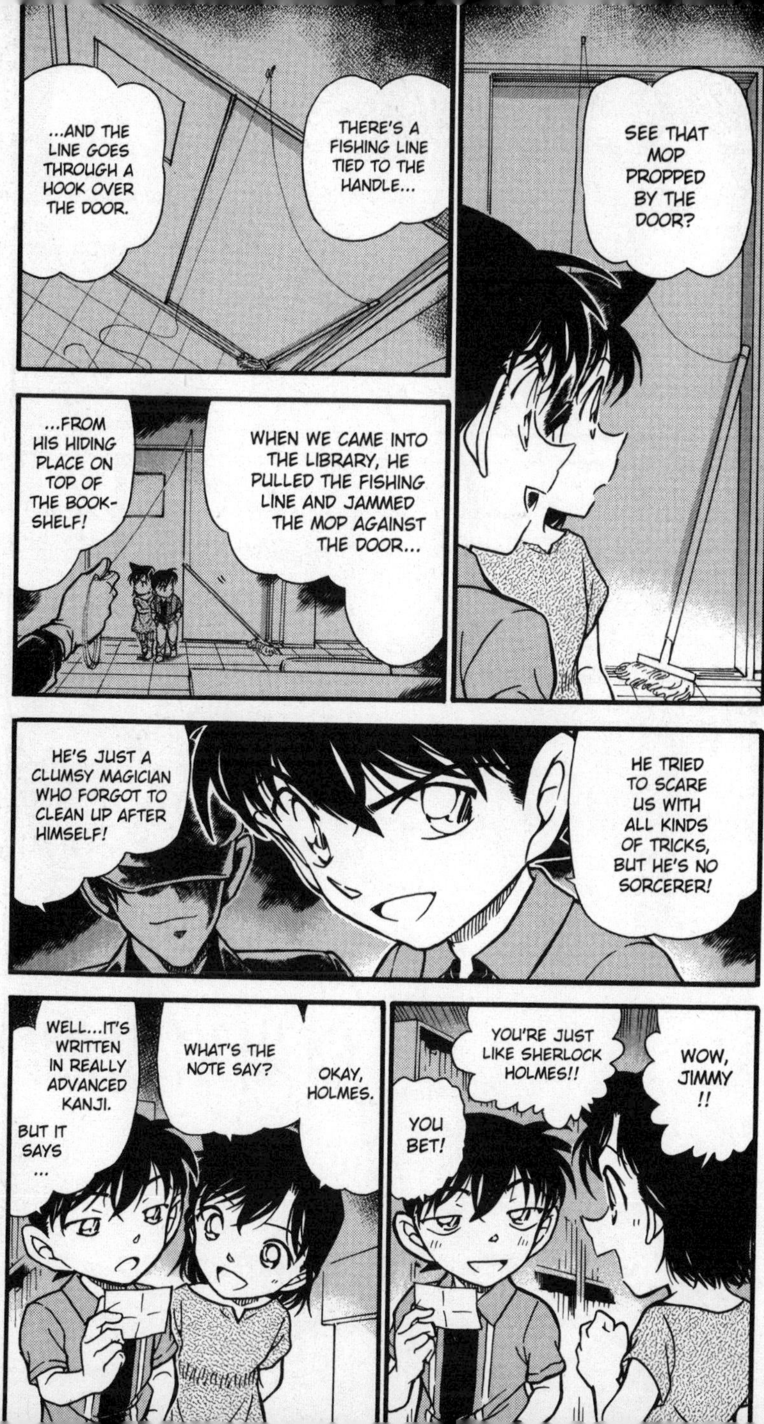
SEE THAT MOP PROPPED BY THE DOOR?
THERE'S A FISHING LINE TIED TO THE HANDLE...
...AND THE LINE GOES THROUGH A HOOK OVER THE DOOR.
WHEN WE CAME INTO THE LIBRARY, HE PULLED THE FISHING LINE AND JAMMED THE MOP AGAINST THE DOOR...
...FROM HIS HIDING PLACE ON TOP OF THE BOOK-SHELF!
HE TRIED TO SCARE US WITH ALL KINDS OF TRICKS, BUT HE'S NO SORCERER!
HE'S JUST A CLUMSY MAGICIAN WHO FORGOT TO CLEAN UP AFTER HIMSELF!
WOW, JIMMY!!
YOU'RE JUST LIKE SHERLOCK HOLMES!!
YOU BET!
OKAY, HOLMES.
WHAT'S THE NOTE SAY?
WELL...IT'S WRITTEN IN REALLY ADVANCED KANJI.
BUT IT SAYS...

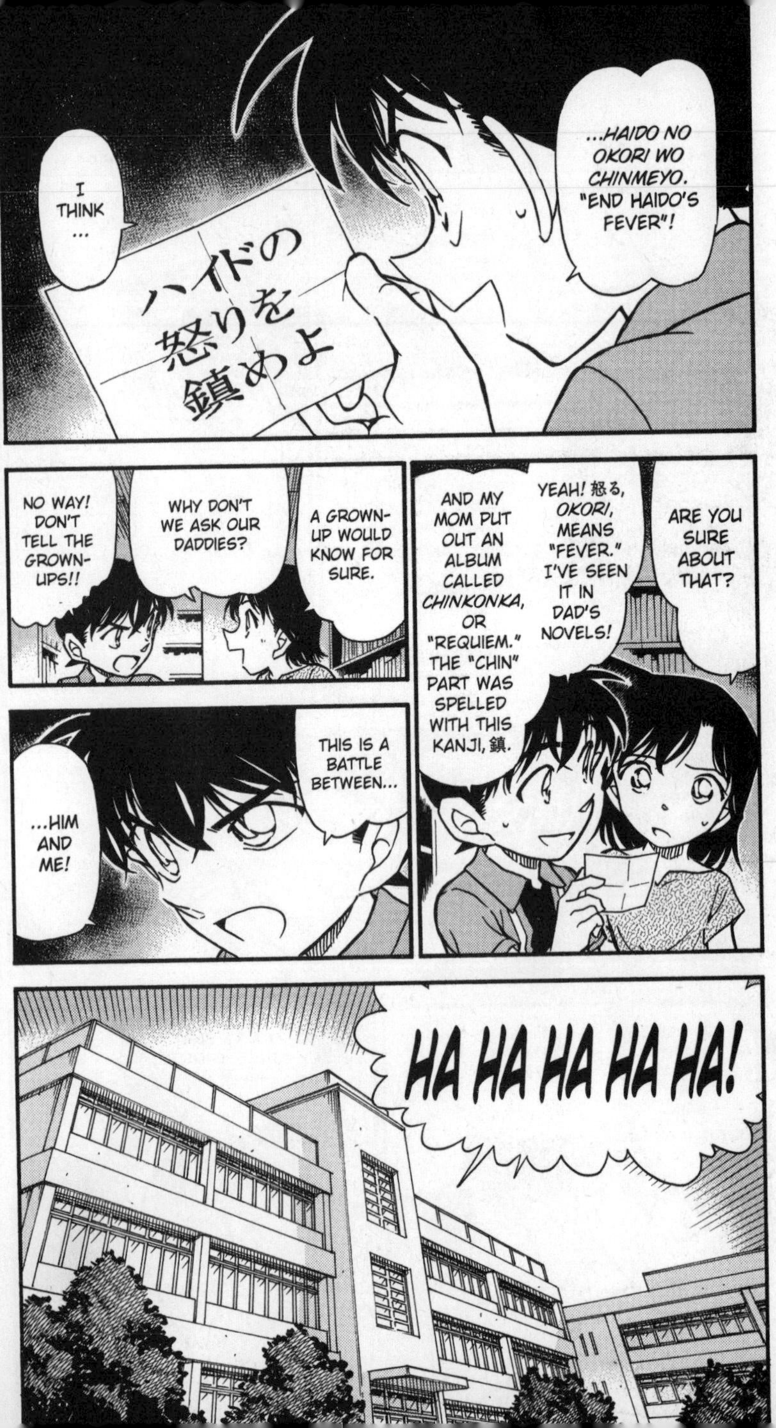
...HAIDO NO OKORI WO CHINMEYO. "END HAIDO'S FEVER"!
I THINK ...
ハイドの怒りを鎮めよ
ARE YOU SURE ABOUT THAT?
YEAH! 怒る, *OKORI*, MEANS "FEVER." I'VE SEEN IT IN DAD'S NOVELS!
AND MY MOM PUT OUT AN ALBUM CALLED *CHINKONKA*, OR "REQUIEM." THE "CHIN" PART WAS SPELLED WITH THIS KANJI, 鎮.
A GROWN-UP WOULD KNOW FOR SURE.
WHY DON'T WE ASK OUR DADDIES?
NO WAY! DON'T TELL THE GROWN-UPS!!
THIS IS A BATTLE BETWEEN...
...HIM AND ME!
HA HA HA HA HA HA!

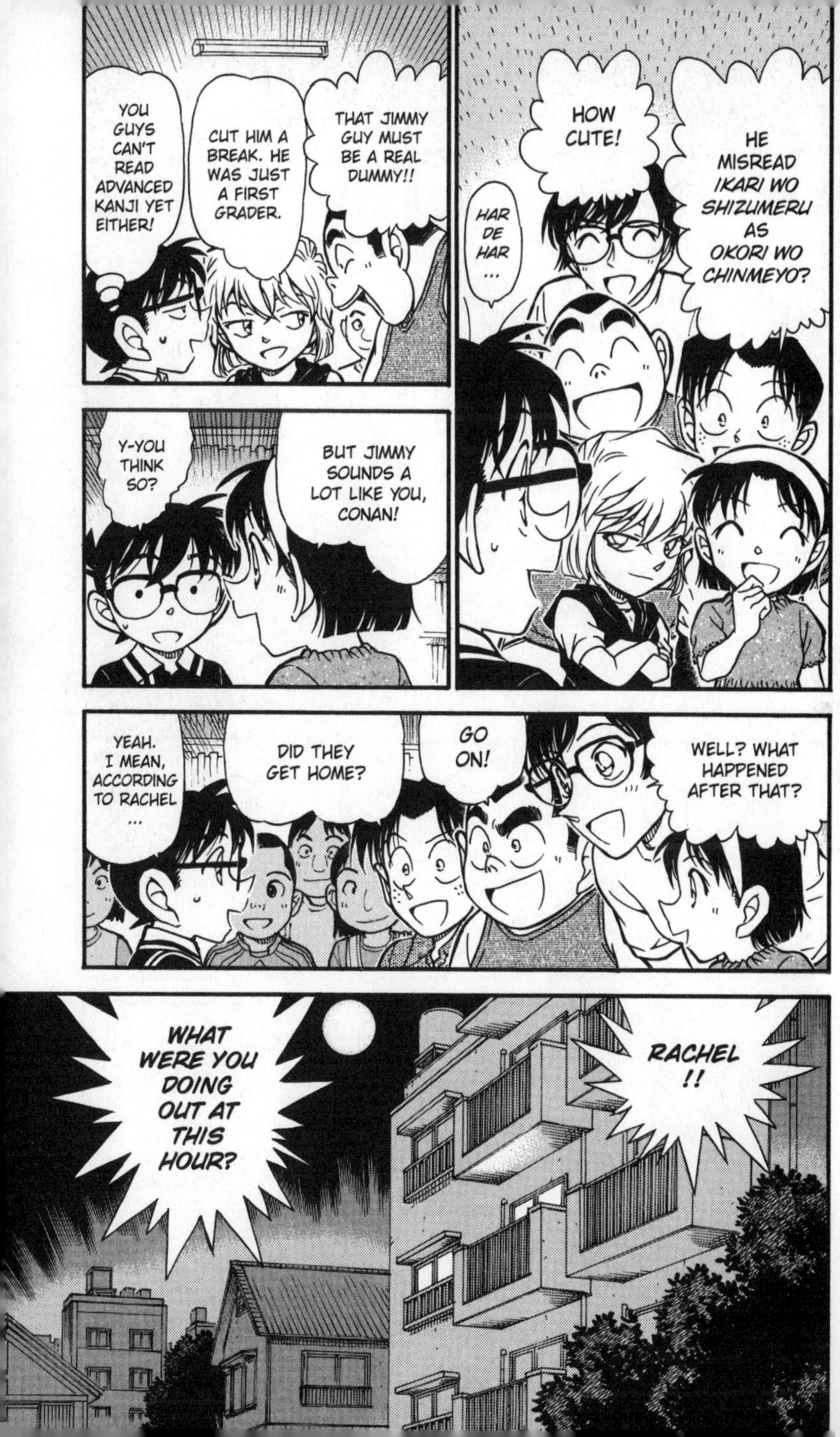

HE MISREAD IKARI WO SHIZUMERU AS OKORI WO CHINMEYO?
HOW CUTE!
HAR DE HAR ...
THAT JIMMY GUY MUST BE A REAL DUMMY!!
CUT HIM A BREAK. HE WAS JUST A FIRST GRADER.
YOU GUYS CAN'T READ ADVANCED KANJI YET EITHER!
BUT JIMMY SOUNDS A LOT LIKE YOU, CONAN!
Y-YOU THINK SO?
WELL? WHAT HAPPENED AFTER THAT?
GO ON!
DID THEY GET HOME?
YEAH. I MEAN, ACCORDING TO RACHEL ...
RACHEL !!
WHAT WERE YOU DOING OUT AT THIS HOUR?

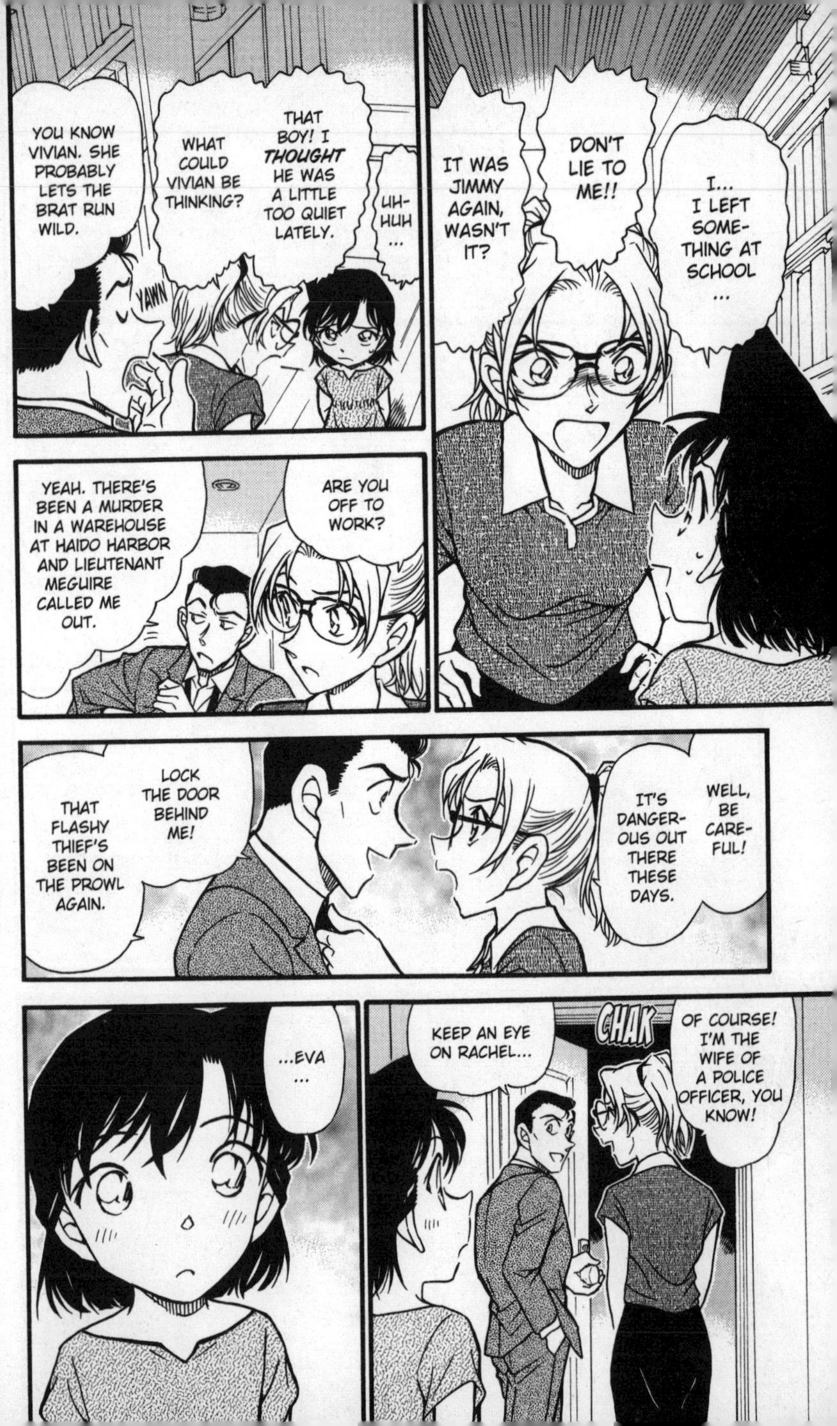
I... I LEFT SOME-THING AT SCHOOL...
DON'T LIE TO ME!!
IT WAS JIMMY AGAIN, WASN'T IT?
UH-HUH...
THAT BOY! I *THOUGHT* HE WAS A LITTLE TOO QUIET LATELY.
WHAT COULD VIVIAN BE THINKING?
YOU KNOW VIVIAN. SHE PROBABLY LETS THE BRAT RUN WILD.
YAWN
ARE YOU OFF TO WORK?
YEAH. THERE'S BEEN A MURDER IN A WAREHOUSE AT HAIDO HARBOR AND LIEUTENANT MEGUIRE CALLED ME OUT.
WELL, BE CARE-FUL!
IT'S DANGER-OUS OUT THERE THESE DAYS.
LOCK THE DOOR BEHIND ME!
THAT FLASHY THIEF'S BEEN ON THE PROWL AGAIN.
OF COURSE! I'M THE WIFE OF A POLICE OFFICER, YOU KNOW!
CHAK
KEEP AN EYE ON RACHEL...
...EVA...

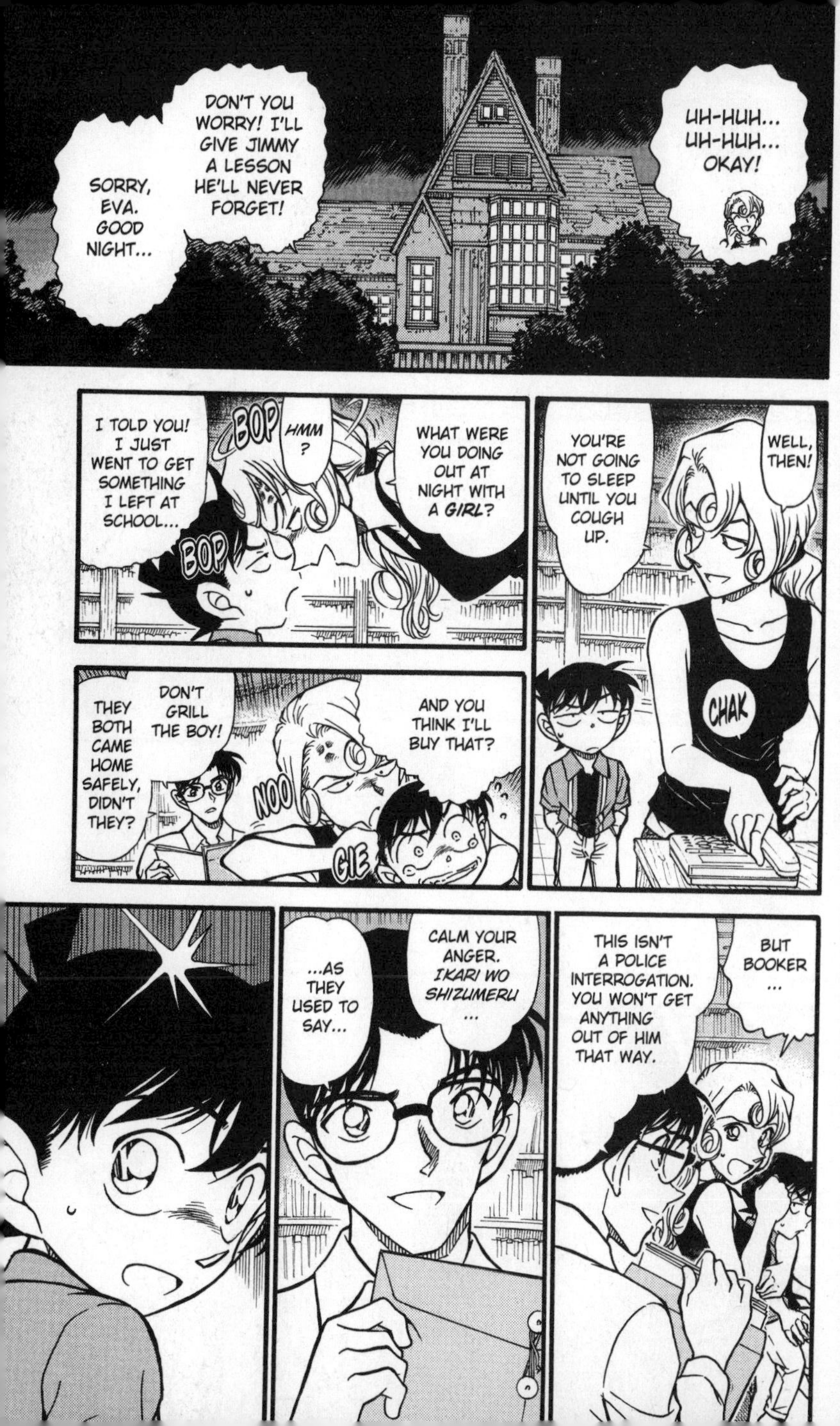
UH-HUH... UH-HUH... OKAY!
DON'T YOU WORRY! I'LL GIVE JIMMY A LESSON HE'LL NEVER FORGET!
SORRY, EVA. GOOD NIGHT...
WELL, THEN!
YOU'RE NOT GOING TO SLEEP UNTIL YOU COUGH UP.
CHAK
WHAT WERE YOU DOING OUT AT NIGHT WITH A *GIRL*?
HMM?
BOP
BOP
I TOLD YOU! I JUST WENT TO GET SOMETHING I LEFT AT SCHOOL...
AND YOU THINK I'LL BUY THAT?
DON'T GRILL THE BOY!
THEY BOTH CAME HOME SAFELY, DIDN'T THEY?
NOO
GIE
BUT BOOKER...
THIS ISN'T A POLICE INTERROGATION. YOU WON'T GET ANYTHING OUT OF HIM THAT WAY.
CALM YOUR ANGER. *IKARI WO SHIZUMERU*...
...AS THEY USED TO SAY...

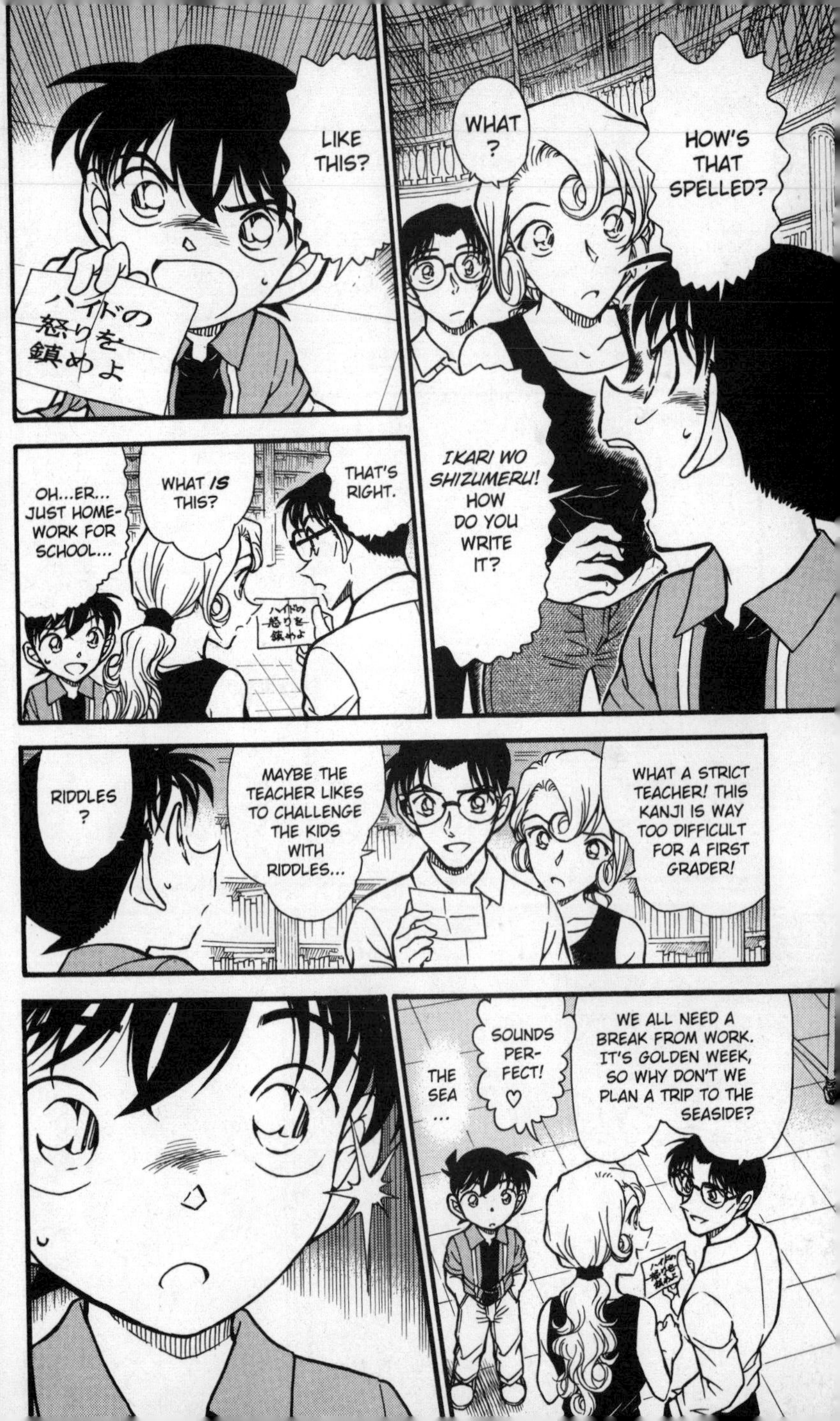
HOW'S THAT SPELLED?
WHAT?
IKARI WO SHIZUMERU! HOW DO YOU WRITE IT?
LIKE THIS?
ハイドの怒りを鎮めよ
THAT'S RIGHT.
WHAT IS THIS?
OH...ER... JUST HOMEWORK FOR SCHOOL...
WHAT A STRICT TEACHER! THIS KANJI IS WAY TOO DIFFICULT FOR A FIRST GRADER!
MAYBE THE TEACHER LIKES TO CHALLENGE THE KIDS WITH RIDDLES...
RIDDLES?
WE ALL NEED A BREAK FROM WORK. IT'S GOLDEN WEEK, SO WHY DON'T WE PLAN A TRIP TO THE SEASIDE?
SOUNDS PERFECT! ♡
THE SEA...

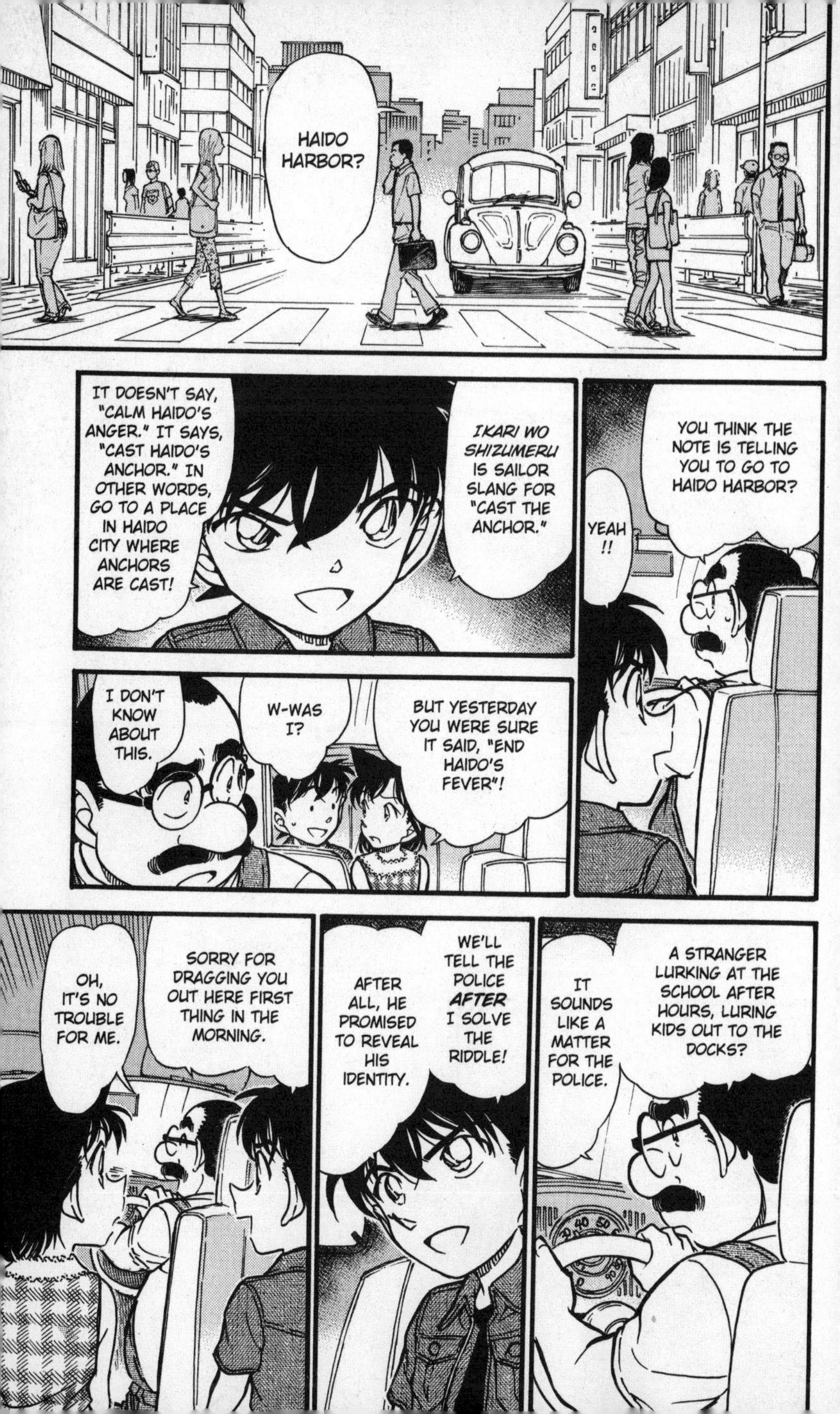
HAIDO HARBOR?
YOU THINK THE NOTE IS TELLING YOU TO GO TO HAIDO HARBOR?
YEAH !!
IKARI WO SHIZUMERU IS SAILOR SLANG FOR "CAST THE ANCHOR."
IT DOESN'T SAY, "CALM HAIDO'S ANGER." IT SAYS, "CAST HAIDO'S ANCHOR." IN OTHER WORDS, GO TO A PLACE IN HAIDO CITY WHERE ANCHORS ARE CAST!
BUT YESTERDAY YOU WERE SURE IT SAID, "END HAIDO'S FEVER"!
W-WAS I?
I DON'T KNOW ABOUT THIS.
A STRANGER LURKING AT THE SCHOOL AFTER HOURS, LURING KIDS OUT TO THE DOCKS?
IT SOUNDS LIKE A MATTER FOR THE POLICE.
WE'LL TELL THE POLICE ***AFTER*** I SOLVE THE RIDDLE!
AFTER ALL, HE PROMISED TO REVEAL HIS IDENTITY.
SORRY FOR DRAGGING YOU OUT HERE FIRST THING IN THE MORNING.
OH, IT'S NO TROUBLE FOR ME.

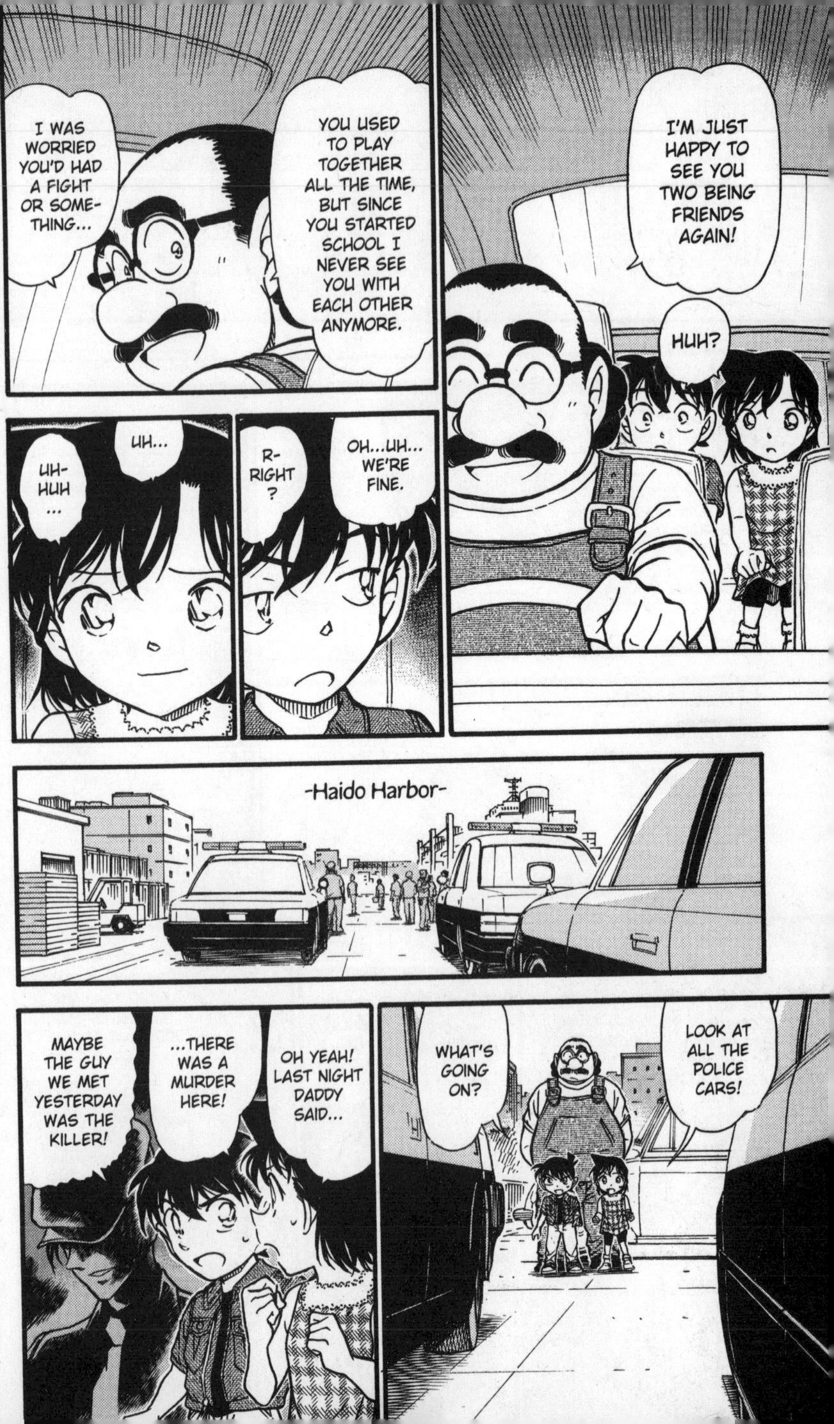
I'M JUST HAPPY TO SEE YOU TWO BEING FRIENDS AGAIN!
HUH?
YOU USED TO PLAY TOGETHER ALL THE TIME, BUT SINCE YOU STARTED SCHOOL I NEVER SEE YOU WITH EACH OTHER ANYMORE.
I WAS WORRIED YOU'D HAD A FIGHT OR SOME-THING...
OH...UH... WE'RE FINE.
R-RIGHT?
UH...
UH-HUH...
-Haido Harbor-
LOOK AT ALL THE POLICE CARS!
WHAT'S GOING ON?
OH YEAH! LAST NIGHT DADDY SAID...
...THERE WAS A MURDER HERE!
MAYBE THE GUY WE MET YESTERDAY WAS THE KILLER!

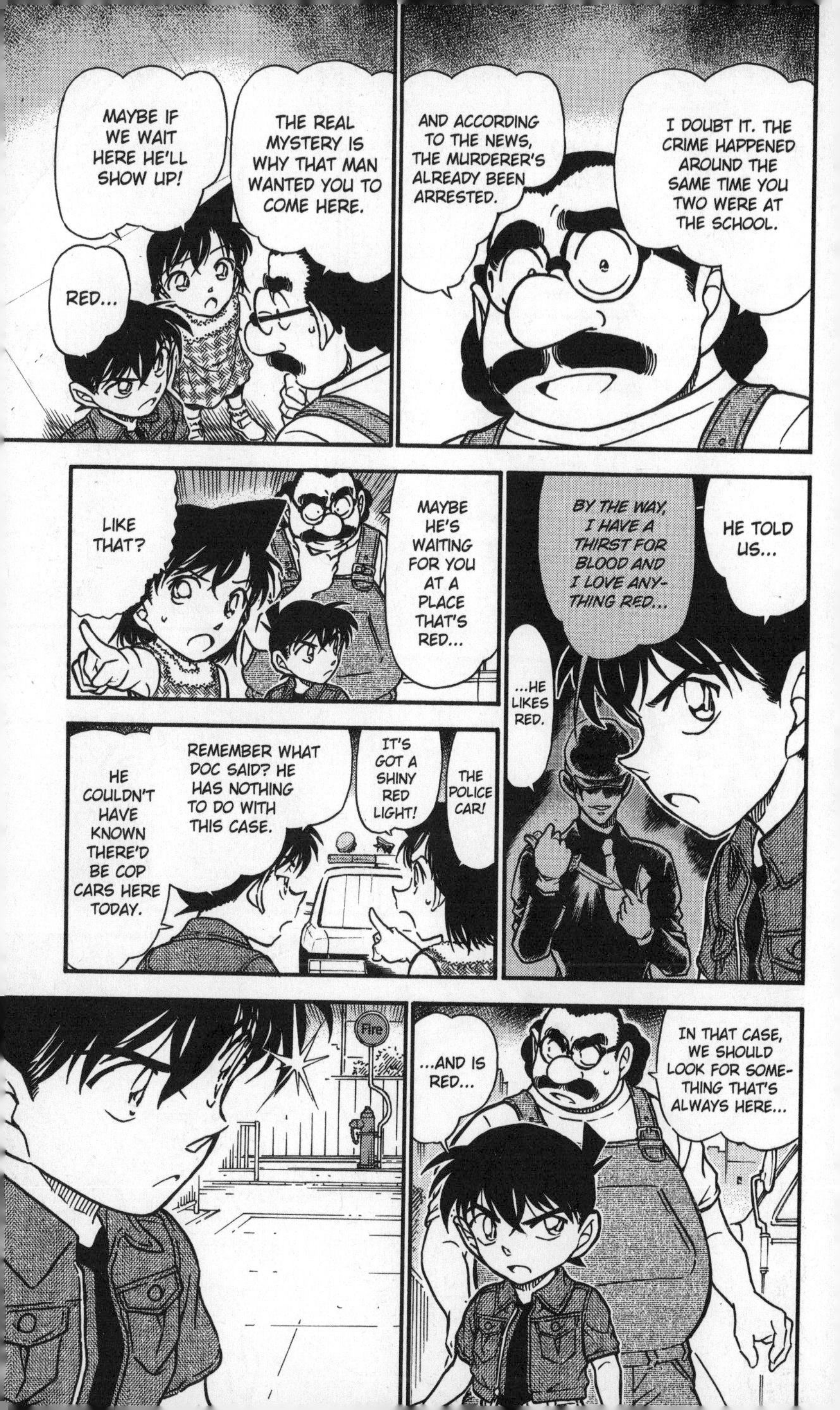
I DOUBT IT. THE CRIME HAPPENED AROUND THE SAME TIME YOU TWO WERE AT THE SCHOOL.
AND ACCORDING TO THE NEWS, THE MURDERER'S ALREADY BEEN ARRESTED.
THE REAL MYSTERY IS WHY THAT MAN WANTED YOU TO COME HERE.
MAYBE IF WE WAIT HERE HE'LL SHOW UP!
RED...
HE TOLD US...
BY THE WAY, I HAVE A THIRST FOR BLOOD AND I LOVE ANYTHING RED...
...HE LIKES RED.
MAYBE HE'S WAITING FOR YOU AT A PLACE THAT'S RED...
LIKE THAT?
THE POLICE CAR!
IT'S GOT A SHINY RED LIGHT!
REMEMBER WHAT DOC SAID? HE HAS NOTHING TO DO WITH THIS CASE.
HE COULDN'T HAVE KNOWN THERE'D BE COP CARS HERE TODAY.
IN THAT CASE, WE SHOULD LOOK FOR SOMETHING THAT'S ALWAYS HERE...
...AND IS RED...
Fire

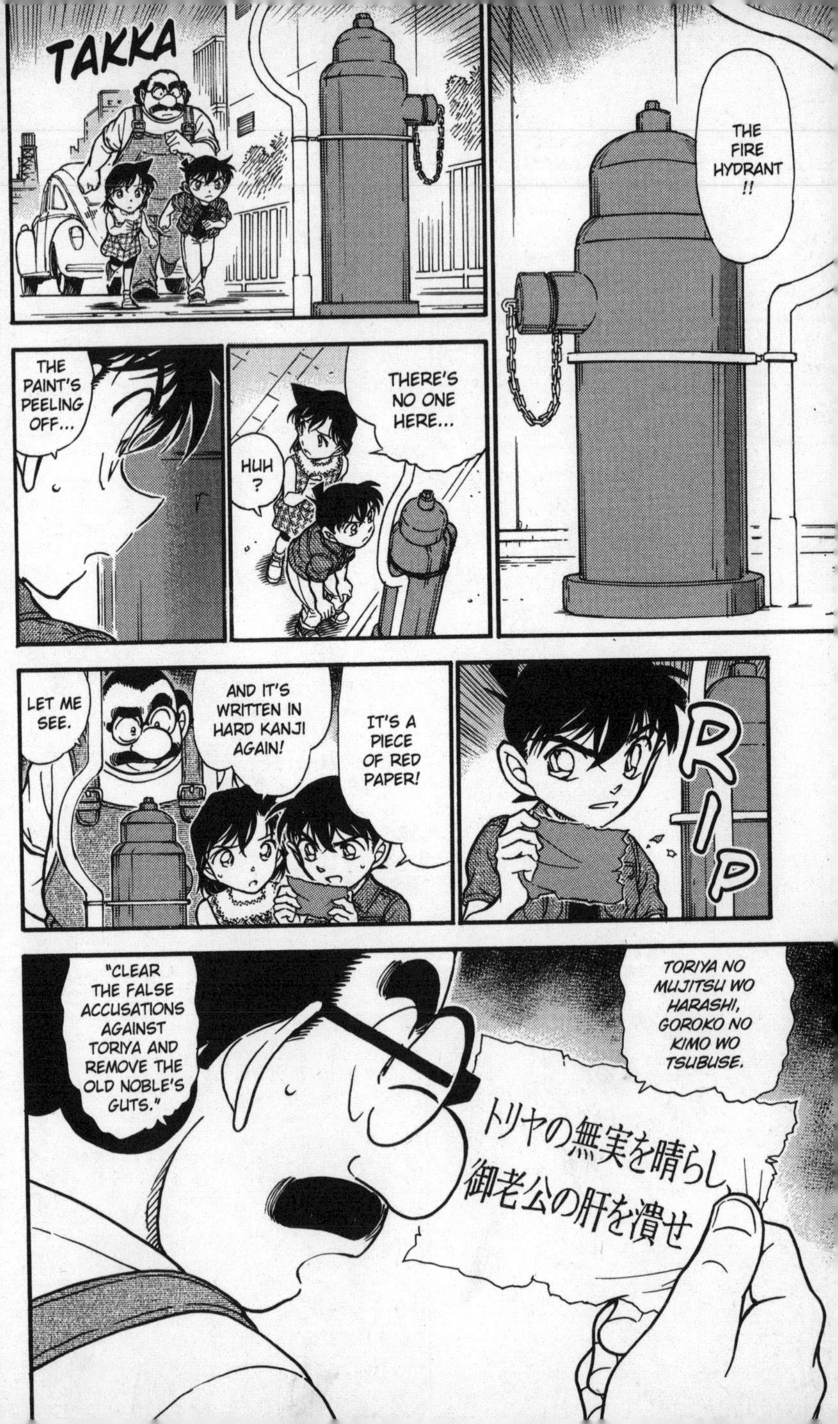
THE FIRE HYDRANT !!
TAKKA
THERE'S NO ONE HERE...
HUH ?
THE PAINT'S PEELING OFF...
RIP
IT'S A PIECE OF RED PAPER!
AND IT'S WRITTEN IN HARD KANJI AGAIN!
LET ME SEE.
TORIYA NO MUJITSU WO HARASHI, GOROKO NO KIMO WO TSUBUSE.
トリヤの無実を晴らし
御老公の肝を潰せ
"CLEAR THE FALSE ACCUSATIONS AGAINST TORIYA AND REMOVE THE OLD NOBLE'S GUTS."

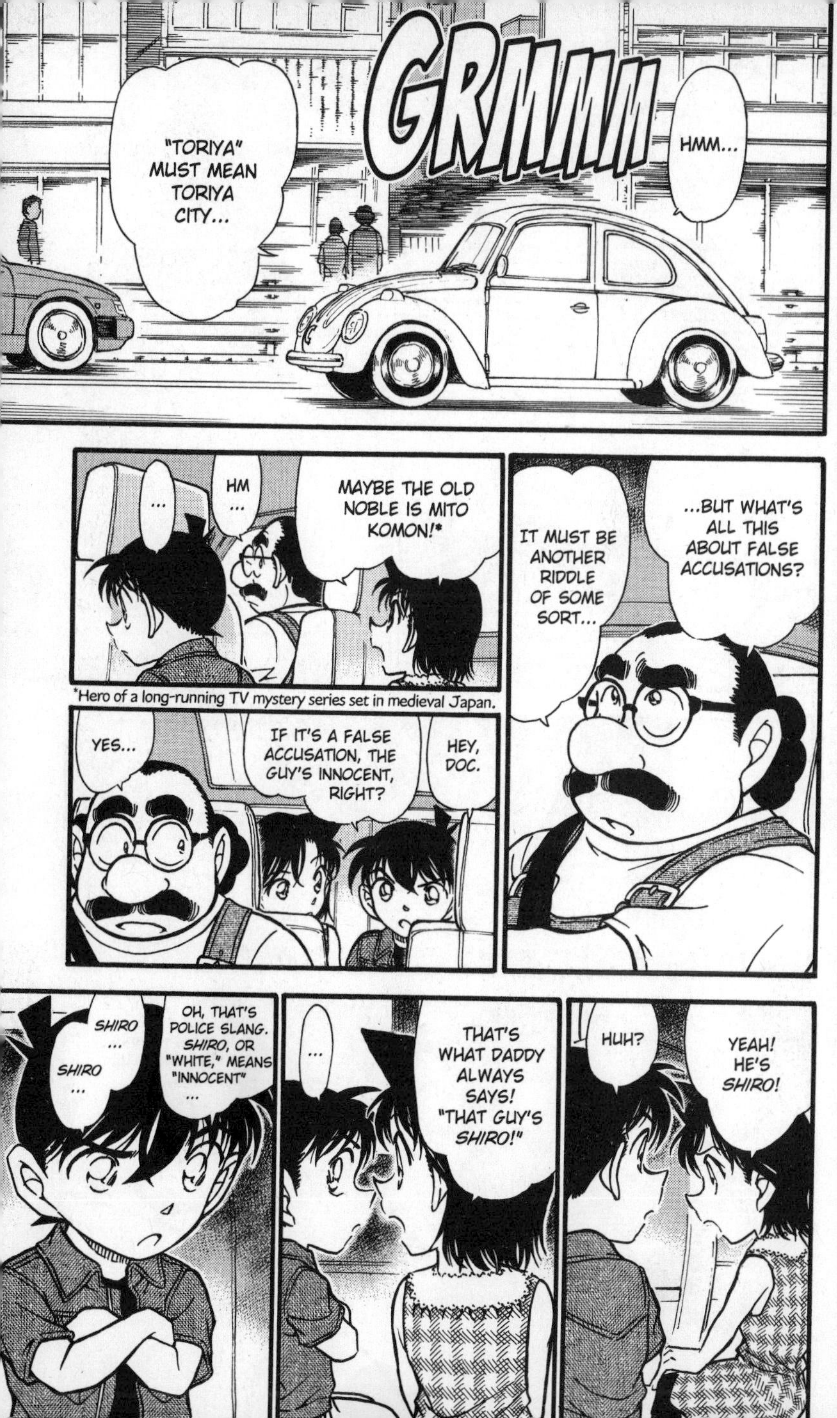
HMM...
GRMMMM
"TORIYA" MUST MEAN TORIYA CITY...
...BUT WHAT'S ALL THIS ABOUT FALSE ACCUSATIONS?
IT MUST BE ANOTHER RIDDLE OF SOME SORT...
MAYBE THE OLD NOBLE IS MITO KOMON!*
HM ...
...
HEY, DOC.
IF IT'S A FALSE ACCUSATION, THE GUY'S INNOCENT, RIGHT?
YES...
YEAH! HE'S *SHIRO*!
HUH?
THAT'S WHAT DADDY ALWAYS SAYS! "THAT GUY'S *SHIRO*!"
...
OH, THAT'S POLICE SLANG. *SHIRO*, OR "WHITE," MEANS "INNOCENT" ...
SHIRO ...
SHIRO ...
*Hero of a long-running TV mystery series set in medieval Japan.

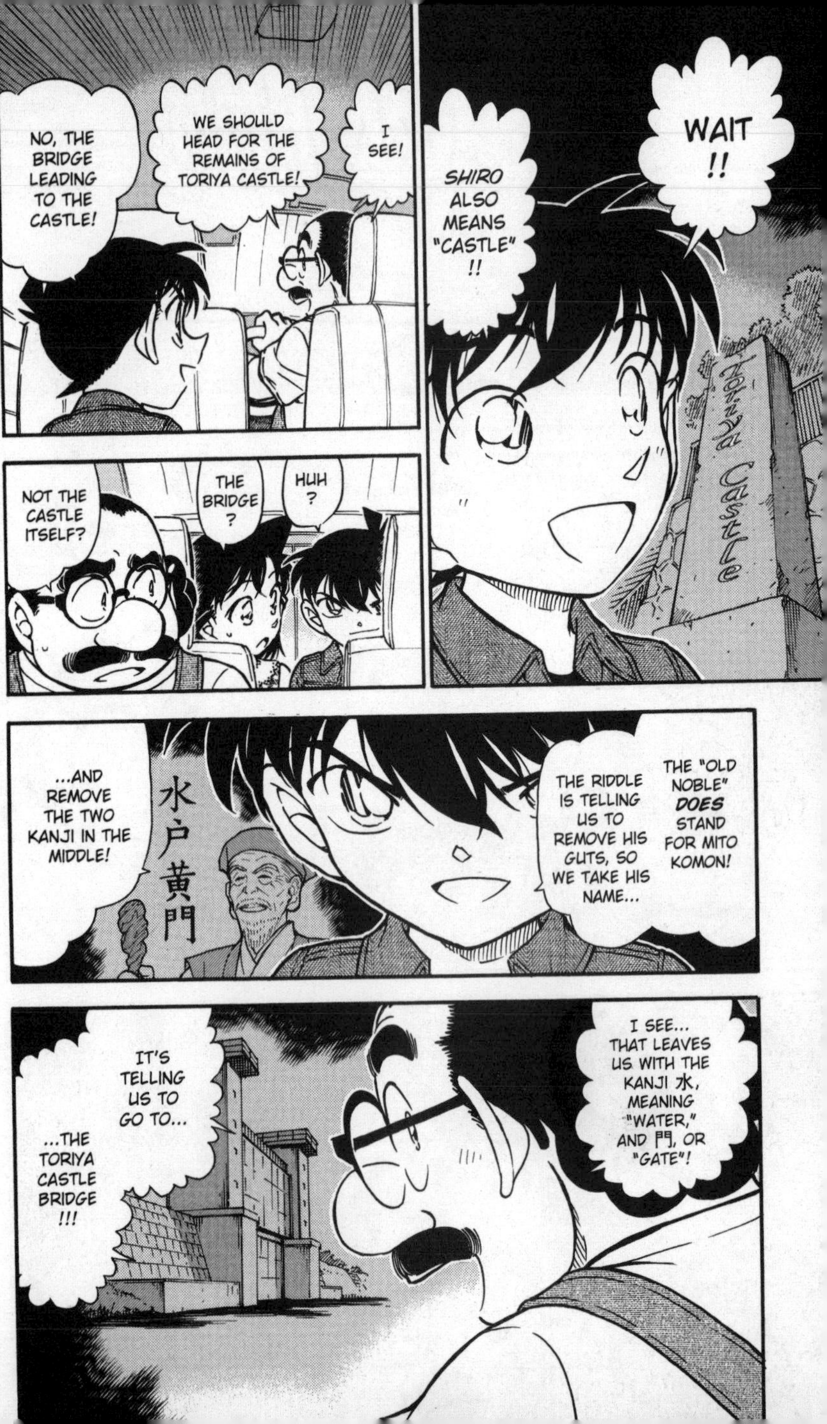
WAIT!!
SHIRO ALSO MEANS "CASTLE"!!
Toriya Castle
I SEE!
WE SHOULD HEAD FOR THE REMAINS OF TORIYA CASTLE!
NO, THE BRIDGE LEADING TO THE CASTLE!
HUH?
THE BRIDGE?
NOT THE CASTLE ITSELF?
THE "OLD NOBLE" *DOES* STAND FOR MITO KOMON!
THE RIDDLE IS TELLING US TO REMOVE HIS GUTS, SO WE TAKE HIS NAME...
水戸黄門
...AND REMOVE THE TWO KANJI IN THE MIDDLE!
I SEE... THAT LEAVES US WITH THE KANJI 水, MEANING "WATER," AND 門, OR "GATE"!
IT'S TELLING US TO GO TO...
...THE TORIYA CASTLE BRIDGE!!!

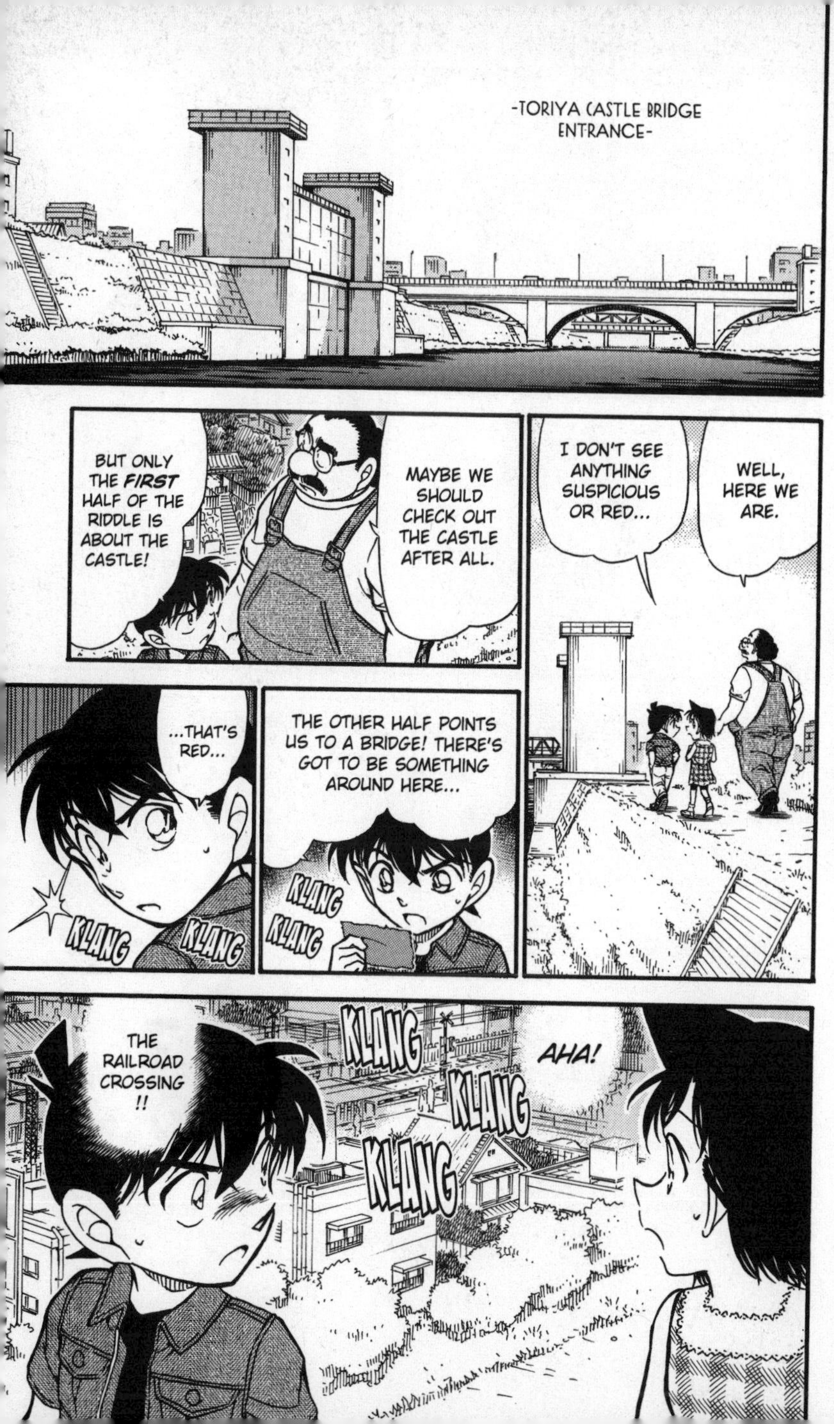
-TORIYA CASTLE BRIDGE ENTRANCE-
WELL, HERE WE ARE.
I DON'T SEE ANYTHING SUSPICIOUS OR RED...
MAYBE WE SHOULD CHECK OUT THE CASTLE AFTER ALL.
BUT ONLY THE FIRST HALF OF THE RIDDLE IS ABOUT THE CASTLE!
THE OTHER HALF POINTS US TO A BRIDGE! THERE'S GOT TO BE SOMETHING AROUND HERE...
KLANG
KLANG
...THAT'S RED...
KLANG
KLANG
AHA!
KLANG
KLANG
KLANG
THE RAILROAD CROSSING !!

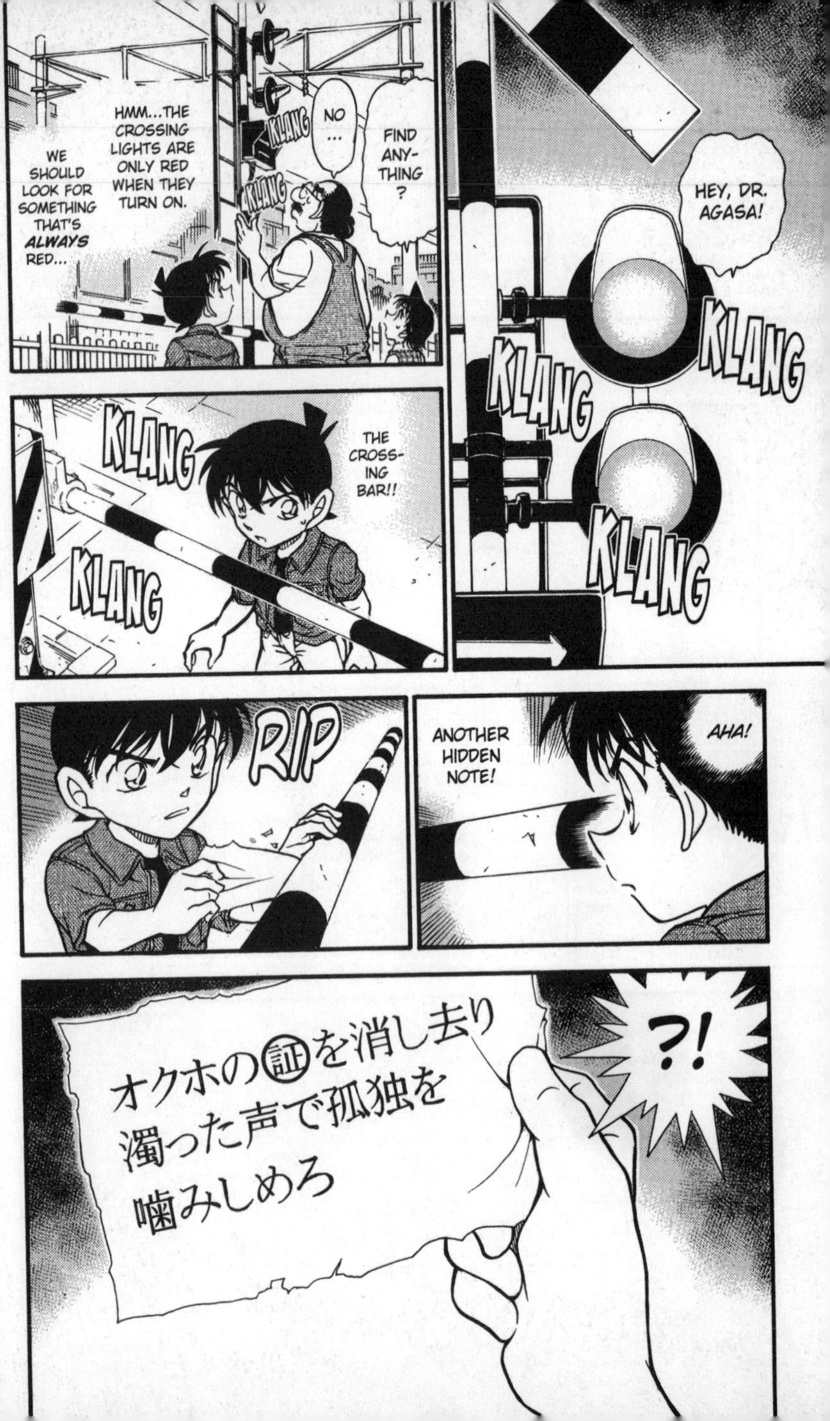
HEY, DR. AGASA!
KLANG
KLANG
KLANG
KLANG
FIND ANY-THING?
NO...
KLANG
KLANG
HMM...THE CROSSING LIGHTS ARE ONLY RED WHEN THEY TURN ON.
WE SHOULD LOOK FOR SOMETHING THAT'S ALWAYS RED...
KLANG
THE CROSS-ING BAR!!
KLANG
AHA!
ANOTHER HIDDEN NOTE!
RIP
?!
オクホの㊟を消し去り
濁った声で孤独を
噛みしめろ

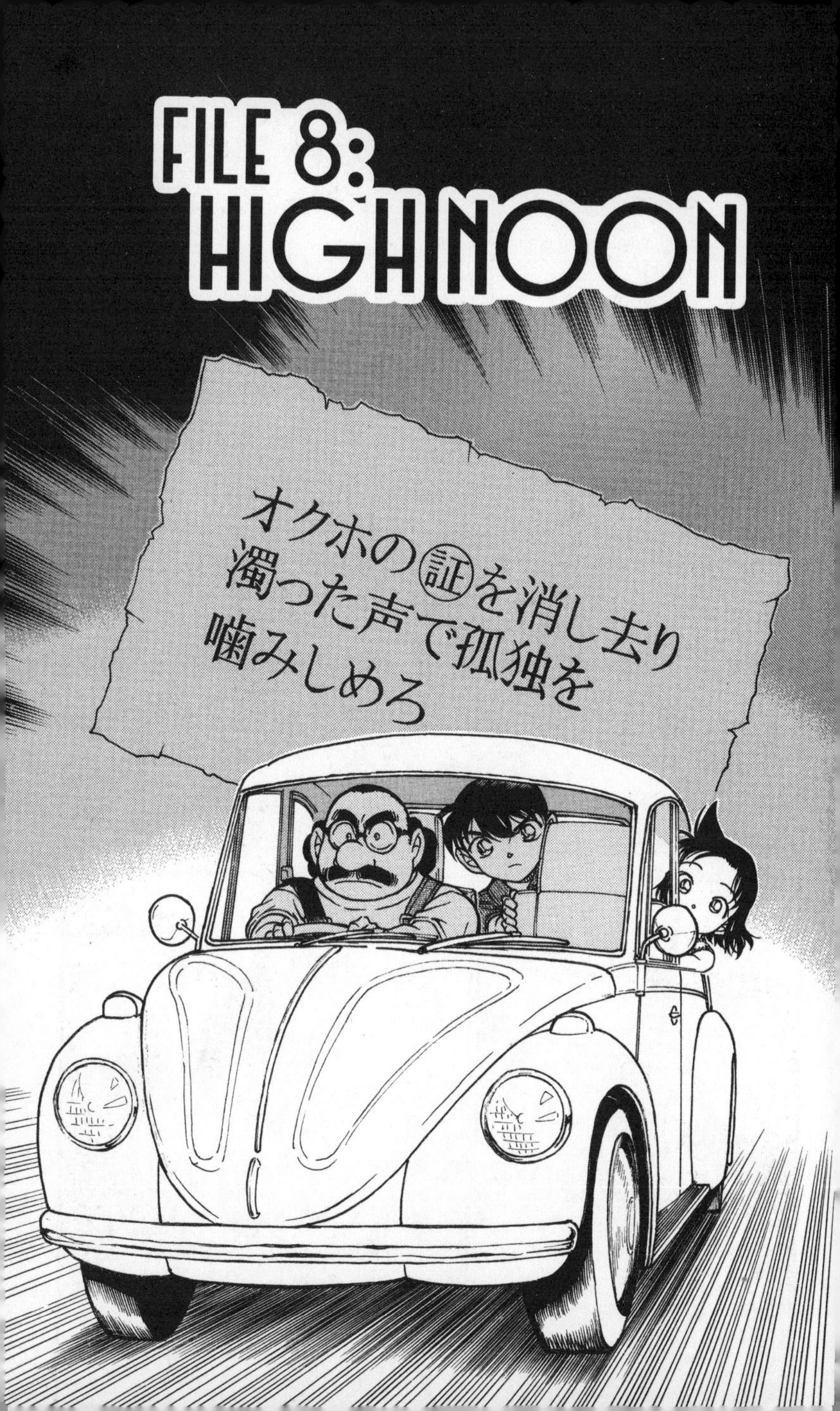
FILE 8:
HIGH NOON
オクホの証を消し去り
濁った声で孤独を
噛みしめろ

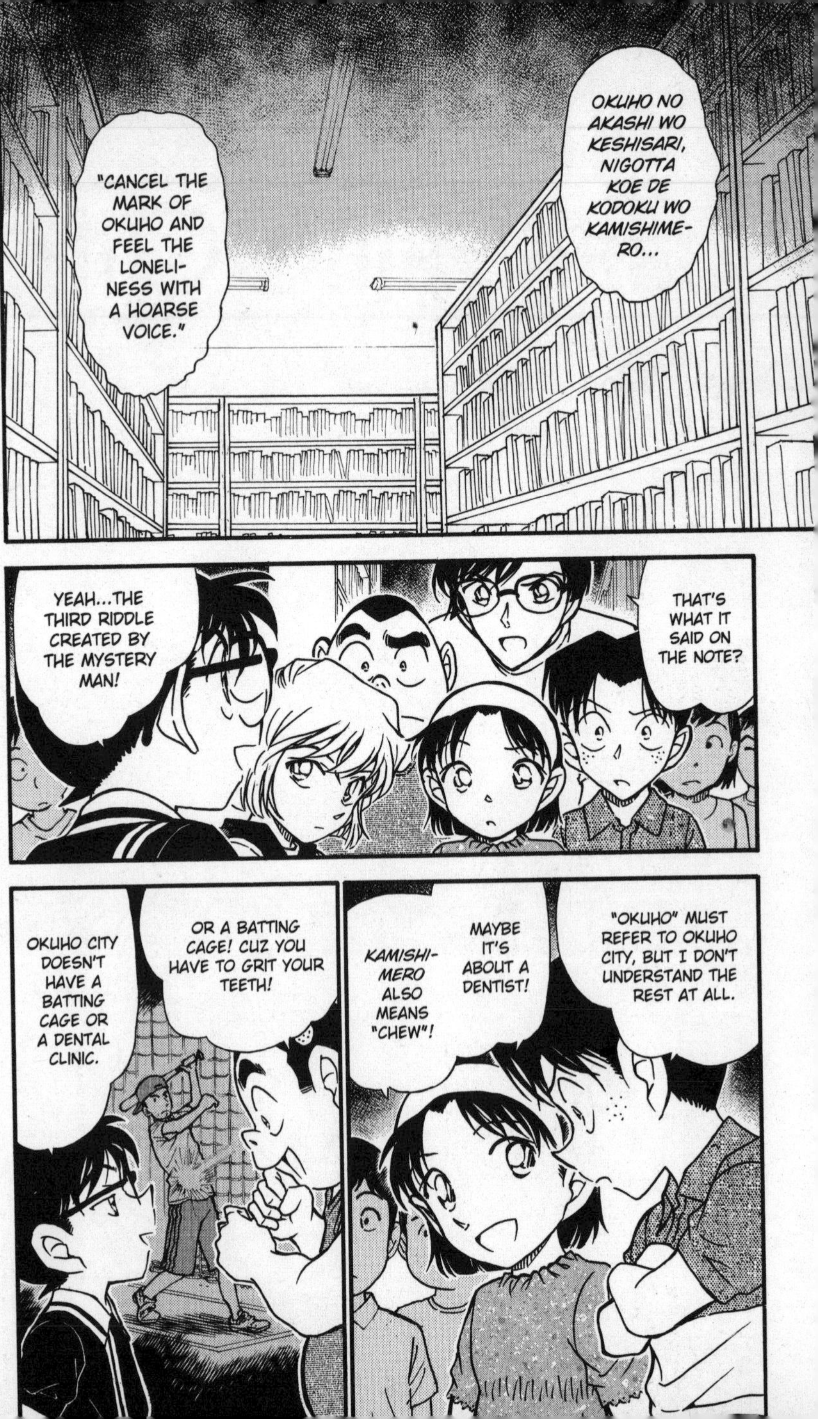
OKUHO NO AKASHI WO KESHISARI, NIGOTTA KOE DE KODOKU WO KAMISHIME-RO...
"CANCEL THE MARK OF OKUHO AND FEEL THE LONELI-NESS WITH A HOARSE VOICE."
THAT'S WHAT IT SAID ON THE NOTE?
YEAH...THE THIRD RIDDLE CREATED BY THE MYSTERY MAN!
"OKUHO" MUST REFER TO OKUHO CITY, BUT I DON'T UNDERSTAND THE REST AT ALL.
MAYBE IT'S ABOUT A DENTIST!
KAMISHI-MERO ALSO MEANS "CHEW"!
OR A BATTING CAGE! CUZ YOU HAVE TO GRIT YOUR TEETH!
OKUHO CITY DOESN'T HAVE A BATTING CAGE OR A DENTAL CLINIC.

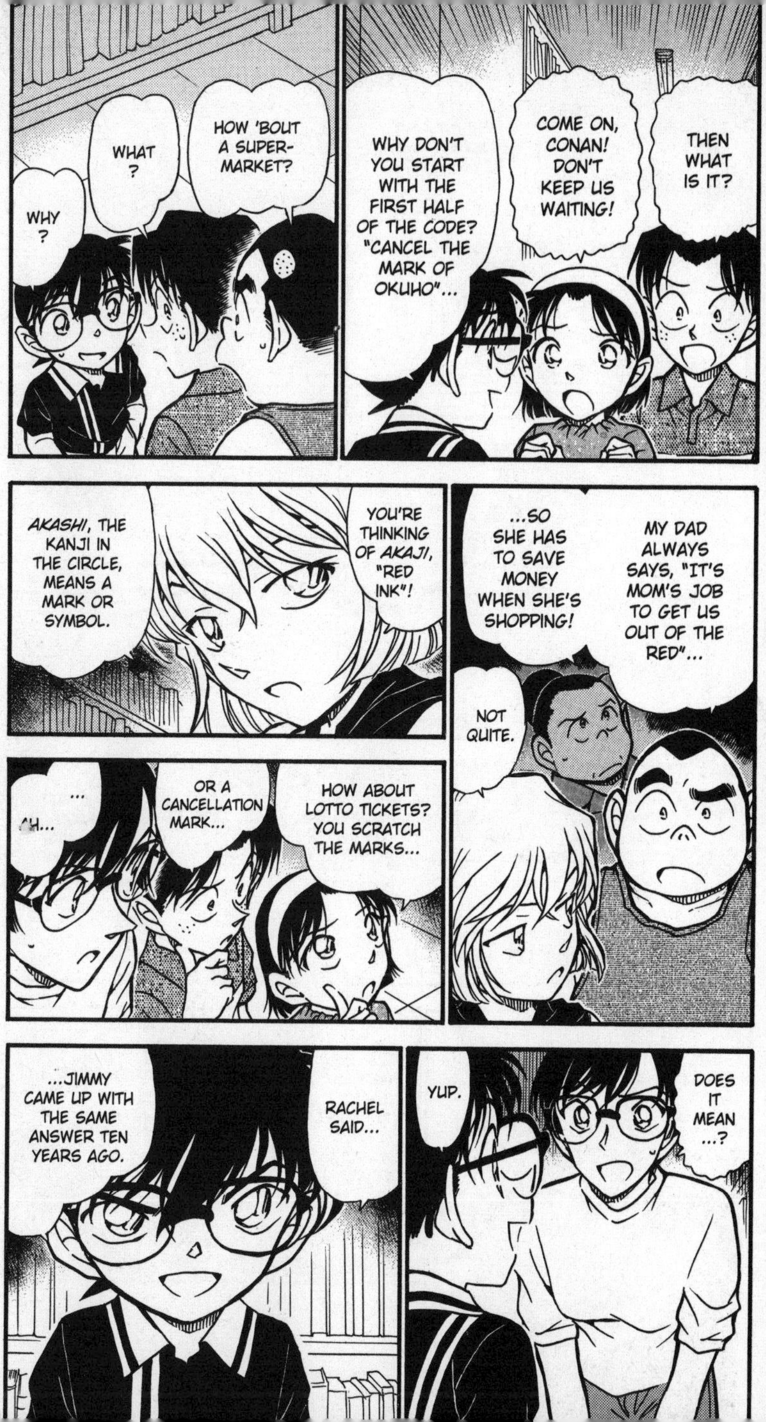
THEN WHAT IS IT?
COME ON, CONAN! DON'T KEEP US WAITING!
WHY DON'T YOU START WITH THE FIRST HALF OF THE CODE? "CANCEL THE MARK OF OKUHO"...
HOW 'BOUT A SUPER-MARKET?
WHAT?
WHY?
MY DAD ALWAYS SAYS, "IT'S MOM'S JOB TO GET US OUT OF THE RED"...
...SO SHE HAS TO SAVE MONEY WHEN SHE'S SHOPPING!
NOT QUITE.
YOU'RE THINKING OF *AKAJI*, "RED INK"!
AKASHI, THE KANJI IN THE CIRCLE, MEANS A MARK OR SYMBOL.
HOW ABOUT LOTTO TICKETS? YOU SCRATCH THE MARKS...
OR A CANCELLATION MARK...
...
AH...
DOES IT MEAN ...?
YUP.
RACHEL SAID...
...JIMMY CAME UP WITH THE SAME ANSWER TEN YEARS AGO.

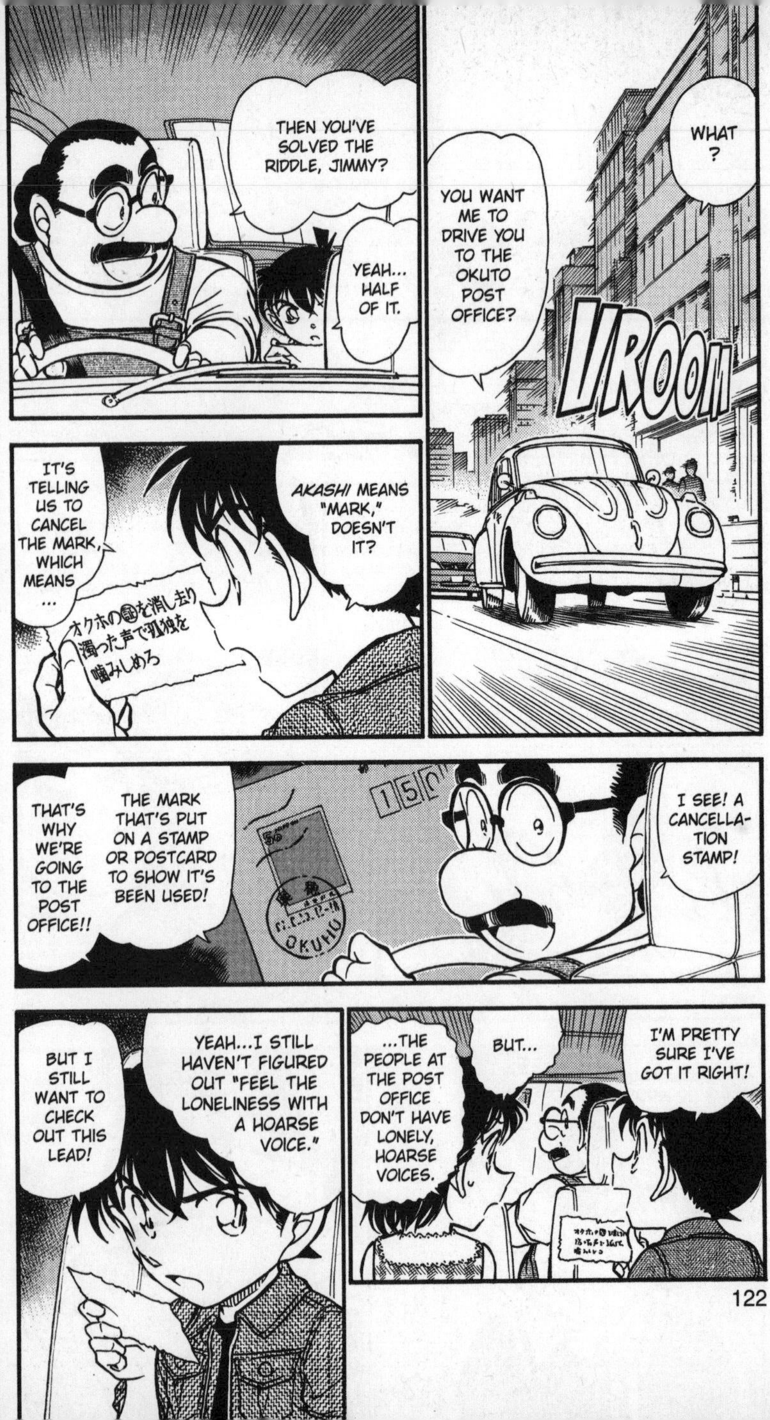
WHAT?
YOU WANT ME TO DRIVE YOU TO THE OKUTO POST OFFICE?
VROOM
THEN YOU'VE SOLVED THE RIDDLE, JIMMY?
YEAH... HALF OF IT.
AKASHI MEANS "MARK," DOESN'T IT?
IT'S TELLING US TO CANCEL THE MARK, WHICH MEANS ...
オクホの㊞を消し去り 濁った声で孤独を 噛みしめろ
I SEE! A CANCELLATION STAMP!
THE MARK THAT'S PUT ON A STAMP OR POSTCARD TO SHOW IT'S BEEN USED!
THAT'S WHY WE'RE GOING TO THE POST OFFICE!!
I'M PRETTY SURE I'VE GOT IT RIGHT!
BUT...
...THE PEOPLE AT THE POST OFFICE DON'T HAVE LONELY, HOARSE VOICES.
YEAH...I STILL HAVEN'T FIGURED OUT "FEEL THE LONELINESS WITH A HOARSE VOICE."
BUT I STILL WANT TO CHECK OUT THIS LEAD!

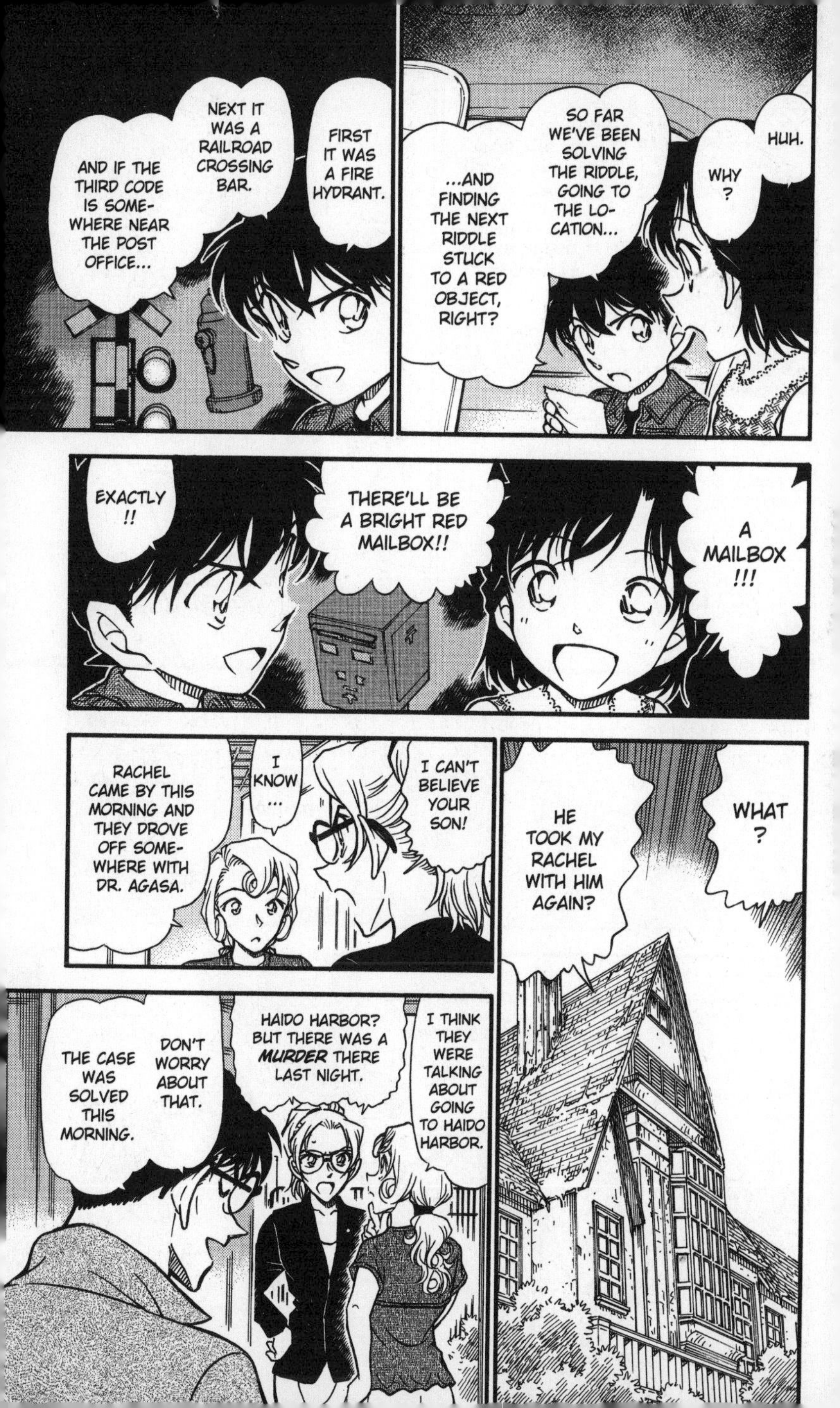
HUH.
WHY?
SO FAR WE'VE BEEN SOLVING THE RIDDLE, GOING TO THE LOCATION...
...AND FINDING THE NEXT RIDDLE STUCK TO A RED OBJECT, RIGHT?
FIRST IT WAS A FIRE HYDRANT.
NEXT IT WAS A RAILROAD CROSSING BAR.
AND IF THE THIRD CODE IS SOMEWHERE NEAR THE POST OFFICE...
A MAILBOX!!!
THERE'LL BE A BRIGHT RED MAILBOX!!
EXACTLY!!
WHAT?
HE TOOK MY RACHEL WITH HIM AGAIN?
I CAN'T BELIEVE YOUR SON!
I KNOW...
RACHEL CAME BY THIS MORNING AND THEY DROVE OFF SOMEWHERE WITH DR. AGASA.
I THINK THEY WERE TALKING ABOUT GOING TO HAIDO HARBOR.
HAIDO HARBOR? BUT THERE WAS A *MURDER* THERE LAST NIGHT.
DON'T WORRY ABOUT THAT.
THE CASE WAS SOLVED THIS MORNING.

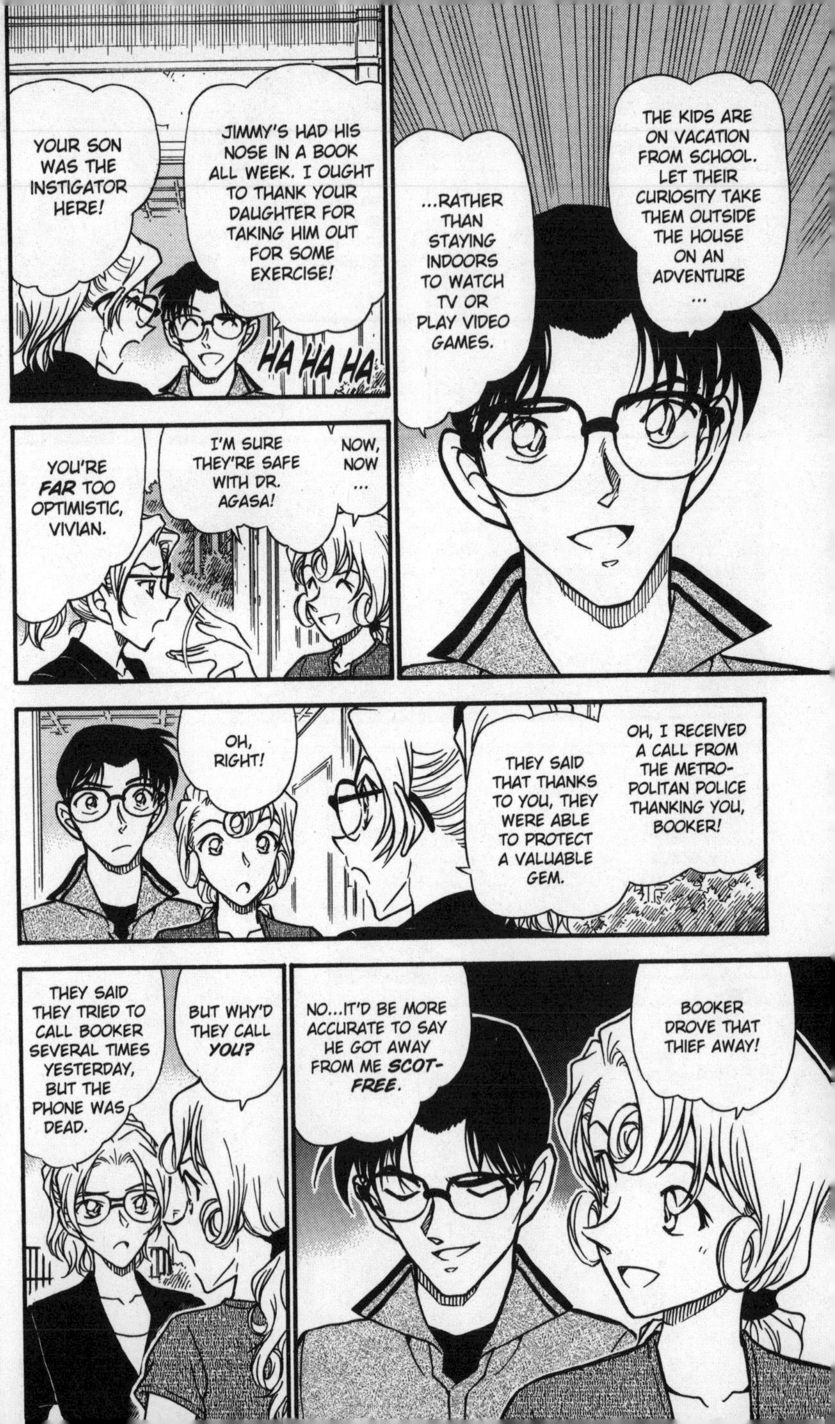
THE KIDS ARE ON VACATION FROM SCHOOL. LET THEIR CURIOSITY TAKE THEM OUTSIDE THE HOUSE ON AN ADVENTURE ...
...RATHER THAN STAYING INDOORS TO WATCH TV OR PLAY VIDEO GAMES.
JIMMY'S HAD HIS NOSE IN A BOOK ALL WEEK. I OUGHT TO THANK YOUR DAUGHTER FOR TAKING HIM OUT FOR SOME EXERCISE!
YOUR SON WAS THE INSTIGATOR HERE!
HA HA HA
NOW, NOW ...
I'M SURE THEY'RE SAFE WITH DR. AGASA!
YOU'RE **FAR** TOO OPTIMISTIC, VIVIAN.
OH, I RECEIVED A CALL FROM THE METRO-POLITAN POLICE THANKING YOU, BOOKER!
THEY SAID THAT THANKS TO YOU, THEY WERE ABLE TO PROTECT A VALUABLE GEM.
OH, RIGHT!
BOOKER DROVE THAT THIEF AWAY!
NO...IT'D BE MORE ACCURATE TO SAY HE GOT AWAY FROM ME **SCOT-FREE**.
BUT WHY'D THEY CALL **YOU?**
THEY SAID THEY TRIED TO CALL BOOKER SEVERAL TIMES YESTERDAY, BUT THE PHONE WAS DEAD.

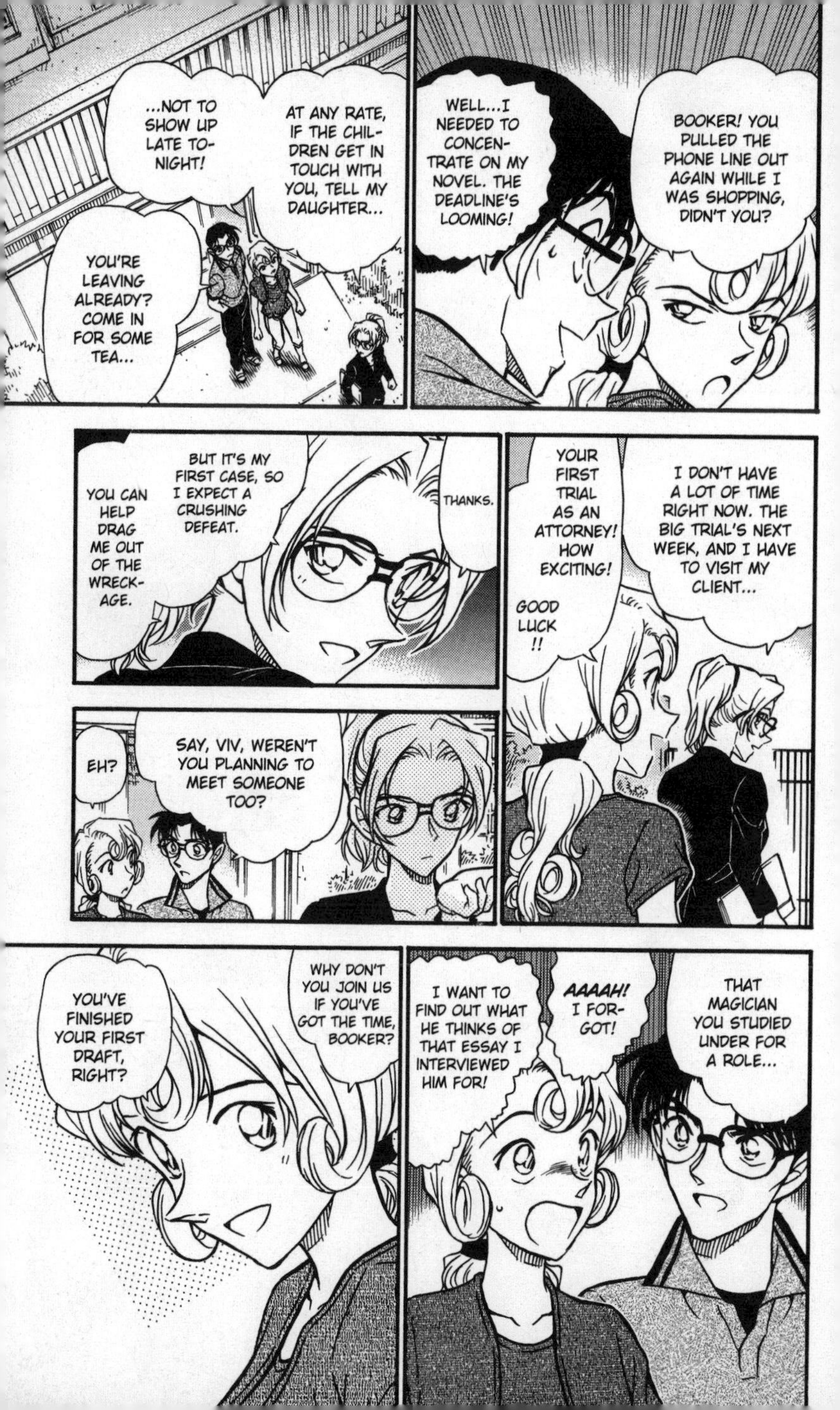

BOOKER! YOU PULLED THE PHONE LINE OUT AGAIN WHILE I WAS SHOPPING, DIDN'T YOU?
WELL...I NEEDED TO CONCENTRATE ON MY NOVEL. THE DEADLINE'S LOOMING!
AT ANY RATE, IF THE CHILDREN GET IN TOUCH WITH YOU, TELL MY DAUGHTER...
...NOT TO SHOW UP LATE TONIGHT!
YOU'RE LEAVING ALREADY? COME IN FOR SOME TEA...
I DON'T HAVE A LOT OF TIME RIGHT NOW. THE BIG TRIAL'S NEXT WEEK, AND I HAVE TO VISIT MY CLIENT...
YOUR FIRST TRIAL AS AN ATTORNEY! HOW EXCITING!
GOOD LUCK !!
THANKS.
BUT IT'S MY FIRST CASE, SO I EXPECT A CRUSHING DEFEAT.
YOU CAN HELP DRAG ME OUT OF THE WRECKAGE.
SAY, VIV, WEREN'T YOU PLANNING TO MEET SOMEONE TOO?
EH?
THAT MAGICIAN YOU STUDIED UNDER FOR A ROLE...
AAAAH! I FORGOT!
I WANT TO FIND OUT WHAT HE THINKS OF THAT ESSAY I INTERVIEWED HIM FOR!
WHY DON'T YOU JOIN US IF YOU'VE GOT THE TIME, BOOKER?
YOU'VE FINISHED YOUR FIRST DRAFT, RIGHT?

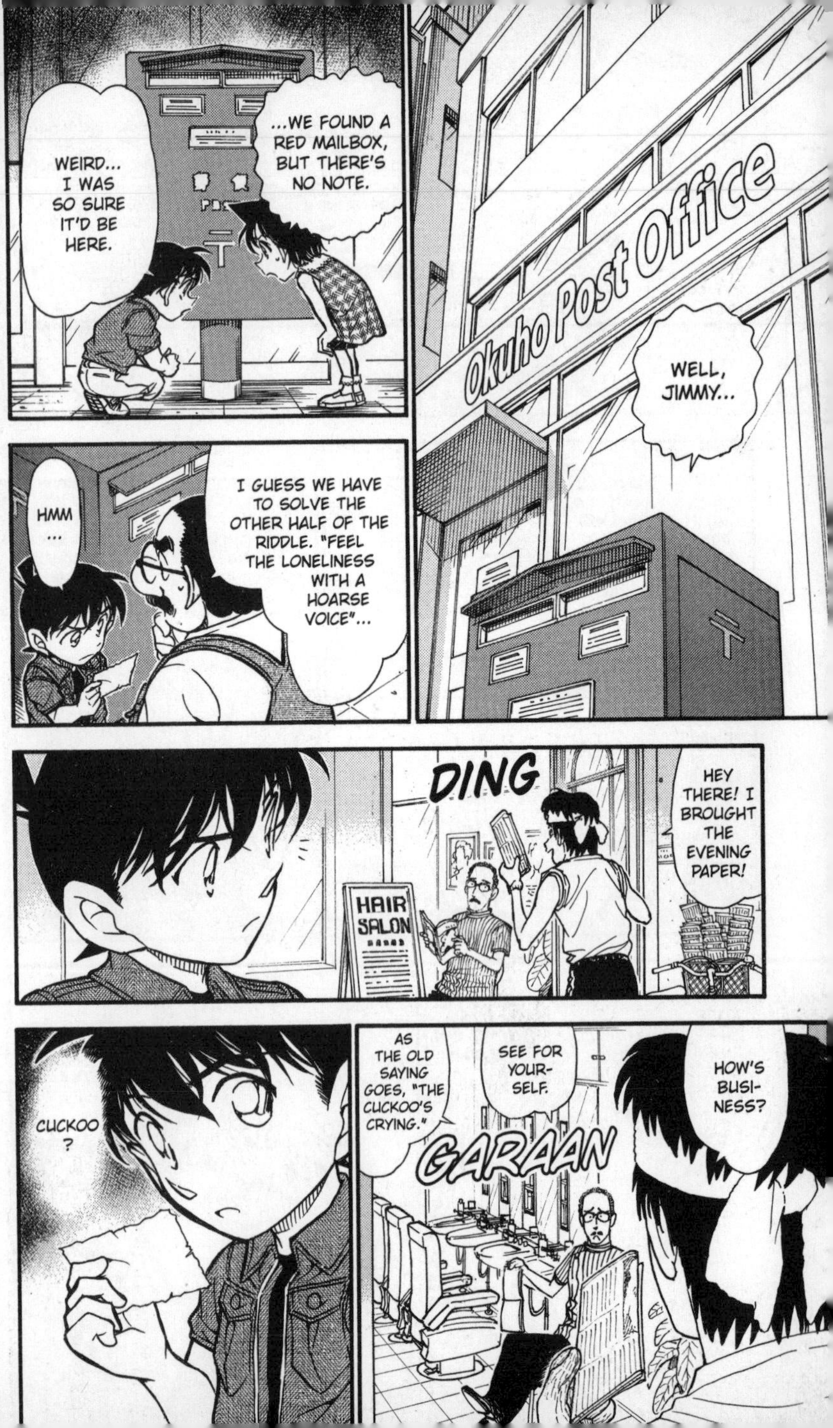
Okuho Post Office
WELL, JIMMY...
...WE FOUND A RED MAILBOX, BUT THERE'S NO NOTE.
WEIRD... I WAS SO SURE IT'D BE HERE.
I GUESS WE HAVE TO SOLVE THE OTHER HALF OF THE RIDDLE. "FEEL THE LONELINESS WITH A HOARSE VOICE"...
HMM...
HEY THERE! I BROUGHT THE EVENING PAPER!
DING
HAIR SALON
HOW'S BUSINESS?
SEE FOR YOURSELF.
AS THE OLD SAYING GOES, "THE CUCKOO'S CRYING."
GARAAN
CUCKOO?

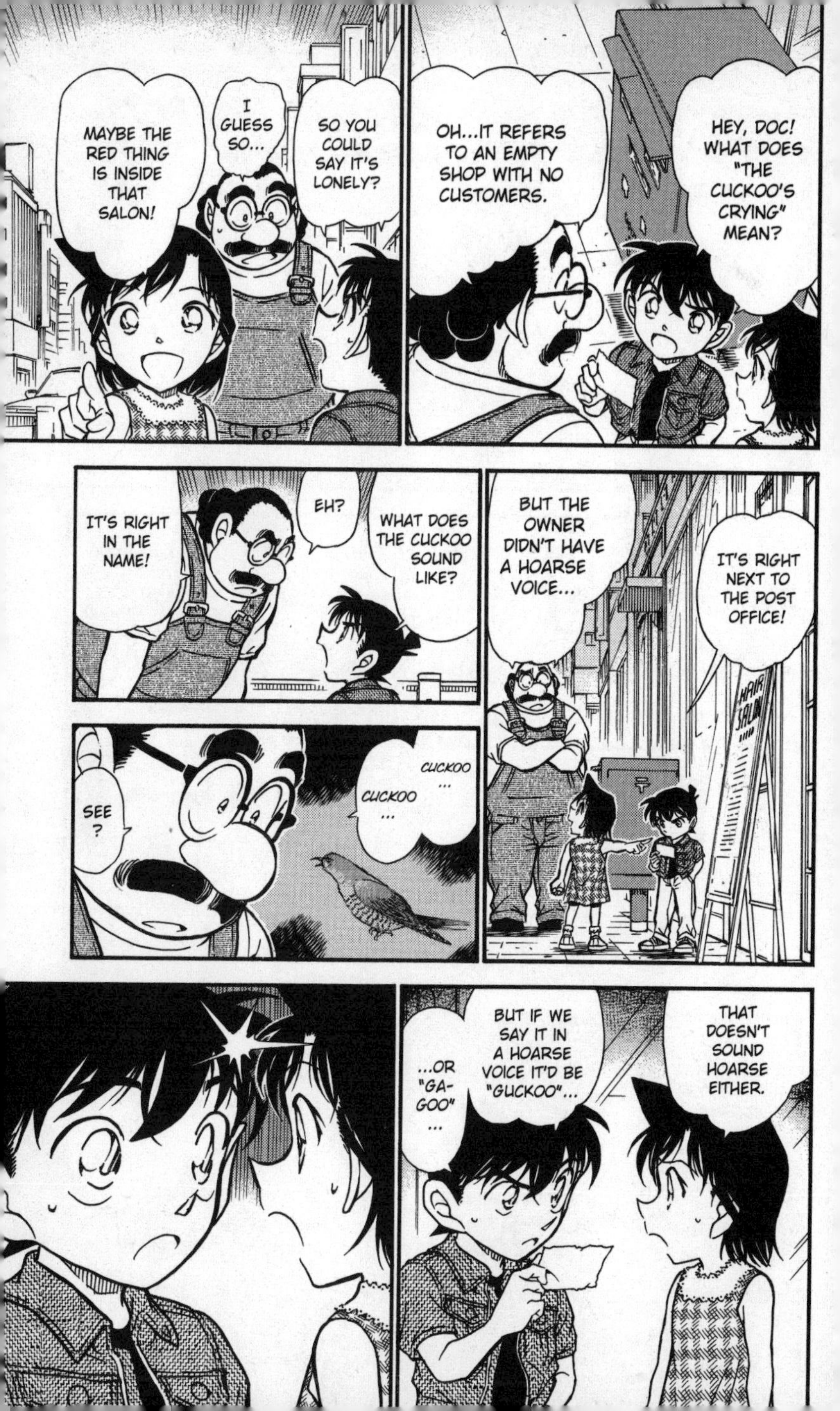
HEY, DOC! WHAT DOES "THE CUCKOO'S CRYING" MEAN?
OH...IT REFERS TO AN EMPTY SHOP WITH NO CUSTOMERS.
SO YOU COULD SAY IT'S LONELY?
I GUESS SO...
MAYBE THE RED THING IS INSIDE THAT SALON!
IT'S RIGHT NEXT TO THE POST OFFICE!
BUT THE OWNER DIDN'T HAVE A HOARSE VOICE...
HAIR SALON
WHAT DOES THE CUCKOO SOUND LIKE?
EH?
IT'S RIGHT IN THE NAME!
CUCKOO...
CUCKOO...
SEE?
THAT DOESN'T SOUND HOARSE EITHER.
BUT IF WE SAY IT IN A HOARSE VOICE IT'D BE "GUCKOO"...
...OR "GA-GOO"...

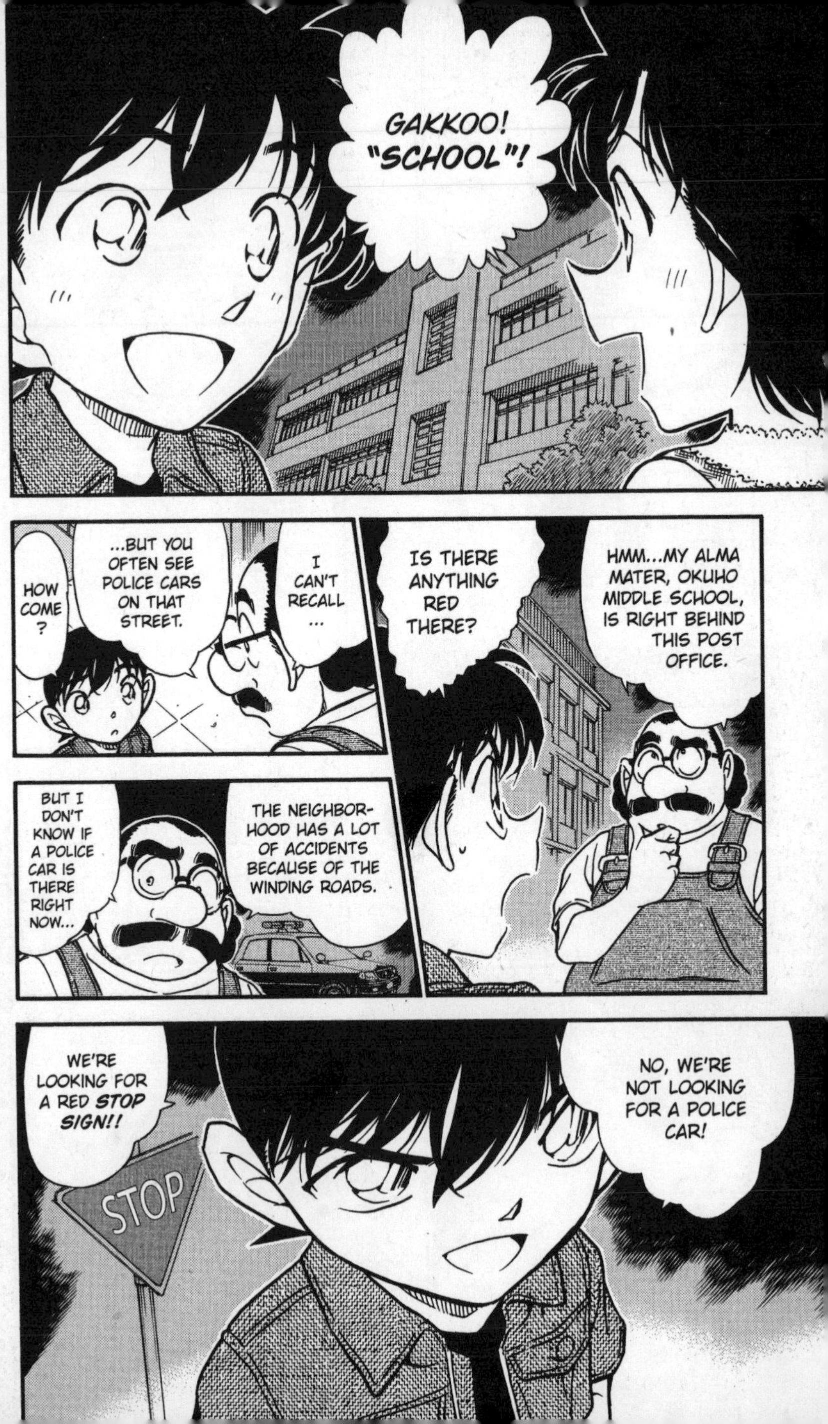
GAKKOO! "SCHOOL"!
HMM...MY ALMA MATER, OKUHO MIDDLE SCHOOL, IS RIGHT BEHIND THIS POST OFFICE.
IS THERE ANYTHING RED THERE?
I CAN'T RECALL ...
...BUT YOU OFTEN SEE POLICE CARS ON THAT STREET.
HOW COME?
THE NEIGHBOR-HOOD HAS A LOT OF ACCIDENTS BECAUSE OF THE WINDING ROADS.
BUT I DON'T KNOW IF A POLICE CAR IS THERE RIGHT NOW...
NO, WE'RE NOT LOOKING FOR A POLICE CAR!
WE'RE LOOKING FOR A RED ***STOP SIGN!!***
STOP

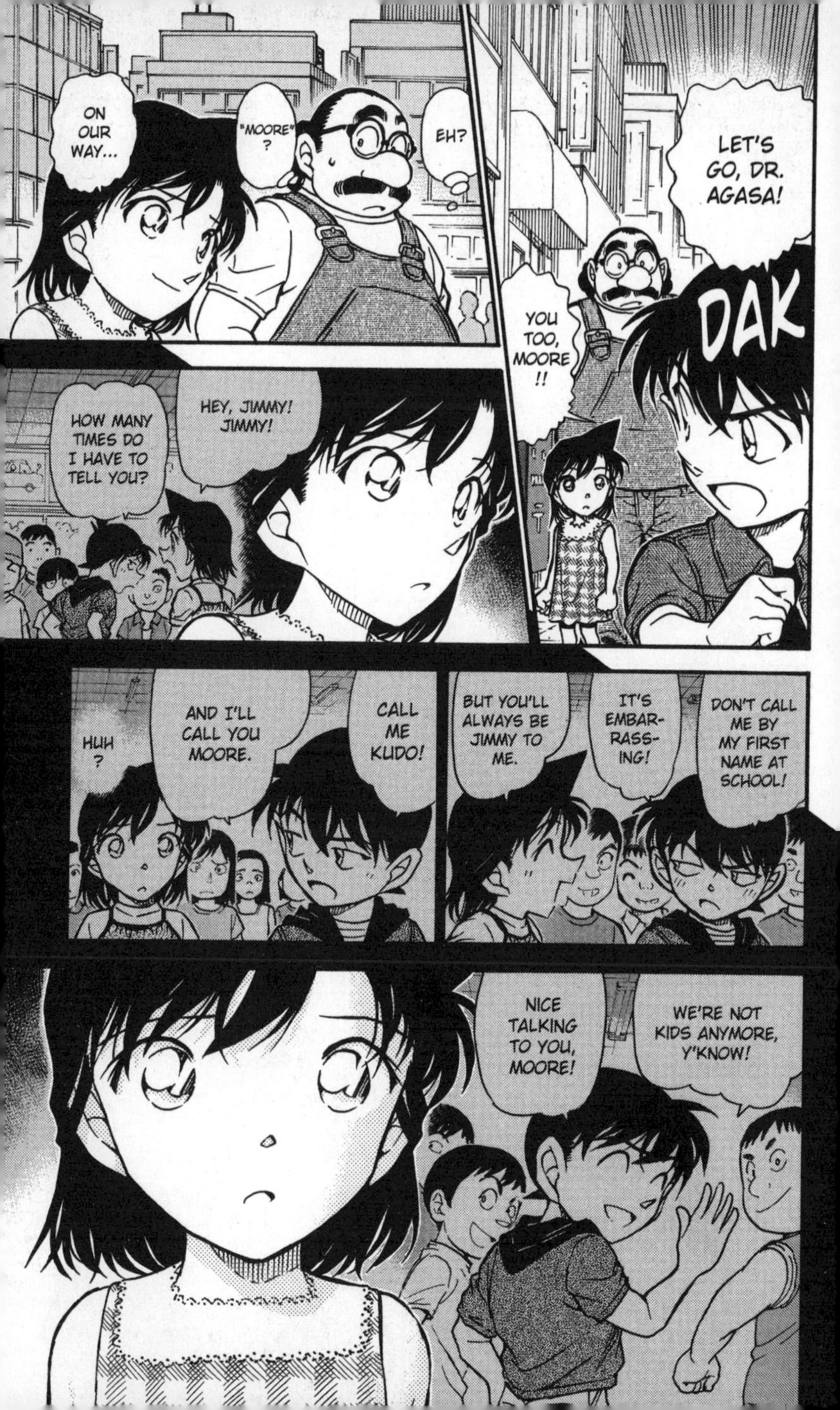
LET'S GO, DR. AGASA!
DAK
YOU TOO, MOORE!!
EH?
"MOORE"?
ON OUR WAY...
HEY, JIMMY! JIMMY!
HOW MANY TIMES DO I HAVE TO TELL YOU?
DON'T CALL ME BY MY FIRST NAME AT SCHOOL!
IT'S EMBARRASSING!
BUT YOU'LL ALWAYS BE JIMMY TO ME.
CALL ME KUDO!
AND I'LL CALL YOU MOORE.
HUH?
WE'RE NOT KIDS ANYMORE, Y'KNOW!
NICE TALKING TO YOU, MOORE!

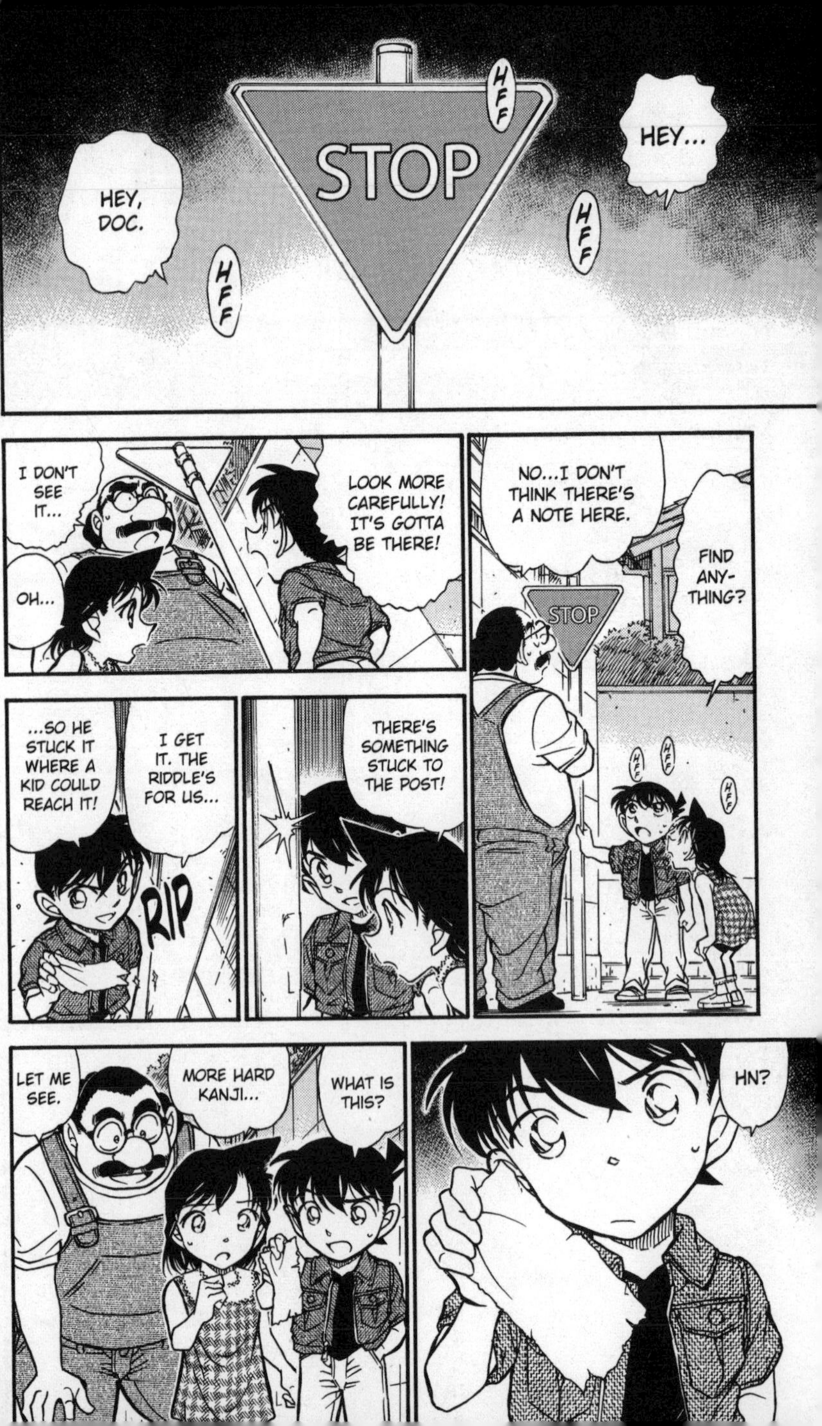
HFF
HEY...
STOP
HFF
HEY, DOC.
HFF
FIND ANY-THING?
NO...I DON'T THINK THERE'S A NOTE HERE.
STOP
HFF
HFF
HFF
LOOK MORE CAREFULLY! IT'S GOTTA BE THERE!
I DON'T SEE IT...
OH...
THERE'S SOMETHING STUCK TO THE POST!
I GET IT. THE RIDDLE'S FOR US...
...SO HE STUCK IT WHERE A KID COULD REACH IT!
RIP
HN?
WHAT IS THIS?
MORE HARD KANJI...
LET ME SEE.

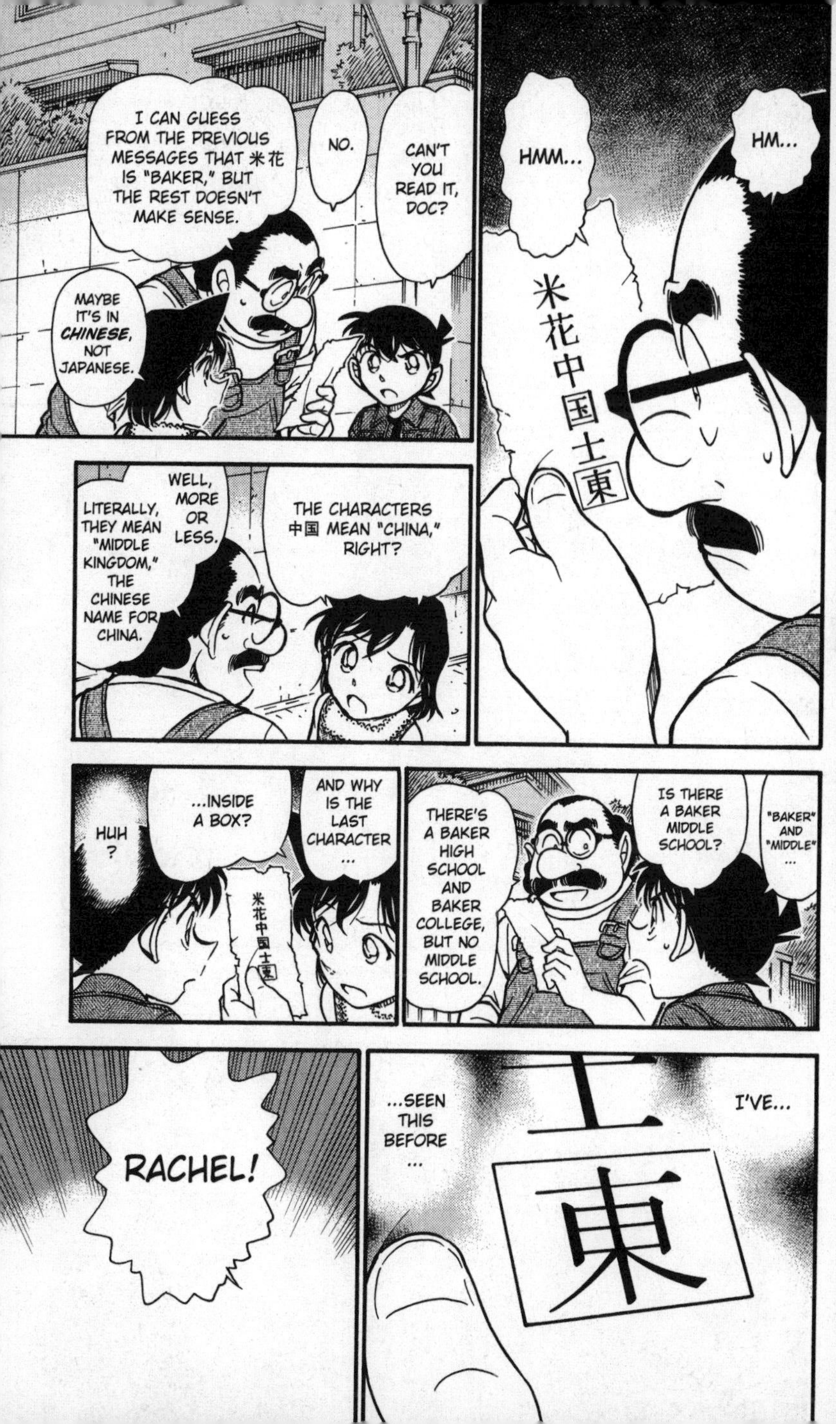
HM...
HMM...
米花中国士東
CAN'T YOU READ IT, DOC?
NO.
I CAN GUESS FROM THE PREVIOUS MESSAGES THAT 米花 IS "BAKER," BUT THE REST DOESN'T MAKE SENSE.
MAYBE IT'S IN ***CHINESE***, NOT JAPANESE.
THE CHARACTERS 中国 MEAN "CHINA," RIGHT?
WELL, MORE OR LESS.
LITERALLY, THEY MEAN "MIDDLE KINGDOM," THE CHINESE NAME FOR CHINA.
"BAKER" AND "MIDDLE"...
IS THERE A BAKER MIDDLE SCHOOL?
THERE'S A BAKER HIGH SCHOOL AND BAKER COLLEGE, BUT NO MIDDLE SCHOOL.
AND WHY IS THE LAST CHARACTER...
...INSIDE A BOX?
HUH?
米花中国士東
I'VE...
...SEEN THIS BEFORE...
士東
RACHEL!

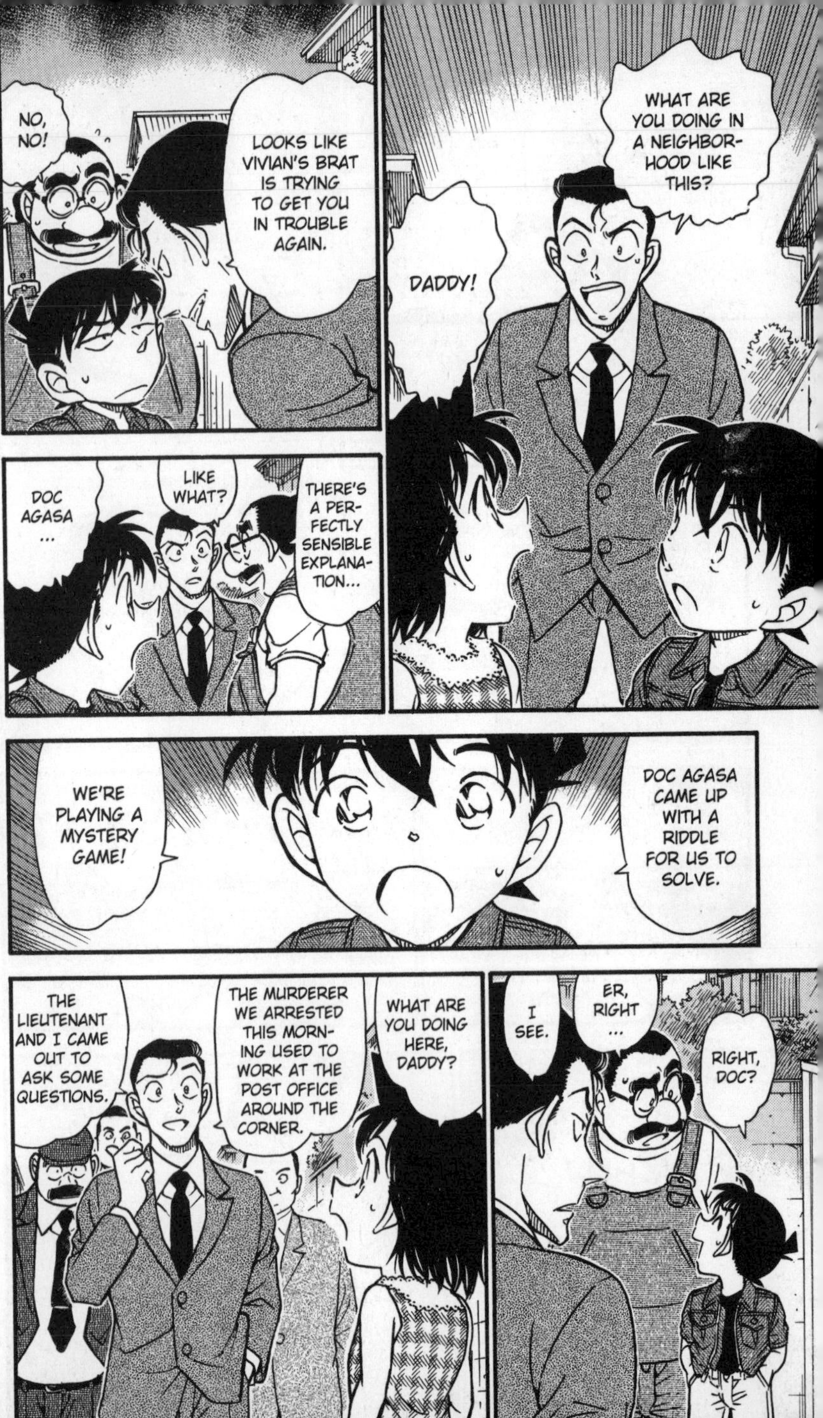

WHAT ARE YOU DOING IN A NEIGHBOR-HOOD LIKE THIS?
DADDY!
LOOKS LIKE VIVIAN'S BRAT IS TRYING TO GET YOU IN TROUBLE AGAIN.
NO, NO!
THERE'S A PER-FECTLY SENSIBLE EXPLANA-TION...
LIKE WHAT?
DOC AGASA ...
DOC AGASA CAME UP WITH A RIDDLE FOR US TO SOLVE.
WE'RE PLAYING A MYSTERY GAME!
RIGHT, DOC?
ER, RIGHT ...
I SEE.
WHAT ARE YOU DOING HERE, DADDY?
THE MURDERER WE ARRESTED THIS MORN-ING USED TO WORK AT THE POST OFFICE AROUND THE CORNER.
THE LIEUTENANT AND I CAME OUT TO ASK SOME QUESTIONS.

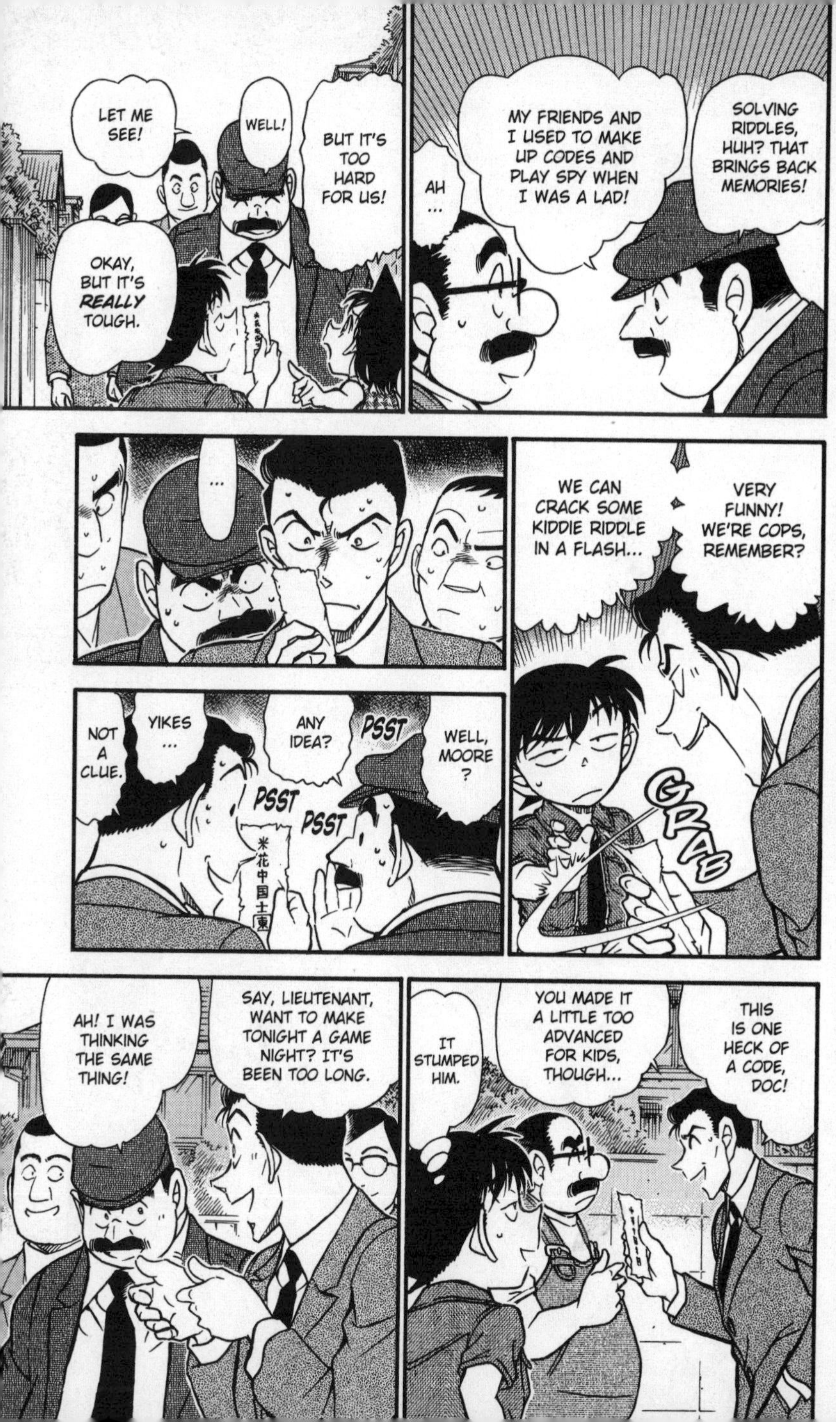
SOLVING RIDDLES, HUH? THAT BRINGS BACK MEMORIES!
MY FRIENDS AND I USED TO MAKE UP CODES AND PLAY SPY WHEN I WAS A LAD!
AH ...
BUT IT'S TOO HARD FOR US!
WELL!
LET ME SEE!
OKAY, BUT IT'S *REALLY* TOUGH.
VERY FUNNY! WE'RE COPS, REMEMBER?
WE CAN CRACK SOME KIDDIE RIDDLE IN A FLASH...
GRAB
...
WELL, MOORE ?
PSST
ANY IDEA?
PSST
PSST
米花中国土東
YIKES ...
NOT A CLUE.
THIS IS ONE HECK OF A CODE, DOC!
YOU MADE IT A LITTLE TOO ADVANCED FOR KIDS, THOUGH...
IT STUMPED HIM.
SAY, LIEUTENANT, WANT TO MAKE TONIGHT A GAME NIGHT? IT'S BEEN TOO LONG.
AH! I WAS THINKING THE SAME THING!

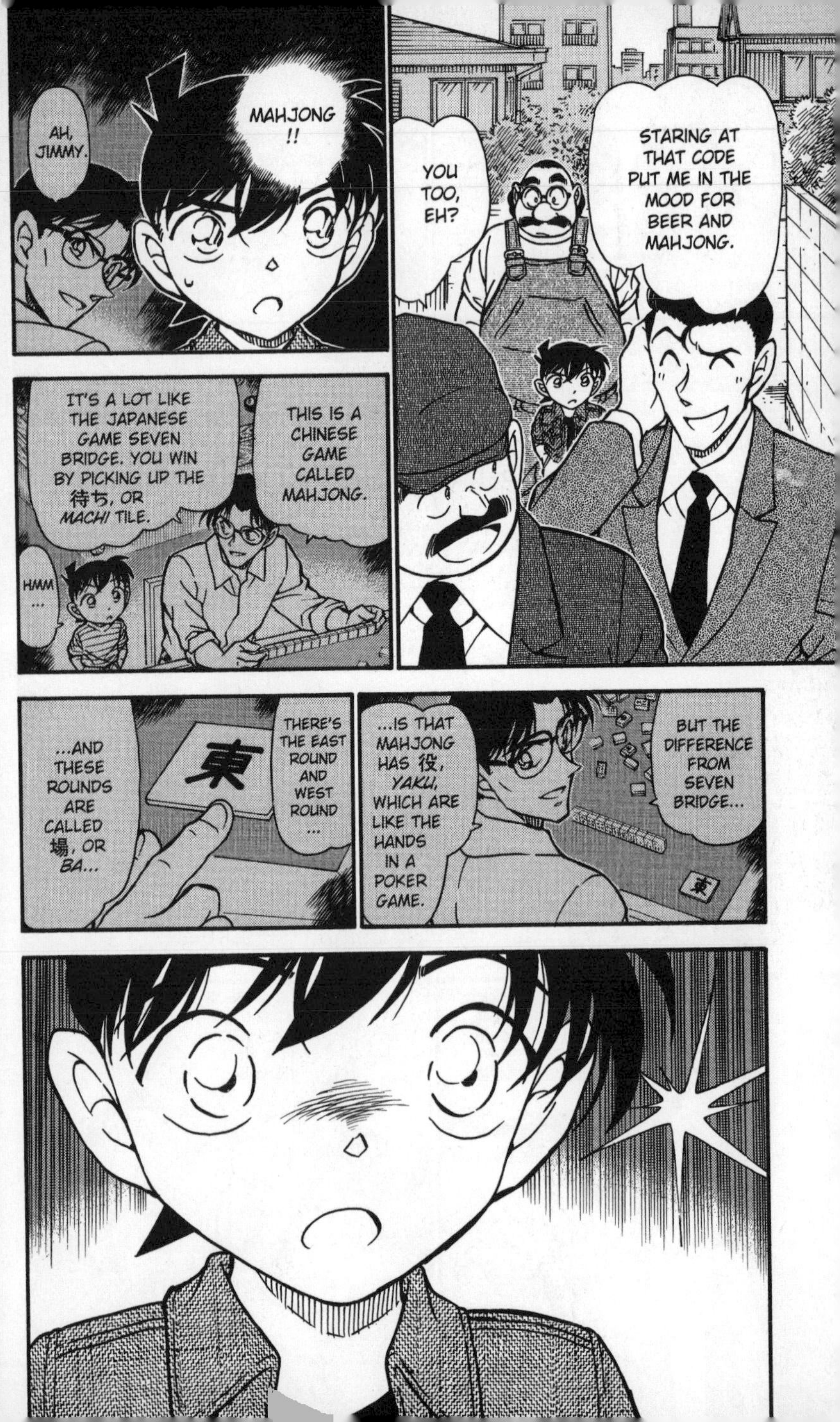
STARING AT THAT CODE PUT ME IN THE MOOD FOR BEER AND MAHJONG.
YOU TOO, EH?
MAHJONG !!
AH, JIMMY.
THIS IS A CHINESE GAME CALLED MAHJONG.
IT'S A LOT LIKE THE JAPANESE GAME SEVEN BRIDGE. YOU WIN BY PICKING UP THE 待ち, OR *MACHI* TILE.
HMM ...
BUT THE DIFFERENCE FROM SEVEN BRIDGE...
...IS THAT MAHJONG HAS 役, *YAKU*, WHICH ARE LIKE THE HANDS IN A POKER GAME.
THERE'S THE EAST ROUND AND WEST ROUND ...
...AND THESE ROUNDS ARE CALLED 場, OR *BA*...

FILE 9: SUNSET

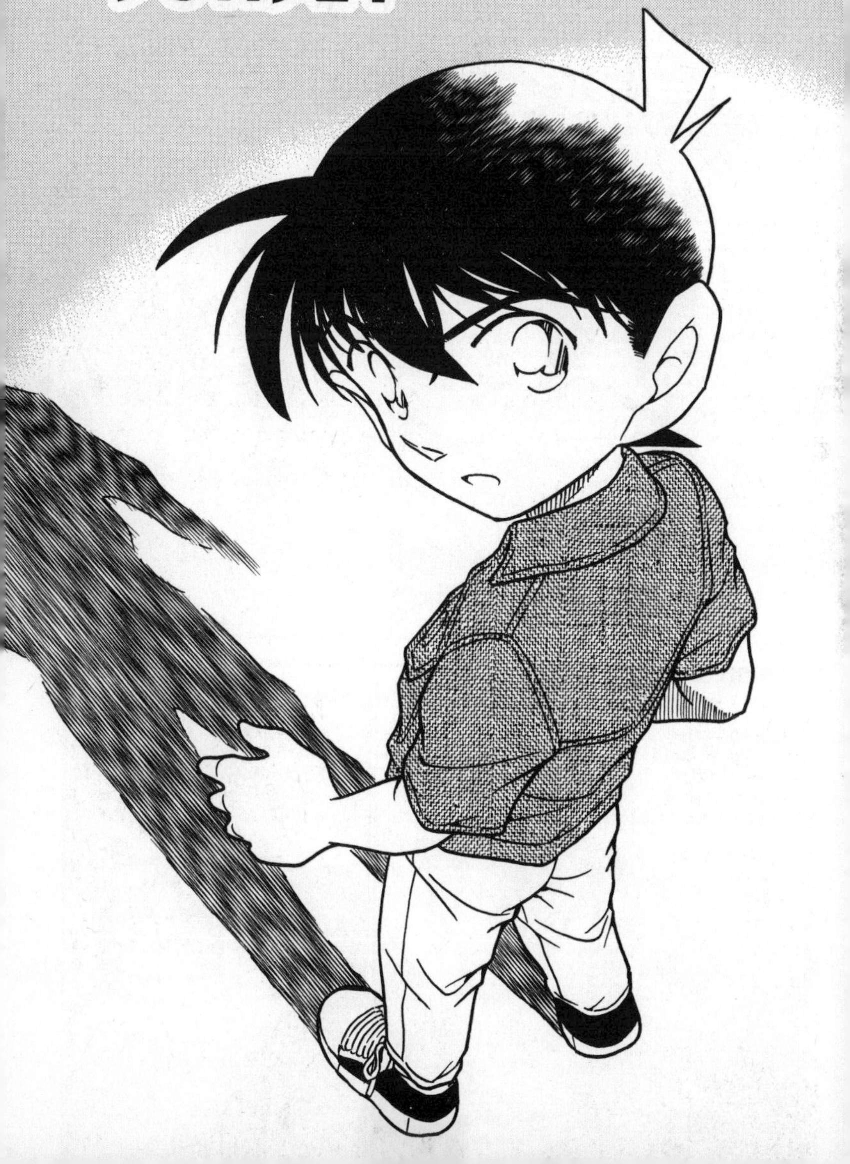

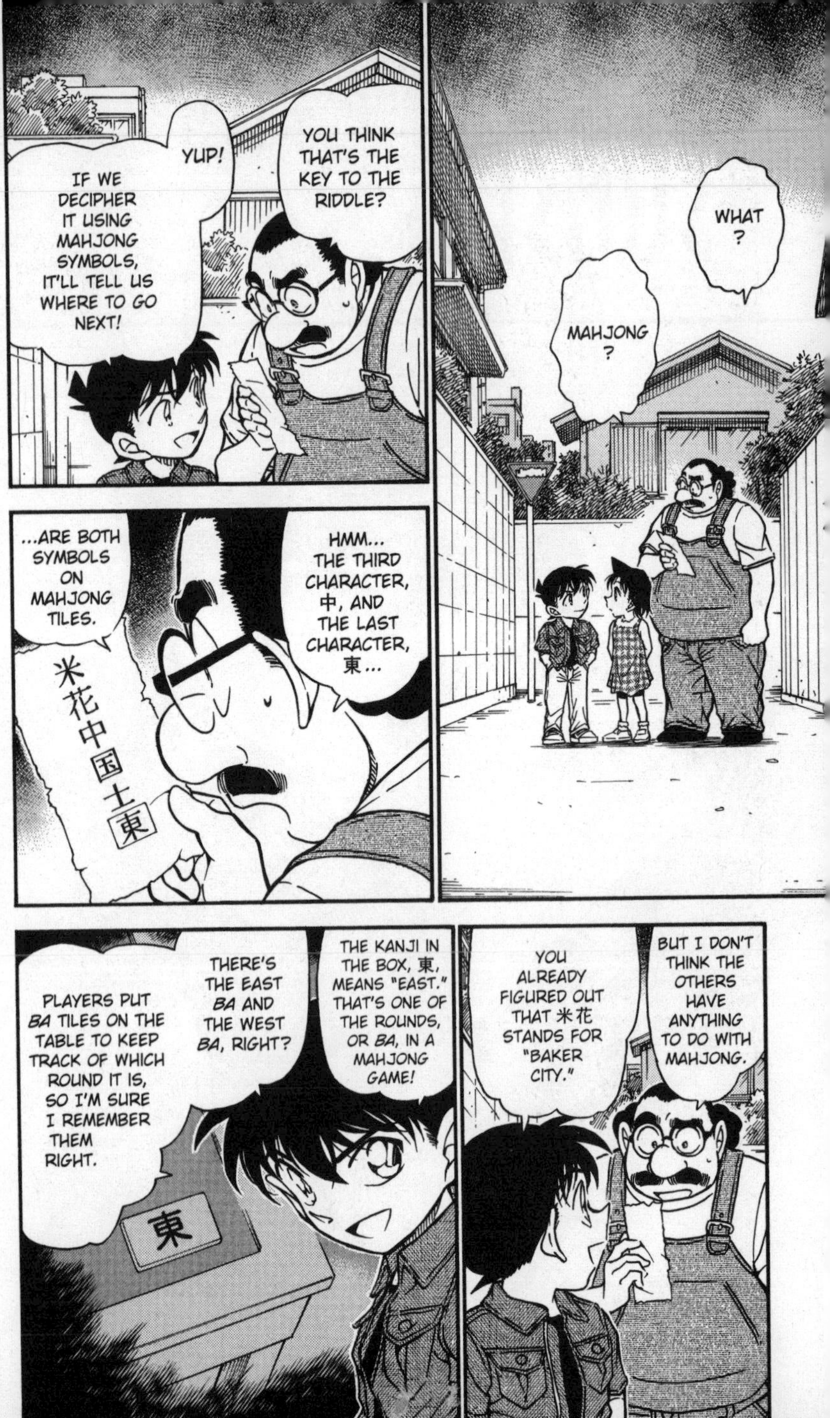
WHAT?
MAHJONG?
YOU THINK THAT'S THE KEY TO THE RIDDLE?
YUP!
IF WE DECIPHER IT USING MAHJONG SYMBOLS, IT'LL TELL US WHERE TO GO NEXT!
HMM... THE THIRD CHARACTER, 中, AND THE LAST CHARACTER, 東...
...ARE BOTH SYMBOLS ON MAHJONG TILES.
米花中国土東
BUT I DON'T THINK THE OTHERS HAVE ANYTHING TO DO WITH MAHJONG.
YOU ALREADY FIGURED OUT THAT 米花 STANDS FOR "BAKER CITY."
THE KANJI IN THE BOX, 東, MEANS "EAST." THAT'S ONE OF THE ROUNDS, OR *BA*, IN A MAHJONG GAME!
THERE'S THE EAST *BA* AND THE WEST *BA*, RIGHT?
PLAYERS PUT *BA* TILES ON THE TABLE TO KEEP TRACK OF WHICH ROUND IT IS, SO I'M SURE I REMEMBER THEM RIGHT.
東

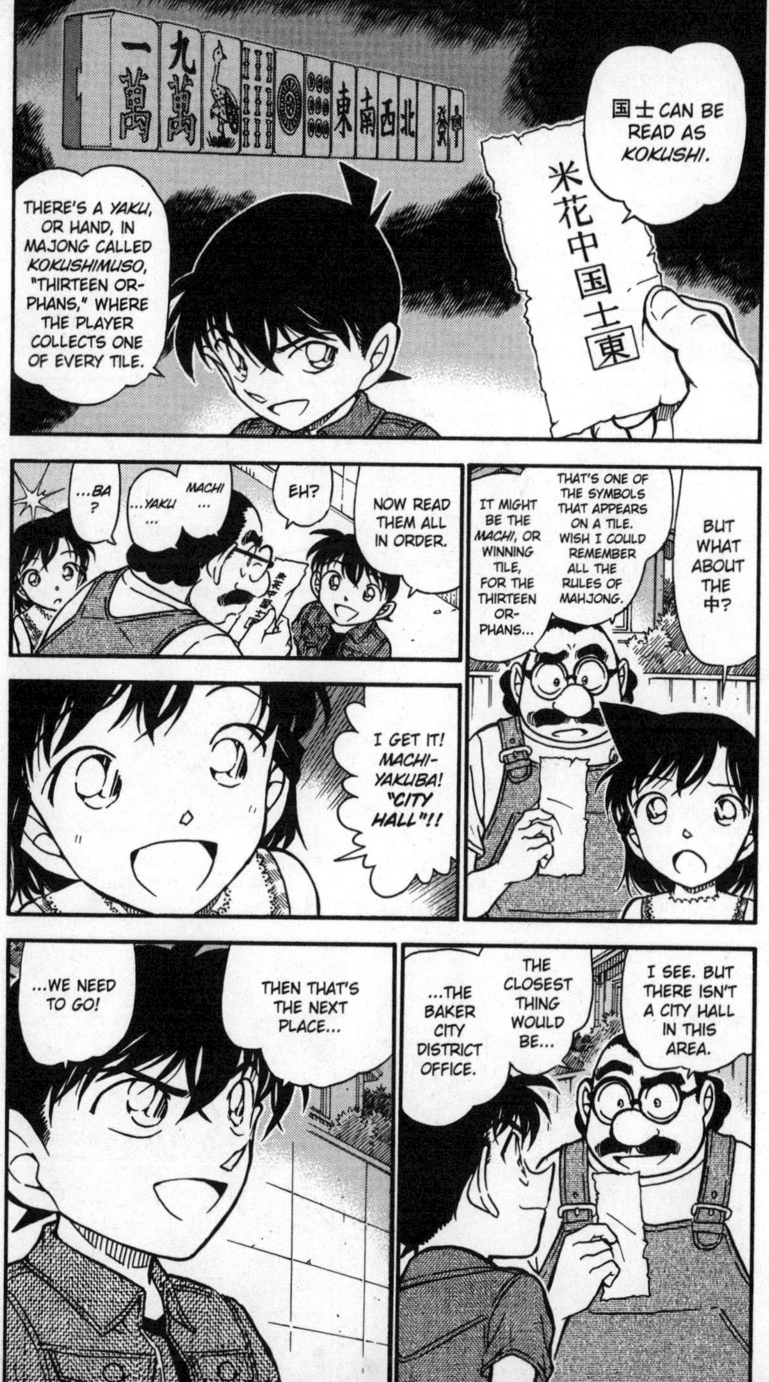

国士 CAN BE READ AS *KOKUSHI*.
米花中国士東
THERE'S A *YAKU*, OR HAND, IN MAJONG CALLED *KOKUSHIMUSO*, "THIRTEEN ORPHANS," WHERE THE PLAYER COLLECTS ONE OF EVERY TILE.
BUT WHAT ABOUT THE 中?
THAT'S ONE OF THE SYMBOLS THAT APPEARS ON A TILE. WISH I COULD REMEMBER ALL THE RULES OF MAHJONG.
IT MIGHT BE THE *MACHI*, OR WINNING TILE, FOR THE THIRTEEN ORPHANS...
NOW READ THEM ALL IN ORDER.
EH?
MACHI ...
...*YAKU* ...
...*BA* ?
I GET IT! *MACHI-YAKUBA*! *"CITY HALL"*!!
I SEE. BUT THERE ISN'T A CITY HALL IN THIS AREA.
THE CLOSEST THING WOULD BE...
...THE BAKER CITY DISTRICT OFFICE.
THEN THAT'S THE NEXT PLACE...
...WE NEED TO GO!

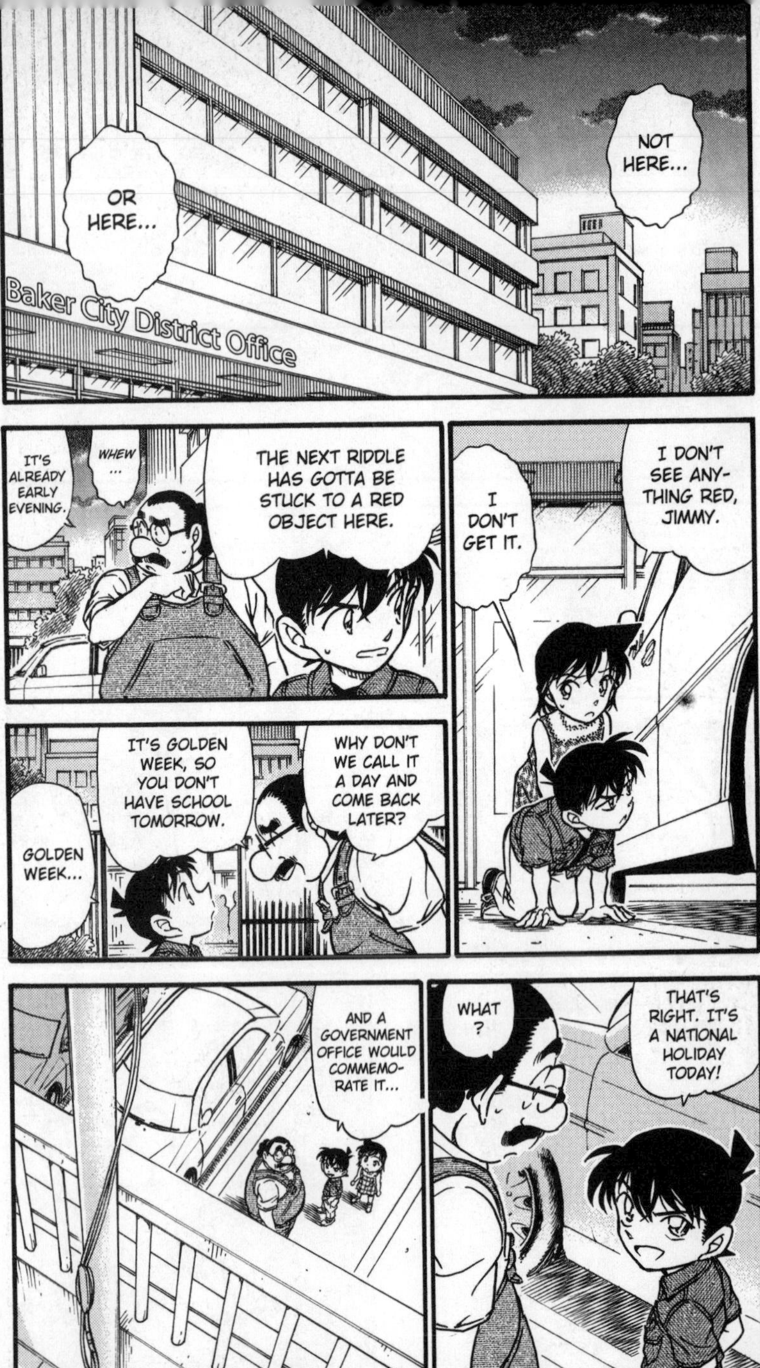
NOT HERE...
OR HERE...
Baker City District Office
I DON'T SEE ANY-THING RED, JIMMY.
I DON'T GET IT.
THE NEXT RIDDLE HAS GOTTA BE STUCK TO A RED OBJECT HERE.
WHEW ...
IT'S ALREADY EARLY EVENING.
WHY DON'T WE CALL IT A DAY AND COME BACK LATER?
IT'S GOLDEN WEEK, SO YOU DON'T HAVE SCHOOL TOMORROW.
GOLDEN WEEK...
THAT'S RIGHT. IT'S A NATIONAL HOLIDAY TODAY!
WHAT ?
AND A GOVERNMENT OFFICE WOULD COMMEMO-RATE IT...

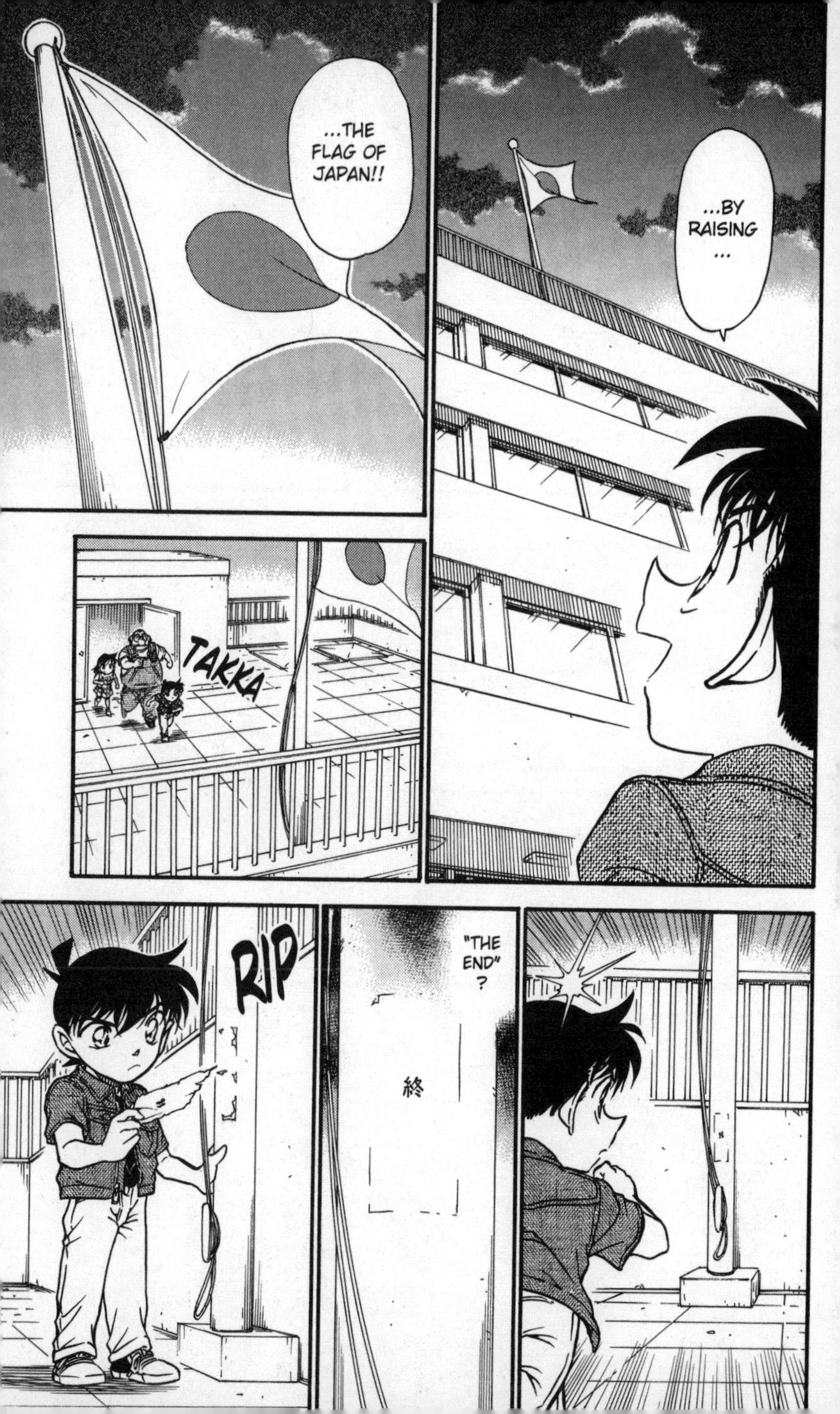
...BY RAISING ...
...THE FLAG OF JAPAN!!
TAKKA
"THE END"?
終
RIP

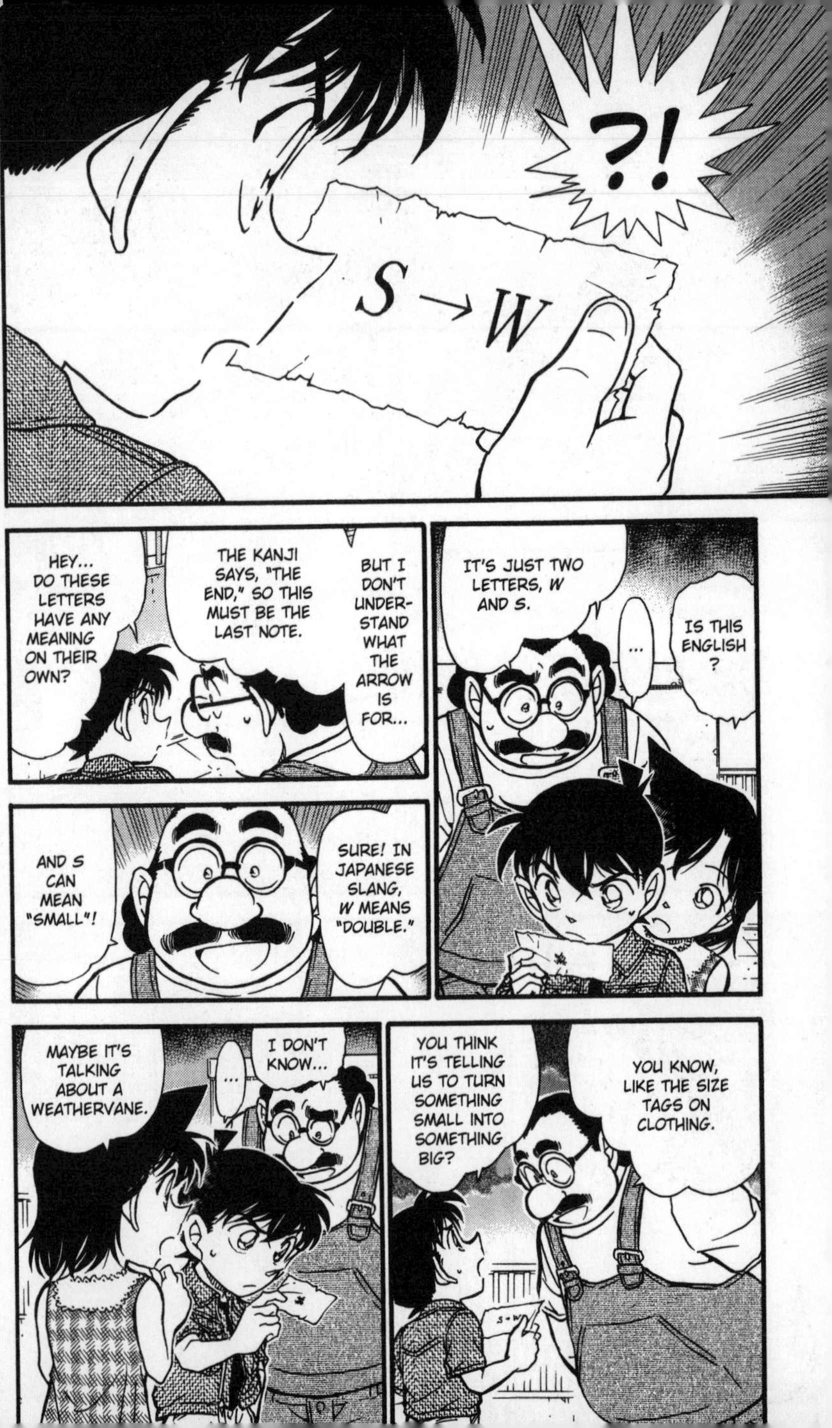

?!
S → W
IS THIS ENGLISH?
...
IT'S JUST TWO LETTERS, W AND S.
BUT I DON'T UNDERSTAND WHAT THE ARROW IS FOR...
THE KANJI SAYS, "THE END," SO THIS MUST BE THE LAST NOTE.
HEY... DO THESE LETTERS HAVE ANY MEANING ON THEIR OWN?
SURE! IN JAPANESE SLANG, W MEANS "DOUBLE."
AND S CAN MEAN "SMALL"!
YOU KNOW, LIKE THE SIZE TAGS ON CLOTHING.
YOU THINK IT'S TELLING US TO TURN SOMETHING SMALL INTO SOMETHING BIG?
I DON'T KNOW...
...
MAYBE IT'S TALKING ABOUT A WEATHERVANE.

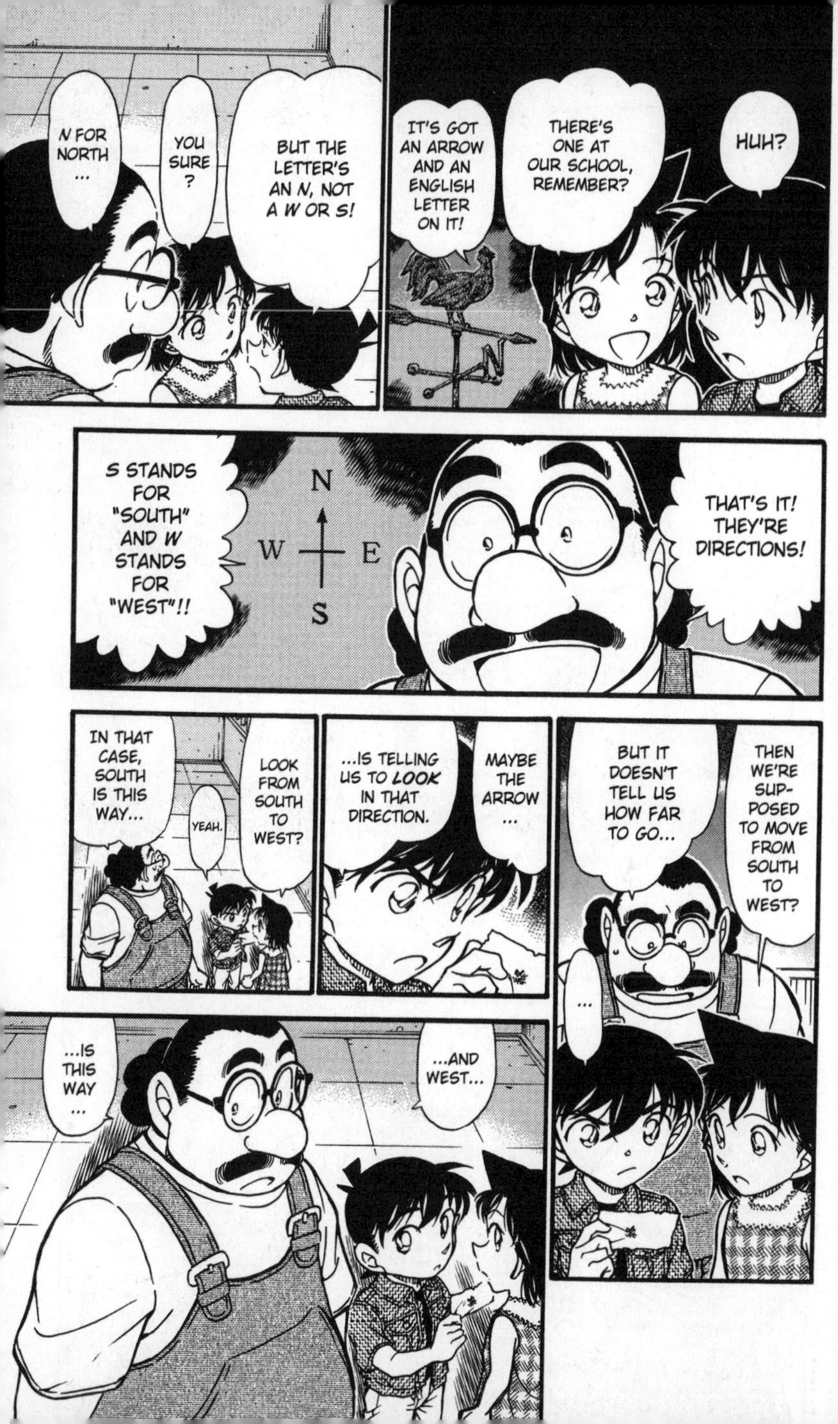
HUH?
THERE'S ONE AT OUR SCHOOL, REMEMBER?
IT'S GOT AN ARROW AND AN ENGLISH LETTER ON IT!
N
BUT THE LETTER'S AN *N*, NOT A *W* OR *S*!
YOU SURE?
N FOR NORTH...
THAT'S IT! THEY'RE DIRECTIONS!
N
W
E
S
S STANDS FOR "SOUTH" AND *W* STANDS FOR "WEST"!!
THEN WE'RE SUP-POSED TO MOVE FROM SOUTH TO WEST?
BUT IT DOESN'T TELL US HOW FAR TO GO...
...
MAYBE THE ARROW...
...IS TELLING US TO ***LOOK*** IN THAT DIRECTION.
LOOK FROM SOUTH TO WEST?
YEAH.
IN THAT CASE, SOUTH IS THIS WAY...
...AND WEST...
...IS THIS WAY...

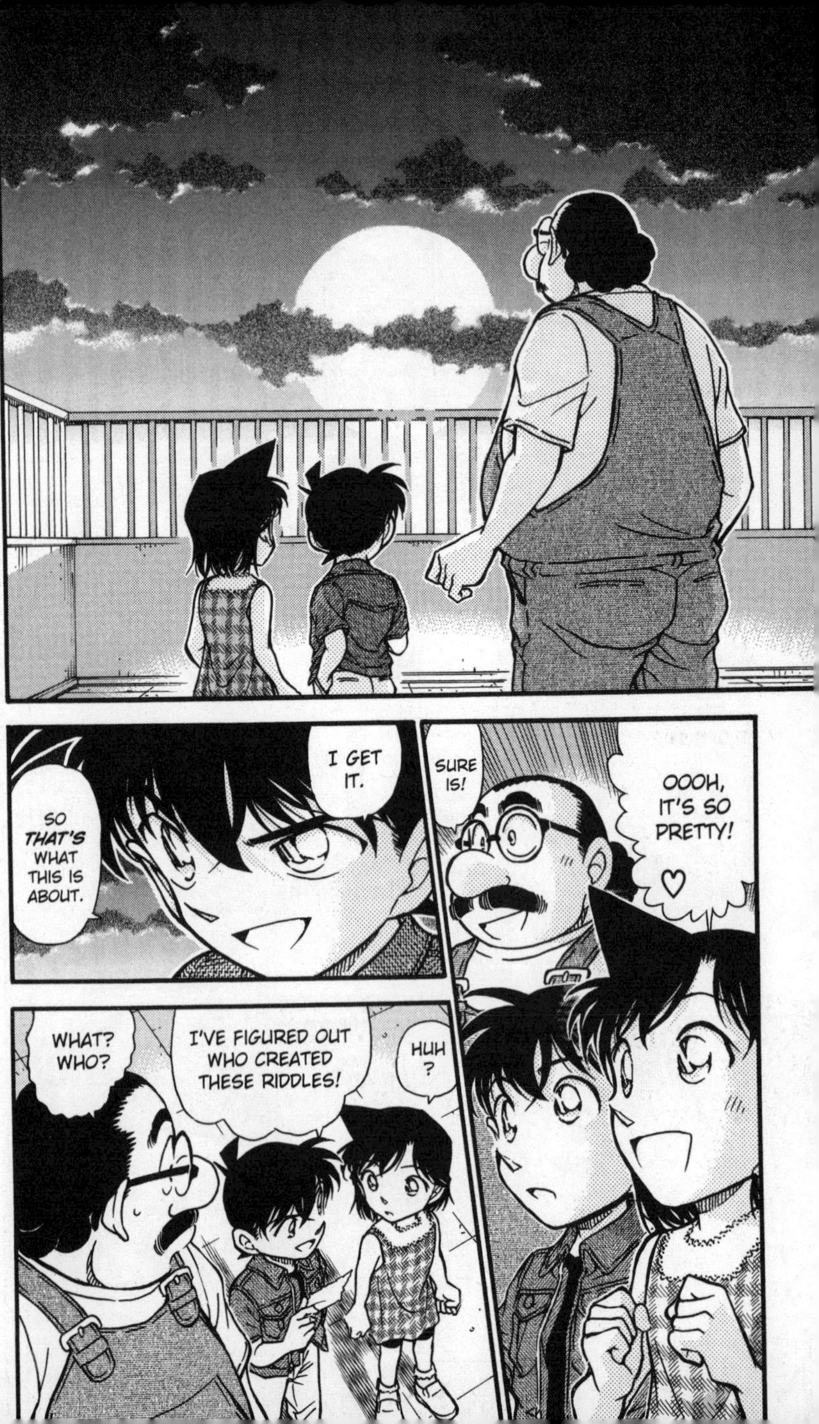
OOOH, IT'S SO PRETTY! ♥
SURE IS!
I GET IT.
SO *THAT'S* WHAT THIS IS ABOUT.
HUH ?
I'VE FIGURED OUT WHO CREATED THESE RIDDLES!
WHAT? WHO?

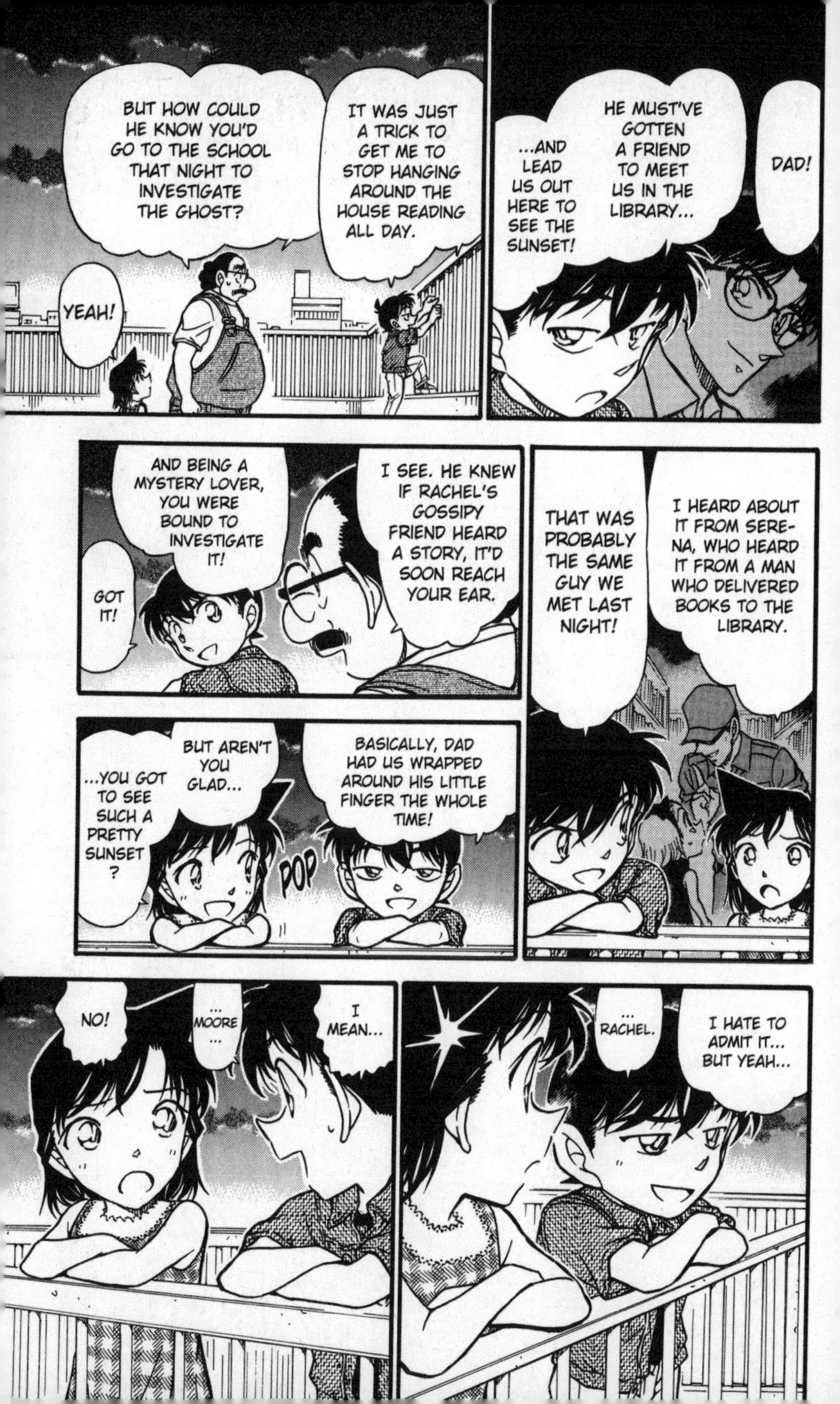
DAD!
HE MUST'VE GOTTEN A FRIEND TO MEET US IN THE LIBRARY...
...AND LEAD US OUT HERE TO SEE THE SUNSET!
IT WAS JUST A TRICK TO GET ME TO STOP HANGING AROUND THE HOUSE READING ALL DAY.
BUT HOW COULD HE KNOW YOU'D GO TO THE SCHOOL THAT NIGHT TO INVESTIGATE THE GHOST?
YEAH!
I HEARD ABOUT IT FROM SERE-NA, WHO HEARD IT FROM A MAN WHO DELIVERED BOOKS TO THE LIBRARY.
THAT WAS PROBABLY THE SAME GUY WE MET LAST NIGHT!
I SEE. HE KNEW IF RACHEL'S GOSSIPY FRIEND HEARD A STORY, IT'D SOON REACH YOUR EAR.
AND BEING A MYSTERY LOVER, YOU WERE BOUND TO INVESTIGATE IT!
GOT IT!
BASICALLY, DAD HAD US WRAPPED AROUND HIS LITTLE FINGER THE WHOLE TIME!
POP
BUT AREN'T YOU GLAD...
...YOU GOT TO SEE SUCH A PRETTY SUNSET?
I HATE TO ADMIT IT... BUT YEAH...
...RACHEL.
I MEAN...
...MOORE...
NO!

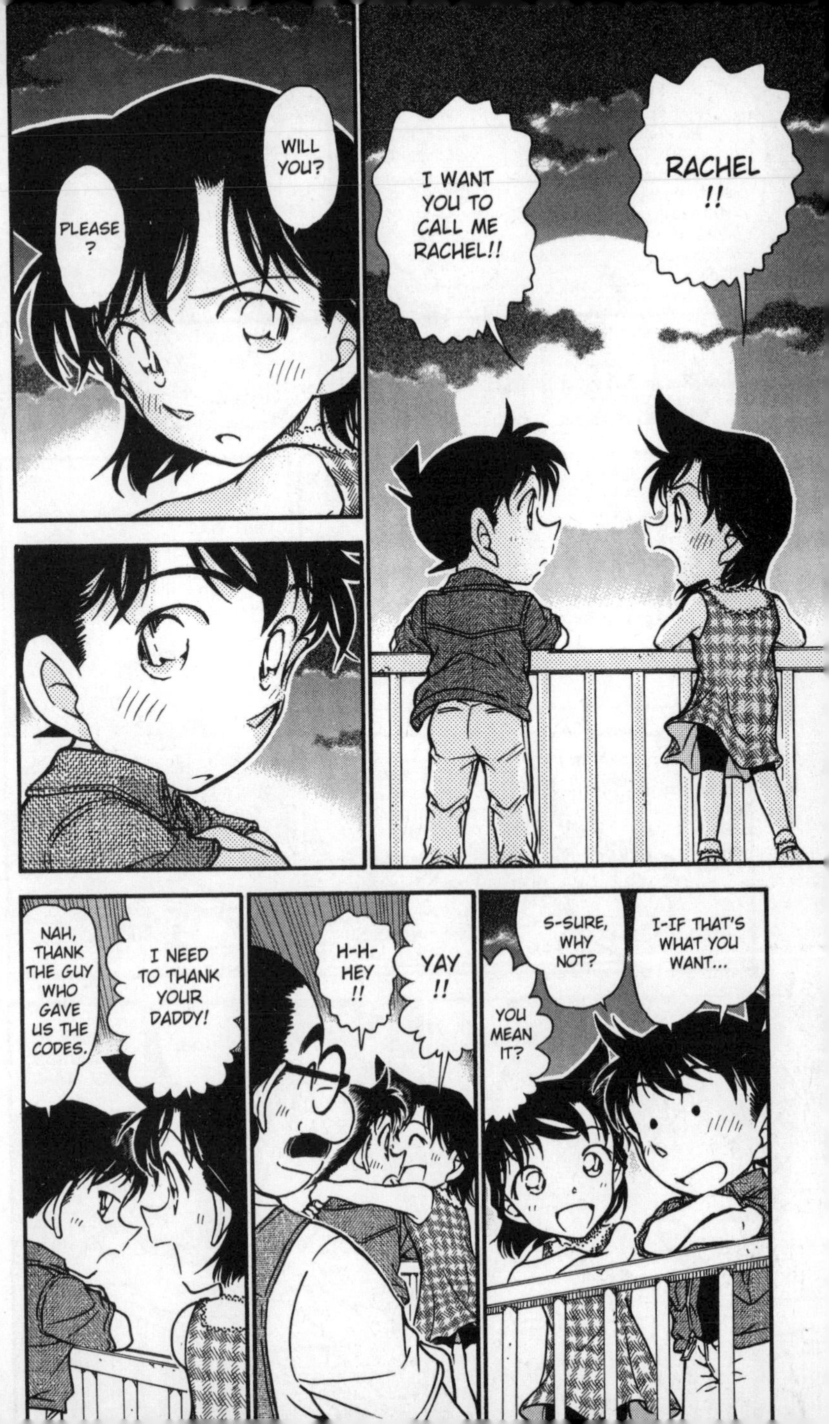
RACHEL !!
I WANT YOU TO CALL ME RACHEL!!
WILL YOU?
PLEASE ?
I-IF THAT'S WHAT YOU WANT...
S-SURE, WHY NOT?
YOU MEAN IT?
YAY !!
H-H-HEY !!
I NEED TO THANK YOUR DADDY!
NAH, THANK THE GUY WHO GAVE US THE CODES.

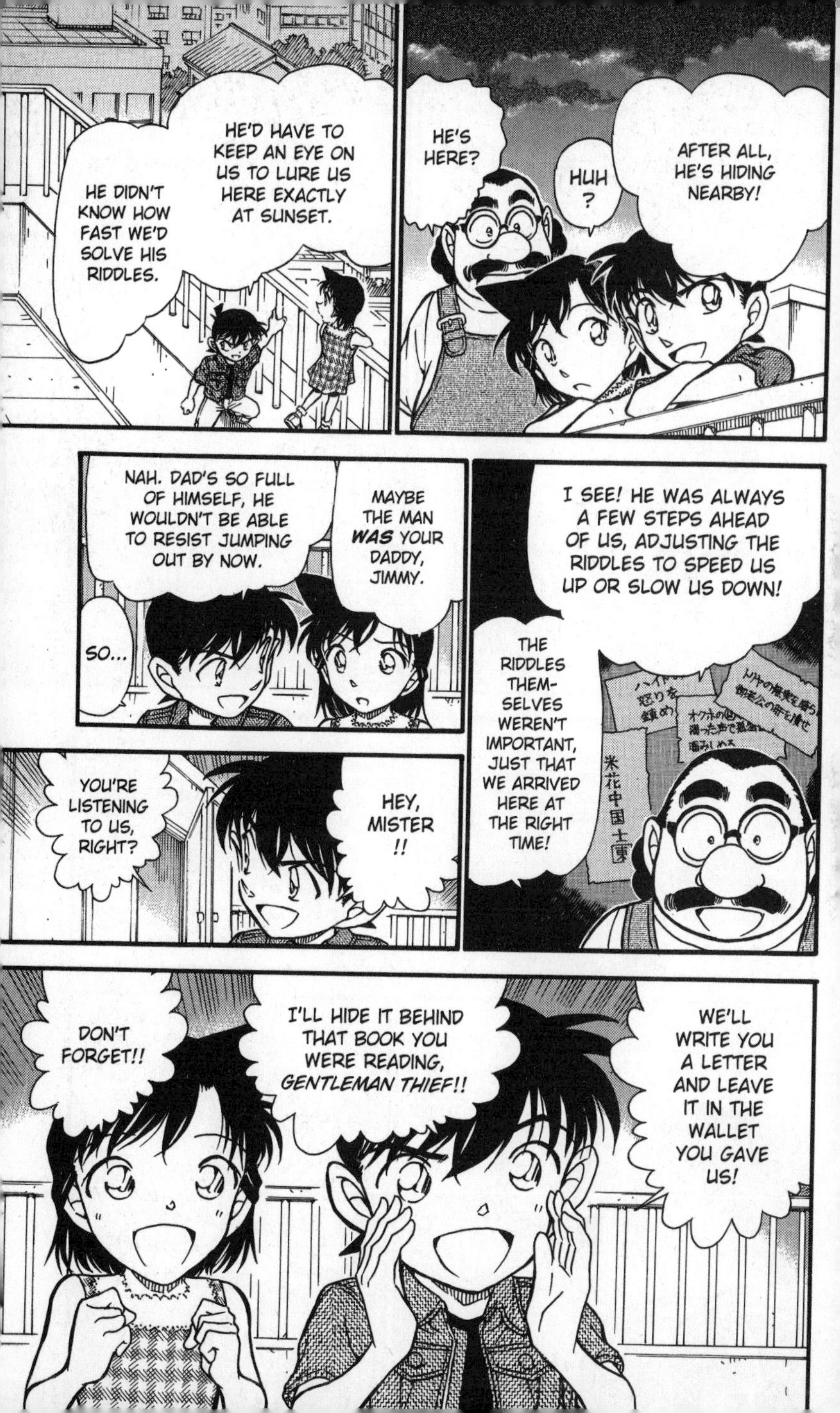
AFTER ALL, HE'S HIDING NEARBY!
HUH?
HE'S HERE?
HE'D HAVE TO KEEP AN EYE ON US TO LURE US HERE EXACTLY AT SUNSET.
HE DIDN'T KNOW HOW FAST WE'D SOLVE HIS RIDDLES.
I SEE! HE WAS ALWAYS A FEW STEPS AHEAD OF US, ADJUSTING THE RIDDLES TO SPEED US UP OR SLOW US DOWN!
THE RIDDLES THEM-SELVES WEREN'T IMPORTANT, JUST THAT WE ARRIVED HERE AT THE RIGHT TIME!
MAYBE THE MAN ***WAS*** YOUR DADDY, JIMMY.
NAH. DAD'S SO FULL OF HIMSELF, HE WOULDN'T BE ABLE TO RESIST JUMPING OUT BY NOW.
SO...
HEY, MISTER!!
YOU'RE LISTENING TO US, RIGHT?
WE'LL WRITE YOU A LETTER AND LEAVE IT IN THE WALLET YOU GAVE US!
I'LL HIDE IT BEHIND THAT BOOK YOU WERE READING, *GENTLEMAN THIEF*!!
DON'T FORGET!!

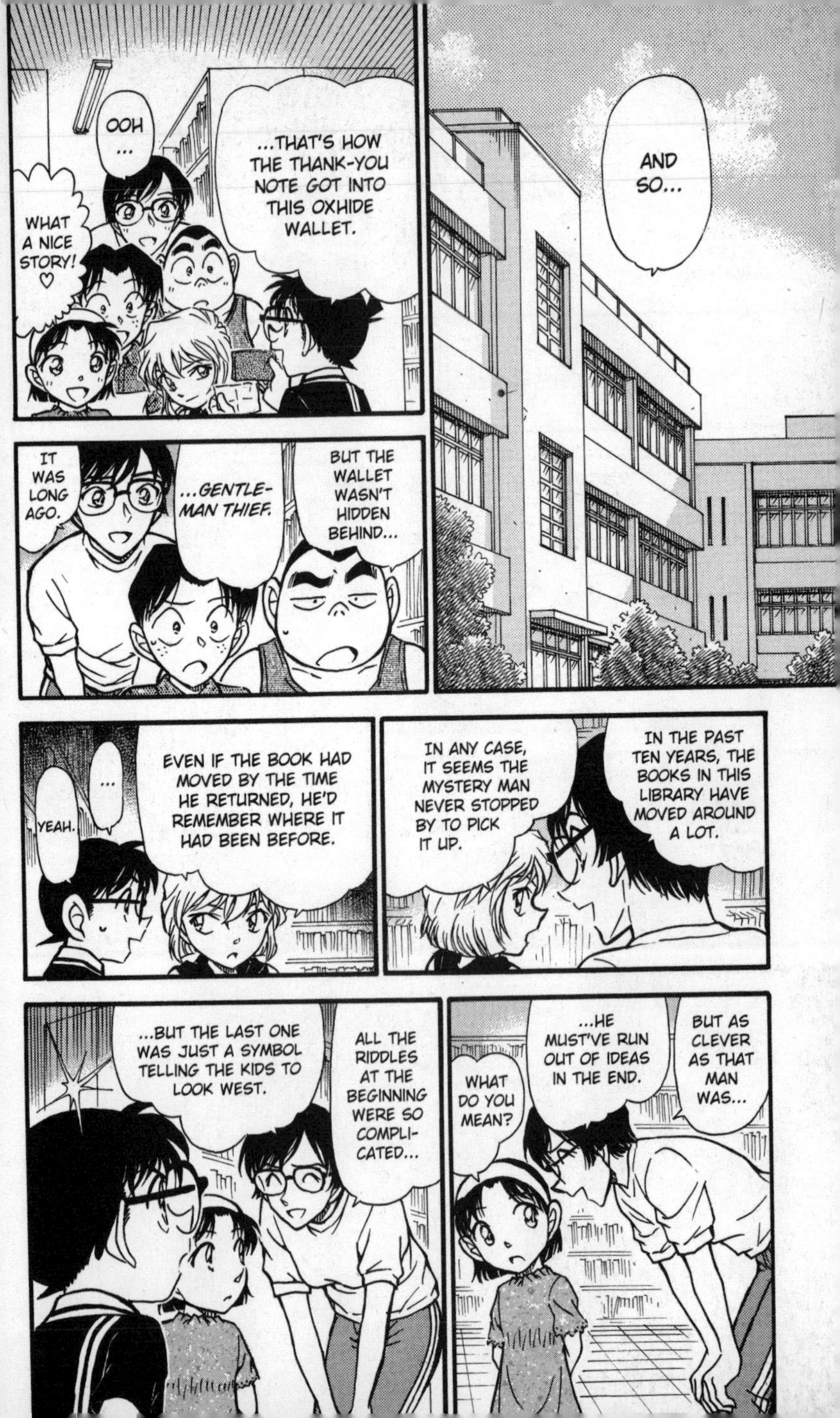
AND SO...
...THAT'S HOW THE THANK-YOU NOTE GOT INTO THIS OXHIDE WALLET.
OOH...
WHAT A NICE STORY! ♡
BUT THE WALLET WASN'T HIDDEN BEHIND...
...GENTLEMAN THIEF.
IT WAS LONG AGO.
IN THE PAST TEN YEARS, THE BOOKS IN THIS LIBRARY HAVE MOVED AROUND A LOT.
IN ANY CASE, IT SEEMS THE MYSTERY MAN NEVER STOPPED BY TO PICK IT UP.
EVEN IF THE BOOK HAD MOVED BY THE TIME HE RETURNED, HE'D REMEMBER WHERE IT HAD BEEN BEFORE.
...
YEAH.
BUT AS CLEVER AS THAT MAN WAS...
...HE MUST'VE RUN OUT OF IDEAS IN THE END.
WHAT DO YOU MEAN?
ALL THE RIDDLES AT THE BEGINNING WERE SO COMPLICATED...
...BUT THE LAST ONE WAS JUST A SYMBOL TELLING THE KIDS TO LOOK WEST.

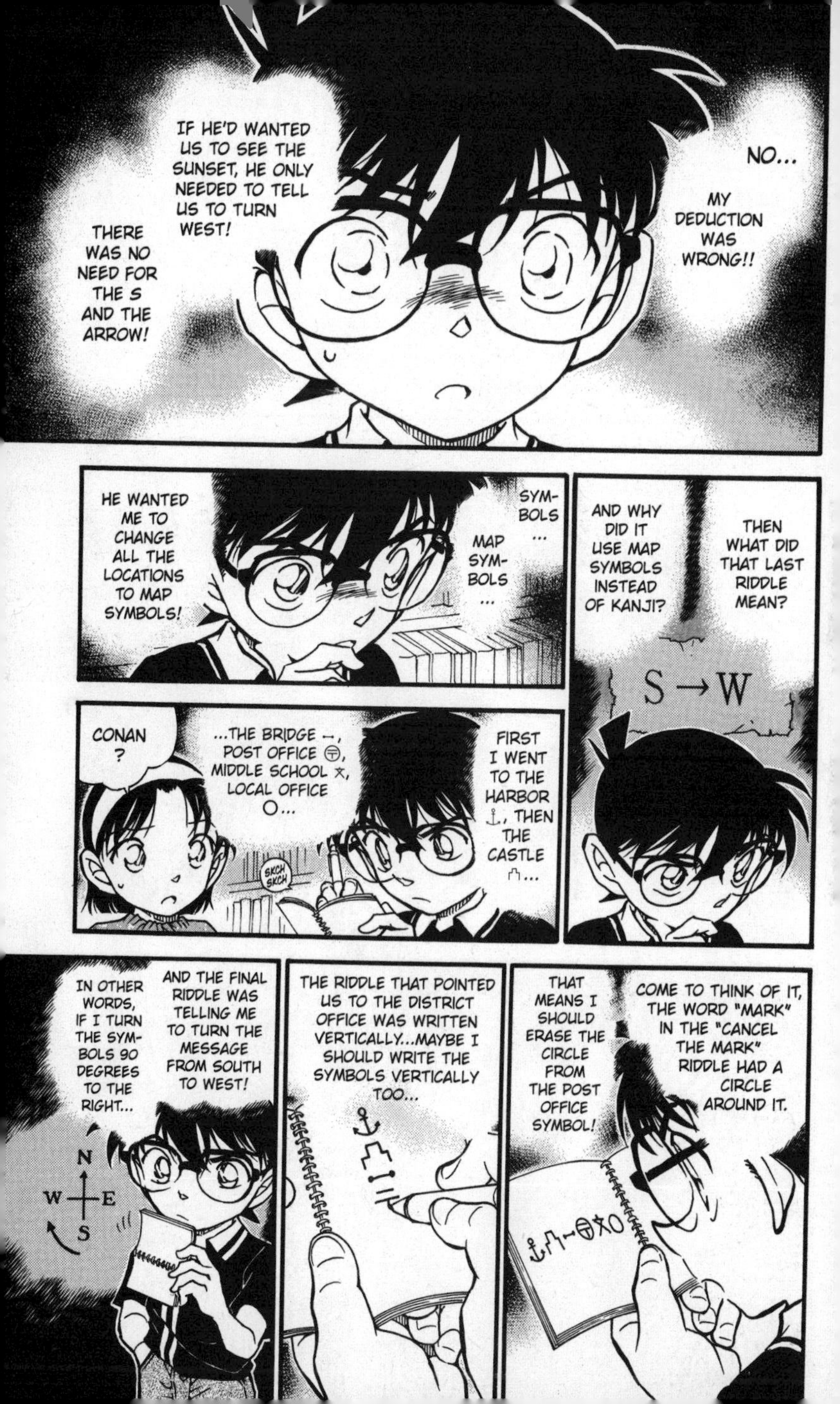
NO...
MY DEDUCTION WAS WRONG!!
IF HE'D WANTED US TO SEE THE SUNSET, HE ONLY NEEDED TO TELL US TO TURN WEST!
THERE WAS NO NEED FOR THE S AND THE ARROW!
THEN WHAT DID THAT LAST RIDDLE MEAN?
AND WHY DID IT USE MAP SYMBOLS INSTEAD OF KANJI?
S → W
SYM-BOLS ...
MAP SYM-BOLS ...
HE WANTED ME TO CHANGE ALL THE LOCATIONS TO MAP SYMBOLS!
FIRST I WENT TO THE HARBOR ⚓, THEN THE CASTLE ...
...THE BRIDGE, POST OFFICE 〒, MIDDLE SCHOOL 文, LOCAL OFFICE ○...
SKCH SKCH
CONAN ?
COME TO THINK OF IT, THE WORD "MARK" IN THE "CANCEL THE MARK" RIDDLE HAD A CIRCLE AROUND IT.
THAT MEANS I SHOULD ERASE THE CIRCLE FROM THE POST OFFICE SYMBOL!
THE RIDDLE THAT POINTED US TO THE DISTRICT OFFICE WAS WRITTEN VERTICALLY...MAYBE I SHOULD WRITE THE SYMBOLS VERTICALLY TOO...
AND THE FINAL RIDDLE WAS TELLING ME TO TURN THE MESSAGE FROM SOUTH TO WEST!
IN OTHER WORDS, IF I TURN THE SYM-BOLS 90 DEGREES TO THE RIGHT...
N
W
E
S

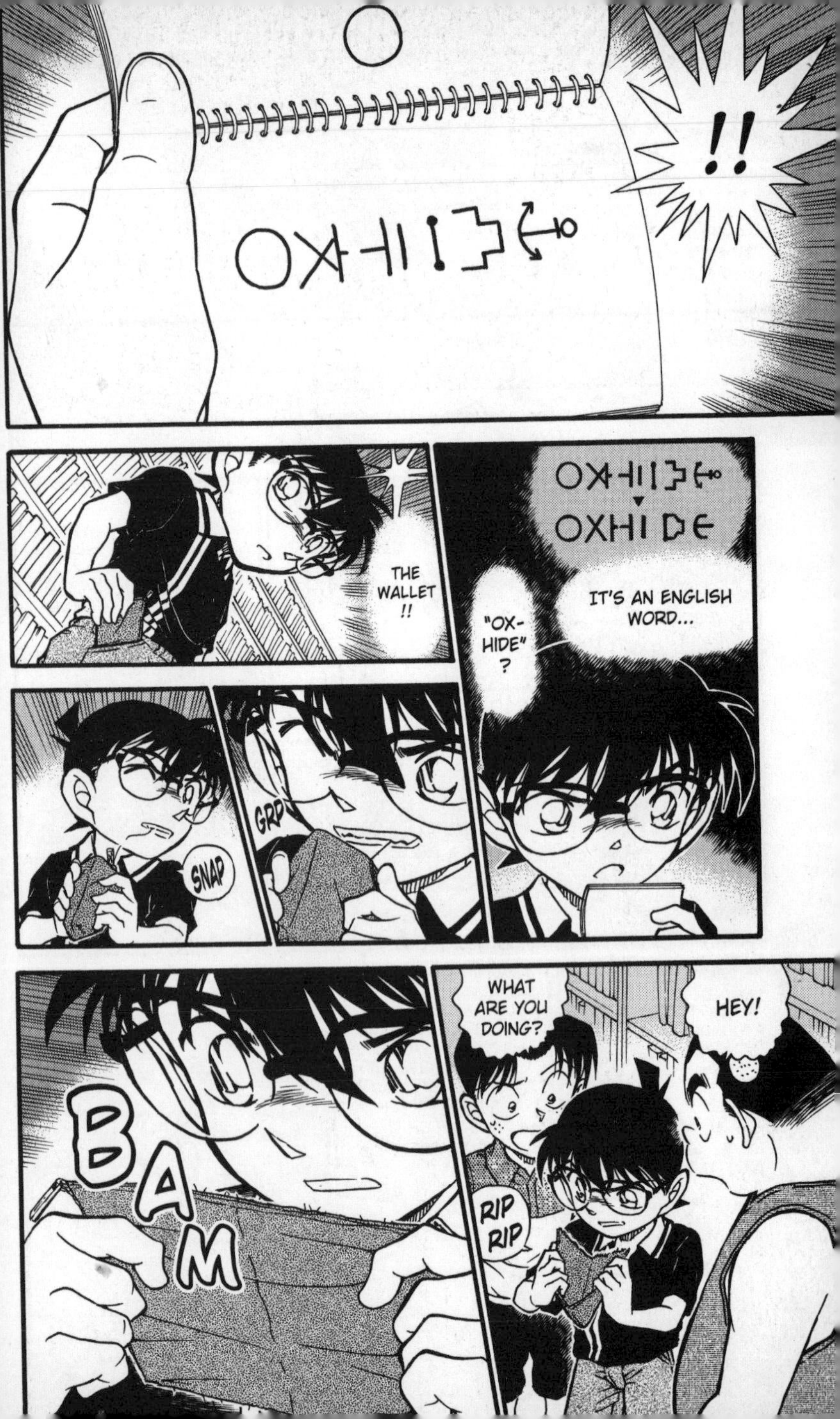
!!
OXHIDE
IT'S AN ENGLISH WORD...
"OX-HIDE"?
THE WALLET!!
GRP
SNAP
HEY!
WHAT ARE YOU DOING?
RIP RIP
BAM

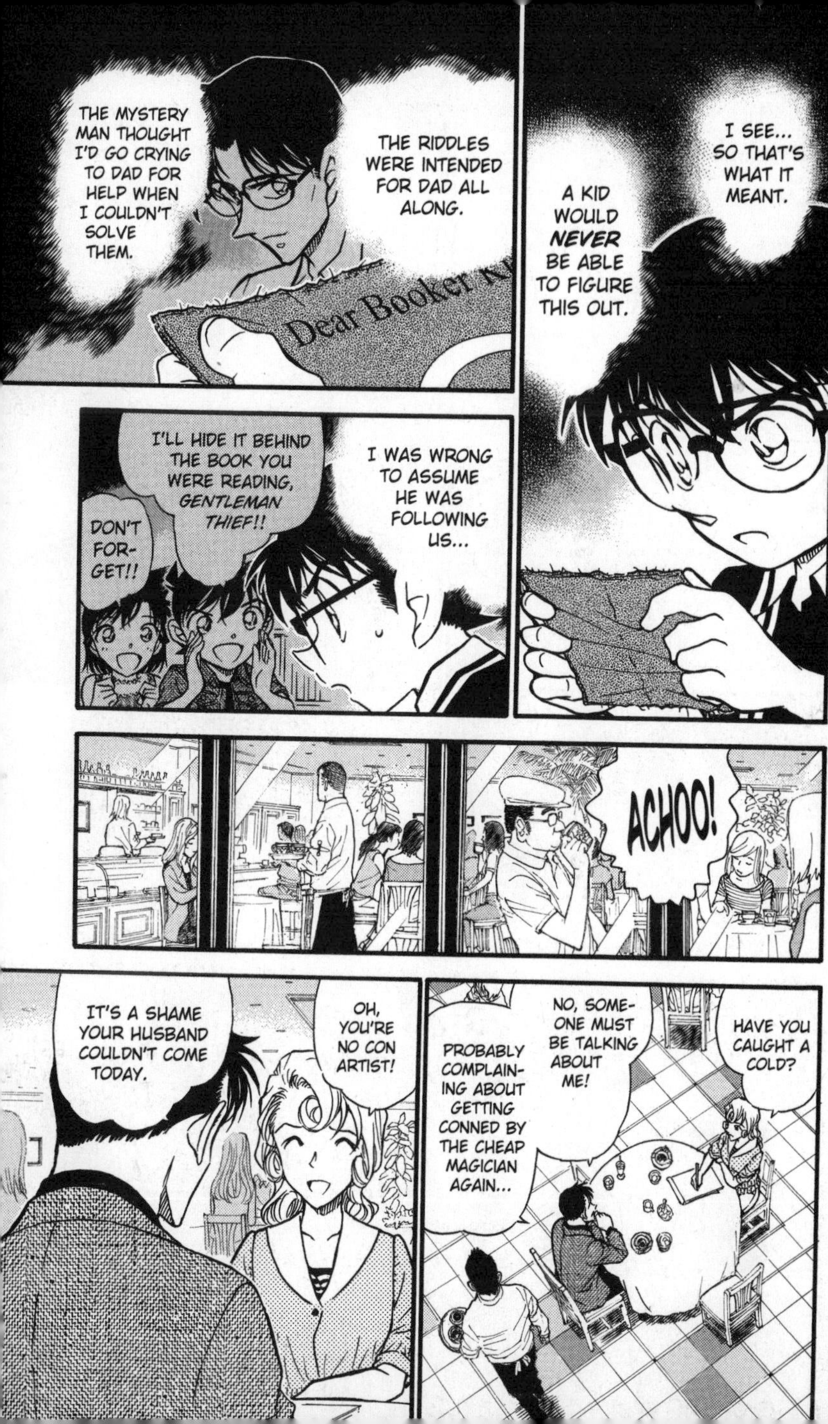
I SEE... SO THAT'S WHAT IT MEANT.
A KID WOULD **NEVER** BE ABLE TO FIGURE THIS OUT.
THE RIDDLES WERE INTENDED FOR DAD ALL ALONG.
THE MYSTERY MAN THOUGHT I'D GO CRYING TO DAD FOR HELP WHEN I COULDN'T SOLVE THEM.
I WAS WRONG TO ASSUME HE WAS FOLLOWING US...
I'LL HIDE IT BEHIND THE BOOK YOU WERE READING, *GENTLEMAN THIEF!!*
DON'T FOR-GET!!
ACHOO!
HAVE YOU CAUGHT A COLD?
NO, SOME-ONE MUST BE TALKING ABOUT ME!
PROBABLY COMPLAIN-ING ABOUT GETTING CONNED BY THE CHEAP MAGICIAN AGAIN...
OH, YOU'RE NO CON ARTIST!
IT'S A SHAME YOUR HUSBAND COULDN'T COME TODAY.

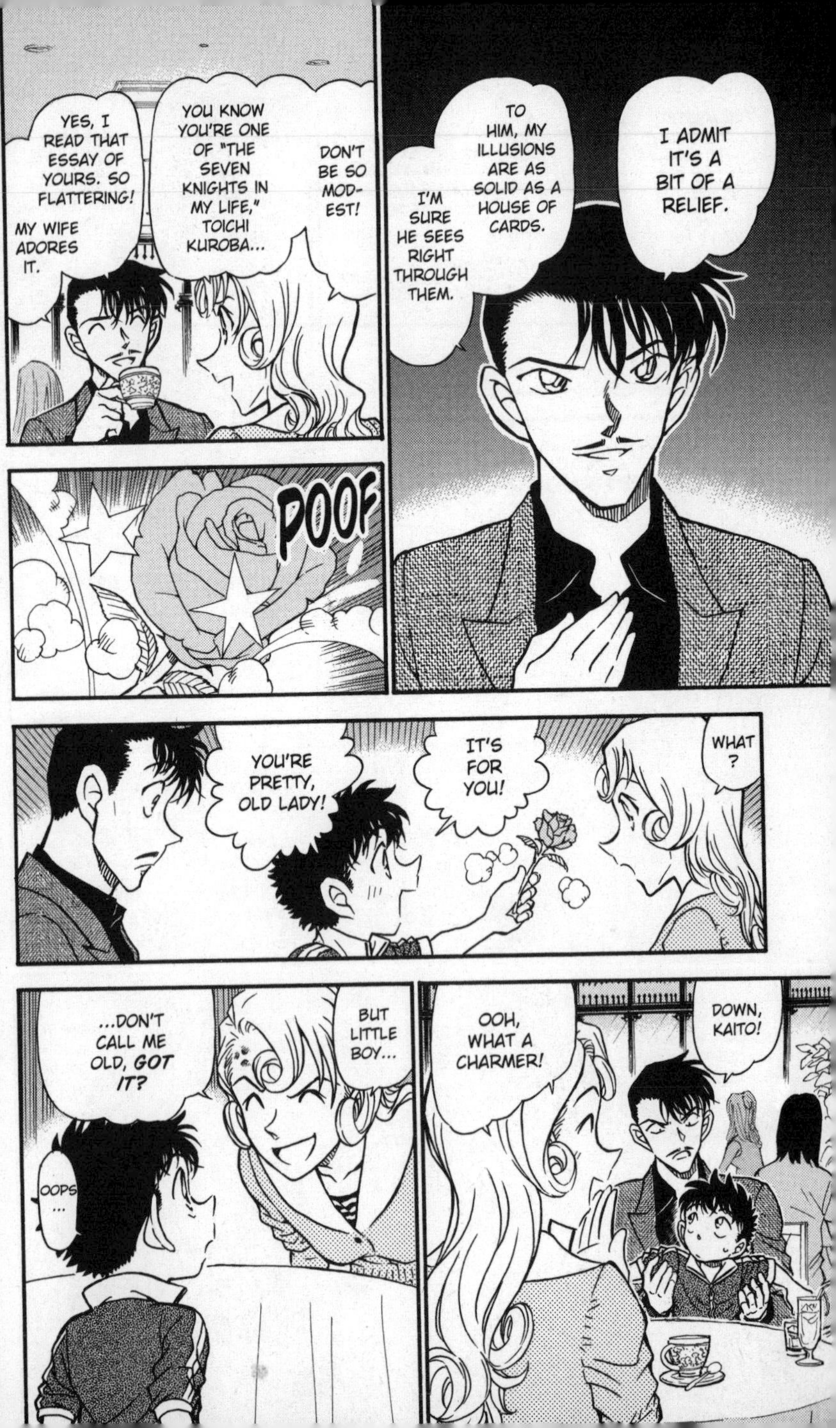
I ADMIT IT'S A BIT OF A RELIEF.
TO HIM, MY ILLUSIONS ARE AS SOLID AS A HOUSE OF CARDS.
I'M SURE HE SEES RIGHT THROUGH THEM.
DON'T BE SO MOD-EST!
YOU KNOW YOU'RE ONE OF "THE SEVEN KNIGHTS IN MY LIFE," TOICHI KUROBA...
YES, I READ THAT ESSAY OF YOURS. SO FLATTERING!
MY WIFE ADORES IT.
POOF
WHAT?
IT'S FOR YOU!
YOU'RE PRETTY, OLD LADY!
DOWN, KAITO!
OOH, WHAT A CHARMER!
BUT LITTLE BOY...
...DON'T CALL ME OLD, ***GOT IT?***
OOPS...

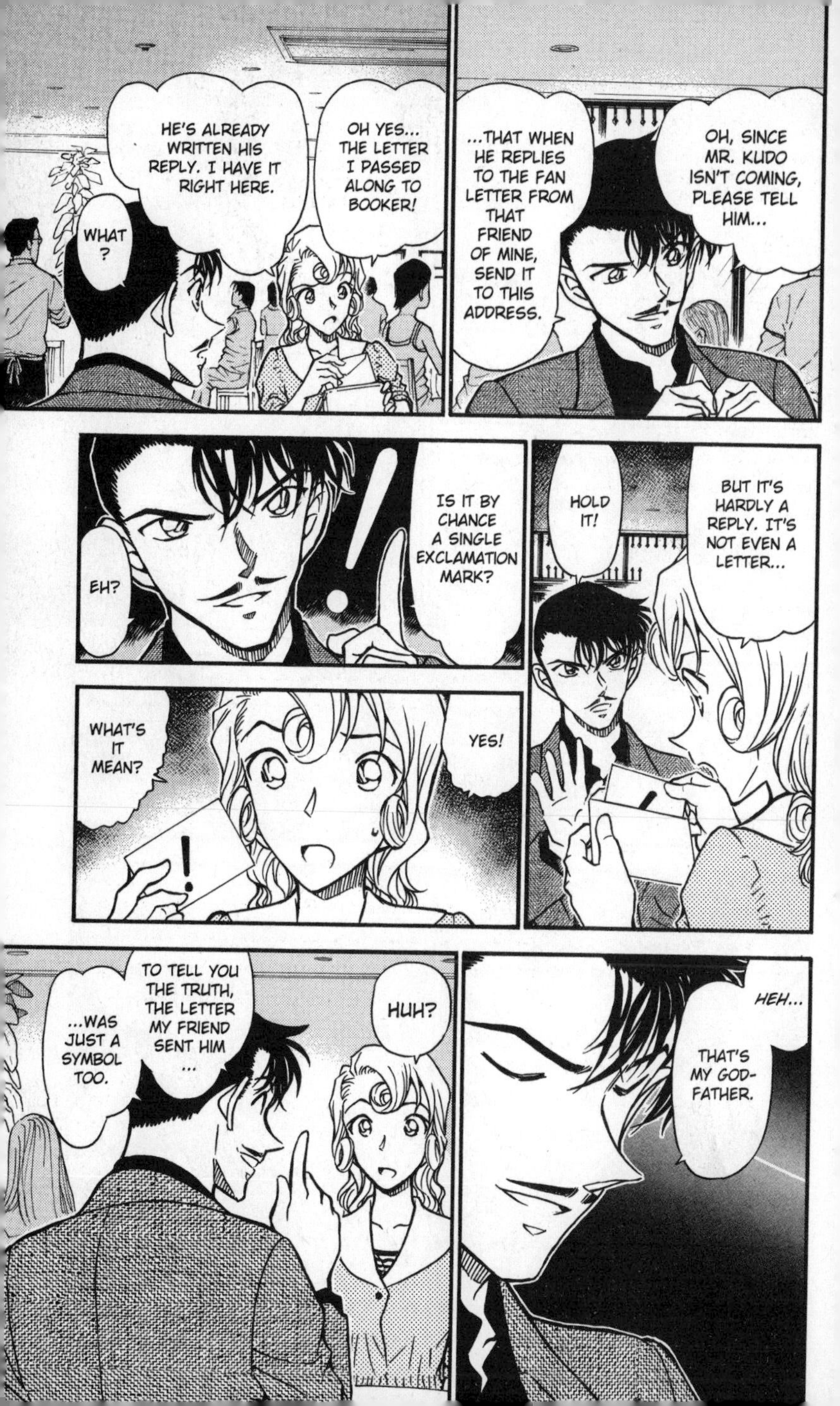
OH, SINCE MR. KUDO ISN'T COMING, PLEASE TELL HIM...
...THAT WHEN HE REPLIES TO THE FAN LETTER FROM THAT FRIEND OF MINE, SEND IT TO THIS ADDRESS.
OH YES... THE LETTER I PASSED ALONG TO BOOKER!
HE'S ALREADY WRITTEN HIS REPLY. I HAVE IT RIGHT HERE.
WHAT?
BUT IT'S HARDLY A REPLY. IT'S NOT EVEN A LETTER...
HOLD IT!
IS IT BY CHANCE A SINGLE EXCLAMATION MARK?
EH?
YES!
WHAT'S IT MEAN?
HEH...
THAT'S MY GOD-FATHER.
HUH?
TO TELL YOU THE TRUTH, THE LETTER MY FRIEND SENT HIM ...
...WAS JUST A SYMBOL TOO.

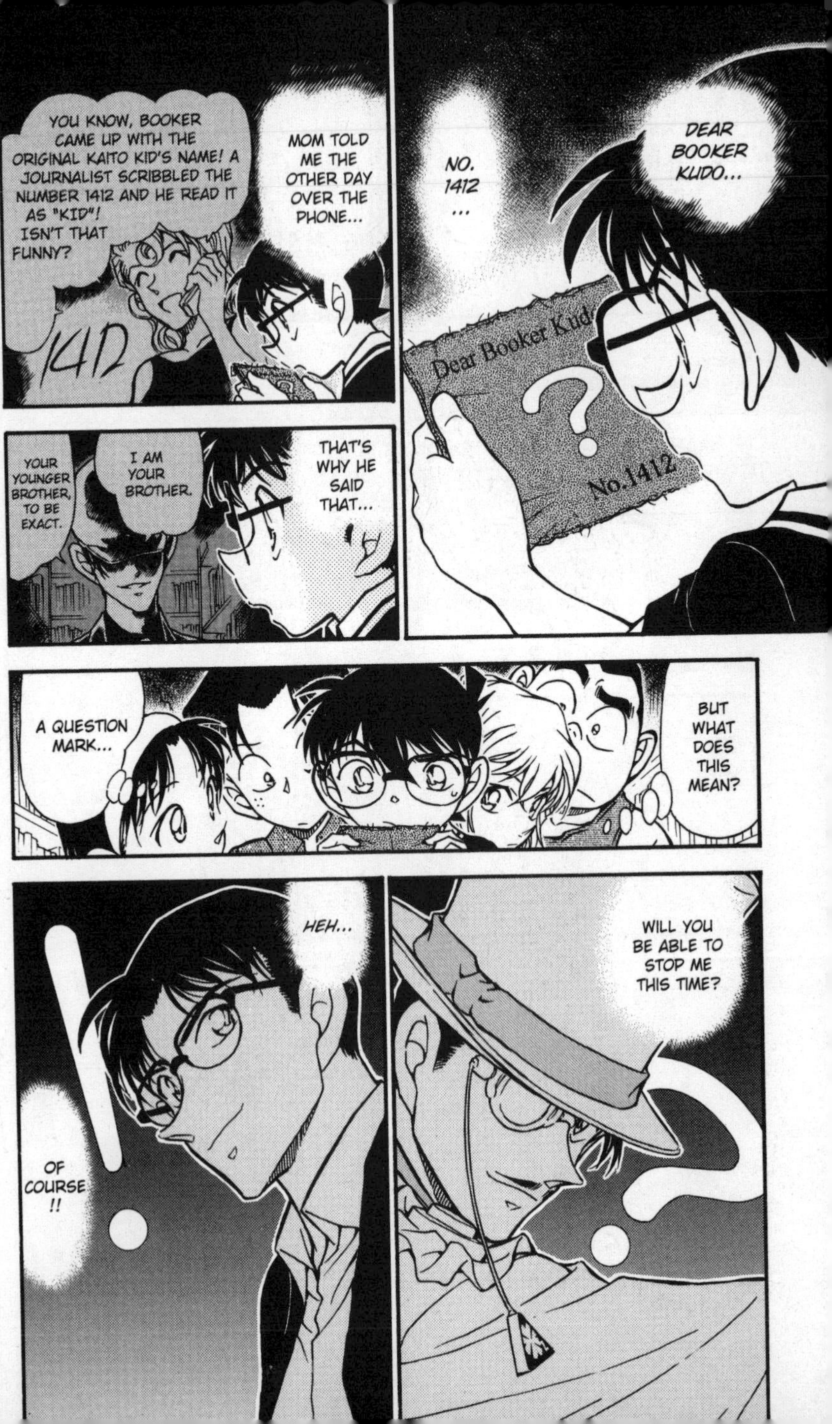
DEAR BOOKER KUDO...
NO. 1412 ...
Dear Booker Kud
No.1412
MOM TOLD ME THE OTHER DAY OVER THE PHONE...
YOU KNOW, BOOKER CAME UP WITH THE ORIGINAL KAITO KID'S NAME! A JOURNALIST SCRIBBLED THE NUMBER 1412 AND HE READ IT AS "KID"! ISN'T THAT FUNNY?
1412
THAT'S WHY HE SAID THAT...
I AM YOUR BROTHER.
YOUR YOUNGER BROTHER, TO BE EXACT.
BUT WHAT DOES THIS MEAN?
A QUESTION MARK...
WILL YOU BE ABLE TO STOP ME THIS TIME?
HEH...
OF COURSE !!

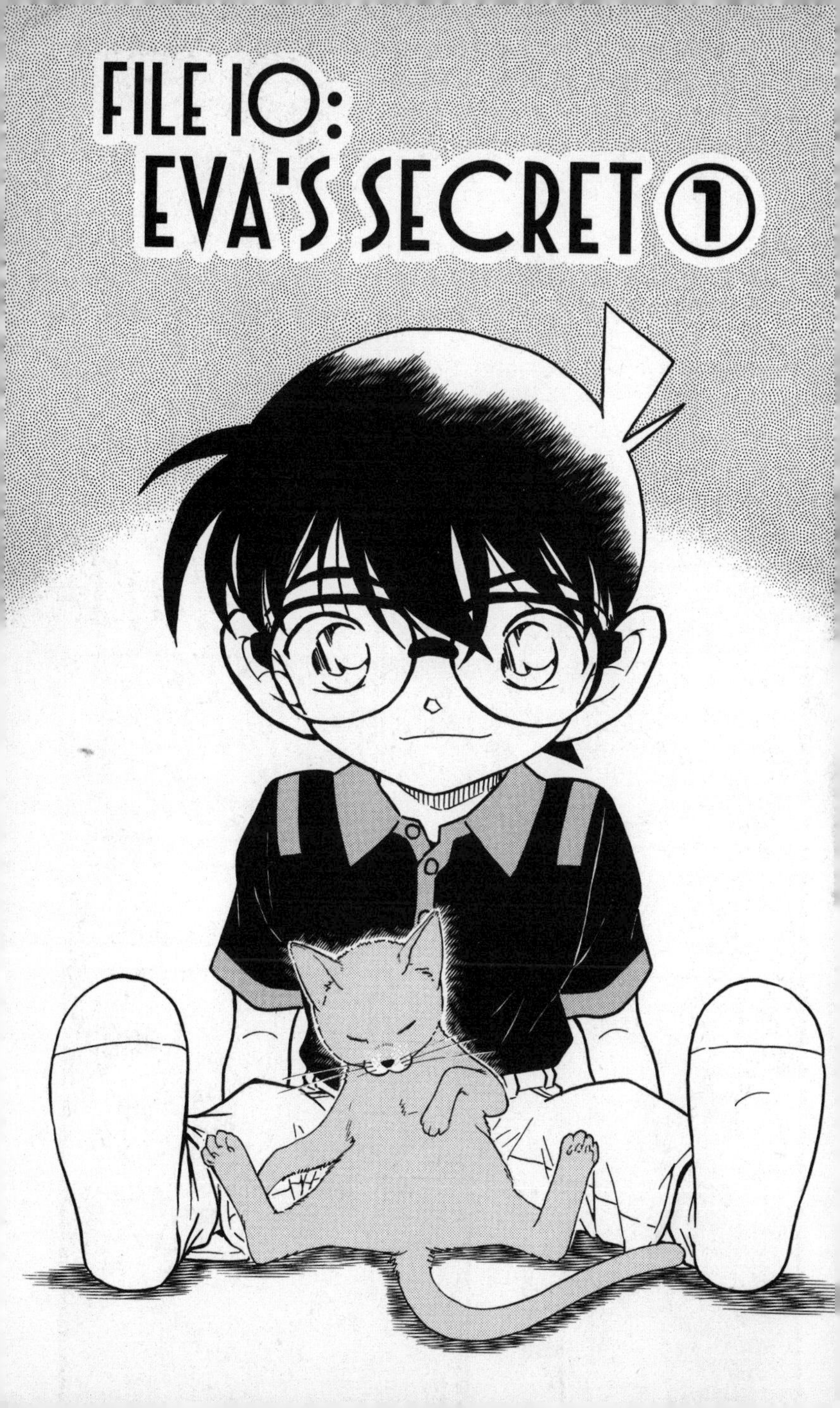
FILE 10:
EVA'S SECRET ①

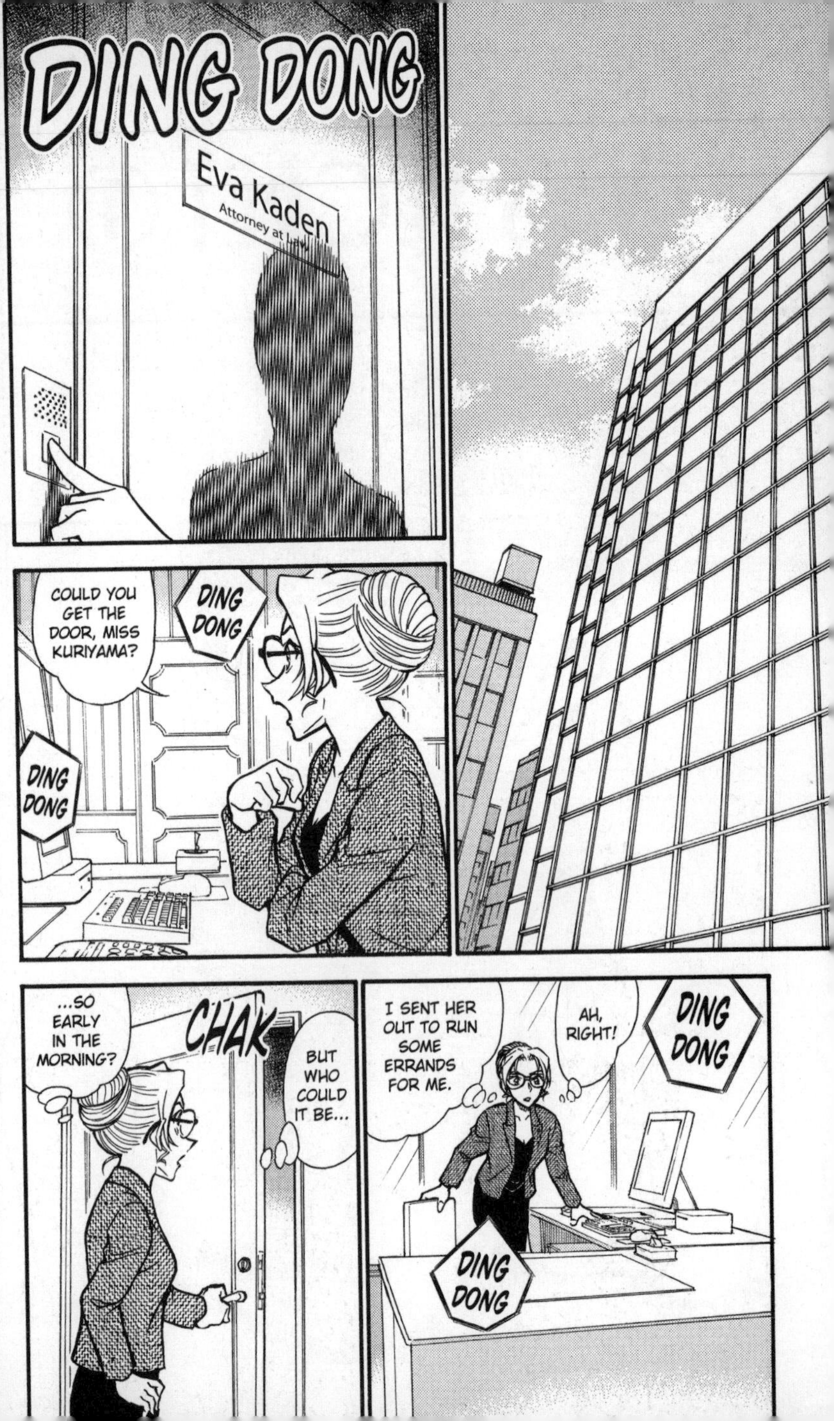
DING DONG
Eva Kaden
Attorney at Law
DING DONG
COULD YOU GET THE DOOR, MISS KURIYAMA?
DING DONG
DING DONG
AH, RIGHT!
I SENT HER OUT TO RUN SOME ERRANDS FOR ME.
DING DONG
CHAK
BUT WHO COULD IT BE...
...SO EARLY IN THE MORNING?

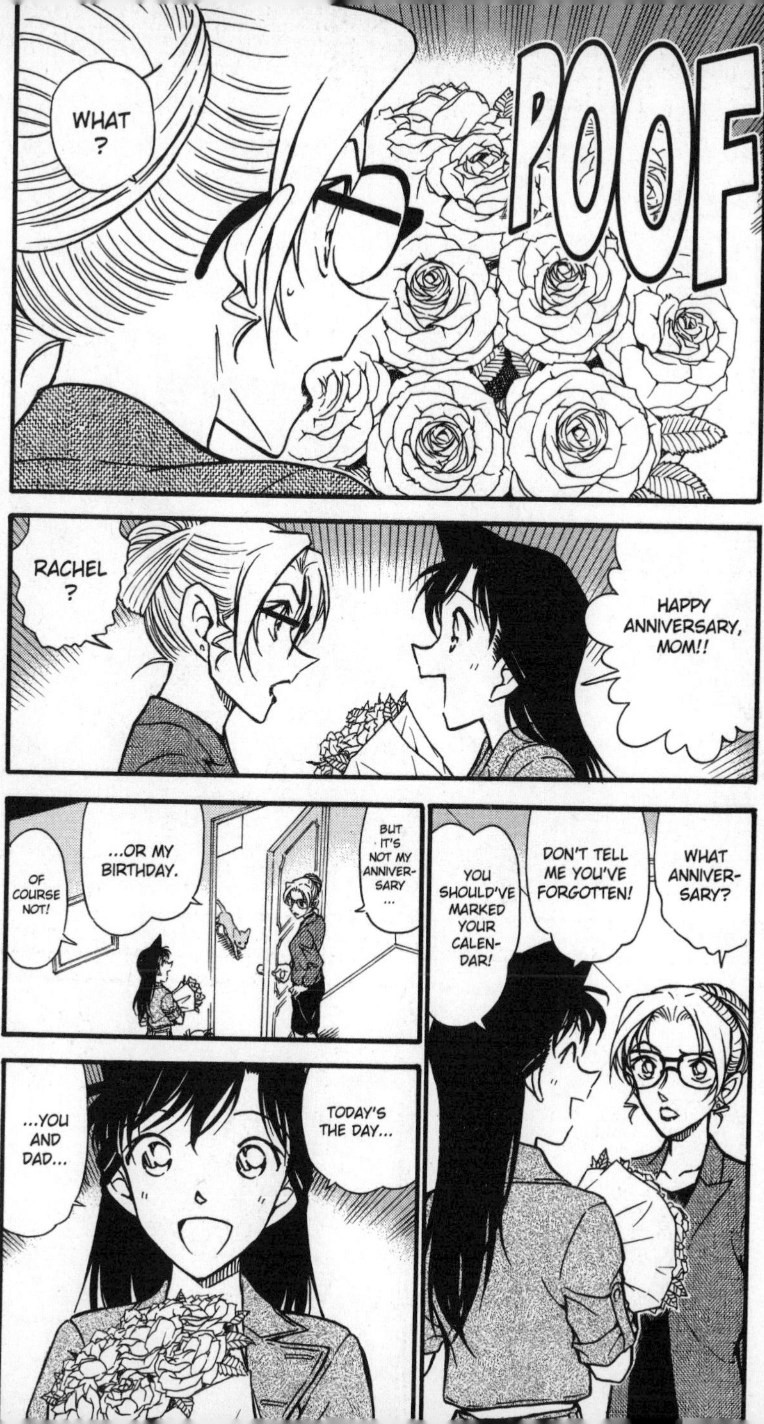

POOF
WHAT ?
HAPPY ANNIVERSARY, MOM!!
RACHEL ?
WHAT ANNIVERSARY?
DON'T TELL ME YOU'VE FORGOTTEN!
YOU SHOULD'VE MARKED YOUR CALENDAR!
BUT IT'S NOT MY ANNIVERSARY...
...OR MY BIRTHDAY.
OF COURSE NOT!
TODAY'S THE DAY...
...YOU AND DAD...

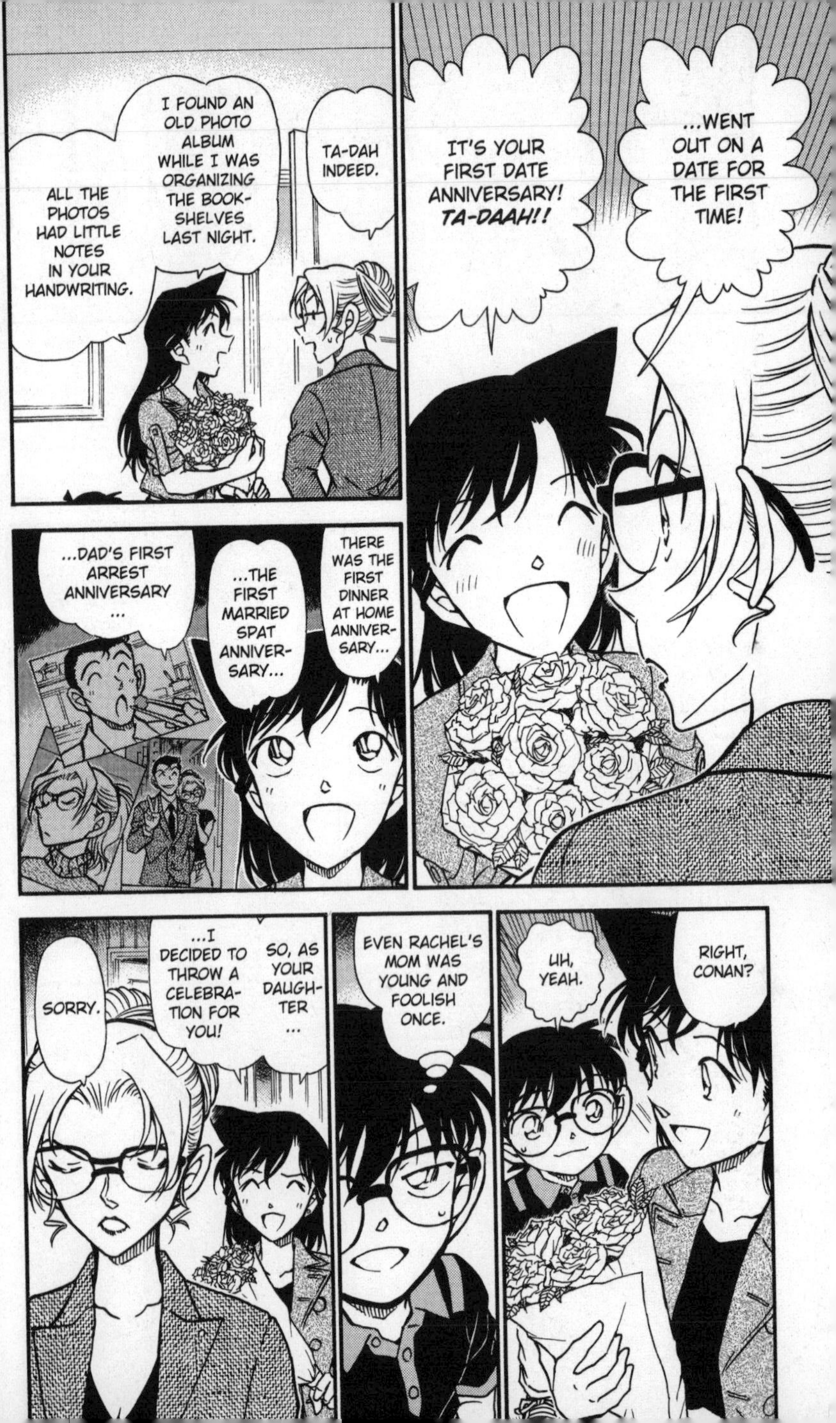
...WENT OUT ON A DATE FOR THE FIRST TIME!
IT'S YOUR FIRST DATE ANNIVERSARY! *TA-DAAH!!*
TA-DAH INDEED.
I FOUND AN OLD PHOTO ALBUM WHILE I WAS ORGANIZING THE BOOK-SHELVES LAST NIGHT.
ALL THE PHOTOS HAD LITTLE NOTES IN YOUR HANDWRITING.
THERE WAS THE FIRST DINNER AT HOME ANNIVER-SARY...
...THE FIRST MARRIED SPAT ANNIVER-SARY...
...DAD'S FIRST ARREST ANNIVERSARY ...
RIGHT, CONAN?
UH, YEAH.
EVEN RACHEL'S MOM WAS YOUNG AND FOOLISH ONCE.
SO, AS YOUR DAUGH-TER ...
...I DECIDED TO THROW A CELEBRA-TION FOR YOU!
SORRY.

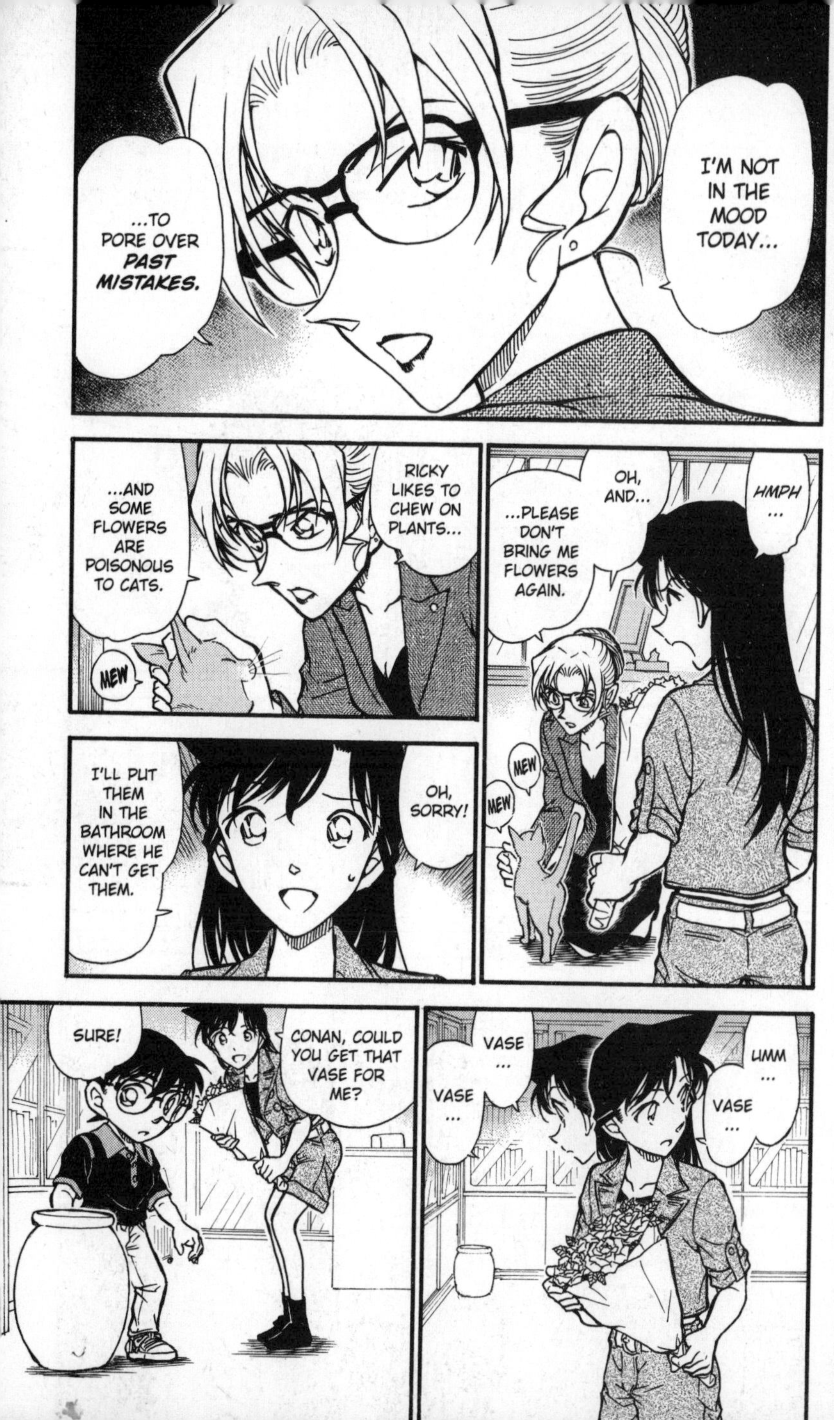
I'M NOT IN THE MOOD TODAY...
...TO PORE OVER PAST MISTAKES.
HMPH...
OH, AND...
...PLEASE DON'T BRING ME FLOWERS AGAIN.
MEW
MEW
RICKY LIKES TO CHEW ON PLANTS...
...AND SOME FLOWERS ARE POISONOUS TO CATS.
MEW
OH, SORRY!
I'LL PUT THEM IN THE BATHROOM WHERE HE CAN'T GET THEM.
UMM... VASE...
VASE...
VASE...
CONAN, COULD YOU GET THAT VASE FOR ME?
SURE!

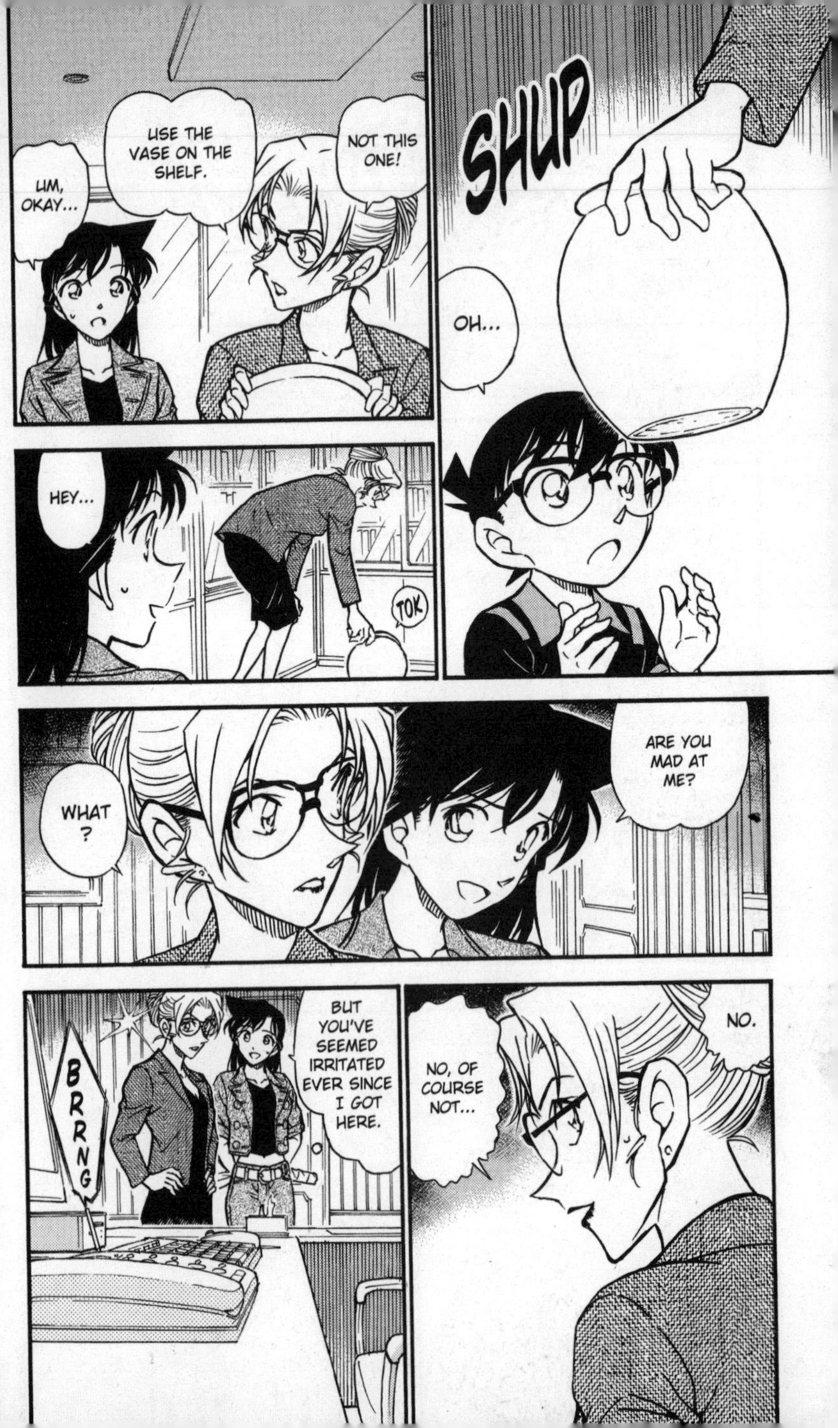
SHUP
OH...
NOT THIS ONE!
USE THE VASE ON THE SHELF.
UM, OKAY...
HEY...
TOK
ARE YOU MAD AT ME?
WHAT?
NO.
NO, OF COURSE NOT...
BUT YOU'VE SEEMED IRRITATED EVER SINCE I GOT HERE.
BRRNG

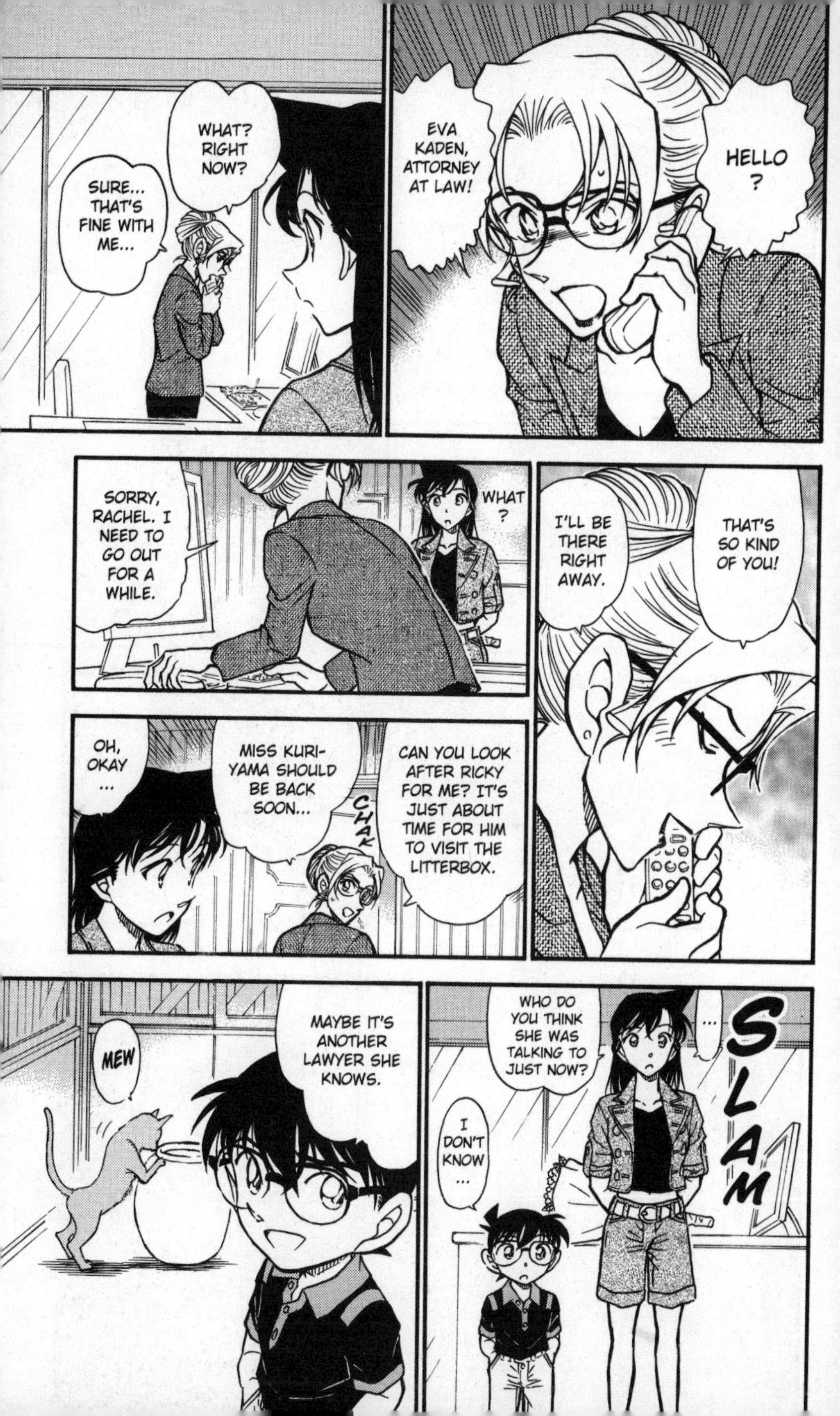
HELLO?
EVA KADEN, ATTORNEY AT LAW!
WHAT? RIGHT NOW?
SURE... THAT'S FINE WITH ME...
THAT'S SO KIND OF YOU!
I'LL BE THERE RIGHT AWAY.
WHAT?
SORRY, RACHEL. I NEED TO GO OUT FOR A WHILE.
CAN YOU LOOK AFTER RICKY FOR ME? IT'S JUST ABOUT TIME FOR HIM TO VISIT THE LITTERBOX.
CHAK
MISS KURI-YAMA SHOULD BE BACK SOON...
OH, OKAY ...
SLAM
...
WHO DO YOU THINK SHE WAS TALKING TO JUST NOW?
I DON'T KNOW ...
MAYBE IT'S ANOTHER LAWYER SHE KNOWS.
MEW

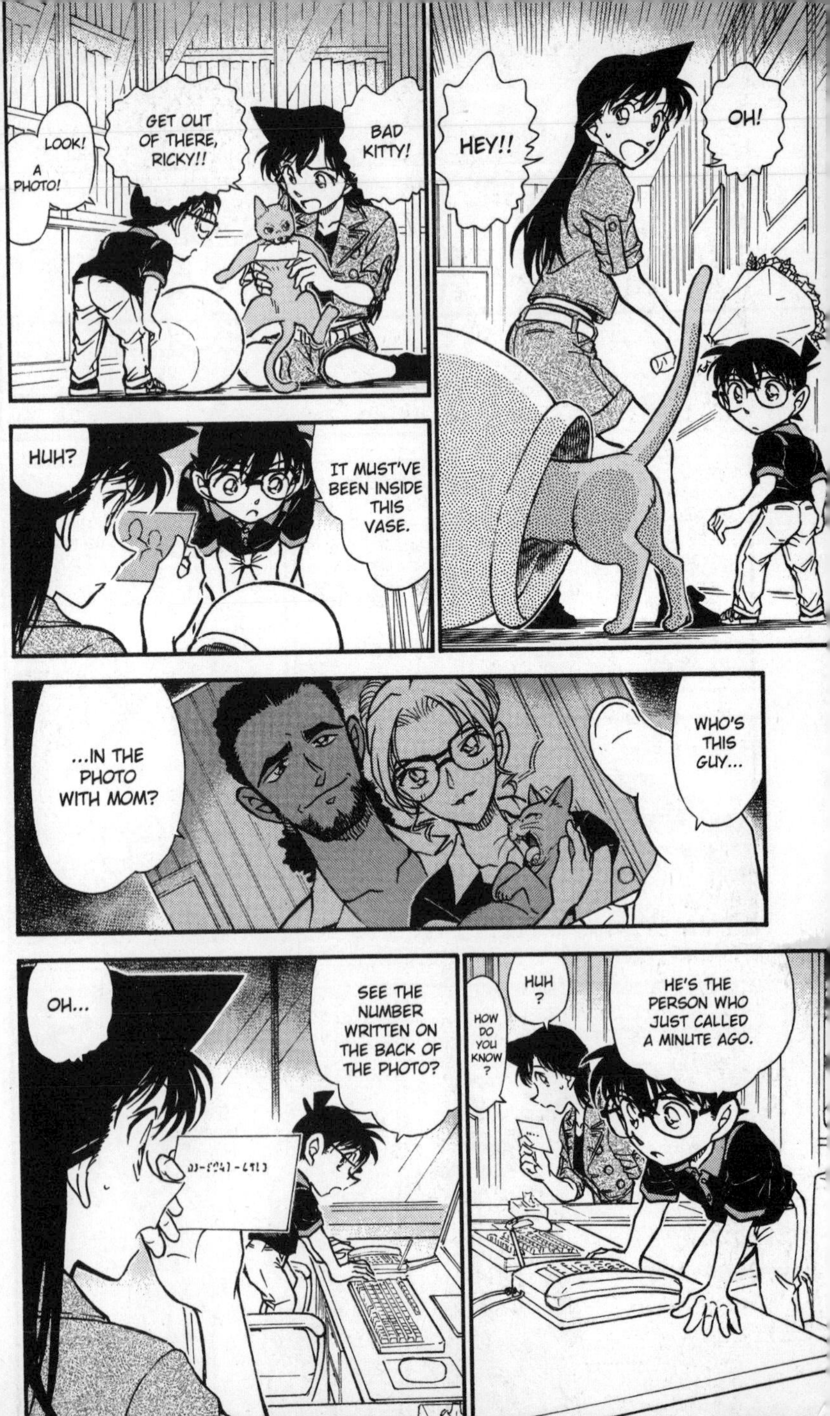
OH!
HEY!!
BAD KITTY!
GET OUT OF THERE, RICKY!!
LOOK!
A PHOTO!
IT MUST'VE BEEN INSIDE THIS VASE.
HUH?
WHO'S THIS GUY...
...IN THE PHOTO WITH MOM?
HE'S THE PERSON WHO JUST CALLED A MINUTE AGO.
HUH?
HOW DO YOU KNOW?
SEE THE NUMBER WRITTEN ON THE BACK OF THE PHOTO?
OH...

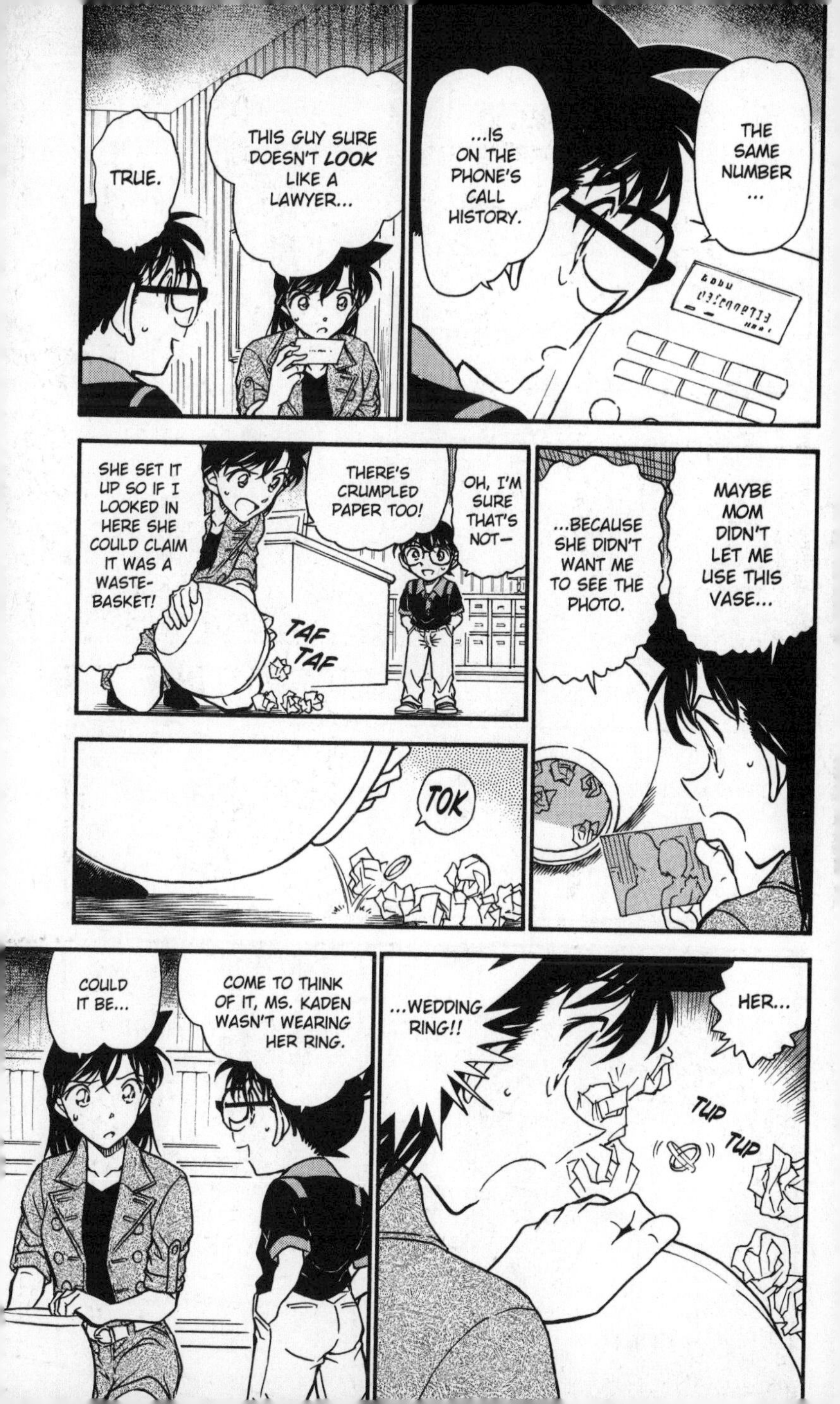
THE SAME NUMBER...
...IS ON THE PHONE'S CALL HISTORY.
THIS GUY SURE DOESN'T LOOK LIKE A LAWYER...
TRUE.
MAYBE MOM DIDN'T LET ME USE THIS VASE...
...BECAUSE SHE DIDN'T WANT ME TO SEE THE PHOTO.
OH, I'M SURE THAT'S NOT—
THERE'S CRUMPLED PAPER TOO!
SHE SET IT UP SO IF I LOOKED IN HERE SHE COULD CLAIM IT WAS A WASTE-BASKET!
TAF TAF
TOK
HER...
...WEDDING RING!!
TUP TUP
COME TO THINK OF IT, MS. KADEN WASN'T WEARING HER RING.
COULD IT BE...

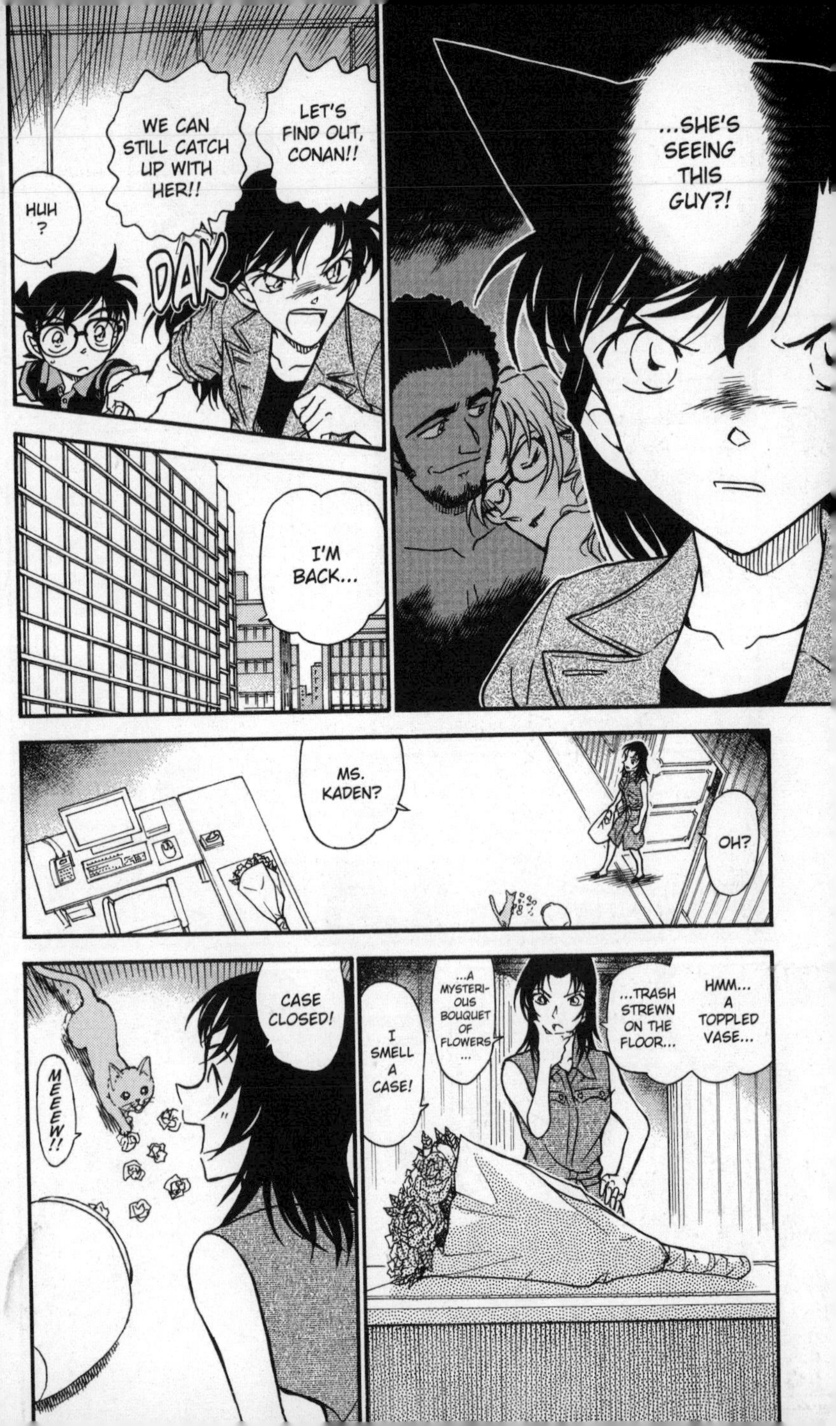
...SHE'S SEEING THIS GUY?!
LET'S FIND OUT, CONAN!!
WE CAN STILL CATCH UP WITH HER!!
DAK
HUH?
I'M BACK...
OH?
MS. KADEN?
HMM... A TOPPLED VASE...
...TRASH STREWN ON THE FLOOR...
...A MYSTERIOUS BOUQUET OF FLOWERS...
I SMELL A CASE!
CASE CLOSED!
MEEEEW!!

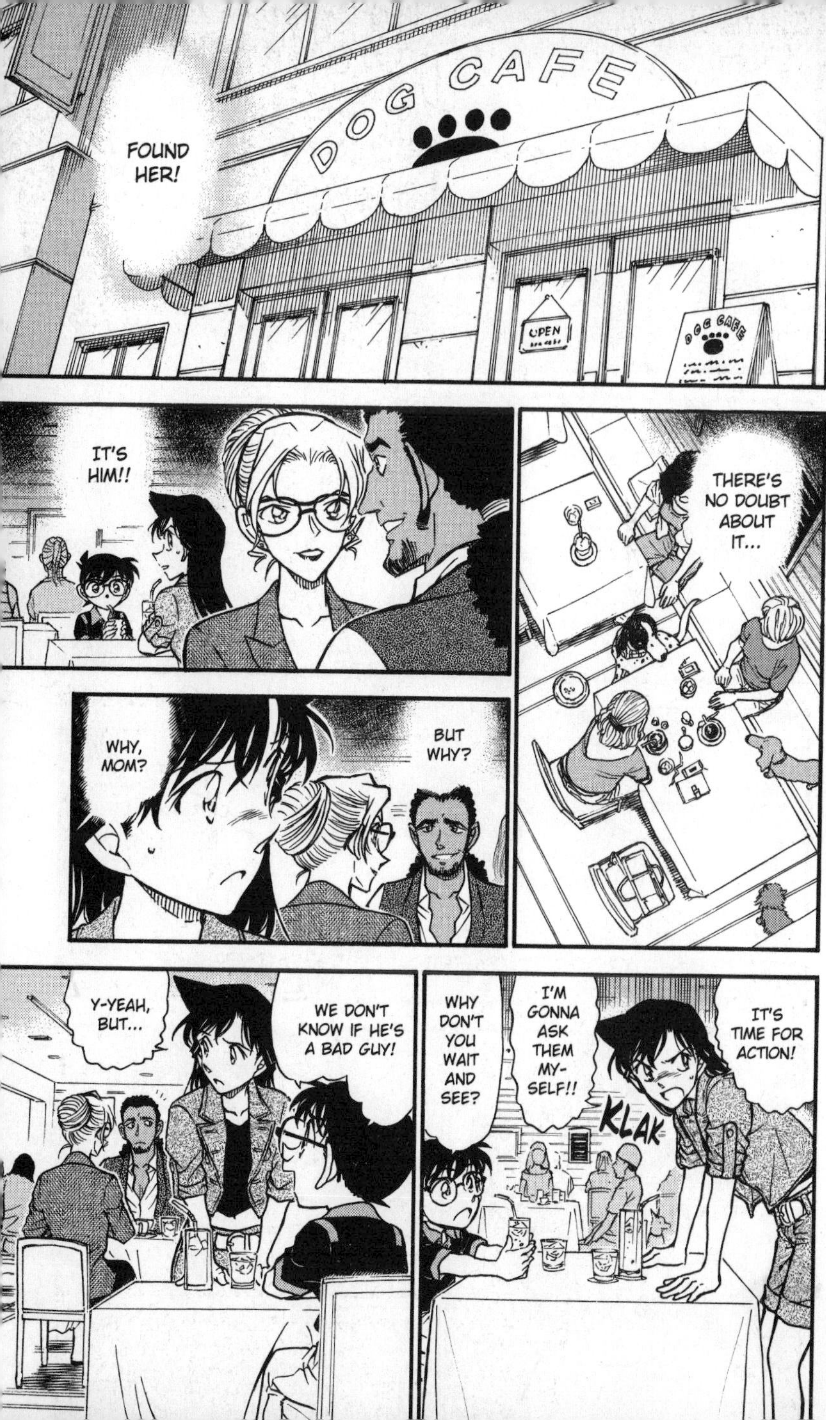
DOG CAFE
FOUND HER!
OPEN
DOG CAFE
THERE'S NO DOUBT ABOUT IT...
IT'S HIM!!
BUT WHY?
WHY, MOM?
IT'S TIME FOR ACTION!
I'M GONNA ASK THEM MY-SELF!!
KLAK
WHY DON'T YOU WAIT AND SEE?
WE DON'T KNOW IF HE'S A BAD GUY!
Y-YEAH, BUT...

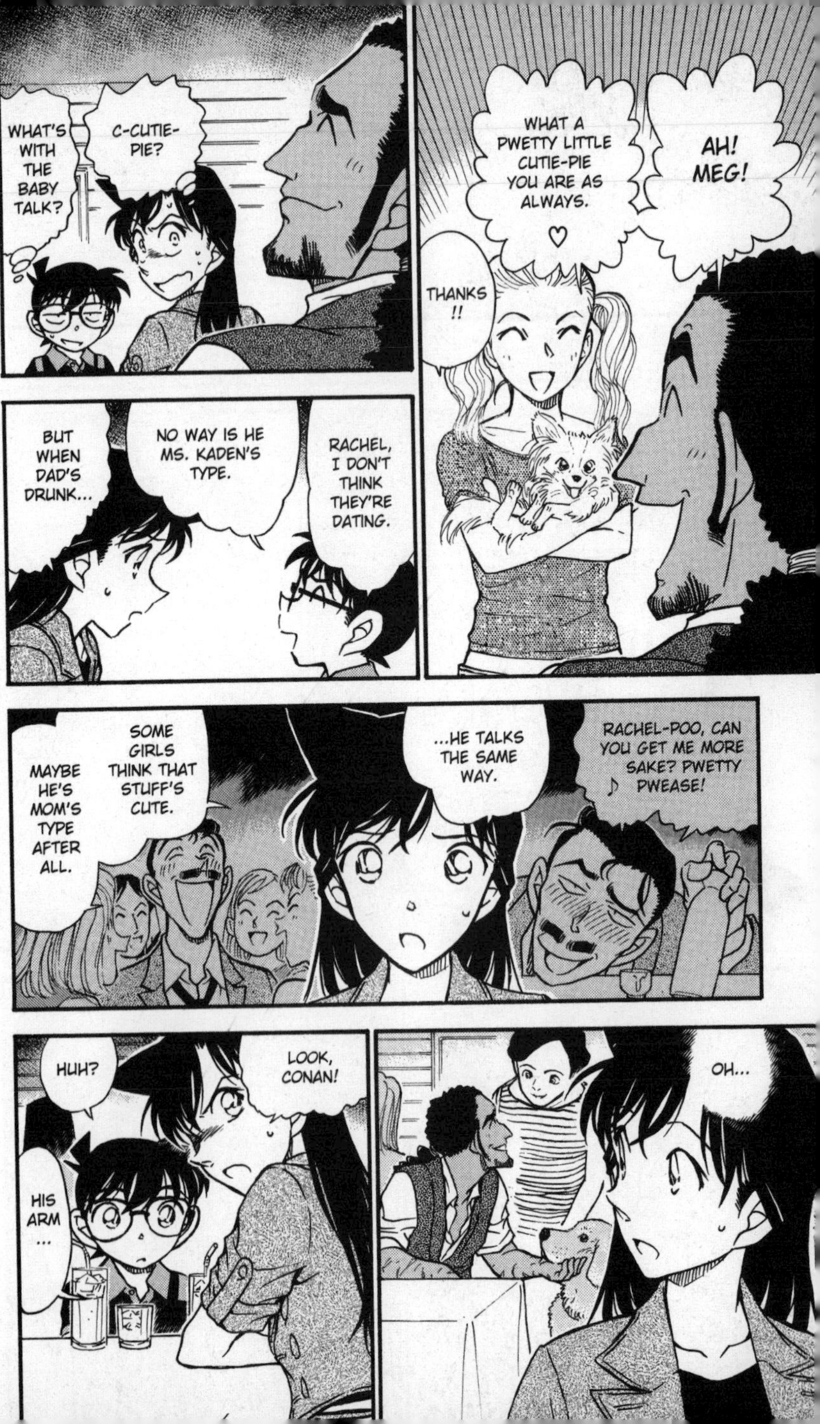
AH! MEG!
WHAT A PWETTY LITTLE CUTIE-PIE YOU ARE AS ALWAYS. ♡
THANKS !!
C-CUTIE-PIE?
WHAT'S WITH THE BABY TALK?
RACHEL, I DON'T THINK THEY'RE DATING.
NO WAY IS HE MS. KADEN'S TYPE.
BUT WHEN DAD'S DRUNK...
RACHEL-POO, CAN YOU GET ME MORE SAKE? PWETTY PWEASE! ♪
...HE TALKS THE SAME WAY.
SOME GIRLS THINK THAT STUFF'S CUTE.
MAYBE HE'S MOM'S TYPE AFTER ALL.
OH...
LOOK, CONAN!
HUH?
HIS ARM ...

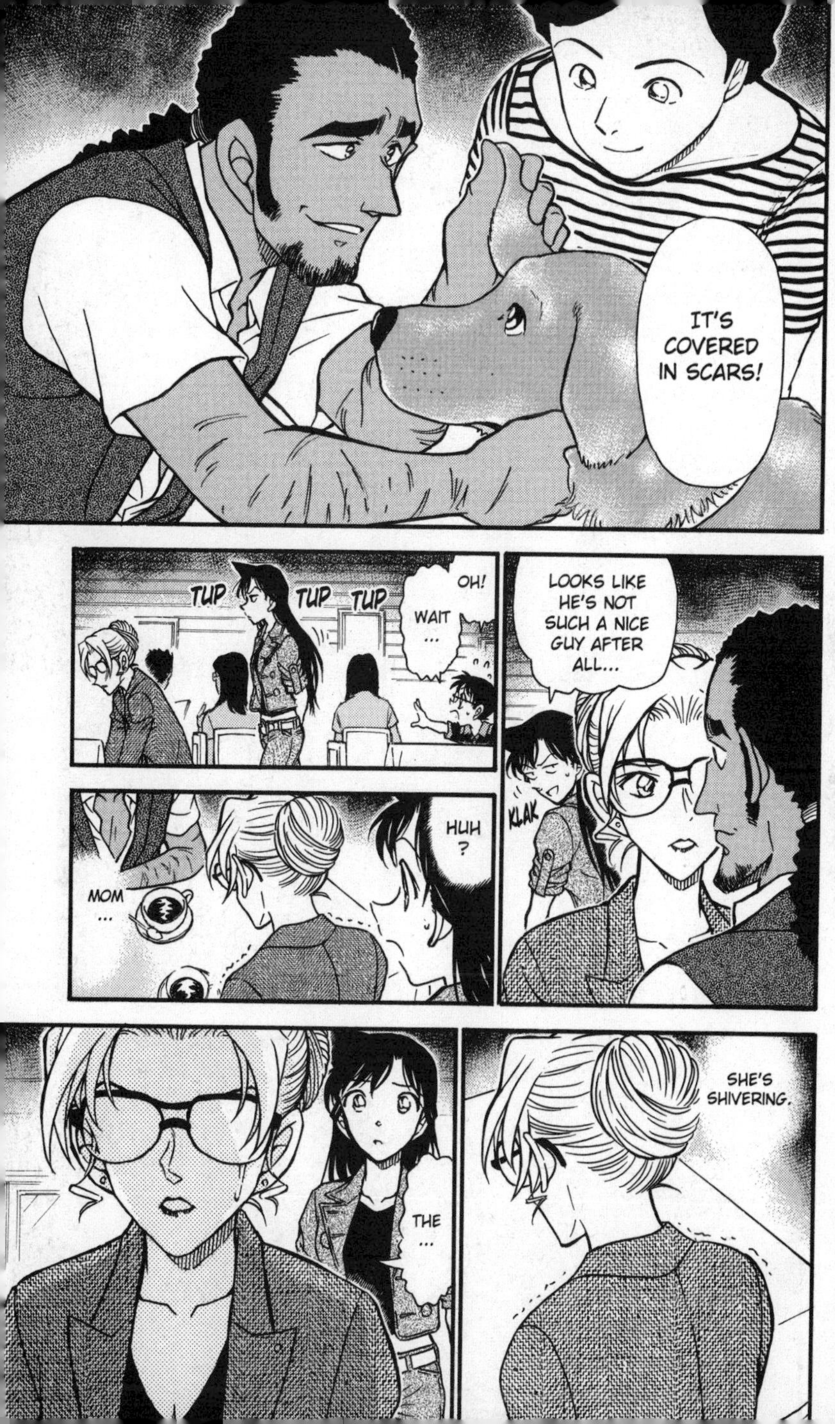
IT'S COVERED IN SCARS!
LOOKS LIKE HE'S NOT SUCH A NICE GUY AFTER ALL...
KLAK
OH!
WAIT ...
TUP
TUP
TUP
TUP
HUH ?
MOM ...
SHE'S SHIVERING.
THE ...

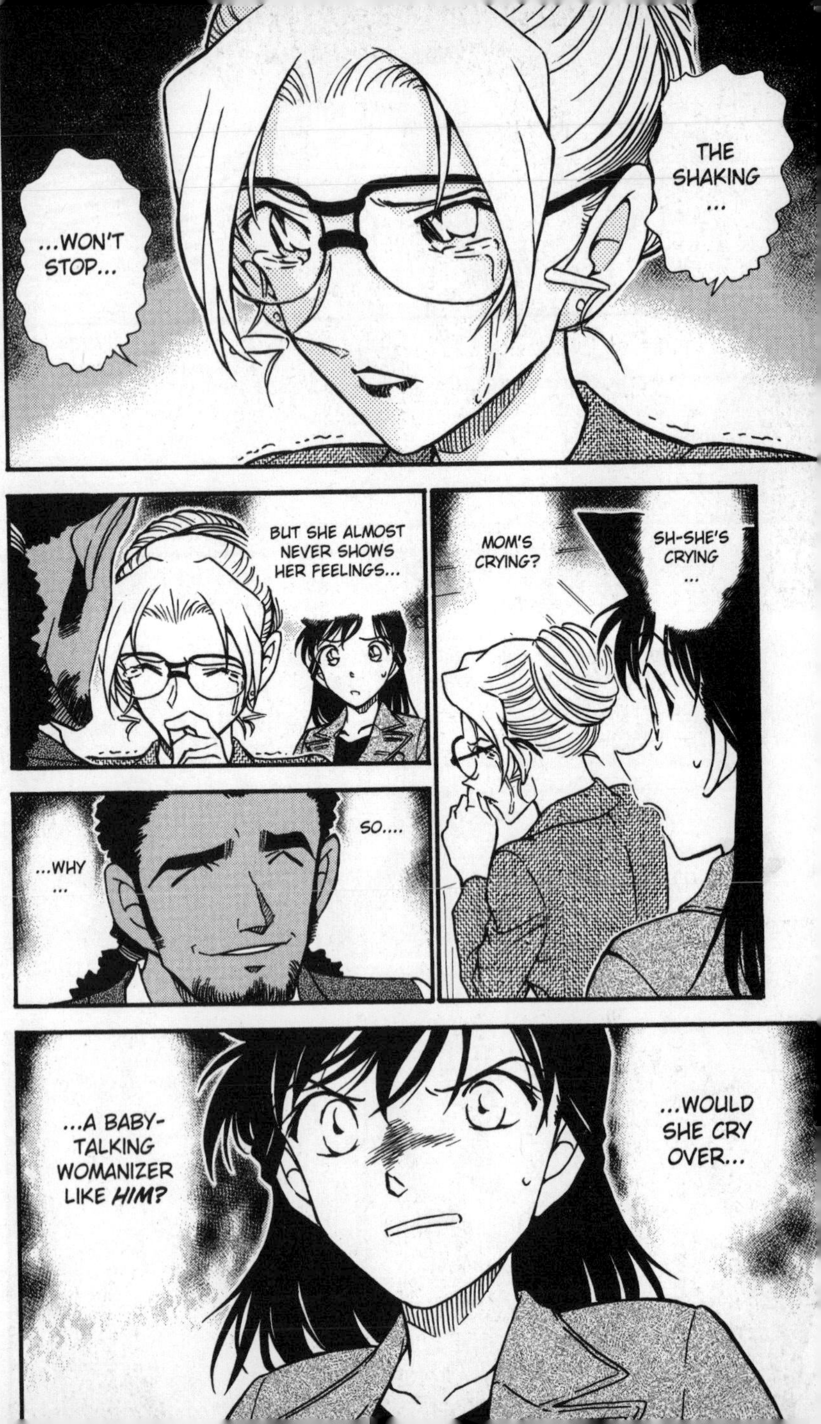
THE SHAKING ...
...WON'T STOP...
SH-SHE'S CRYING ...
MOM'S CRYING?
BUT SHE ALMOST NEVER SHOWS HER FEELINGS...
SO....
...WHY ...
...WOULD SHE CRY OVER...
...A BABY-TALKING WOMANIZER LIKE *HIM*?

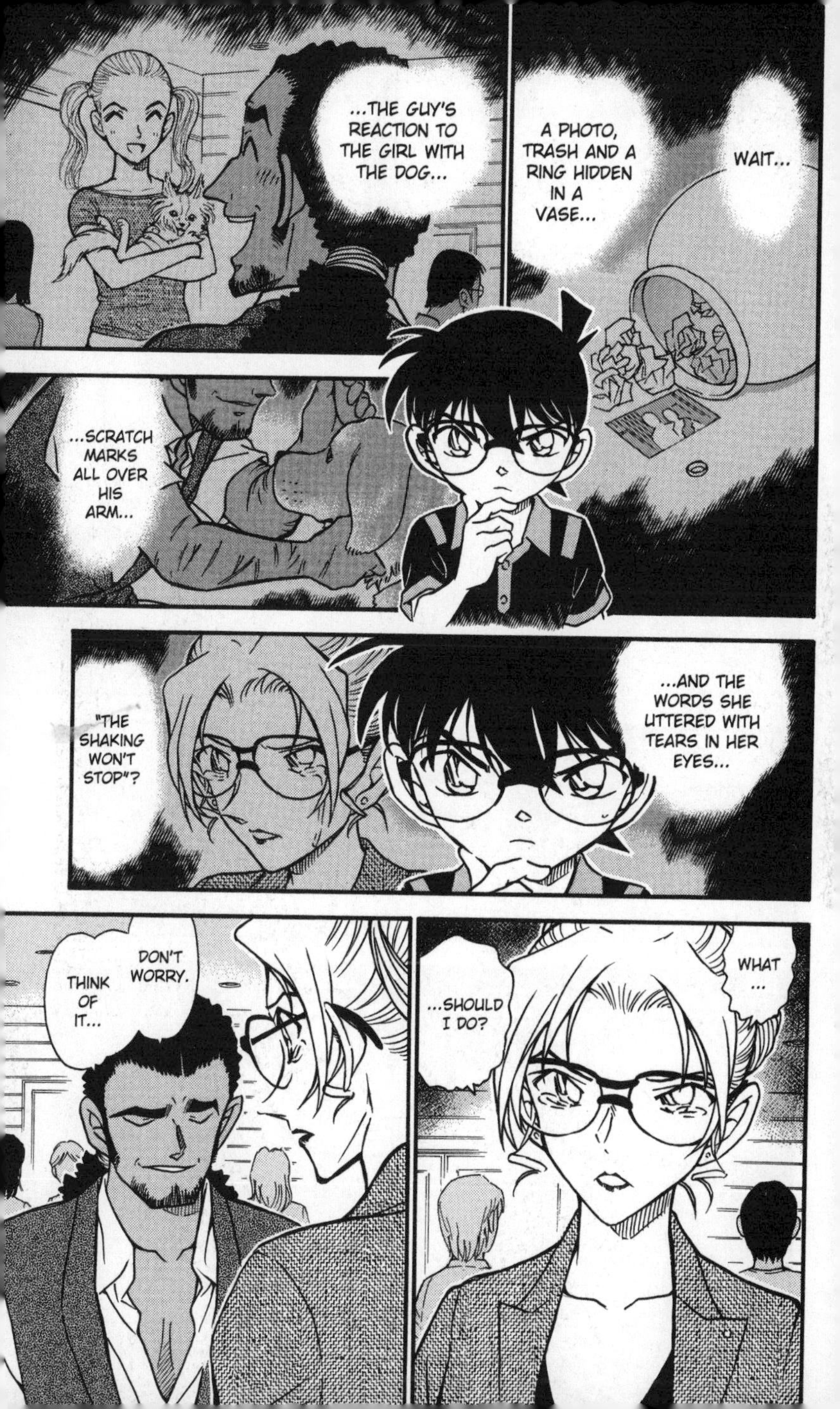
WAIT...
A PHOTO, TRASH AND A RING HIDDEN IN A VASE...
...THE GUY'S REACTION TO THE GIRL WITH THE DOG...
...SCRATCH MARKS ALL OVER HIS ARM...
...AND THE WORDS SHE UTTERED WITH TEARS IN HER EYES...
"THE SHAKING WON'T STOP"?
WHAT ...
...SHOULD I DO?
DON'T WORRY.
THINK OF IT...

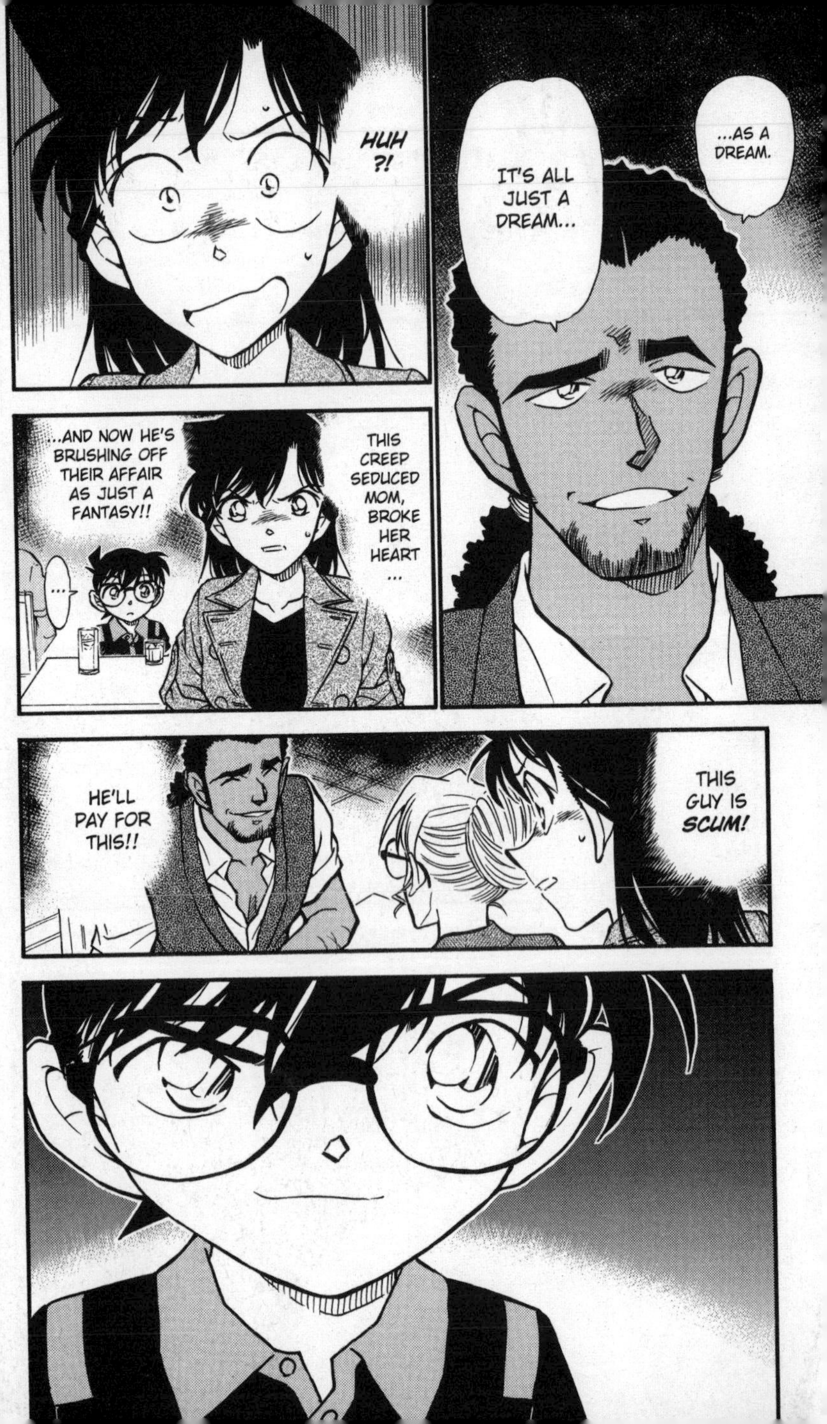
IT'S ALL JUST A DREAM...
...AS A DREAM.
HUH ?!
THIS CREEP SEDUCED MOM, BROKE HER HEART ...
...AND NOW HE'S BRUSHING OFF THEIR AFFAIR AS JUST A FANTASY!!
...
THIS GUY IS SCUM!
HE'LL PAY FOR THIS!!

FILE 11: EVA'S SECRET ②

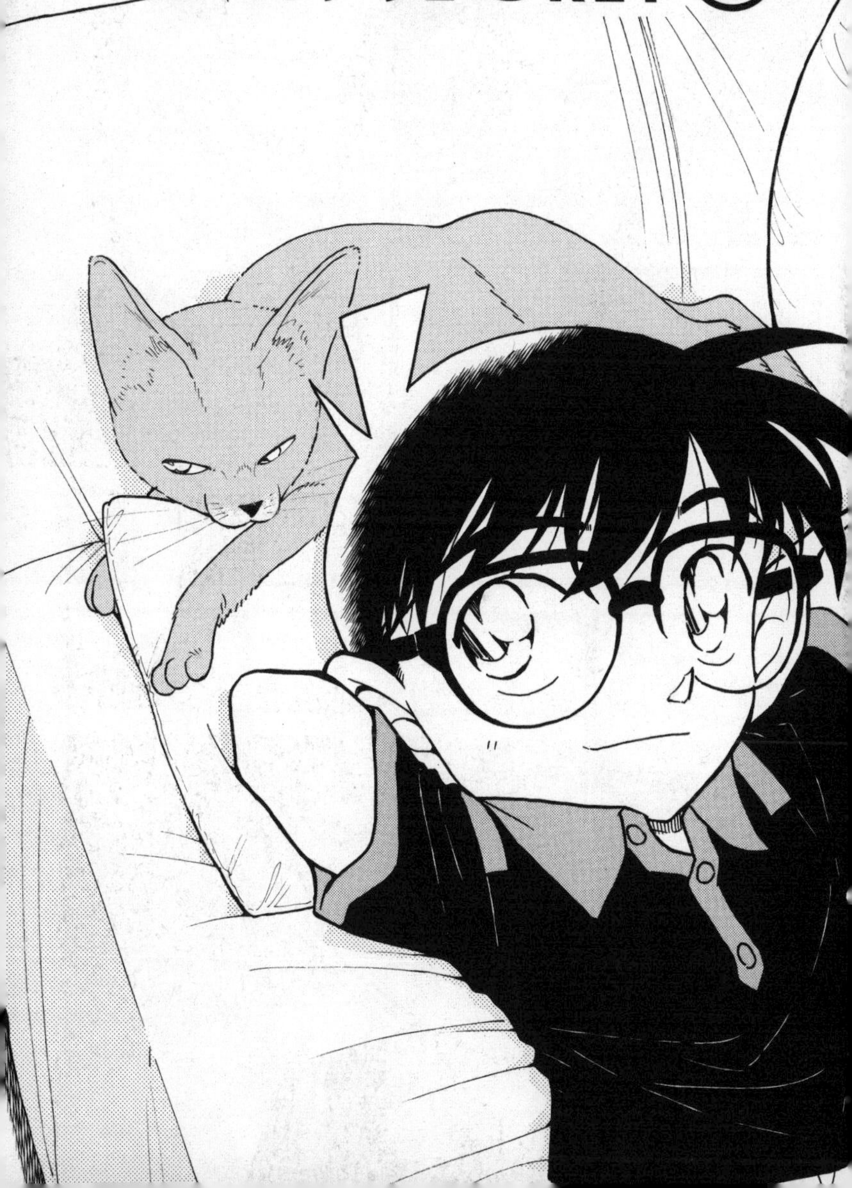

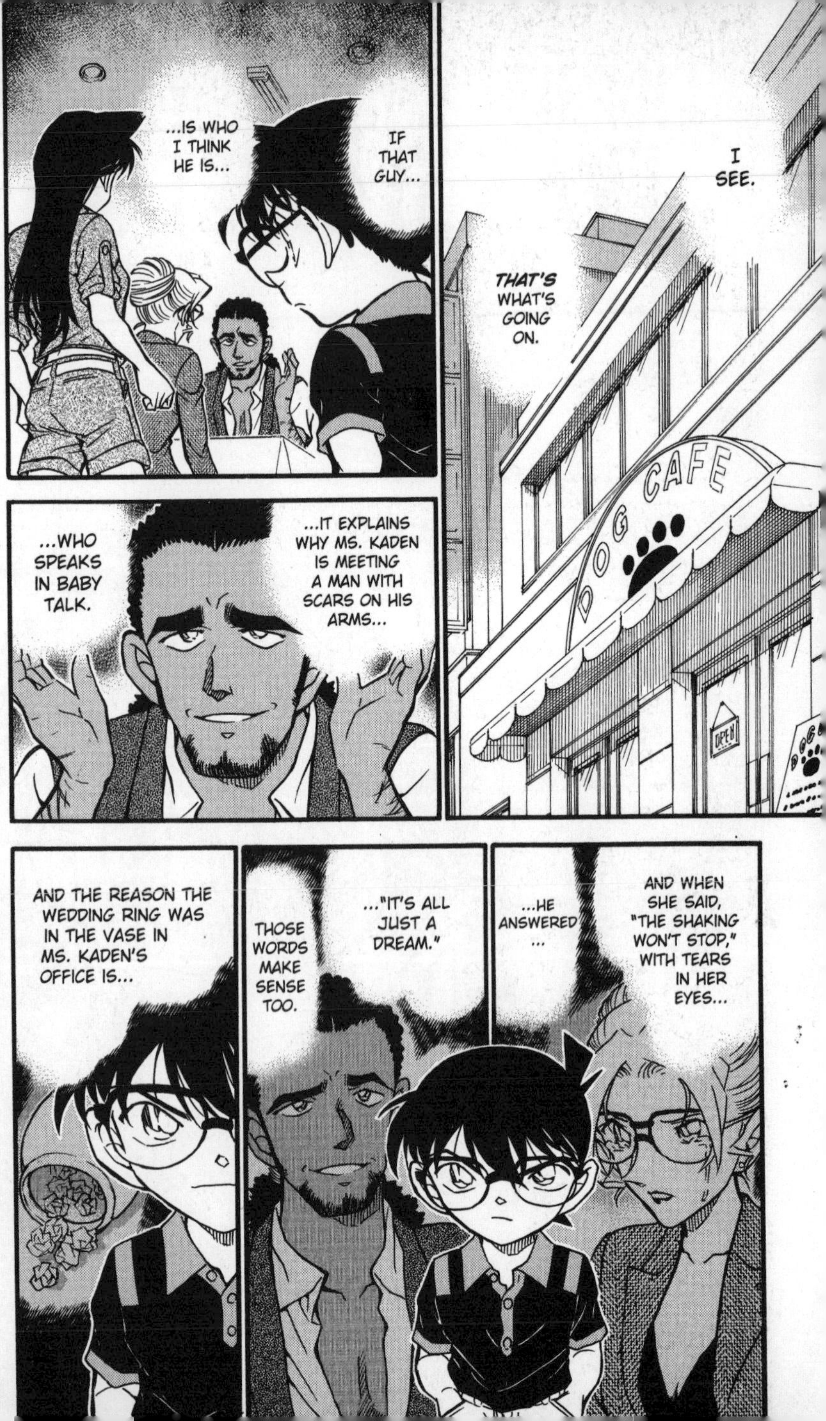
I SEE.
THAT'S WHAT'S GOING ON.
DOG CAFE
OPEN
IF THAT GUY...
...IS WHO I THINK HE IS...
...IT EXPLAINS WHY MS. KADEN IS MEETING A MAN WITH SCARS ON HIS ARMS...
...WHO SPEAKS IN BABY TALK.
AND WHEN SHE SAID, "THE SHAKING WON'T STOP," WITH TEARS IN HER EYES...
...HE ANSWERED...
..."IT'S ALL JUST A DREAM."
THOSE WORDS MAKE SENSE TOO.
AND THE REASON THE WEDDING RING WAS IN THE VASE IN MS. KADEN'S OFFICE IS...

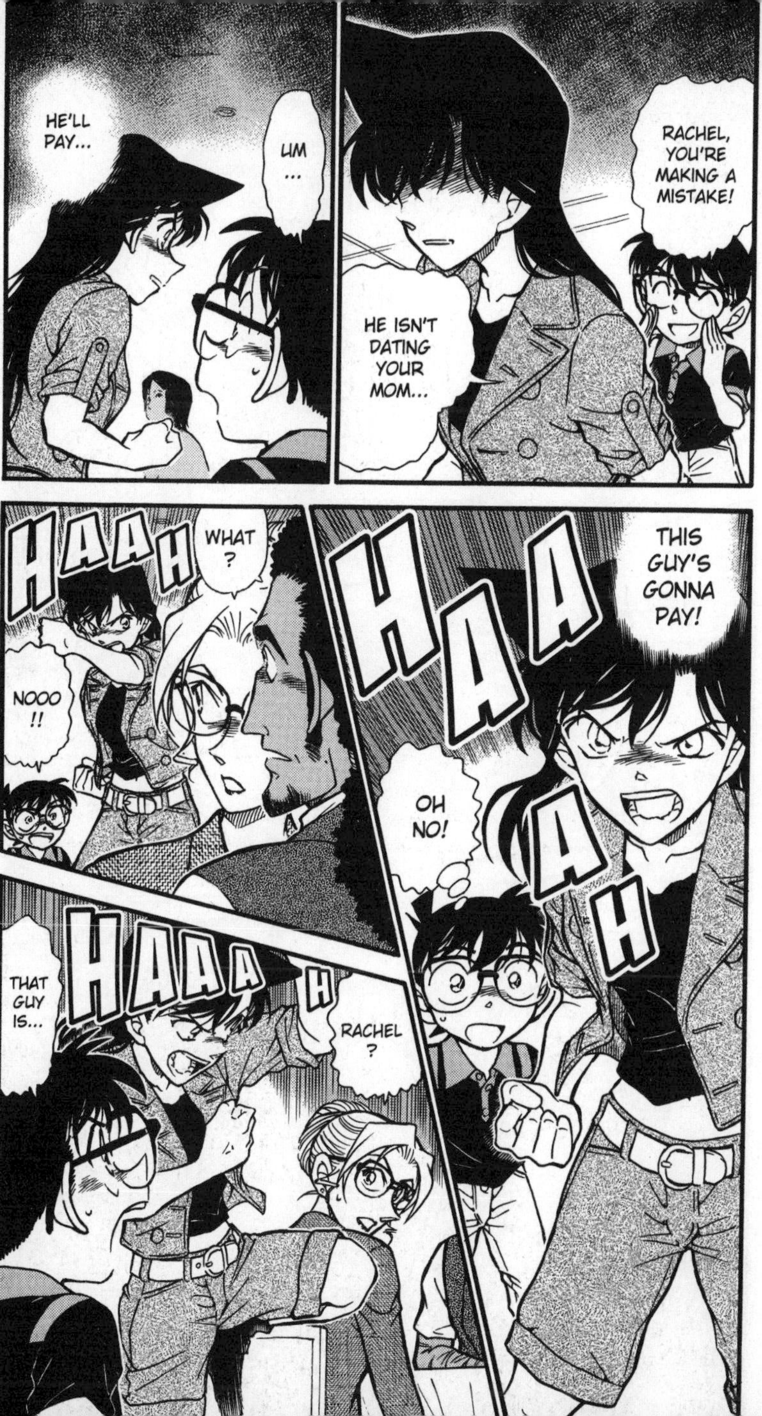
RACHEL, YOU'RE MAKING A MISTAKE!
HE ISN'T DATING YOUR MOM...
UM ...
HE'LL PAY...
HAAAAH
THIS GUY'S GONNA PAY!
OH NO!
WHAT ?
HAAH
NOOO !!
RACHEL ?
HAAAAH
THAT GUY IS...

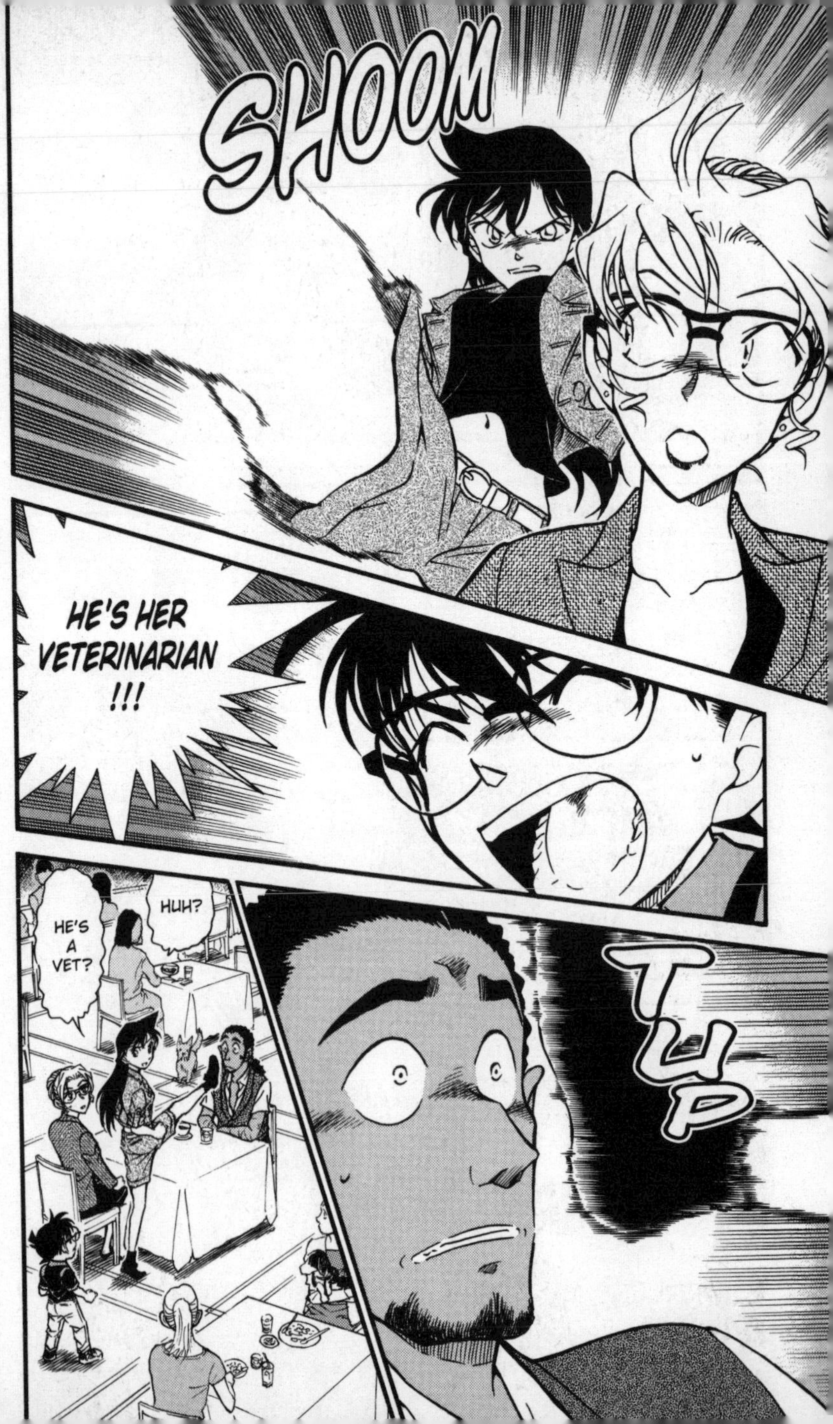
SHOOM
HE'S HER VETERINARIAN!!!
TUP
HUH?
HE'S A VET?

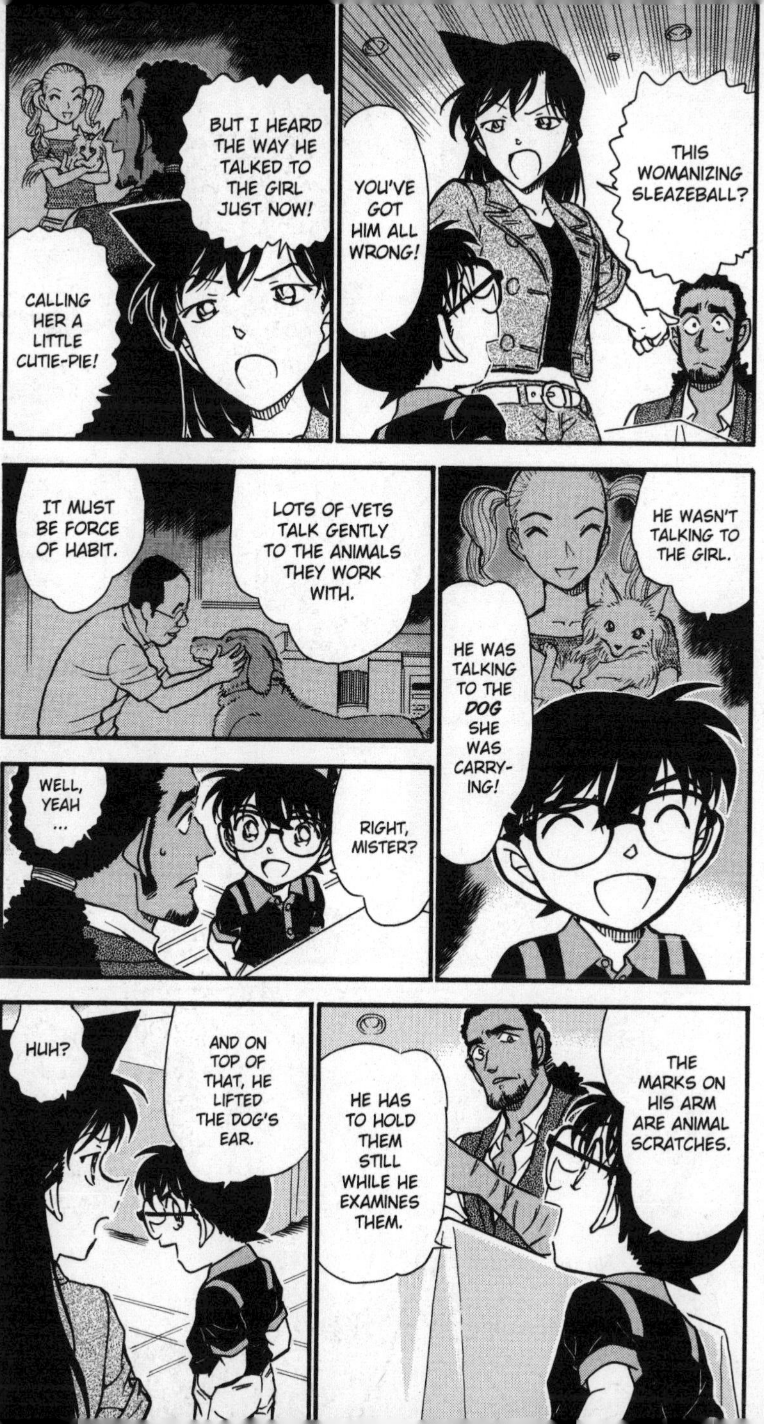
THIS WOMANIZING SLEAZEBALL?
YOU'VE GOT HIM ALL WRONG!
BUT I HEARD THE WAY HE TALKED TO THE GIRL JUST NOW!
CALLING HER A LITTLE CUTIE-PIE!
HE WASN'T TALKING TO THE GIRL.
HE WAS TALKING TO THE *DOG* SHE WAS CARRY-ING!
LOTS OF VETS TALK GENTLY TO THE ANIMALS THEY WORK WITH.
IT MUST BE FORCE OF HABIT.
RIGHT, MISTER?
WELL, YEAH ...
THE MARKS ON HIS ARM ARE ANIMAL SCRATCHES.
HE HAS TO HOLD THEM STILL WHILE HE EXAMINES THEM.
AND ON TOP OF THAT, HE LIFTED THE DOG'S EAR.
HUH?

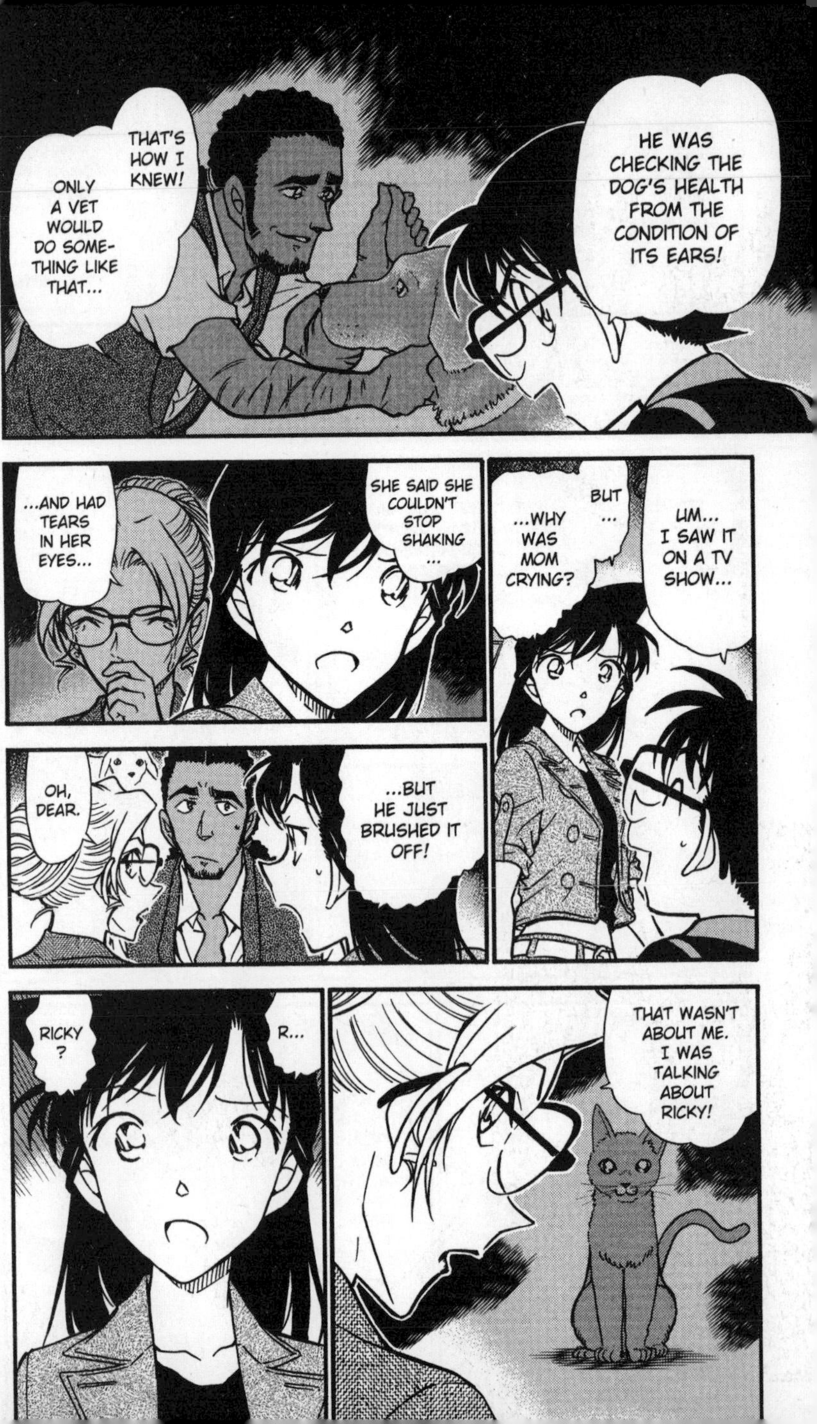
HE WAS CHECKING THE DOG'S HEALTH FROM THE CONDITION OF ITS EARS!
THAT'S HOW I KNEW!
ONLY A VET WOULD DO SOME-THING LIKE THAT...
UM... I SAW IT ON A TV SHOW...
BUT ...
...WHY WAS MOM CRYING?
SHE SAID SHE COULDN'T STOP SHAKING ...
...AND HAD TEARS IN HER EYES...
...BUT HE JUST BRUSHED IT OFF!
OH, DEAR.
THAT WASN'T ABOUT ME. I WAS TALKING ABOUT RICKY!
R...
RICKY ?

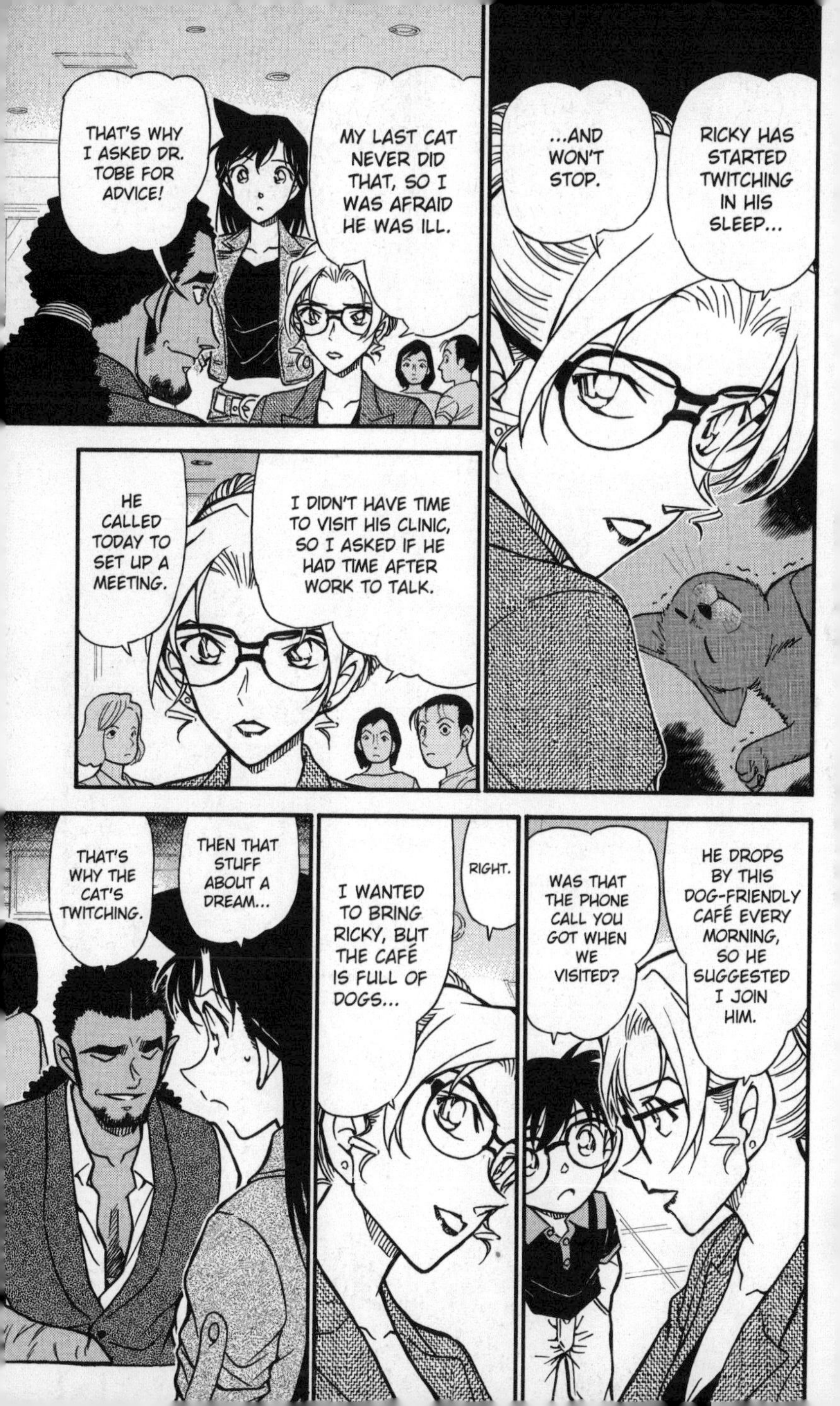
RICKY HAS STARTED TWITCHING IN HIS SLEEP...
...AND WON'T STOP.
MY LAST CAT NEVER DID THAT, SO I WAS AFRAID HE WAS ILL.
THAT'S WHY I ASKED DR. TOBE FOR ADVICE!
I DIDN'T HAVE TIME TO VISIT HIS CLINIC, SO I ASKED IF HE HAD TIME AFTER WORK TO TALK.
HE CALLED TODAY TO SET UP A MEETING.
HE DROPS BY THIS DOG-FRIENDLY CAFÉ EVERY MORNING, SO HE SUGGESTED I JOIN HIM.
WAS THAT THE PHONE CALL YOU GOT WHEN WE VISITED?
RIGHT.
I WANTED TO BRING RICKY, BUT THE CAFÉ IS FULL OF DOGS...
THEN THAT STUFF ABOUT A DREAM...
THAT'S WHY THE CAT'S TWITCHING.

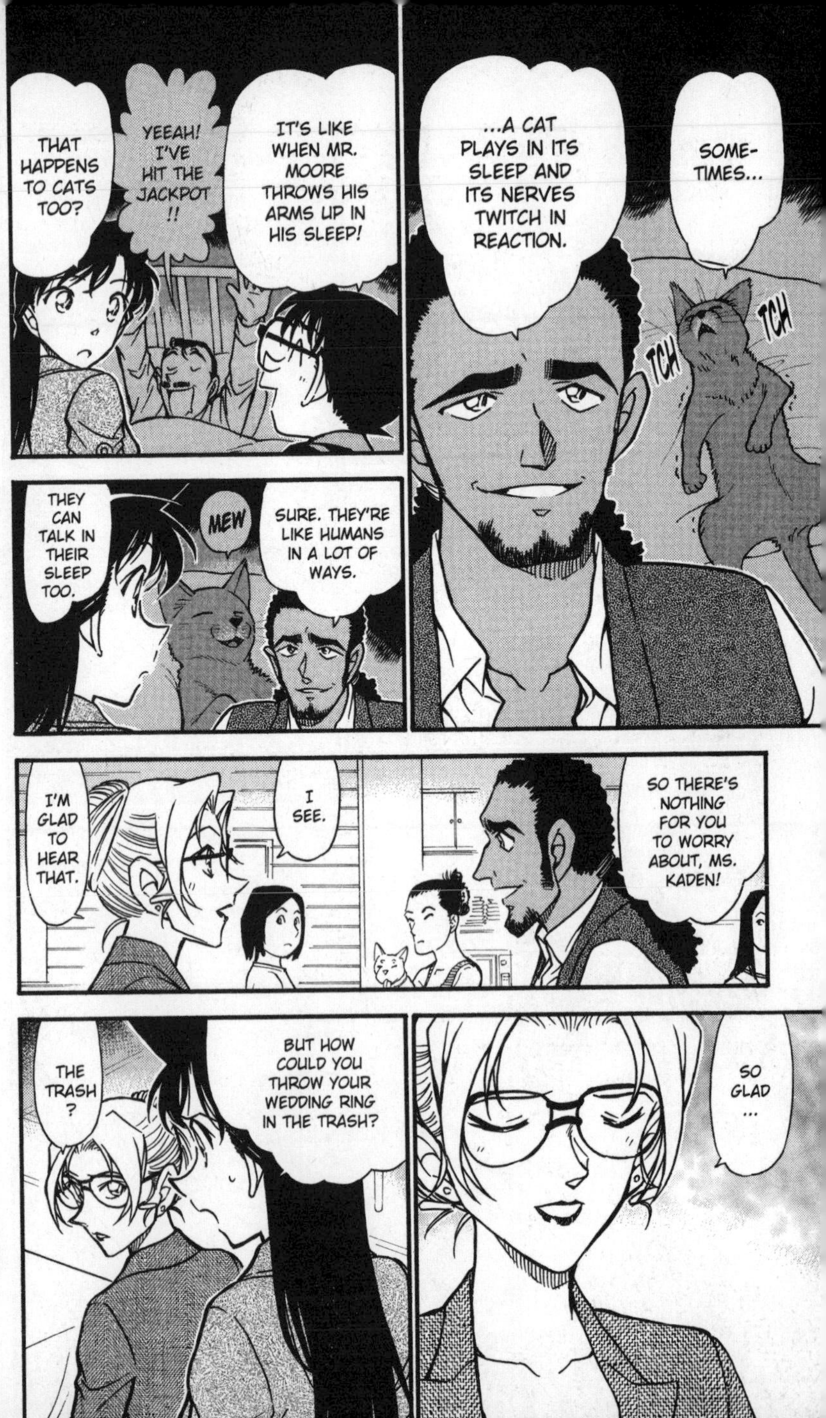
SOMETIMES...
...A CAT PLAYS IN ITS SLEEP AND ITS NERVES TWITCH IN REACTION.
TCH
TCH
IT'S LIKE WHEN MR. MOORE THROWS HIS ARMS UP IN HIS SLEEP!
YEEAH! I'VE HIT THE JACKPOT!!
THAT HAPPENS TO CATS TOO?
SURE. THEY'RE LIKE HUMANS IN A LOT OF WAYS.
MEW
THEY CAN TALK IN THEIR SLEEP TOO.
SO THERE'S NOTHING FOR YOU TO WORRY ABOUT, MS. KADEN!
I SEE.
I'M GLAD TO HEAR THAT.
SO GLAD...
BUT HOW COULD YOU THROW YOUR WEDDING RING IN THE TRASH?
THE TRASH?

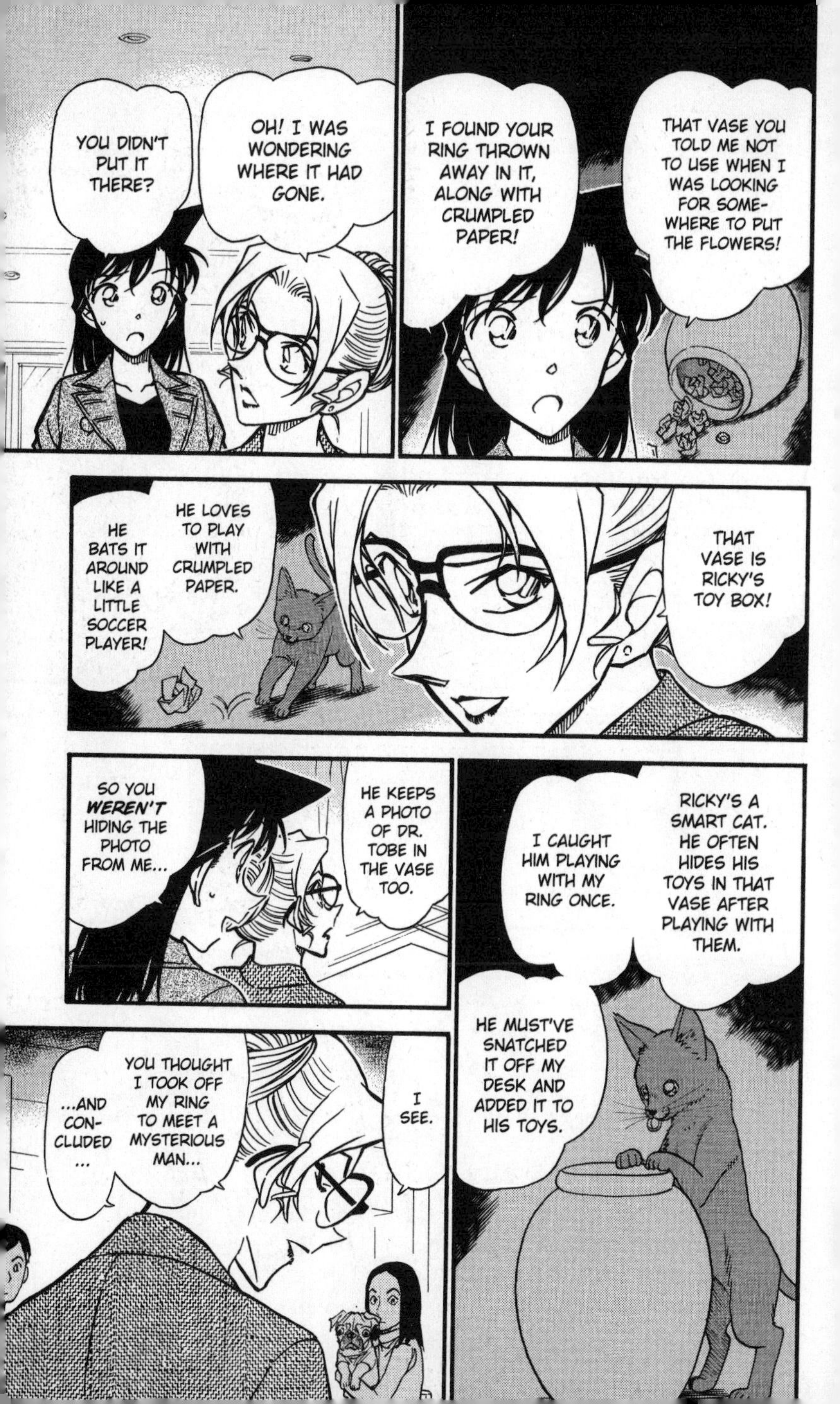
THAT VASE YOU TOLD ME NOT TO USE WHEN I WAS LOOKING FOR SOME-WHERE TO PUT THE FLOWERS!
I FOUND YOUR RING THROWN AWAY IN IT, ALONG WITH CRUMPLED PAPER!
OH! I WAS WONDERING WHERE IT HAD GONE.
YOU DIDN'T PUT IT THERE?
THAT VASE IS RICKY'S TOY BOX!
HE LOVES TO PLAY WITH CRUMPLED PAPER.
HE BATS IT AROUND LIKE A LITTLE SOCCER PLAYER!
RICKY'S A SMART CAT. HE OFTEN HIDES HIS TOYS IN THAT VASE AFTER PLAYING WITH THEM.
I CAUGHT HIM PLAYING WITH MY RING ONCE.
HE MUST'VE SNATCHED IT OFF MY DESK AND ADDED IT TO HIS TOYS.
HE KEEPS A PHOTO OF DR. TOBE IN THE VASE TOO.
SO YOU *WEREN'T* HIDING THE PHOTO FROM ME...
I SEE.
YOU THOUGHT I TOOK OFF MY RING TO MEET A MYSTERIOUS MAN...
...AND CON-CLUDED ...

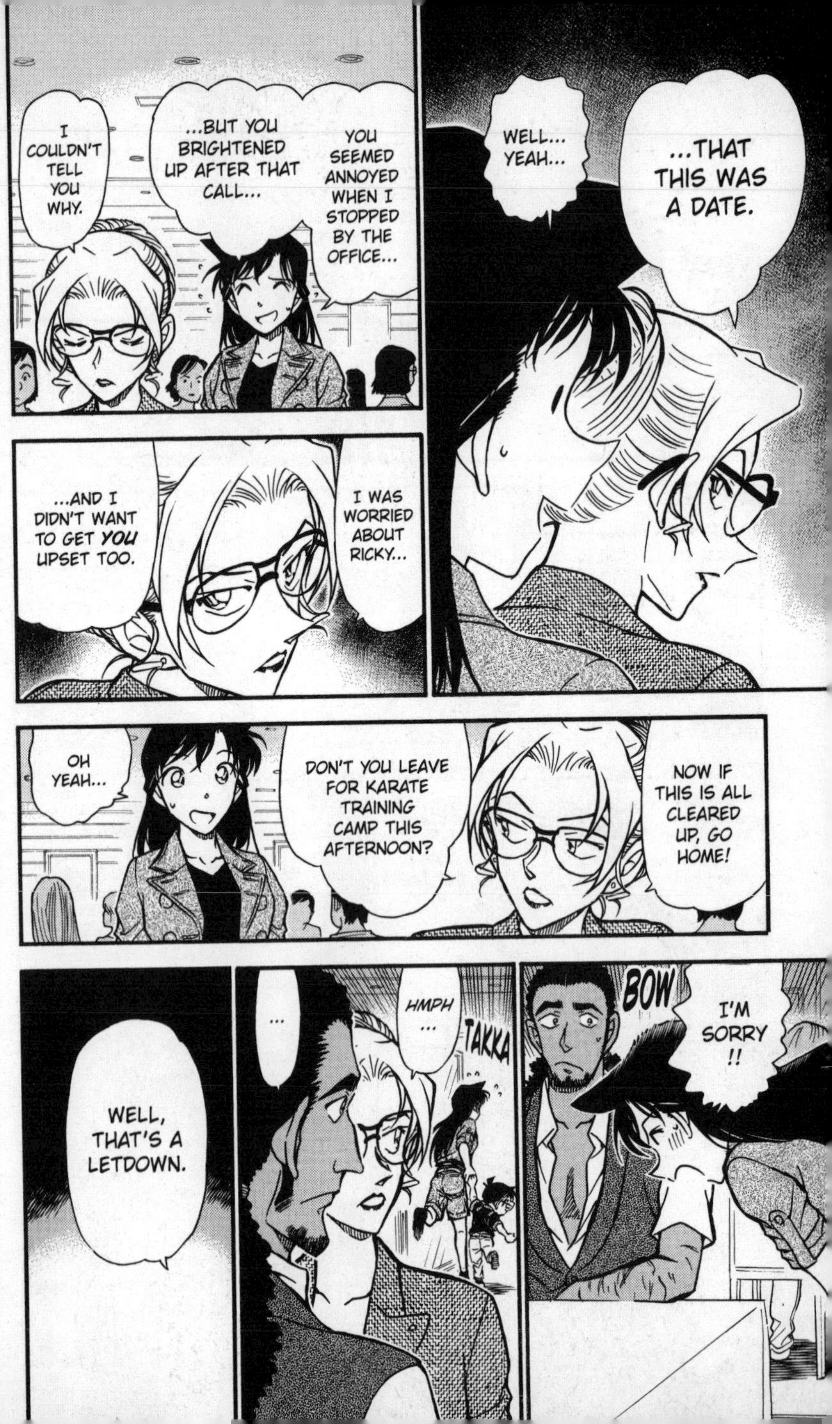
...THAT THIS WAS A DATE.
WELL... YEAH...
YOU SEEMED ANNOYED WHEN I STOPPED BY THE OFFICE...
...BUT YOU BRIGHTENED UP AFTER THAT CALL...
I COULDN'T TELL YOU WHY.
I WAS WORRIED ABOUT RICKY...
...AND I DIDN'T WANT TO GET *YOU* UPSET TOO.
NOW IF THIS IS ALL CLEARED UP, GO HOME!
DON'T YOU LEAVE FOR KARATE TRAINING CAMP THIS AFTERNOON?
OH YEAH...
I'M SORRY !!
BOW
TAKKA
HMPH ...
...
WELL, THAT'S A LETDOWN.

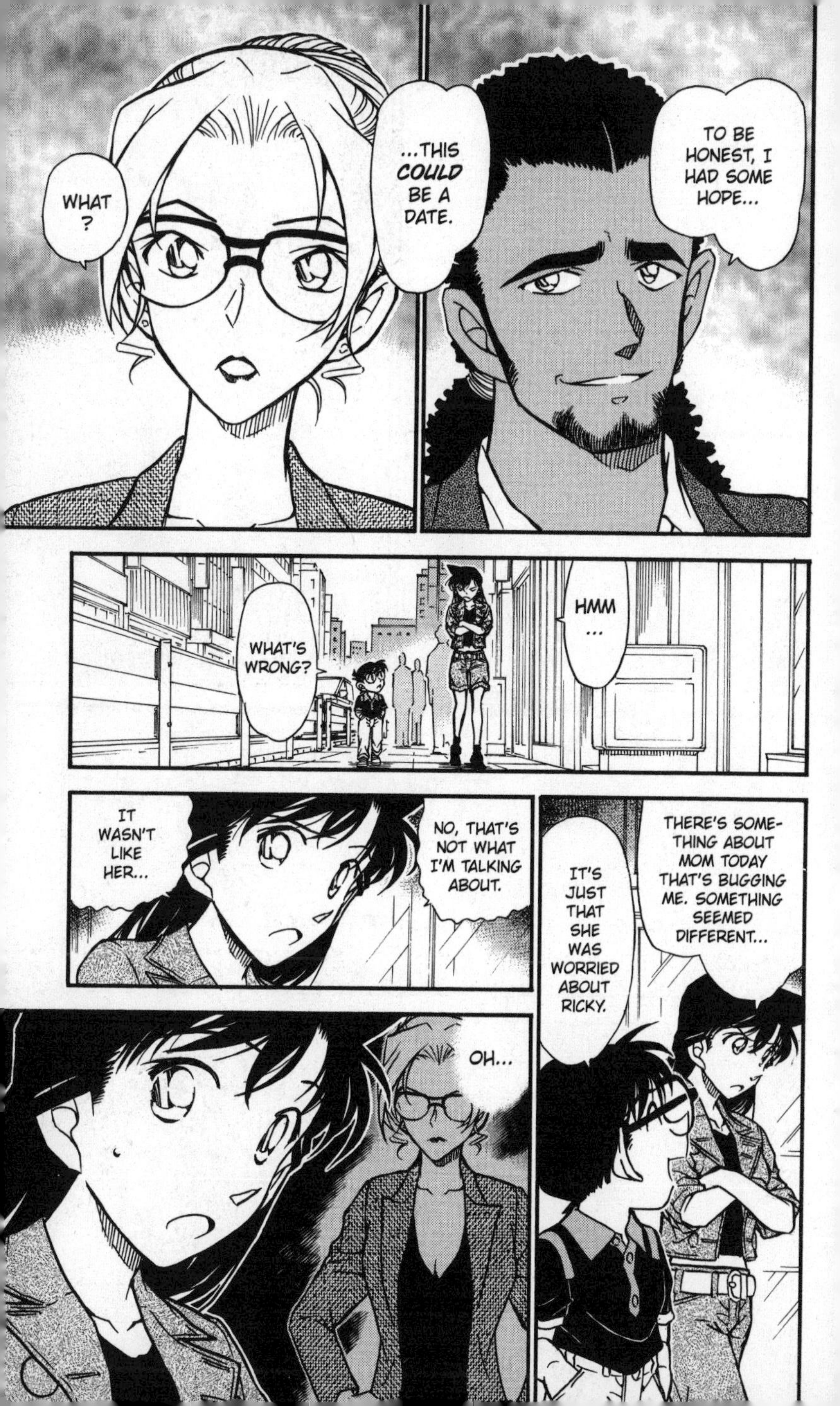
TO BE HONEST, I HAD SOME HOPE...
...THIS COULD BE A DATE.
WHAT ?
HMM ...
WHAT'S WRONG?
THERE'S SOME-THING ABOUT MOM TODAY THAT'S BUGGING ME. SOMETHING SEEMED DIFFERENT...
IT'S JUST THAT SHE WAS WORRIED ABOUT RICKY.
NO, THAT'S NOT WHAT I'M TALKING ABOUT.
IT WASN'T LIKE HER...
OH...

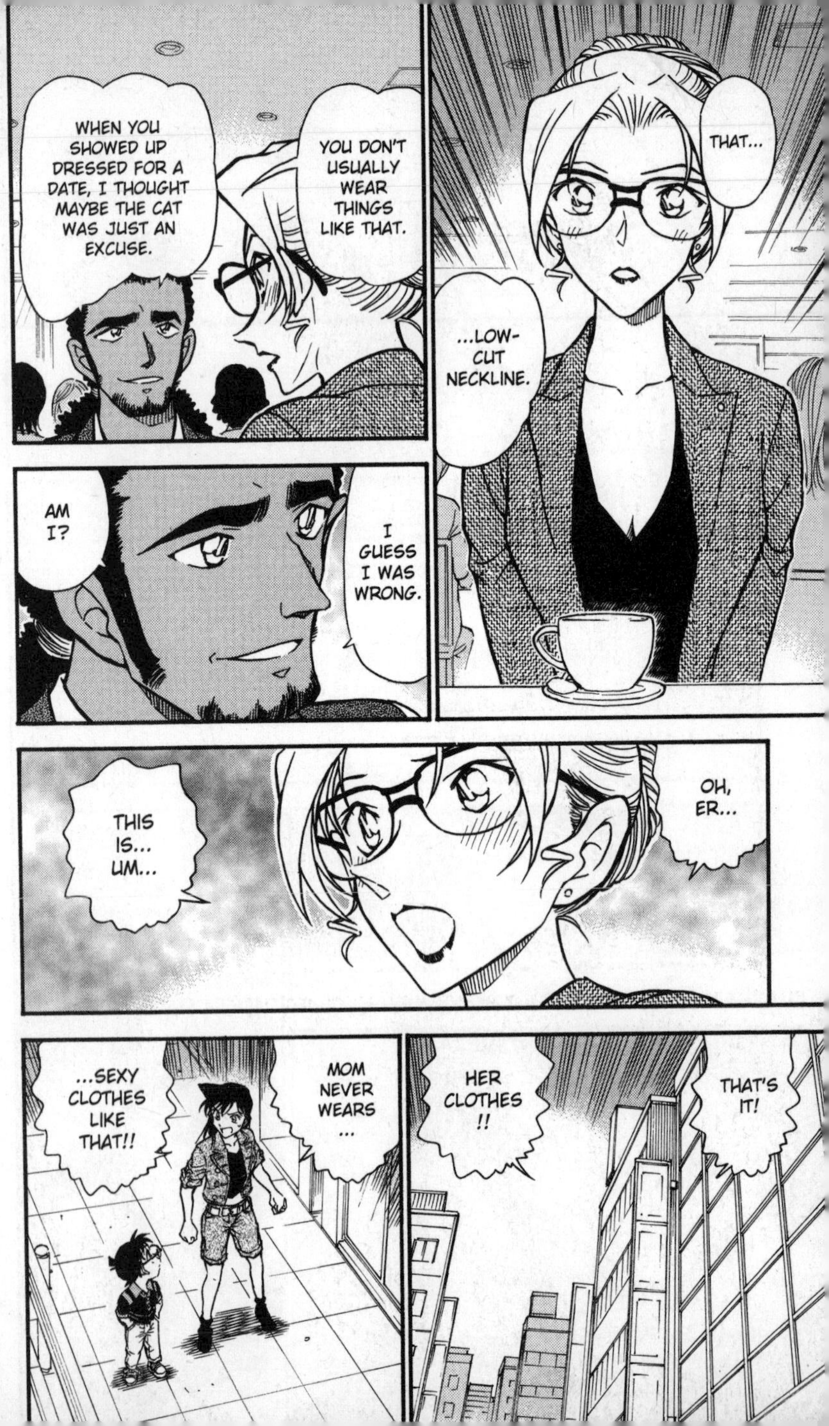
THAT...
...LOW-CUT NECKLINE.
YOU DON'T USUALLY WEAR THINGS LIKE THAT.
WHEN YOU SHOWED UP DRESSED FOR A DATE, I THOUGHT MAYBE THE CAT WAS JUST AN EXCUSE.
I GUESS I WAS WRONG.
AM I?
OH, ER...
THIS IS... UM...
THAT'S IT!
HER CLOTHES!!
MOM NEVER WEARS...
...SEXY CLOTHES LIKE THAT!!

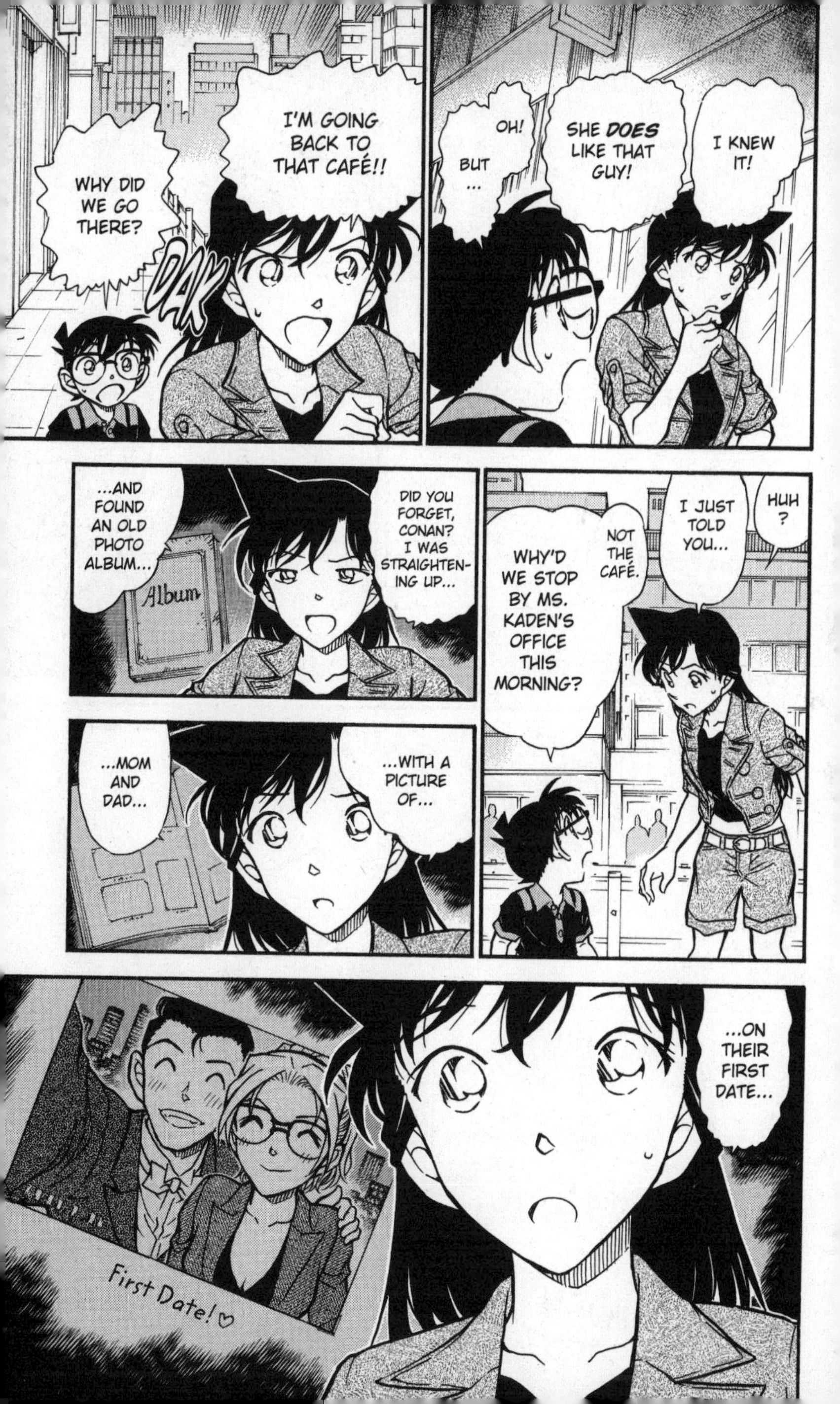
I KNEW IT!
SHE **DOES** LIKE THAT GUY!
OH!
BUT ...
I'M GOING BACK TO THAT CAFÉ!!
DAK
WHY DID WE GO THERE?
HUH?
I JUST TOLD YOU...
NOT THE CAFÉ.
WHY'D WE STOP BY MS. KADEN'S OFFICE THIS MORNING?
DID YOU FORGET, CONAN? I WAS STRAIGHTENING UP...
...AND FOUND AN OLD PHOTO ALBUM...
Album
...WITH A PICTURE OF...
...MOM AND DAD...
...ON THEIR FIRST DATE...
First Date! ♡

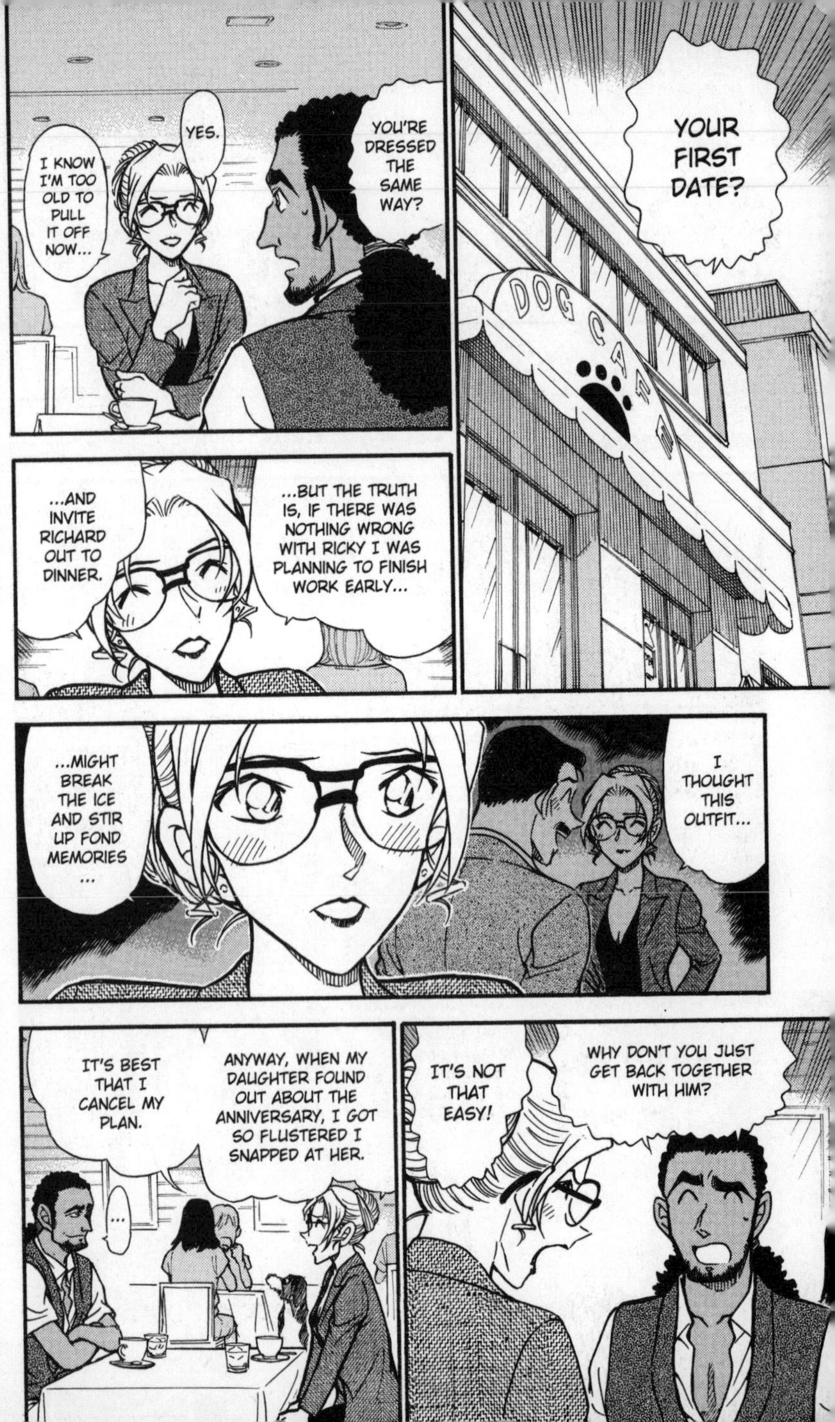
YOUR FIRST DATE?
DOG CAFE
YOU'RE DRESSED THE SAME WAY?
YES.
I KNOW I'M TOO OLD TO PULL IT OFF NOW...
...BUT THE TRUTH IS, IF THERE WAS NOTHING WRONG WITH RICKY I WAS PLANNING TO FINISH WORK EARLY...
...AND INVITE RICHARD OUT TO DINNER.
I THOUGHT THIS OUTFIT...
...MIGHT BREAK THE ICE AND STIR UP FOND MEMORIES ...
WHY DON'T YOU JUST GET BACK TOGETHER WITH HIM?
IT'S NOT THAT EASY!
ANYWAY, WHEN MY DAUGHTER FOUND OUT ABOUT THE ANNIVERSARY, I GOT SO FLUSTERED I SNAPPED AT HER.
IT'S BEST THAT I CANCEL MY PLAN.
...

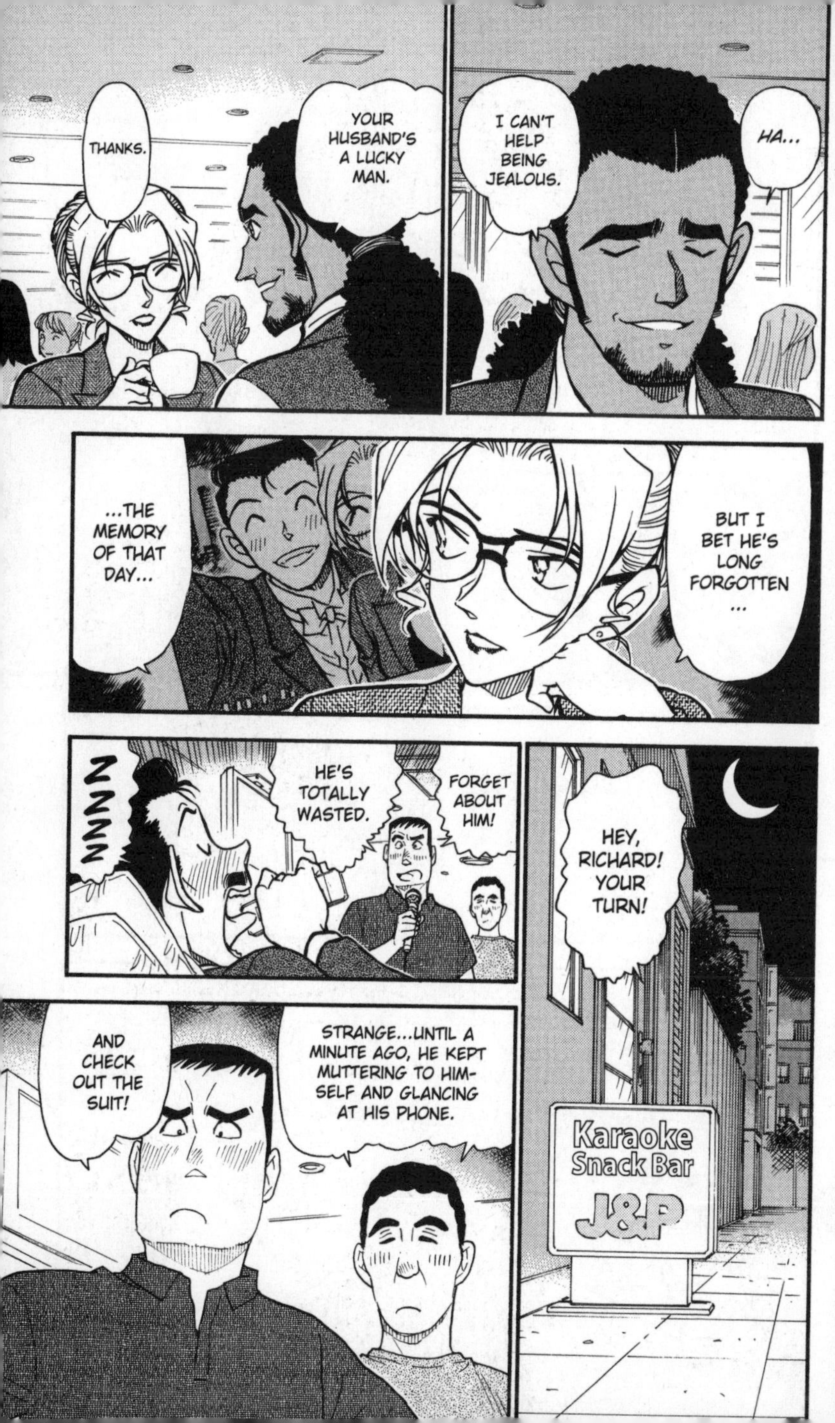
HA...
I CAN'T HELP BEING JEALOUS.
YOUR HUSBAND'S A LUCKY MAN.
THANKS.
BUT I BET HE'S LONG FORGOTTEN ...
...THE MEMORY OF THAT DAY...
HEY, RICHARD! YOUR TURN!
Karaoke Snack Bar J&P
FORGET ABOUT HIM!
HE'S TOTALLY WASTED.
ZZZZ
STRANGE...UNTIL A MINUTE AGO, HE KEPT MUTTERING TO HIMSELF AND GLANCING AT HIS PHONE.
AND CHECK OUT THE SUIT!

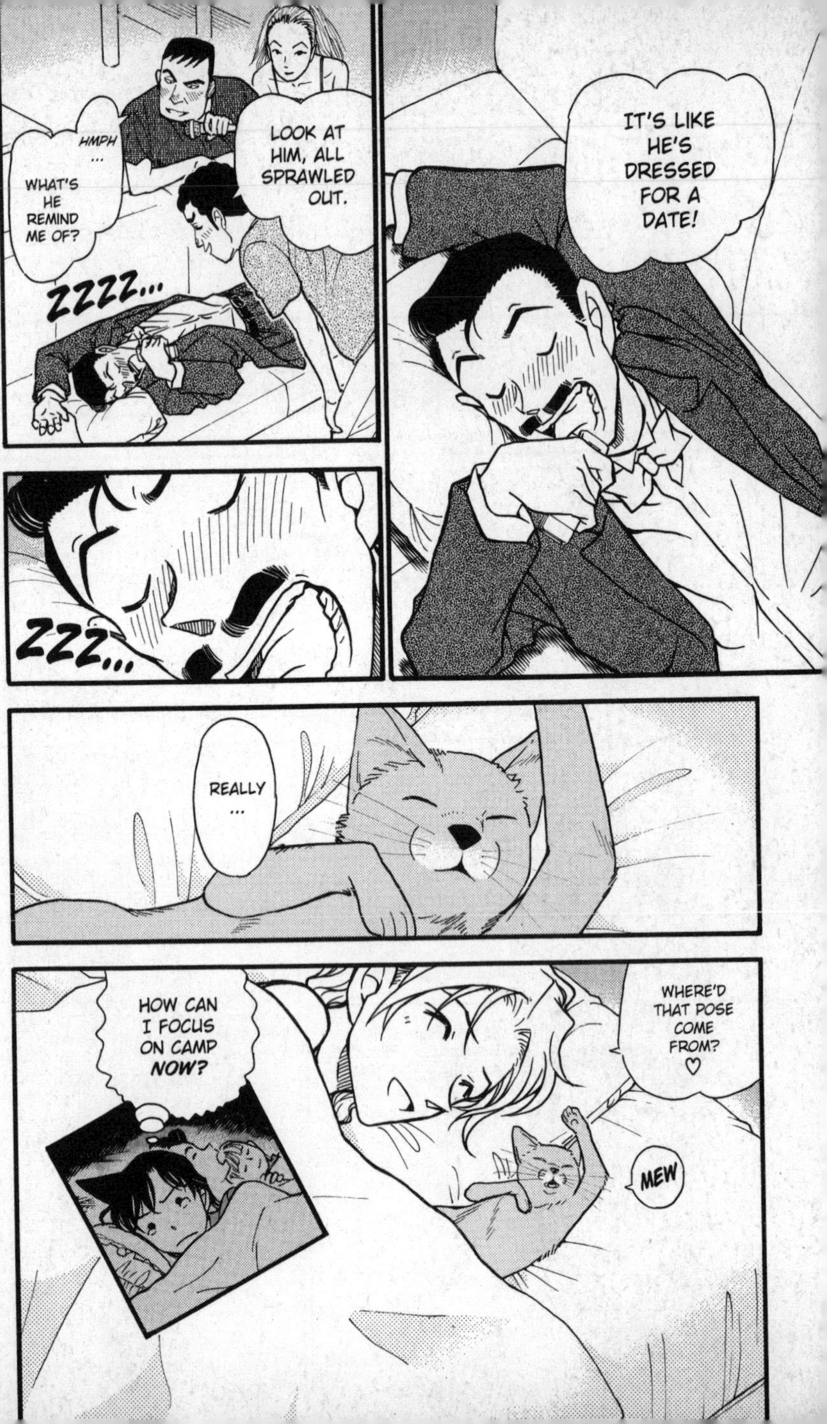
IT'S LIKE HE'S DRESSED FOR A DATE!
LOOK AT HIM, ALL SPRAWLED OUT.
HMPH ... WHAT'S HE REMIND ME OF?
ZZZZ...
ZZZ...
REALLY ...
WHERE'D THAT POSE COME FROM? ♡
MEW
HOW CAN I FOCUS ON CAMP NOW?

Hello, Aoyama here.

I receive many requests from readers. This time I caved in (heh) and decided to do a story about the young Jimmy and Rachel! But who could've guessed the mastermind behind the whole case was the guy on the back cover trying to pick the keyhole with a piece of wire?

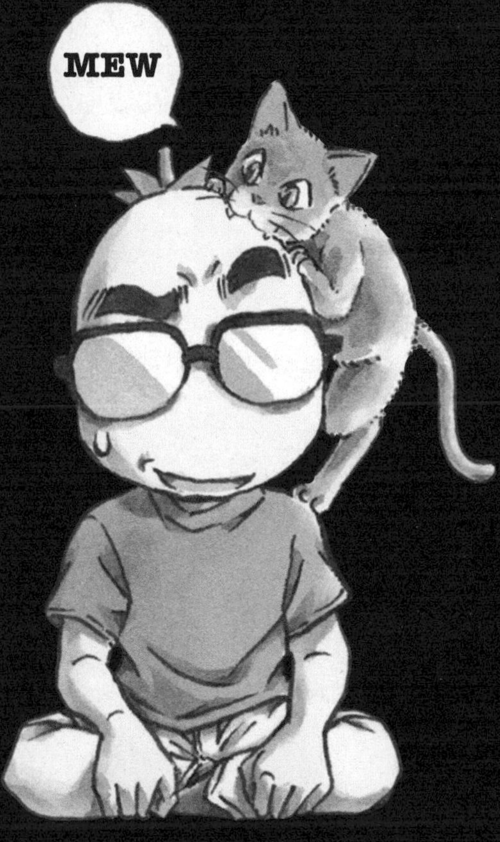
MEW

Gosho Aoyama's Mystery Library

55

THE CONTINENTAL OP

There are many hard-boiled detectives, but this time I'd like to introduce you to the Continental Op, the progenitor of the entire genre. A muscular middle-aged man who likes to drink and smoke, he's an operative for the San Francisco Continental Detective Agency, but he never reveals his true name and works under a variety of aliases. He's willing to use any means necessary to get the job done, even resorting to force. The only person he fears is his boss at the agency, "the Old Man." He always sweats over writing a report to present to the boss after he solves a case with his reckless methods.

Author Dashiell Hammett is also the creator of Sam Spade. He pioneered hard-boiled detective fiction, while the best I can do is soft-boiled...

I recommend *Blood Money*.

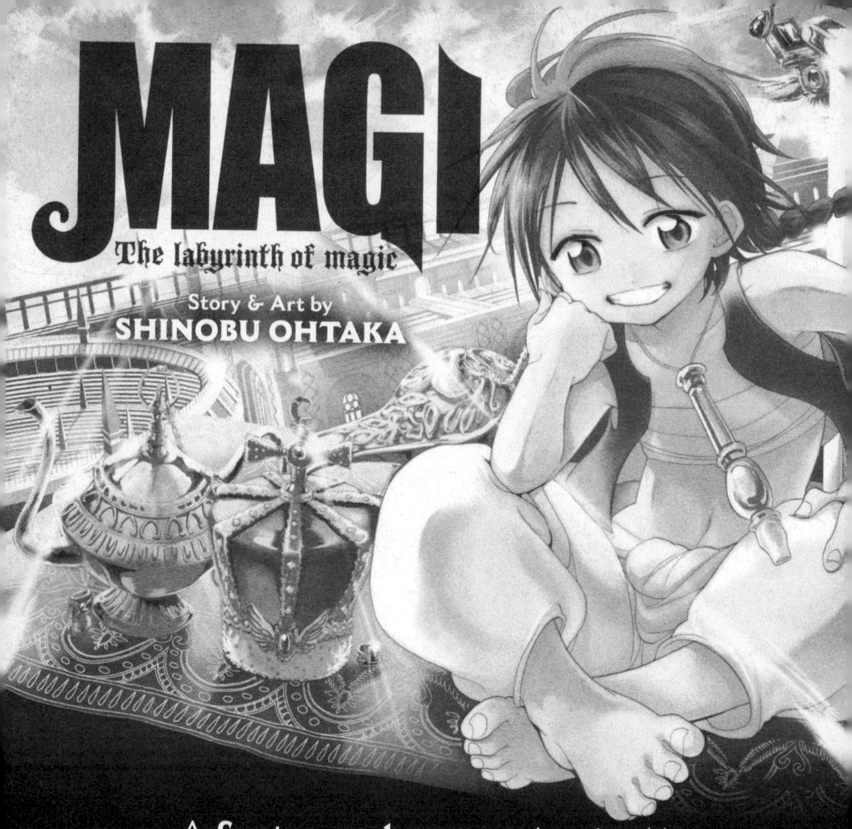
MAGI
The labyrinth of magic
Story & Art by
SHINOBU OHTAKA

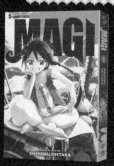

CASE CLOSED IS A STEAL
THE PROOF IS IN THE PRICE

CATCH THE CAPERS ON DVD FOR UNDER $30 A SEASON!

You should be watching funimation.com/case-closed

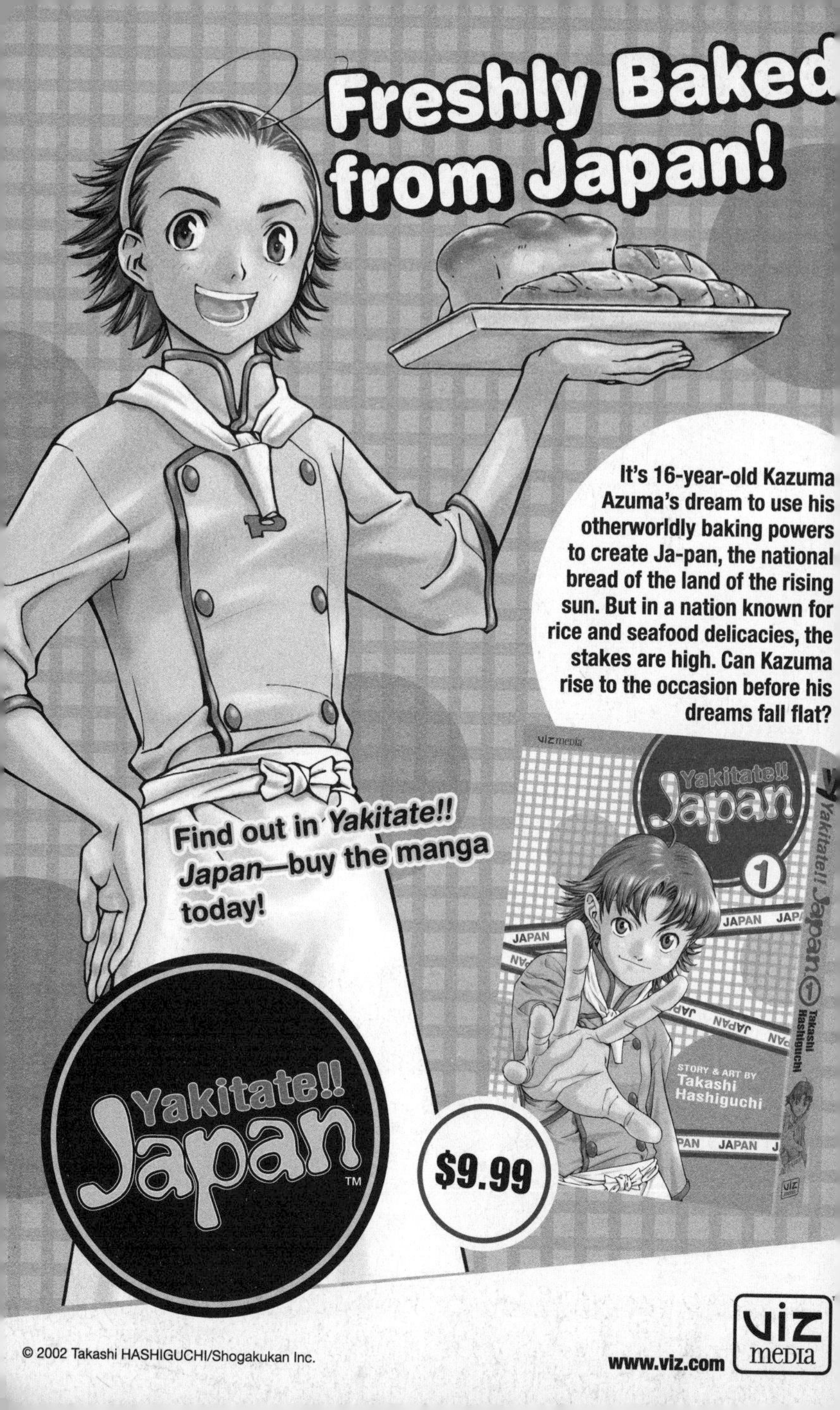
Freshly Baked from Japan!
It's 16-year-old Kazuma Azuma's dream to use his otherworldly baking powers to create Ja-pan, the national bread of the land of the rising sun. But in a nation known for rice and seafood delicacies, the stakes are high. Can Kazuma rise to the occasion before his dreams fall flat?
Find out in Yakitate!! Japan—buy the manga today!
Yakitate!! Japan™
$9.99
viz media
Yakitate!! Japan™
1
JAPAN
STORY & ART BY Takashi Hashiguchi
Yakitate!! Japan 1 Takashi Hashiguchi
© 2002 Takashi HASHIGUCHI/Shogakukan Inc.
www.viz.com
viz media